The Revelation:
Ready or Not

Dr. Bo Wagner

Word of His Mouth Publishers
Mooresboro, NC

All Scripture quotations are taken from the **King James Version** of the Bible.

ISBN: 978-1-941039-27-4
Printed in the United States of America
©2022 Dr. Bo Wagner

Word of His Mouth Publishers
Mooresboro, NC
www.wordofhismouth.com

All rights reserved. No part of this publication may be reproduced in any form without the publisher's prior written permission except for quotations in printed reviews.

Table of Contents

1	An Electrifying Opening	5
2	The Emperor's Errors	15
3	You Only Thought You Knew Him	23
4	Prophecy and Practice in the Fallen Church	35
5.	Prophecy and Practice in the Faithful Church	47
6.	Prophecy and Practice in the Fluctuating Church	55
7.	Prophecy and Practice in the Fornicating Church	65
8.	Prophecy and Practice in the Fake Church	75
9.	Prophecy and Practice in the Favored Church	85
10	Prophecy and Practice in the Foul Church	95
11	The Throne Room of God, 01	101
12	The Throne Room of God, 02	115
13	Tears and Triumph	127
14	The Four Horsemen of the Apocalypse	137
15.	The Fifth and Sixth Seal	147
16	The Calm That Is a Storm	155
17	The Seventh Seal	165
18	Four Trumpets and Fatal Thirds	171
19	The Opening of the Pit	179
20.	the Army Like No Other	185
21	The Final Countdown	193
22	The Measuring Day	201
23	The Two Witnesses	207
24	Capital G	217
25	The Devil's Tale	223
26	History's Biggest Failure	233
27	The Rise of the Beast	241
28	The Unholy Spirit	251
29	the Mark of the Beast	259
30	Purity on Display	267
31	Three More Preachers	275
32	Approaching Armageddon	287
33	Peace in the Storm	295
34	The First Four Vials	305
35	The Fifth and Sixth Vials	315
36	The Seventh Vial	321
37	Hell's Harlot	325
38	It Takes an angel to Explain a Woman	335
39	The Fall of Babylon	343

40	The Shouting Before the Showing	353
41	The Second Coming	361
42	The Millennial Reign of Christ	371
43	God's Sewage System	379
44	The Message I Want the Devil to Hear	385
45	The Great White Throne Judgment	391
46	All Things New	401
47	Alpha and Omega	405
48	Showing Off the Bride	411
49	A Little Slice of Heaven	419
50	Settling into Eternity	425
51	The End	433
	Works Cited	441

Chapter One
An Electrifying Opening

Revelation 1:1 *The Revelation of Jesus Christ, which God gave unto him, to shew unto his servants things which must shortly come to pass; and he sent and signified it by his angel unto his servant John:* **2** *Who bare record of the word of God, and of the testimony of Jesus Christ, and of all things that he saw.* **3** *Blessed is he that readeth, and they that hear the words of this prophecy, and keep those things which are written therein: for the time is at hand.* **4** *John to the seven churches which are in Asia: Grace be unto you, and peace, from him which is, and which was, and which is to come; and from the seven Spirits which are before his throne;* **5** *And from Jesus Christ, who is the faithful witness, and the first begotten of the dead, and the prince of the kings of the earth. Unto him that loved us, and washed us from our sins in his own blood,* **6** *And hath made us kings and priests unto God and his Father; to him be glory and dominion for ever and ever. Amen.* **7** *Behold, he cometh with clouds; and every eye shall see him, and they also which pierced him: and all kindreds of the earth shall wail because of him. Even so, Amen.* **8** *I am Alpha and Omega, the beginning and the ending, saith the Lord, which is, and which was, and which is to come, the Almighty.*

When we were little children, we played a game called Hide and Seek. Almost everyone would run and hide while one person closed their eyes and counted to some predetermined number. Then, once the count was done, he would shout, "Ready or not, here I come!"

Something a lot like that happens here in the book of The Revelation, not one or two times, but four times:

Revelation 3:11 *Behold, **I come quickly**: hold that fast which thou hast, that no man take thy crown.*

Revelation 22:7 *Behold, **I come quickly**: blessed is he that keepeth the sayings of the prophecy of this book.*

Revelation 22:12 *And, **behold, I come quickly**; and my reward is with me, to give every man according as his work shall be.*

Revelation 22:20 *He which testifieth these things saith, **Surely I come quickly**. Amen. Even so, come, Lord Jesus.*

Four times in the last book of the Bible, He says this, and one of those four verses is the next to the last verse in the entire Bible. You get the sense that He is coming, whether we are ready or not!

But before we get to the last book of the Bible, we really should look back at the very first verse of the very first book of the Bible to get a bit of needed perspective on it.

Genesis 1:1 *In the beginning God created the heaven and the earth.*

Do you know what is really interesting about Genesis 1:1? It was spoken about 4,100 years before the book of The Revelation was written. When it was later written down by Moses, there were still nearly 1,600 years until the book of The Revelation would be written. During that 1,600-year span, books of the Bible kept coming, and coming, and coming. And they always seemed to look forward to a time when there would be more books, and more books, and more. They often came in the form of letters and then ended up as books of the Bible. Then one day, a fairly decent-sized letter arrived in Asia Minor. The year was approximately A.D. 96, and the letter that showed up had a couple of unique twists to it. First of all, it was actually seven letters in one. The pastor of the church opened it up and found letters to six other churches in Asia Minor, with the instruction for everybody to read the entire letter, even the parts addressed to other churches. Then, this letter to these churches stopped talking about the churches altogether and instead unveiled the remainder of God's plan for the rest of time and eternity. The pastor and the church realized that what they were holding was the last bit of Scripture that would ever be written. Can you imagine! This is it; the Bible is done; I'm the first one to ever see the last thing that God will ever write! Everything that God began in those first sixty-five books was wrapped up and finished in this last one, the sixty-sixth. I suspect the pastor understood right away that that was the reason for the name God gave this book right in the first few words:

Revelation 1:1a *The Revelation of Jesus Christ...*

This was not The Revelation given by and about "St. John the Divine" or "John the Revelator," this was The Revelation given by and about Jesus Christ, finishing everything that He began back in Genesis 1:1. The pastor looked at that letter and realized that what he was reading contained vital information that was still future to him. As we begin to read it again today, it still contains information that is future even to us, but it is now very clearly something that is in our very near future. So let's take the first eight verses that the pastor read, the introduction to this book, and start with them.

The purpose of the book

Revelation 1:1a *The Revelation of Jesus Christ, which God gave unto him, to shew unto his servants things which must shortly come to pass...*

There is a very ominous sounding word in our English language, the word *apocalypse*. That word, derived from the Greek language, is actually the very first word of the book of The Revelation. Rather than being ominous, it is truly quite amazing. It means to reveal, to make known, to show that which has been hidden, to unveil. You see, this book is not the first one that dealt with the subject of the end times, and John was not the first one to be given details about the last days. Hundreds of years before John was even born, God gave a man named Daniel one of the most remarkable books of prophecy ever written. He showed Daniel the entire course of Gentile world powers up until the end of time. He told Daniel about Jesus, the coming King, and how He would set up an everlasting kingdom. Daniel is a companion book to the book of The Revelation. But God did not tell Daniel all that He could have told him, nor did He even allow Daniel to explain all that he had written. In fact, God told Daniel to write it, then to seal up what he had written and leave it alone!

Daniel 12:4 *But thou, O Daniel, shut up the words, and seal the book, even to the time of the end: many shall run to and fro, and knowledge shall be increased.*

Daniel writes this amazing prophecy under the inspiration of the Holy Ghost, and then he will not talk about it, explain it, or expound on it. He dies a year or so later, a very old man in a foreign land where he had been taken captive, and takes what he knew about what he had written but had never said to the grave with him.

Hundreds of years pass. Christ is born of a virgin in Bethlehem of Judaea. He grows up, fulfills His public ministry, dies for mankind's sin, raises the third day, and ascends into Heaven. His followers go across the known world spreading the gospel, and one by one, the apostles die out. Finally, there is just one left, John the beloved. Like Daniel, he is now likely more than ninety years old. Like Daniel, he is held captive in a foreign land. Like Daniel, he is visited by someone from Heaven and given a message. But where Daniel was given a prophecy and told to seal it up, John is now told to take the prophecy that Daniel began and, using the final and fuller parts of information given in these twenty-two chapters, unveil that which had been hidden for all these years. Using what Daniel sealed up and what John unveiled, we are now seeing the truth of what God told Daniel would happen:

Daniel 12:4 *But thou, O Daniel, shut up the words, and seal the book, even to the time of the end: many shall run to and fro, and knowledge shall be increased.*

God told Daniel that in the last days, people would "run to and fro." In the last century, that has become a reality. For roughly 5,900 years, men walked or rode animals. In the last one hundred years, we now find people riding three hundred at a time on massive passenger jets around the world, hundreds of millions at a time in eight-cylinder cars down the freeways, and even going to the moon and back. There are multiple companies that, within the next few years, are going to start offering space tourism to the general public. Many are running to and fro, and knowledge is now being exponentially increased. We are in the information age, the Bible called it the time of the end, and it will not last long. It is in our day that people are taking Daniel's veiled book, studying it along with John's unveiled book, and enjoying the purpose of the book of The Revelation. The purpose of this book is *"to shew unto his servants things which must shortly come to pass."* In other words, the purpose of this book is to tell us the future.

The penman of the book

Revelation 1:1b... *and he sent and signified it by his angel unto his servant John:* **2** *Who bare record of the word of God, and of the testimony of Jesus Christ, and of all things that he saw.*

The John referred to here is, as we have already seen, John the apostle. He started off as a hot-headed disciple whom Jesus nicknamed, along with James, his brother, "Boanerges," meaning the sons of thunder. He ended up as Jesus' closest follower, even going to Calvary when everyone else ran for cover.

After the resurrection, John almost fades into the background as Peter, Paul, Barnabas, and Silas take center stage. Even people who had not been of the original twelve were out writing books about Jesus, but John was not. John was doing exactly what Jesus asked him to do, tending to Mary, His mother. It was not until everybody else was dead and gone that John finally put pen to paper and gave us the gospel of John, the three epistles of John, and last of all, The Revelation of Jesus Christ. I know that every word of every Bible book is inspired, but somehow it still seems that God and John saved the best for last.

The promises of the book

Revelation 1:3 *Blessed is he that readeth, and they that hear the words of this prophecy, and keep those things which are written therein: for the time is at hand.*

Blessed is he that readeth... that phrase is found just one time in all the Bible, and this is it. It is the beginning of one of the two promises found in this verse associated with this book. This is the only book in the Bible that God gives a promise quite like this: *if you will read, and hear, and keep the words of this book, the book of The Revelation, you will be blessed*! Why would God need to make a promise like that? Because people tend to avoid the book of The Revelation like it is one of the plagues written about within it. Their reasoning usually goes something like, "Well, we'll be gone before any of that stuff happens; why should we bother to read and study it?" Why? Because God promised to bless those who would read and study it. That must mean it is pretty important.

The second promise He gives in verse three concerning this book is that when it comes to the things written about within it, *the time is at hand.* He has already said something very similar in verse one, telling us that these things would be coming to pass *shortly.* These phrases, especially the words *at hand* mean "something whose beginning is soon to come, though the end may be far into the future." (Linder, Barnes)

God told seven churches by the hand of John that the last days were right around the corner. But all of the people who read that eventually grew old and died, as did their children, and their children's children. Was God wrong? Of course not. Try to remember that what we think about "soon" and what God thinks about "soon" are about as similar as what we think about "soon" and what our kids think about "soon!" When our daughters say, "Mom, dad, when can I start letting boys call me?" We say "soon." What we mean by *soon* is a few years, and for us, that is really soon! But for our daughters, a few years is not soon; it is an eternity! We just do not have the same idea of *soon* as they do. That missed truth is what has caused a lot of people to scoff at and openly doubt God's Word on the subject of the second coming. Peter wrote about people like that:

2 Peter 3:1 *This second epistle, beloved, I now write unto you; in both which I stir up your pure minds by way of remembrance:* **2** *That ye may be mindful of the words which were spoken before by the holy prophets, and of the commandment of us the apostles of the Lord and Saviour:* **3** *Knowing this first, that there shall come in the last days scoffers, walking after their own lusts,* **4** *And saying, Where is the promise of his coming? for since the fathers fell asleep, all things continue as they were from the beginning of the creation.*

Even in Peter's day, people were saying, "I thought you said He was coming soon? He's not coming; everything is just like it has always been." Peter then went on to tell them why they were wrong:

2 Peter 3:8 *But, beloved, be not ignorant of this one thing, that one day is with the Lord as a thousand years, and a thousand years as one day.* **9** *The Lord is not slack concerning his promise, as some men count slackness; but is longsuffering to us-ward, not willing that any should perish, but that all should come to repentance.* **10** *But the day of the Lord will come as a thief in the night; in the which the heavens shall pass away with a great noise, and the elements shall melt with fervent heat, the earth also and the works that are therein shall be burned up.*

The nearly 2,000 years that we have gone through as a world since John wrote that all of this was *at hand* is only a couple of days in the mind of God. It may seem like forever to us, but not to Him! To Him, it is all very soon, even at the door. And now, to us, it is also very soon. You see, what Daniel wrote about the last days being the time when knowledge shall be increased, and men shall run to and fro, marks for us the beginning of the very last of the last days! God did not put a date on it, but it is pretty easy to figure out that somewhere around the year 1900, we truly entered the last of the last days. For 5,900 years or so, men walked, now we fly and drive, and people are running to and fro. For 5,900 years or so, what people knew changed very little from generation to generation, but now every field of knowledge is advancing at the speed of light. We are in the age of quantum physics, the theory of relativity, the mapping of human DNA, computer processing, and even theology has advanced more than ever before, specifically in the field of prophecy. For 1,900 years since the time of Christ, prophecy was rarely mentioned, hardly studied, and only sporadically written about. But in the last one hundred years, prophecy has become the dominant topic of theological reading, writing, and study. Why now? Why now, after 1,900 years of nearly complete silence, why now is everybody everywhere talking about the Rapture, and the Tribulation, and the Antichrist, and the mark of the beast? Because we have entered the last of the last days

The point of the book

Revelation 1:4 *John to the seven churches which are in Asia: Grace be unto you, and peace, from him which is, and which was, and which is to come; and from the seven Spirits which are before his throne;* **5** *And from Jesus Christ, who is the faithful witness, and the first begotten of the dead, and the prince of the kings of the earth. Unto him that loved us, and washed us from our sins in his own blood,* **6** *And hath made us kings and priests unto God and his Father; to him be glory and dominion for ever and ever. Amen.* **7** *Behold, he cometh with clouds; and every eye shall see him, and they also which pierced him: and all kindreds of the earth shall wail because of him. Even so, Amen.* **8** *I am Alpha and Omega, the beginning and the ending, saith the Lord, which is, and which was, and which is to come, the Almighty.*

When people think of the book of Revelation, their mind almost invariably goes to the Antichrist, the mark of the beast, cataclysmic judgments, Armageddon. All of those things are in this book, starting in chapter four and going all the way through chapter twenty-two. But none of those things are the point of this book. The focal point, the center of attention, is that which has been intentionally ignored by kings and slaves, rich and poor, black and white, sinners of every type for thousands of years. The point of this book is Jesus Christ, the Lamb of God, the all-conquering King, the Lord of lords. Look at how He is described in verses four through eight, and understand that even though His name does not appear until verse five, everything in verses four through eight is talking about Him:

He is the One who gives grace and peace:

Revelation 1:4a *John to the seven churches which are in Asia: Grace be unto you, and peace...*

These two things did not come from John. They never come from any man at all. They came from and come from Christ alone.

He is the One who is, and was, and is to come:

Revelation 1:4b... *from him which is, and which was, and which is to come...*

Yes, this points to the fact that Christ was presently alive to meet with John there on Patmos, was alive on earth before His crucifixion, and will be coming again to receive us and culminate all things. But this phrase is even bigger than all of that. It means the One who is "everlasting, embracing all duration, past, present, and (future)." (Linder, Barnes) That should sound familiar to you:

Hebrews 13:8 *Jesus Christ the same yesterday, and to day, and for ever.*

The Jesus of Bethlehem is also the Jehovah of Mount Sinai. The Christ of Calvary is also the Elohim of Genesis 1:1. Jesus is not held by time; He is the holder of time.

He is the One who has seven spirits before His throne:

Revelation 1:4c... *and from the seven Spirits which are before his throne;*

We will see more about these seven Spirits later; it is enough for now that we know that if anyone but the Almighty God Himself were sitting on that throne, those Spirits would not be standing in allegiance before it.

He is the faithful witness:

Revelation 1:5a *And from Jesus Christ, who is the faithful witness...*

This means that Jesus is the witness whose testimony is always true and infallible. Everything He says is right. A witness can be a false witness either by telling an intentional lie or by simply making a mistake. But Jesus never does either of those things, and therefore, He is always the faithful witness, the witness whose testimony is always true and infallible.

<u>He is the first begotten of the dead:</u>

Revelation 1:5b... *and the first begotten of the dead...*

This phrase *"first begotten of the dead"* means that He is the first one to raise from the dead, never to die again. He was the first one whose resurrection was permanent, foreshadowing the permanent resurrection of all who believe on Him. Lazarus rose from the dead, but he eventually died again. The same thing is true of the widow of Nain's son. But Jesus rose from the dead, never to die again.

<u>He is the prince of the kings of the earth:</u>

Revelation 1:5c... *and the prince of the kings of the earth...*

In our Western minds, we automatically think of kings as being higher in rank than princes. This was not necessarily so in Eastern cultures and not so in Biblical theology either. This word prince is the word *arkown*, and it indicates a superior, not an inferior. Literally, Jesus is the prince who is *over* the kings of the earth. Do they like this arrangement? No, and the Bible tells us of a time when they decided that they would show God that they were boss:

Psalm 2:1 *Why do the heathen rage, and the people imagine a vain thing?* **2** *The kings of the earth set themselves, and the rulers take counsel together, against the LORD, and against his anointed, saying,* **3** *Let us break their bands asunder, and cast away their cords from us.*

How well did their plan work?

Psalm 2:4 *He that sitteth in the heavens shall laugh: the Lord shall have them in derision.*

This matter has already been settled. Modern-day heathens can rage all they want, but Jesus is still in charge.

<u>He is the one who loved us enough to die for us:</u>

Revelation 1:5d... *Unto him that loved us, and washed us from our sins in his own blood,*

The King of kings with power *over* us is also the Lamb of God who took pity *on* us. We who are saved have had our sins washed away by the blood that Jesus shed on Calvary.

<u>He is the one who took slaves and made kings and priests out of them:</u>

Revelation 1:6 *And hath made us kings and priests unto God and his Father...*

When God found us, we were nothing. We were slaves in the bondage of sin with the devil as our taskmaster. God bought us up, cleaned us up, and brought us up to the lofty position of kings and priests in His kingdom.

He is the one who has and deserves glory and dominion forever:

Revelation 1:6 ... *to him be glory and dominion for ever and ever. Amen.*

Glory is from the word *doxa*, and it means splendor and brightness. It is an indication that He deserves to be verbally and enthusiastically praised. Dominion is from the word *kratos*, and it means force and strength and power and might. He has all of that, and He deserves all of that, not just now but forever.

He is the One who is coming back and who will be seen by every eye of all history:

Revelation 1:7 *Behold, he cometh with clouds; and every eye shall see him, and they also which pierced him: and all kindreds of the earth shall wail because of him. Even so, Amen.*

We know that there will be a portion of His coming that only believers are even aware of, and the word we use for that is the Rapture. But there will be another portion of His coming in which every eye of those living and dead will see Him clearly as He arrives in clouds of glory. It will be a time when people wail in anguish and fear because they know time is up, and they have rejected their sovereign God. Among those eyes that will behold Him will be the eyes of a small group of Roman soldiers who have been in hell for nearly 2,000 years. They will look up from the flames in horror and see the One that their own hands pierced with cruel nails. The prophet Zechariah said the same thing in Zechariah 12:10 before it even happened. The last time those soldiers saw Him, He was hanging lifeless on a cross. The next time they see Him, He will be riding on a white horse, with the armies of Heaven following Him. When John thought of that, his reaction was a very appropriate AMEN!

He is all in all, A to Z:

Revelation 1:8 *I am Alpha and Omega, the beginning and the ending, saith the Lord, which is, and which was, and which is to come, the Almighty.*

Alpha is the first letter of the Greek alphabet; Omega is the last letter of the Greek alphabet. We say, "From A-Z," they would say, "From Alpha to Omega." This basically means that He is all in all, and all you really need to know. If you do not know Him, you have missed everything that is really important, and you have either wittingly or unwittingly lined up against the almighty God. You never could afford to do that before, but here, now, in the last of the last days, you really cannot afford to do it.

As the pastor of that church read the opening part of this letter, His hands had to be shaking as he realized he was holding the last book of the Bible ever to be written, and he was looking at what would happen in the future. That future never took place during his lifetime, but there is no way to escape the sense that it most likely will take place in ours. Are you ready?

Chapter Two
The Emperor's Errors

Revelation 1:9 *I John, who also am your brother, and companion in tribulation, and in the kingdom and patience of Jesus Christ, was in the isle that is called Patmos, for the word of God, and for the testimony of Jesus Christ.* **10** *I was in the Spirit on the Lord's day, and heard behind me a great voice, as of a trumpet,* **11** *Saying, I am Alpha and Omega, the first and the last: and, What thou seest, write in a book, and send it unto the seven churches which are in Asia; unto Ephesus, and unto Smyrna, and unto Pergamos, and unto Thyatira, and unto Sardis, and unto Philadelphia, and unto Laodicea.*

In A.D. 51, John the apostle was in his mid-50s, in the prime of life, and though much in the background as compared to Peter and others, in the prime of his ministry. The work that Christ started had about twenty years under its belt and was now numbering in the hundreds of thousands of followers. But on October 24 of that year, in Rome, a baby was born that would one day impact the apostle John in ways he could never have imagined. That baby's name was Domitian, He had an older brother named Titus, and he was the youngest son of Vespasian, who by A.D. 69 would be Emperor Vespasian. A few short years later, Vespasian, his father, named Titus the older brother as his successor, which he actually became when Vespasian died in A.D. 79. Little brother Domitian was given a series of menial government jobs with no real power, while his brother was hailed as one of Rome's greatest rulers. But in A.D. 81, Titus died. Domitian hurried to the camp to see his brother breathe his last breath and then had to endure only a day's wait before the Roman Senate proclaimed him as the new Emperor. He finally had the attention and the power that he had always craved. It truly seemed like nothing could go wrong... (Chilver, 2022)

But one day, about A.D. 90 or so, Domitian became aware of an old man, up past ninety years old. This old man was a preacher, and to Domitian, he was the worst kind of preacher. You see, Domitian was absolutely sold on the paganism of Rome, and he would not tolerate anybody who said that Jupiter and Minerva (to whom he kept a personal shrine in his bedroom) were not true gods. But this old man, John, went all across the Roman Empire, Domitian's empire, preaching that Jesus alone was God and the only way of salvation! (Anistoriton)

And that was not the only thing that Domitian hated about John. You see, late in A.D. 85, Domitian had proclaimed himself *censor perpetuus*, censor for perpetuity, meaning that he was the one who got to decide what was right and wrong, moral or immoral. And then here came this John, telling the world that God's Word alone could tell you what was right or wrong, moral or immoral. Young Domitian and old John did not see eye to eye on anything! And to top it all off, where most people in the empire were scared to death of the emperor and his power, this weak old man did not have an ounce of fear of Domitian or anyone else. He would point-blank disagree with him and kept on preaching all of the things that Domitian told him not to. Talk about nerve!

Domitian figured he did not have to put up with this. Old man or not, John was going to have to learn the hard way who was boss. So Domitian arranged for one of his favorite methods of killing "religious fanatics." He had his servants prepare a vat of boiling hot oil, and he had ninety-plus-year-old John immersed in it. I guess that would teach John a thing or two!

Except for the fact that John did not die. A frail, wizened old man took the worst that Domitian had to offer, and he lived through it. The God who can stop the lions from eating Daniel can also stop the oil from cooking John.

Now Domitian was in a bind. He was getting embarrassed by all of this. What good Roman Emperor, especially one so power-hungry that both Suetonius and Cassius Dio say officially gave himself the title of Dominus et Deus, meaning "Lord and God," cannot kill a feeble ninety-year-old? There had to be a way to make this problem go away.

And then he thought of it. Banishment! There was an island named Patmos out in the Aegean Sea that was perfect for situations like this. It was only about ten miles long, just a few miles wide, had no trees, no natural edible vegetation, just a barren, rocky outpost. And so in A.D. 95, Eusebius tells us that Domitian determined to send John away to Patmos into exile.

He had a plan.

But it is hard to imagine any plan that failed as miserably as Domitian's did.

Here were his errors.

Domitian assumed that John was just like him, thinking only of himself.

Revelation 1:9a *I John, who also am your brother, and companion in tribulation, and in the kingdom and patience of Jesus Christ,*

Knowing the arrogance of the entire family of Domitian, there is no question whatsoever that if he had been "put down" to the same degree that aged John had been put down, he would have been utterly wallowing in the mire of self-pity. And there is no way whatsoever that he believed John was better or emotionally stronger than himself. So when Domitian put him on that barren rock to wither and die, he very clearly expected John to feel every ounce of the emotional weight being poured on him as his life dripped away day by day.

The last thing, the very last thing he would ever have expected, would be for a letter to come out of all that containing the words, "*I John, who also am your brother, and companion in tribulation, and in the kingdom and patience of Jesus Christ*,"

As bad as John himself had suffered and was suffering, he thought of folks in the church going through so much, and he wanted them to know that he was right there with them. He called himself their brother, which he absolutely was through their mutual kinship to Christ. But he also called himself their companion in tribulation, which was an indication that he knew he was not suffering alone. Christians everywhere were suffering, and he wanted them to know that he understood their pain and had not forgotten about them. This is a level of compassion and awareness Domitian never would have had.

But he also wanted him to know that he was their companion "*in the kingdom and patience of Jesus Christ.*"

It is evident that everyone with any good sense would be perfectly fine with being a companion in the kingdom of Jesus Christ—but that word kingdom is inextricably joined to the word patience. Adam Clarke gives a good sense of what John was saying when he spoke of the patience of Jesus Christ, "Meekly bearing all indignities, privations, and sufferings, for the sake and after the example of our Lord and Master." (Clarke, 6: 971)

That is exactly what Jesus did for us, and it is exactly what the Christians to whom John was writing were doing, and it is exactly what John himself was then doing, and it is exactly what God still expects us to be doing. We are still to be companions in the patience of Jesus Christ; we are still to be meekly bearing all indignities, privations, and sufferings for the sake and after the example of our Lord and Master.

Domitian would never have done any of that for his own false gods, let alone for the real God, whom he did not believe in to begin with.

Domitian assumed that great difficulties would shake John out of what he believed and where he stood.

Revelation 1:9b *I John, who also am your brother, and companion in tribulation, and in the kingdom and patience of Jesus*

Christ, was in the isle that is called Patmos, **for the word of God, and for the testimony of Jesus Christ.**

Domitian did not believe that what John and the other followers of Christ were preaching and writing was the Word of God, and that is a prominent reason why John was on Patmos.

Domitian did not believe in the testimony of Jesus Christ as the Son of God and God the Son and the One who rose from the dead three days after being put to death by Rome. That also is a very big reason why John was on Patmos.

This banishment, among other things, was designed to shake John out of all those "faulty beliefs." Instead, John held to those beliefs so very tightly that he wrote about them from that very island of banishment, focusing on *"the word of God and the testimony of Jesus Christ."*

Domitian assumed that he was going to be in union with his gods in the palace and John was going to be forsaken by his God on that barren island.

As we have already observed, Domitian was very much a worshipper of the gods of Rome, especially Jupiter and Minerva. He had a shrine to Minerva in his bedroom. He also deified his brother, Titus, after his death. Union with his "gods" was a big thing to Domitian. And yet John kept on claiming to be a follower of Jesus Christ who was the Son of God and somehow also the one true God along with his Father and the Holy Spirit.

So when Domitian sent John to Patmos, it was at least partially to establish the "right pattern" in his mind where he, Domitian, could once again be in undisturbed "union" with his gods in the palace, gods that John kept denying, and that irritating old man, John, could be abandoned by his "so-called god" on a barren island. But then, lo and behold, we read this from John:

Revelation 1:10a *I was in the Spirit on the Lord's day,*

We find this phrase "the Lord's Day" just once in Scripture, right here in the book of The Revelation. It is how the early church referred to Sunday, their day of worship, the day that Jesus rose from the dead. Albert Barnes said, "The term was used generally by the early Christians to denote the first day of the week. It occurs twice in the Epistle of Ignatius to the Magnesians (about A.D. 101,) who calls the Lord's Day 'the queen and prince of all days.' Chrysostom (on Psalms 119) says, 'It was called the Lord's Day because the Lord rose from the dead on that day.' " (Linder, Barnes)

So it was Sunday, and John, whom Domitian would have assumed to be abandoned and alone, was instead "in the Spirit" on the Lord's Day. God, in some miraculous way, made Himself so very real to John on that island, some would call it a divine prophetic state, that John knew he was in the literal presence of God Himself while on that little barren speck of dirt in the midst of the Aegean Sea.

For all of his marble shrines, there was never one ounce of real communion between Domitian and his handmade gods there in the palace. But there on that island, God, the real God, came down and met with a ninety-year-old man who had loved Him for so very long.

And oh, how He met with him!

Revelation 1:10b *and heard behind me a great voice, as of a trumpet,* **11** *Saying, I am Alpha and Omega, the first and the last...*

There were some things that Domitian just **knew.** For instance, he just **knew** that Jesus was dead, and he just **knew** Jesus was not coming back. And the only problem with what he knew was that everything he knew was completely wrong.

When John was in the Spirit on the Lord's Day on that island, he heard a great voice behind him, a voice as if it were a trumpet blaring out the words, "*I am Alpha and Omega, the first and the last...*"

Those first two words, all by themselves, are utterly significant. Jesus did not say, "I was." He said, "I am." The One that Domitian was quite sure was just a past tense individual destined to be blown off the pages of history as if fine sand blown away by the winds of time, was instead a very real and present and living person destined to still be remembered and worshipped for all of the eternity in which the name of Domitian will be forever forgotten.

But He followed up those amazing words by saying [I am] *"the Alpha and Omega, the first and the last."* We saw those very words just a couple of verses ago in verse eight. This was Jesus giving Himself the justly deserved title of Alpha and Omega, A to Z, the first and the last. This title is an indication that Jesus is not a part of creation along with everything else; He is over and above the entirety of creation. This title is an indication that Jesus is not just a part of the story, not even just the choicest part of the story. As far as existence itself goes, He is the story, and we are merely in it. Everything else, including ourselves, is merely a supporting part; Jesus Christ is the Alpha and Omega; He is the omnipresent, self-existent God.

And that God showed up for one old man on a barren island in the middle of the sea.

Domitian assumed that once he got John to that island, his service for Christ was over.

There is not one thing about John's life work and ministry that Domitian appreciated or was even willing to tolerate. Everything that John stood for was antithetical to everything that Domitian believed. So when he put him on that island, one very definite thought on his heart was to shut John up and bring his ministry to an end forever.

And that was going to work out just exactly as well for him as everything else did in this matter. Look at what Jesus said to John when He began to speak to him:

Revelation 1:11b *...and, What thou seest, write in a book, and send it unto the seven churches which are in Asia; unto Ephesus, and unto Smyrna, and unto Pergamos, and unto Thyatira, and unto Sardis, and unto Philadelphia, and unto Laodicea.*

Let me use geography to paint an important picture in your mind at this point. Yes, Patmos was a barren rock in the midst of the Aegean Sea. But it was a mountainous, barren rock. Its highest point is 883 feet above sea level. And from that high vantage point, John could easily look just thirty miles to the east, and do you know what he would see? All of the areas that Jesus was describing to him in this verse, the region often called Asia Minor.

The John, whose ministry was supposed to be over as far as Domitian thought, and quite likely as far as John himself probably thought, instead had the Son of God Himself show up to him on that island and say in so many words, "John, look off to the east. Do you see that area over there, Ephesus, Smyrna, Pergamos, Thyatira, Sardis, Philadelphia, Laodicea? I need you to write something down for them. I want to send a letter apiece to every single one of them, John. And I want those seven letters to actually be one overarching letter that will tell everyone about every last thing they need to know about the past, the present, and even the future. John, you get to write the very last book of the Bible."

Child of God, this should be encouraging to you. If you can still see the need, and if you can still hear the sweet voice of the God who can meet the need, your service for Christ is not over yet.

Domitian assumed that he would hear of John's death and not the other way around.

What did Domitian intend for John? Ironically, there really is not any doubt of that, especially because of where he sent him. The name Patmos means "My Killing." Can you imagine trying to drum up any tourist business with a name like that?

Domitian, young, healthy, and in his mind all-powerful, very much expected his servants to bring him word just any day of the death of old John. But instead, on September 18, A.D. 96, eighteen months after he sent John to Patmos, Domitian was assassinated and was succeeded on the very same day by Cocceius Nerva, who then released John from exile. But then, John knew this was going to happen. Look at what Jesus told him after He told him to write those letters:

Revelation 10:11 *And he said unto me, Thou must prophesy again before many peoples, and nations, and tongues, and kings.*

John's last years were not retiring years; they were re-firing years. It really did not matter in the least that Domitian was done with John because Jesus was not done with John.

This is what I call a story with a happy ending. But it is also a story whose ending could have actually been much happier still. You see, Jesus, who came to speak to John on the Isle of Patmos, actually loved Domitian. In fact, He loved him so much that He died for him. He also loved him so much that He sent His very favorite apostle, the one who had once laid his head on His own breast, the one to whom He had entrusted the care of His own mother, to speak to Domitian personally and tell him about Jesus. There could have been no better soul-winner on earth to send to Domitian than John.

And yet Domitian is burning in hell, even though he once stood in the presence of that old man who could easily have led him to the Christ who could have taken him to Heaven.

That is the greatest error a person can possibly make.

Chapter Three
You Only Thought You Knew Him

Revelation 1:12 *And I turned to see the voice that spake with me. And being turned, I saw seven golden candlesticks;* **13** *And in the midst of the seven candlesticks one like unto the Son of man, clothed with a garment down to the foot, and girt about the paps with a golden girdle.* **14** *His head and his hairs were white like wool, as white as snow; and his eyes were as a flame of fire;* **15** *And his feet like unto fine brass, as if they burned in a furnace; and his voice as the sound of many waters.* **16** *And he had in his right hand seven stars: and out of his mouth went a sharp twoedged sword: and his countenance was as the sun shineth in his strength.* **17** *And when I saw him, I fell at his feet as dead. And he laid his right hand upon me, saying unto me, Fear not; I am the first and the last:* **18** *I am he that liveth, and was dead; and, behold, I am alive for evermore, Amen; and have the keys of hell and of death.* **19** *Write the things which thou hast seen, and the things which are, and the things which shall be hereafter;* **20** *The mystery of the seven stars which thou sawest in my right hand, and the seven golden candlesticks. The seven stars are the angels of the seven churches: and the seven candlesticks which thou sawest are the seven churches.*

It is amazing how many times in life you find out you did not really know people. This happens a lot, in bad ways and good ways. There have been times I was just sure that I knew people and then found out, to my detriment, that I really did not. But there have also been times when I thought I knew people and found out that they were actually a whole lot more impressive than I had ever imagined!

But if there was anyone on earth who could truly lay claim to knowing Jesus, it was John the Beloved.

He was one of Jesus' inner circle.

He was one of only three who got to see Jesus transfigured.

He was the disciple who leaned on Jesus' breast at supper.

He was the only disciple at the cross with Jesus.

He was the one who took Mary, the mother of Jesus, into his home.

John, it could be said, knew Jesus as well as any man could have known Him.

Fast forward many years to John as an old man on the same Isle of Patmos we looked at in the last chapter. He has been sent there to die and probably thinks he is going to. But then he hears a voice behind him; Jesus has stepped on the scene. He turns to see the person speaking, and when he does, he sees Jesus like he has never seen Him before! John "knew" Jesus in the sense that he was saved and had been a follower of Christ for many years. But he was about to find out that though he knew Jesus, he really did not *know* Jesus.

It would probably do all of us good to see Jesus once again but like we have never seen Him before. If we do, we will learn things about Him that we all desperately need to know. We do not need to settle for just being saved. Just like Paul said in Philippians 3:10, we need to *know* Him.

And this text can help us to do so.

If you did not know how He feels about the local church, then you only thought you knew Him.

Revelation 1:12 *And I turned to see the voice that spake with me. And being turned, I saw seven golden candlesticks;* **13a** *And in the midst of the seven candlesticks one like unto the Son of man...*

As John turned to see who was speaking to him, it quickly became evident that he was seeing things that were not "natural." He turned around on this barren island and saw something that had not been there just a second ago, seven golden candlesticks. They just instantly appeared from out of nowhere. In the middle of those candlesticks, there was someone standing, someone that John sort of recognized, someone that he called "*the Son of man.*" That is a title that Jesus used for Himself over and over again. John was seeing his beloved Jesus, but in a whole new way—a way that had intense meaning to it.

John said that he saw Jesus in the midst of the golden candlesticks. In other words, Jesus could have portrayed Himself to John any way that He so chose, and He chose to portray Himself this way. He chose to have John see Him in the middle of all these candlesticks.

Do you figure that maybe, just maybe, this was important? Oh yes, very important. Remember, this is the first time in about sixty years that John has seen Jesus. How you portray yourself to someone after a sixty-year absence is pretty important!

So what was Jesus saying? Well, to know that we need to know what those candlesticks represented. Fortunately, the Bible tells us exactly what they represented:

Revelation 1:20 *The mystery of the seven stars which thou sawest in my right hand, and the seven golden candlesticks. The seven stars are the angels of the seven churches: and* **the seven candlesticks which thou sawest are the seven churches**.

After a sixty-year absence, the first way that Jesus, the Son of God, portrays Himself to John is as the One who is walking in the midst of the churches! Not the synagogue, not the temple, not the home, not the workplace, not the palace, not the White House, not the little league game, not the scouts, not the county fair, the churches! Jesus portrayed Himself as walking in the midst of the literal local churches of that day.

Many people who call themselves Christians today do not seem to have any clue how the Christ they claim to follow feels about the local church. This was not some "universal church," some "brotherhood of believers" He was standing in the midst of; it was seven local churches. God highly prizes the local church. We are supposed to highly prize it as well!

Look at what Paul said to the elders of the local church at Ephesus:

Acts 20:28 *Take heed therefore unto yourselves, and to all the flock, over the which the Holy Ghost hath made you overseers, to feed the church of God, which he hath purchased with his own blood.*

It should be readily obvious that these local elders living in Ephesus were not being tasked with spiritually feeding the "universal church," all the believers around the world. They were specifically being tasked with feeding the local church at Ephesus, and it was that local church, that local assembly of saved believers, that Christ purchased with His own blood. Every real, local church, every assembly of saved believers is what Christ purchased with His own blood. God has always expected those who believe in Him to faithfully meet together as a local body to worship Him, and real believers have always understood that and been glad to do so:

Hebrews 10:25 *Not forsaking the assembling of ourselves together, as the manner of some is; but exhorting one another: and so much the more, as ye see the day approaching.*

Psalm 122:1 *I was glad when they said unto me, Let us go into the house of the LORD.*

Nehemiah 10:39b *...and we will not forsake the house of our God.*

Psalm 84:1 *How amiable are thy tabernacles, O LORD of hosts! 2 My soul longeth, yea, even fainteth for the courts of the LORD: my heart and my flesh crieth out for the living God. 3 Yea, the sparrow hath found an house, and the swallow a nest for herself, where she may lay her young, even thine altars, O LORD of hosts, my King, and my God. 4 Blessed are they that dwell in thy house: they will be still praising thee. Selah. 5 Blessed is the man whose strength is in thee; in whose heart are the ways of them. 6 Who passing through the valley of Baca make it a well; the rain also filleth the pools. 7 They go from strength to strength, every one of them in Zion appeareth before God. 8 O LORD God of hosts,* *hear my prayer: give ear, O God of Jacob. Selah.* **9** *Behold, O God our shield, and look upon the face of thine anointed.* **10** *For a day in thy courts is better than a thousand. I had rather be a doorkeeper in the house of my God, than to dwell in the tents of wickedness.*

God's house has always been precious to God and to any people who truly love God.

So if you did not know how Jesus feels about the local church, you only thought you knew Him.

If you did not know that He is the great High Priest, then you only thought you knew Him.

Revelation 1:13b *...clothed with a garment down to the foot, and girt about the paps with a golden girdle.*

In life, John saw Jesus day after day. On almost all of those days, he saw Jesus wearing the simple robes of a common laborer. That is how he was used to seeing Jesus. But when Jesus appeared to him on the Isle of Patmos, John saw Him dressed in a way that he had never seen Him before:

...clothed with a garment down to the foot, and girt about the paps with a golden girdle.

This was the garment of the High Priest. Laborers wore shorter robes. The priest's girdle was interlaced with gold; the girdle of Christ was all of gold. Jesus was portraying Himself to John as our Great High Priest:

Hebrews 6:20 *Whither the forerunner is for us entered, even Jesus, made an high priest for ever after the order of Melchisedec.*

Hebrews 4:14 *Seeing then that we have a great high priest, that is passed into the heavens, Jesus the Son of God, let us hold fast our profession.* **15** *For we have not an high priest which cannot be touched with the feeling of our infirmities; but was in all points tempted like as we are, yet without sin.*

1 Timothy 2:5 *For there is one God, and one mediator between God and men, the man Christ Jesus;*

Way back in the book of Job, Job, at one point, complained that there was no daysman, no mediator, no priest between God and man. He learned just a few chapters later that there actually is one! And we now know that there is a God in Heaven, who came down to earth, wrapped Himself in flesh, died as the sacrifice for our sins, rose from the dead, went back to Heaven, placed His own blood on the Mercy Seat, then sat down at the right hand of God, and ever liveth to make intercession for us! John said:

1 John 2:1 *My little children, these things write I unto you, that ye sin not. And if any man sin, we have an advocate with the Father, Jesus Christ the righteous:*

That is our Jesus, our advocate, our Great High Priest. When Jesus showed up to John after a sixty-year absence, it was in a way that let John know that He was walking in the midst of the seven churches and in clothing that let John know that He is our great high priest.

Up in West Virginia, where I preached a revival a few years ago, there is a Catholic Church just a block or so away. It is a tiny community; everyone knows everyone else. So when the priest was found out in public, falling down drunk, the local sheriff came and picked him up, took him home, told him to sleep it off, and left. That's nice, I think; after all, he is a man of the cloth! People need him to dry out and crawl back into his little box so they can get him to forgive their sins!

I trust you grasp the sarcasm in all of that.

You have no need of an earthly priest. I have no need of an earthly priest. They are no more holy or special than anyone else.

Further, while pastors and deacons and other servants are needed by man and designated by God for offices and services in the local church of today, we also do not need any pastor or deacon or anyone else to act as a mediator for us between God and man. In other words, not only do we not need any priests at all, we also do not need people in other legitimate offices acting like priests. A pastor is a pastor, not your mediator. You need him to preach to you and feed you and guard the flock, but you do not need him to take your sins before God to get them dealt with.

So, Jesus Christ is our Great High priest, and if you did not know that, then you only thought you knew Him!

If you did not know that He is the Ancient of Days, you only thought you knew Him.

Revelation 1:14a *His head and his hairs were white like wool, as white as snow...*

This is a unique view of Jesus that John was given. It had been sixty years or so. Remember that the last time John saw Jesus, Jesus was in His early thirties. He would have still had very dark hair at that time. Now John sees Him with hair like wool, as white as snow. That is important because that description has been used previously in the Bible:

Daniel 7:9 *I beheld till the thrones were cast down, and the Ancient of days did sit, whose garment was white as snow, and the hair of his head like the pure wool: his throne was like the fiery flame, and his wheels as burning fire.*

This is a vision of Jehovah God that Daniel saw. Several hundred years later, John saw the exact same person. Only he knew Him by another name, the name Jesus. The Jesus of Revelation 1 is the Ancient of Days of Daniel 7.

What does that name, the Ancient of Days, mean? The One who is eternal and eternally God!

There really are some things people ought to know about Jesus. For instance, He did not come into being at Bethlehem, He is not a created being, and He is not just a good man.

Jesus Christ is eternal and eternally God. He is the Son of God, and He is God the Son. He has always been; He will always be. He is the God of all power; He is the Ancient of days.

All of this is good to know since we are depending on Him!

If you did not know that nothing is hidden from His eyes, then you only thought you knew Him.

Revelation 1:14b *...and his eyes were as a flame of fire;*

What a sight that must have been to John. Just think about that. He was used to seeing the tender, compassionate, human eyes of Jesus. Now he turns around, he sees Jesus, but His eyes are so very different. His eyes are now as a flame of fire. This was His way of saying, "I see everything. I see beneath the surface. I see into your very heart and soul and mind."

Proverbs 15:3 *The eyes of the LORD are in every place, beholding the evil and the good.*

Job 34:21 *For his eyes are upon the ways of man, and he seeth all his goings.*

Hebrews 4:13 *Neither is there any creature that is not manifest in his sight: but all things are naked and opened unto the eyes of him with whom we have to do.*

We so often think of this truth in the negative sense, and it is true: God sees every bad thing we do.

But may I remind you that John, who saw Him like this for the very first time, was a good old man who was suffering intensely because he was doing right! That tells me that God does not just see every bad thing we do, but He also sees every good thing we do! Those things we do that no one ever sees and that we never receive credit for, God sees them all.

Whatever you do for the Lord, mark it down, I may never know about it, your family and friends may never know about it, but God sees it, and God knows it. Nothing is hidden from His fiery eyes! And if you did not know that, you only thought you knew Him!

If you did not know that every part of Him is perfectly pure, then you only thought you knew Him.

  Revelation 1:15a *And his feet like unto fine brass, as if they burned in a furnace...*

  John turned and saw Jesus, and he wrote about what he saw. Now, when you and I see people, there are things about them that we are not likely to ever notice or comment on. Their feet, for instance. When I met Dana, I did not notice her feet at all! Truthfully, I cannot remember the first time I ever did take notice of them. Feet are just sort of there.

  So for John to have taken notice of His feet, there had to be something exceptionally special about them. And there was. His feet were as bright as brass in a furnace!

  When I worked in jewelry, we used mainly silver and gold and platinum. But on occasion, we were called on to make something out of brass. I remember some pretty big brass horses that we would make out of molds. We would put that heated mold in a centrifuge and then put a pile of brass in the crucible beside it. We would put the torch to that brass and melt it into liquid. I found that when doing so, unlike when I did so with silver or gold, I actually had to wear sunglasses. That brass was intensely, painfully bright.

  That is what Jesus' feet looked like to John! Why was it like that? Why did Jesus portray Himself in that way? The feet are now, but especially were then, the dirtiest parts of the body. People walked everywhere on dusty roads wearing open sandals. That is why every household of any means had a hired servant that would wash the feet of anyone who came in.

  But on Jesus, that which should have been the dirtiest was utterly, intensely, painfully bright and pure.

  When the Bible says that Jesus was without sin, it actually means it.

  He never sinned in His words.
  He never sinned in His actions.
  He never sinned in His thoughts.
  He never sinned in His attitudes.

  So, Jesus was and is utterly, totally, thoroughly pure, and if you did not know that, you only thought you knew Him!

If you did not know that His voice can overpower anything in existence, then you only thought you knew Him.

  Revelation 1:15b *...and his voice as the sound of many waters.*

  When he turned, John did not just see Jesus; he also heard Him. And he described His voice as being like that of "*many waters.*" One of the loudest things on earth is the sound of water crashing and splashing together. If you get near just an average-sized waterfall, the noise is amazing. Get around a huge waterfall or a couple of bodies of water crashing together, and it is deafening. Niagara Falls, just one body of water, comes in at ninety-two decibels, which is loud enough to make a person go deaf if they listen to it unprotected for a long period of time. Imagine "many waters" and how loud it would be! Imagine the waters crashing across the earth during Noah's flood!

Just the voice of Jesus is enough to overpower His enemies. He does not have to scream and holler and use a megaphone; His voice has to be tempered and lowered at all times just to keep from hurting us, and if you did not know this, you only thought you knew Him!

If you did not know that He holds His men in His hand, then you only thought you knew Him.

Revelation 1:16a *And he had in his right hand seven stars...*

A few moments ago, we saw that He was walking in the midst of seven golden candlesticks. Now we see that number seven again; we see Him holding seven stars in His hands. What are these stars?

Revelation 1:20 *The mystery of the seven stars which thou sawest in my right hand, and the seven golden candlesticks.* **The seven stars are the angels of the seven churches**: *and the seven candlesticks which thou sawest are the seven churches.*

That English word "angels" is from the Greek word *angelos*, and it can be either human or spirit, depending on the context, because it means a messenger. In this case, it is not talking about spirit angels but human angels. This becomes very clear when we see John writing actual physical letters to those "angels" in chapters two and three.

Commentator Adam Clarke said, "The stars are afterwards interpreted as representing the seven angels, messengers, or bishops of the seven Churches. Their being in the right hand of Christ shows that they are under his special care and most powerful protection." (Clarke, 6: 973)

He is correct. This is talking about the messengers to the churches, and by that, it does mean the pastors! I know you have always suspected this, and you are right; I am in fact, an angel...

In all seriousness, the fact that God is holding His men in His hand presents a very sobering, two-part truth to us. One, God's men ought to always be very, very careful what they do. Two, God's people ought to always be very, very careful what they do with God's man.

So, John saw Jesus as the One who was holding His men in His hand, and if you did not know that, you only thought you knew Him!

If you did not know that all He needs to do is speak to win, then you only thought you knew Him

Revelation 1:16b *...and out of his mouth went a sharp twoedged sword...*

The Greek word for this word sword is *romphaia*, and it indicates a long, heavy, broad sword. We find that word again near the end of the book of The Revelation:

Revelation 19:21 *And the remnant were slain with the sword of him that sat upon the horse, which sword proceeded out of his mouth: and all the fowls were filled with their flesh.*

Twice, John saw his beloved Jesus, the One who had spoken with such compassion to so many while John was walking with him, as having a sword coming out of His mouth. The symbolism was inescapable and not at all complicated. The Jesus who came the first time and spoke words of love and compassion, the Jesus who said, *"Come unto me, all ye that labor and are heavy laden, and I will give you rest,"* (Matthew 11:28) is going to come the second time and speak words of judgment and destruction.

The Jesus who came the first time saying in so many words, "Come while there is time," is going to come the second time saying, "Time's up." He is coming, as it were, with a sword in his mouth; He will simply speak the words, and His enemies will be devastated.

I would hate to be an enemy of God.

Anyone who can simply speak a word and win the battle is not someone to be tangled with. And if you did not know that, you only thought you knew Him.

If you did not know that you cannot even handle the sight of Him with your natural eyes, then you only thought you knew Him.

Revelation 1:16c *...and his countenance was as the sun shineth in his strength.*

John used a descriptive term here to describe what Jesus looked like when he saw Him there on the Isle of Patmos. He specifically said that His countenance, His appearance, was like the sun when it is shining in its strength. In other words, the sun when it is at its highest point and completely unobstructed by clouds or anything else. A few seconds of looking directly at the sun like that will cause scarring on the retinas and blind spots that may be temporary but could be permanent. Look at the sun in its unobstructed strength for more than a minute or so and you absolutely will go blind. It is too bright for us to handle. And that is how bright Jesus appeared to John, who was seeing Him for the first time in sixty years. The last time he saw Him, He looked pretty normal, and John could gaze on Him for hours with no risk. But now, the similitude was put away, and Jesus was appearing as He really is in all of His glory.

Jesus is not like any other person. When He walked among us on earth and went up onto the mount of transfiguration, Him revealing His glory and shining like the sun was not the miracle. The miracle was that He walked day by day, veiling that glory, allowing men to see Him!

If you did not know that you cannot even handle the sight of Him with your natural eyes, you only thought you knew Him.

If you did not know that Jesus is the One who can make every mystery understandable, then you only thought you knew Him.

John saw all of these things, he saw the Jesus that he thought he knew, and he realized that he had not even scratched the surface in his knowledge of Jesus. When He saw all of this and when he realized that he only thought he knew Jesus, it had an impact on John:

Revelation 1:17a *And when I saw him, I fell at his feet as dead...*

You may have had some little emotional religious experience, but that is quite different from being reduced to nothing before His glory. When we truly get close to Christ and even begin to see Him as He is, all of our pride, arrogance, and boasting will drain away, and we will fear before Him. That is what happened to John. But Jesus, the Jesus that He was learning about all over again, was not going to leave him on his face in the dust:

Revelation 1:17b *...And he laid his right hand upon me, saying unto me, Fear not; I am the first and the last:*

I find something very interesting at this point: Jesus laid His *right* hand on John. This is the same right hand that held the seven active pastors of the seven churches. But John was not a pastor anymore; he was an exiled old man. Does it encourage you as it does me to realize that God still wants to touch us, even when we are old, sick, frail, and in our minds, useless?

He laid His right hand on John, and then for the third time in this one chapter and in this one conversation, called Himself "the first and the last" and told John not to be afraid.

Jesus then continued speaking to John:

Revelation 1:18 *I am he that liveth, and was dead; and, behold, I am alive for evermore, Amen; and have the keys of hell and of death.*

There is an amen in the middle of the verse. It marks a division in thought, and it divides something that John knew, the first part of the verse, from something he did not know, the second part of the verse. John knew quite well that his Jesus was the One who was living, died on the cross, came back to life, and would never die again throughout the endless ages. But now, he was learning a little about what Jesus did during those three days in the grave. Jesus paid a visit to death and hell, and He took their keys! The child of God never needs to fear getting locked behind the doors of either one because Jesus forever holds the keys.

But Jesus did not come to Patmos just to scare John with His new look or even just let him know about the keys He was carrying. Jesus had a task for John to do. He had already told John to write letters to the seven churches, and now He was going to give John an outline to go by:

Revelation 1:19 *Write the things which thou hast seen, and the things which are, and the things which shall be hereafter;*

This verse gave John and us a basic outline for the book of The Revelation. Chapter one is about the things that John saw, the past. Chapters two and three are the things which are, the things of the present. Chapters four through twenty-two are the things which shall be hereafter, the things of the future.

As Jesus began to wrap up His re-introduction to John, He said and did one more thing:

Revelation 1:20 *The mystery of the seven stars which thou sawest in my right hand, and the seven golden candlesticks. The seven stars are the angels of the seven churches: and the seven candlesticks which thou sawest are the seven churches.*

This was Jesus clearing up a mystery for John. He was unveiling the mystery, meaning the symbolism that He was using in His appearance. The seven golden candlesticks represented the seven churches that John was supposed to write to, and the seven stars were the angels, the pastors of those churches.

John did not know what these things were until Jesus told Him. But Jesus did tell him. Jesus is the One who will answer every question you have in His own time and make every mystery understandable.

If you did not know all of these things; if Jesus was just a sweet religious teacher to you and not the sovereign God and of incomprehensible glory, then you only thought you knew Him.

Chapter Four
Prophecy and Practice in the Fallen Church

Revelation 2:1 *Unto the angel of the church of Ephesus write; These things saith he that holdeth the seven stars in his right hand, who walketh in the midst of the seven golden candlesticks;* **2** *I know thy works, and thy labour, and thy patience, and how thou canst not bear them which are evil: and thou hast tried them which say they are apostles, and are not, and hast found them liars:* **3** *And hast borne, and hast patience, and for my name's sake hast laboured, and hast not fainted.* **4** *Nevertheless I have somewhat against thee, because thou hast left thy first love.* **5** *Remember therefore from whence thou art fallen, and repent, and do the first works; or else I will come unto thee quickly, and will remove thy candlestick out of his place, except thou repent.* **6** *But this thou hast, that thou hatest the deeds of the Nicolaitans, which I also hate.* **7** *He that hath an ear, let him hear what the Spirit saith unto the churches; To him that overcometh will I give to eat of the tree of life, which is in the midst of the paradise of God.*

God does some very remarkable things in the book of The Revelation. For instance, He makes extensive use of certain words to symbolize a truth He wants to convey. One of those words is the number *seven*. The word seven occurs fifty-four times in this book! That is amazing when you consider that the word seven only occurs four hundred sixty-three times in the entire Bible. In other words, the book of The Revelation, only twenty-two chapters long, contains nearly twelve percent of the "sevens" in the entire Bible.

The number seven is a number that symbolizes perfection, completion, or a perfect representation of the whole. That will come into play right now as we begin to look at the churches of Asia Minor. Notice again what John said as he opened the book:

Revelation 1:4 *John to the **seven** churches which are in Asia...*

John mentioned the *seven* churches of Asia. What is so significant about that? The significance is that there were more than seven churches in Asia. In addition to Ephesus, Smyrna, Pergamos, Thyatira, Sardis, Philadelphia, and Laodicea, which Jesus and John did mention, there were also churches at Phrygia, Pamphylia, Galatia, Pontus, Cappadocia, and many other regions of Asia Minor. The fact that God hand-picked seven, not six, and not eight, but seven of them lets us know that they were not only literal churches, but they were also seven churches that accurately represented all of the churches of that day. No matter what church you would have gone into across the world of that day, you could have looked at it for a while and said, "This church is a Sardis type of church. This church is an Ephesus type of church, etc."

Not only do they accurately represent the churches of that day, though, they also accurately represent the churches of our day. No matter what church you walk into today, you could observe it for a while and say, "This church is a Pergamos type of church. This church is a Smyrna type of church, etc." But even though these churches primarily represent the literal seven churches that existed in that day and can secondarily represent the conditions that can be found in churches throughout the years, these churches also accurately represent the general spiritual stages of the church from the time of the apostles until the trumpet sounds ending the church age. No matter what century a person lived in from the time of the apostles until now, that person could examine the totality of the churches in existence, and though all of those churches would be different and unique, he would still be able to say, "The church as a whole, at this particular point in history, is a Philadelphia type of a church, or a Laodicea type of a church, etc." That means that each one of these literal churches is significant both in practice and in prophecy.

Some churches are abundantly blessed by a series of godly pastors, one after the other. But I seriously doubt that any church ever had it quite as good as Ephesus did. The church of Ephesus was founded in Acts 19 by the Apostle Paul. Their third pastor was Paul's protege, Timothy.

But what about the second pastor? Here is the interesting thing: as John began to write to the church that was the nearest to the Isle of Patmos, he was also writing to the church that was the nearest to his heart. You see, church history and commentators tell us that John himself was the second pastor of the church of Ephesus.

Matthew Henry says that Paul started the church at Ephesus, and then "afterwards [it was] watered and governed by John, who had his residence very much there." (1123)

Can you imagine that? Paul, then John, then Timothy as the first three pastors of your church! That is what makes the letter to this church all the more startling, for this blessed church, just a few decades after its founding, was addressed by God as the *fallen church,* the church that had left its first love. John the apostle, the former pastor of that church, had to write to it and address it as such.

The prophecy of the fallen church

Everything God does, He does for a reason. He picked seven churches out of the many that were available for a reason. And He also addressed them in the order that He addressed them for a reason. The nearest church to where John was geographically was Ephesus. But it was also the nearest church to him chronologically. What I mean by that is this: Ephesus is the church that most closely mirrors the overall spiritual state of the church as a whole from the time of the apostles until the apostles and those who learned directly from them died out. And John was the last of the apostles. Notice what the Bible says of this church:

Revelation 2:2 *I know thy works, and thy labour, and thy patience, and how thou canst not bear them which are evil: and thou hast tried them which say they are apostles, and are not, and hast found them liars:* **3** *And hast borne, and hast patience, and for my name's sake hast laboured, and hast not fainted.*

That is all positive! When this church began, and for the first many years of its existence, it was on fire for God and in love with God. But look what comes next:

Revelation 2:4 *Nevertheless I have somewhat against thee, because thou hast left thy first love.*

In such a short period, this church saw its love for God fizzle out.

This is an excellent representation of the church as a whole from about A.D. 30 until A.D. 170. The Ephesian church age, if you will, was a time when the church as a whole, worldwide, started off in love with God and ended up forsaking Him for other loves. While the apostles were around, while everything was exciting and new, everything went fine. But their love cooled, events changed, and the church as a whole, in about A.D. 100[*], stopped looking like the church at Ephesus and started looking much more like the church of Smyrna, which we will examine in the next chapter of this book.

The practice of the fallen church

Each one of these letters is written in the exact same format as if God laid out a template for John to follow. In every one of them, we will see the description of Christ, the discernment of Christ, the direction of Christ, and the delight of Christ.

<u>The description of Christ</u>

Revelation 2:1 *Unto the angel of the church of Ephesus write; These things saith he that holdeth the seven stars in his right hand, who walketh in the midst of the seven golden candlesticks;*

When this letter arrived, it arrived at the most important city in all of Asia. The name Ephesus means "desirable." And not only was

---

[*] Note, the dates given of the "church ages" are approximates and educated opinions. God did not put up a sign at any point saying, "Now leaving the Ephesian church age!"

there much that made this church desirable to God, there was much that made the city desirable to man as well. It had an artificial harbor accessible to the largest ships that rivaled the famed harbor at Miletus. It stood at the entrance of the valley, which reaches far into the interior of Asia Minor, and, connected by highways with the chief cities of the province, Ephesus was the most easily accessible city in Asia, both by land and sea. It was a center of religious, political, and commercial development. The city stood upon the sloping sides and at the base of two hills, Prion and Coressus, and had a breathtaking view. Its climate was exceptionally fine, and the soil of the valley was unusually fertile.

But aside from the natural beauty and the famous harbor, what really made Ephesus stand out was the temple of the famed goddess Diana. It was one of the seven wonders of the ancient world and was widely regarded as the most beautiful structure on earth. Antipater of Sidon said, "Lo, apart from Olympus, the Sun never looked on aught so grand." (Nevres, 2021)

The foundation of the temple was rectangular in form, and the building was made of marble, with a decorated facade overlooking a spacious courtyard. Marble steps surrounding the building platform led to the high terrace, which was approximately 260 feet by 430 feet. The columns were 60 feet high with carved circular sides. There were 127 columns in total, holding up a colonnade roof. (Nostalgia, 2021)

The temple housed many works of art, including four ancient bronze statues of Amazons sculpted by the finest artists at the time. Among the paintings was one by the famous Apelles, a native of Ephesus, representing Alexander the Great hurling a thunderbolt. When Paul visited the city, the temple was adorned with golden pillars and silver statuettes, and in the center of it all was the image of Diana herself, who was the goddess of fertility. Here is the really interesting part: it was also a sanctuary for the criminal, a kind of city of refuge. No one could be arrested for any crime when within a bowshot of its walls. Because of that, a village sprang up around the temple in which the thieves and murderers and other criminals made their homes. (Orr, 961) Because the temple was their only protection, they guarded it carefully. *They held it in their hands*, if you will. That is one thing that makes the description of Christ so unique here. He describes Himself as *"he that holdeth the seven stars in his right hand, who walketh in the midst of the seven golden candlesticks;"*

The great temple and the priests of the goddess Diana were held in the hands of thieves and murderers. The fledgling baby church in Ephesus was held in the hands of the almighty God. The criminals at Ephesus hung around outside the walls of the house of their god; the churches had the very God of the universe walking in the midst of them! Seeing that, it is no wonder that things have turned out like they have. Christ and Diana (sometimes called Artemis) went head-to-head when Paul got to Ephesus, and things did not look good initially:

Acts 19:23 *And the same time there arose no small stir about that way.* **24** *For a certain man named Demetrius, a silversmith, which made silver shrines for Diana, brought no small gain unto the craftsmen;* **25** *Whom he called together with the workmen of like occupation, and said, Sirs, ye know that by this craft we have our wealth.* **26** *Moreover ye see and hear, that not alone at Ephesus, but almost throughout all Asia, this Paul hath persuaded and turned away much people, saying that they be no gods, which are made with hands:* **27** *So that not only this our craft is in danger to be set at nought; but also that the temple of the great goddess Diana should be despised, and her magnificence should be destroyed, whom all Asia and the world worshippeth.* **28** *And when they heard these sayings, they were full of wrath, and cried out, saying, Great is Diana of the Ephesians.* **29** *And the whole city was filled with confusion: and having caught Gaius and Aristarchus, men of Macedonia, Paul's companions in travel, they rushed with one accord into the theatre.* **30** *And when Paul would have entered in unto the people, the disciples suffered him not.* **31** *And certain of the chief of Asia, which were his friends, sent unto him, desiring him that he would not adventure himself into the theatre.* **32** *Some therefore cried one thing, and some another: for the assembly was confused; and the more part knew not wherefore they were come together.* **33** *And they drew Alexander out of the multitude, the Jews putting him forward. And Alexander beckoned with the hand, and would have made his defence unto the people.* **34** *But when they knew that he was a Jew, all with one voice about the space of two hours cried out, Great is Diana of the Ephesians.* **35** *And when the townclerk had appeased the people, he said, Ye men of Ephesus, what man is there that knoweth not how that the city of the Ephesians is a worshipper of the great goddess Diana, and of the image which fell down from Jupiter?* **36** *Seeing then that these things cannot be spoken against, ye ought to be quiet, and to do nothing rashly.* **37** *For ye have brought hither these men, which are neither robbers of churches, nor yet blasphemers of your goddess.* **38** *Wherefore if Demetrius, and the craftsmen which are with him, have a matter against any man, the law is open, and there are deputies: let them implead one another.* **39** *But if ye enquire any thing concerning other matters, it shall be determined in a lawful assembly.* **40** *For we are in danger to be called in question for this day's uproar, there being no cause whereby we may* *give an account of this concourse.* **41** *And when he had thus spoken, he dismissed the assembly.*

When Paul's teachings hit these men in the wallet, they stirred up a riot. They made sure that no one would ever forget that Diana was a god and that the church was a temporary, fleeting, false thing. But the temple of Diana, that great structure, was burned to the ground in A.D. 262 and never re-built. Yet all over the world, at this very moment, people are meeting together in churches to preach and teach about Christ. Why did the temple of Diana fall while the church of the living God is still going strong? It is exactly what Christ said would happen:

Matthew 16:18b *...and upon this rock I will build my church; and the gates of hell shall not prevail against it.*

Think of Diana worship then as being like Islam now. The worshippers of Diana wanted Christianity destroyed, and they were not able to do it. They were the most powerful thing going, and they could not do it. Muhammad and Islam will find the same thing to be true: Christ has promised to preserve His church, and He will!

The temple and priests of Diana were held in the hands of common criminals outside her walls. The men of the living God are held in the hand of God, who is every moment walking in the midst of the churches.

The discernment of Christ

Revelation 2:2 *I know thy works, and thy labour, and thy patience, and how thou canst not bear them which are evil: and thou hast tried them which say they are apostles, and are not, and hast found them liars:* **3** *And hast borne, and hast patience, and for my name's sake hast laboured, and hast not fainted.*

Please see that Christ *knows* what is happening in the churches. He does not have to guess, or investigate, or rely on scouting reports. He *knows* what is happening. It is pleasant to observe that which He knew about this church:

He knew their works and labor. Works and labor... those two words sound a bit redundant, don't they? But they are not redundant; they are progressive. The word work is from *ergon*, and it simply means hard work. But labor is from the word *kopos*, and it means labor unto weariness. In other words, this was a church full of people who worked for God until most average people would quit, and then they kept on going and going and going and going. If you needed anything done, somebody in the church of Ephesus could get it done for you, no matter how large the task. If there was a mountain to be moved, and all they had to work with was a spoon, you better look out for flying dirt.

What a commendation! What a character trait. How I wish that we here in America were breeding people like this today instead of the whiny, self-anointed victims that our liberal public schools and colleges are producing.

But it is bad enough when people out in the world are whiny and lazy; it is absolutely inexcusable when it is people in the house of God behaving like a bunch of victims. Emulate the Ephesian church! When God looks at you, let Him see that you are *working and laboring.*

He knew their patience. This word means endurance through trials. In other words, He saw something He liked in them. He saw that they did not quit when things got hard. I talk to pastors all over, and people like that are getting rarer and rarer! But parents, hear me: if you run when things get hard, you will teach your children to do the same. And you may only run from the house of God, but if you have taught them to run when things get hard there, they will go farther than you and run from the God of the house.

This church at Ephesus was made up of stayers, not runners, and God liked that about them.

He knew that they could not bear evil people. Look again at the exact words He used in verse two, *"and how thou canst not bear them which are evil"* What a commendation! Especially if it can be said of a church in our day when a large majority of woke evangelical churches absolutely *can* bear those that are evil. In fact, they welcome them in, put them in leadership positions, and call you "uncharitable" if you speak out against it.

Churches all around are ordaining and marrying gays, bringing active adulterers into membership, promoting abortion, even embracing pedophiles. The Ephesian church "could not bear" a crowd like that, and neither can any true church today. They and we could and can love them enough to confront them over their sin and try to win them to Christ, but we cannot simply "wrap graceful arms around them" and act as if nothing is wrong with what they are doing.

He knew that they had tried them which said they were apostles, and were not, and had found them liars. Even in John's day, new religious leaders were springing up everywhere. Apostle Smith, Bishop Jones, Elder Brown. Yet this church had the audacity to check the credentials of every would-be religious leader. They figured anybody could buy a business card or print out a doctorate. They ignored those things and checked what people believed, and how they behaved, and what they knew about the Bible, and whether they were after the money. They sorted out the true from the liars, and they did not hesitate to call a liar a liar.

He knew that they did everything they did for Christ's name, not their own. Notice something carefully:

Revelation 2:3 *And hast borne, and hast patience, and for my name's sake hast laboured, and hast not fainted.*

Did you notice the Proverbs-like parallelism? In verse two, you see the terms labor, patience, and bear. Then in verse three, you see those same terms in reverse order, borne, patience, labor. It is the same list. Here, though, he adds something that tells us *why* they did *what* they did. They did it all for His name's sake. They were not the least bit interested in any credit.

What could be accomplished if people were not so concerned about getting credit? How good can the pulpit, or the sound booth, or the singing, or the bus ministry be if all we care about is glorifying God, and we never get defensive, and we never expect people to put our name up in lights? What a great group of things to know about a church.

If only it could stop there. But unfortunately, there was also something negative that Christ knew about this church.

He knew they had left their first love.

Revelation 2:4 *Nevertheless I have somewhat against thee, because thou hast left thy first love.*

Oh, how grieved we ought to be to ever realize that our Savior has something against us! How our eyes ought to fill with tears and our hearts nearly break until everything is made right!

The church at Ephesus read this letter and found out that Christ had something against them. Outwardly, everything was still in order. Their doctrine was right, their behavior was right, their looks were right. But inwardly, the very heart had died within the body. This church had left its first love. The word left is from *aphaykas,* and it means to neglect, to overlook, to let die away. It was not as if these people were spitting in God's face. Quite the contrary. They still respected Him as much as ever. But they got so busy *doing* that they forgot to be *loving.* They let their service become a hollow duty rather than a happy devotion. They remembered the what and forgot the Who.

Every Sunday school class needs teachers who will *do.* I mean people who will have class activities and call the students who are out and recruit new students. But doing for God, as good as it is, can never take the place of loving God. And if you love Him, your doing will take on new meaning, new life, new vibrancy. Whatever you are doing for God, let it be done out of a heart of love toward God.

Do, church. Do and do and do. Work for the night is coming. But above all, love. Love and love and love the God who saved you, and your doing will be so much easier, and the God who made you will be much happier with you than ever before. This church, the church at Ephesus, had left its first love.

And that brings us to:

The direction of Christ

Revelation 2:5 *Remember therefore from whence thou art fallen, and repent, and do the first works; or else I will come unto thee quickly, and will remove thy candlestick out of his place, except thou repent.* **6** *But this thou hast, that thou hatest the deeds of the Nicolaitans, which I also hate.*

A man sits alone in his darkened living room. He has behaved in such a way that his family does not even like to be around him anymore. His wife goes to bed hours before he does. The kids get out of the house as early as they can in the morning and come in as late in the evening as they can get by with. He wonders what in the world went wrong and what he can do to fix it. He picks up a book off of the shelf and opens it to read a bit. When he does, a picture falls out of it. It is from a few years ago. All of the family was in a group photo, a picture that was taken at the zoo. Everybody in it is smiling, having a great time. The memories of how things were come flooding back to him. He notices that he was holding his wife's hand in that picture. "That's right, isn't it," he thinks, "I used to hold my wife's hand." In his other arm, he is holding one of the kids, and the other two are snuggled up close to his legs. What a flood of memories. Memories of how he used to love his family and how they used to love him right back.

That is the idea behind what Jesus is saying. If you have grown cold on God, if you used to be so devoted, but now you are so apathetic, you need to remember. You need to pick up a mental photo of how things once were. You need to think back to the sweet times and find out where you left that pathway so that you can get back onto it again. For some, a bit of hurt feelings cooled their love for God. For some, they got to hanging around a crowd of people that were always bitter, and negative, and abrasive, and they picked up those same poisoned attitudes. The love they once had for God is about to die by neglect, and they need to revive it quickly. If you do not, God said, if you do not go back and do those first works, get back in at the basics where you started, the candlestick will eventually be removed out of its place.

Do you remember what that candlestick represented? You need to remember it because when you do, you will realize that this is one of the most frightening statements in the entire Bible. Revelation 1:20 said that the seven candlesticks are the seven churches. So when God told that church that if they did not rekindle their first love, God would remove their candlestick, He was saying that He would remove their church.

A church can be removed from the place that God assigned it to or even become non-existent. No church is ever promised perpetuity. Many churches that used to be living and vibrant are now dead and gone. Every member of every church ought to realize the responsibility they have in this!

This was written to the angel of the church for him to communicate to the entire church. Every person in the pew will either by their devotion contribute to the continuity of a church or by their apathy contribute to the death of a church.

This thing of leaving your first love is a sin, *a sin*. God said in verse five that it is something to be repented of!

You can take your first love with you all of your life. Or you can wake up one day as an old man or an old woman and realize in horror that the love you had for God at youth camp, and in Sunday School, and in the bus ministry, and in the youth programs has been gone for years, and you did not even miss it, but you did miss and lose a lot of important things along the way.

That is a hard, cutting truth. And I believe that is why God did something unusual at this point. What He had said doubtless cut them to the soul, as it should. But then He turned, after the negative, and pointed out one more positive:

Revelation 2:6 *But this thou hast, that thou hatest the deeds of the Nicolaitans, which I also hate.*

Could God not have included this positive with the first list of positives in verses two and three? Absolutely. But instead, He chose to sandwich the negative between two positives. I am glad that God in mercy thinks of things like that.

This positive is that the Ephesian church hated the deeds of the Nicolaitans, which God also hated. The word *nikao* means *to conquer*, and *laos* means *the people*. The Nicolaitans were people who treated their "inferiors" like dirt and lorded their authority over them.

Some years ago, I ran across a very appropriate and personal example of this type of thing. I was speaking to my grandmother, who was a devout member of the local Catholic Church. Suddenly she said, "Oh dear, I need to go. It is my day to go to the priest's home and empty his kitty litter box. He says it is beneath a man of his station to do it."

I advised her to keep the kitty litter and throw out the priest.

I think also of a very popular modern woke evangelical pastor who spent a lot of time talking about humility and accountability in leadership. But then, when a church election for elders did not go his way, he went full progressive leftist on everyone and accused them of "being used by Satan."

Do not ever let that kind of a snobby, elitist attitude take hold in a church. If you are in any area of leadership, remember this statement, "People in the pews are not here for us; we are here for them."

The delight of Christ

Revelation 2:7 *He that hath an ear, let him hear what the Spirit saith unto the churches; To him that overcometh will I give to eat of the tree of life, which is in the midst of the paradise of God.*

It is God's delight that we hear, that we pay attention to what He has said. Nobody likes to be ignored, least of all God.

It is God's delight that we overcome. In this case, overcoming means that we recapture that first love, that we rekindle the fire that has burned down to embers, that we remember how hot our love for God used to be, and crawl up to an altar and make it so again. Sweep the sin out of the way, cut the ties with whoever or whatever has made you grow cold, and add the love back to your labor.

It is God's delight that whoever overcomes will be given to eat of the tree of life, which is in the middle of the paradise of God.

The tree of life is mentioned only six times in the Bible. Three are in Genesis, and then we never read of it again until the last three times, all of which are found in the book of The Revelation. In Genesis, fallen man was barred from having any of it. In Revelation 22, redeemed man is given the right to it. Those who go to Heaven can reach out and take as much of the fruit of the tree of life as they want. But here in Revelation 2, something extra, something special, is added. To those who overcome, those who retain, or regain, that hot love for God, God said that He Himself would give that person to eat of the tree of life.

The overcomer arrives in Heaven battered from the storms of life, having started out the Christian race in love with God, having ended the Christian race in love with God, having worked, and labored, and been patient. And when He steps on shore, Jesus takes him by the hand, leads him to the tree of life, reaches up with His nail-scarred hand, and plucks him off a choice fruit. He turns and smiles and looks into the face of a saint who is weeping for all they have passed through. He wipes away those tears and then gives that overcomer that fruit from the tree. All of the bitter taste that this life has left in that saint's mouth is drowned out and washed away by the sweet nectar of Heaven, and that hot love grows so strong that if we were not in a glorified body, our hearts would literally burst with the joy of that moment.

Chapter Five
Prophecy and Practice in the Faithful Church

Revelation 2:8 *And unto the angel of the church in Smyrna write; These things saith the first and the last, which was dead, and is alive;* **9** *I know thy works, and tribulation, and poverty, (but thou art rich) and I know the blasphemy of them which say they are Jews, and are not, but are the synagogue of Satan.* **10** *Fear none of those things which thou shalt suffer: behold, the devil shall cast some of you into prison, that ye may be tried; and ye shall have tribulation ten days: be thou faithful unto death, and I will give thee a crown of life.* **11** *He that hath an ear, let him hear what the Spirit saith unto the churches; He that overcometh shall not be hurt of the second*

In the last chapter, we looked at the prophecy and practice of Ephesus, the fallen church. Now we will turn our attention to the city and church of Smyrna, the faithful church.

The prophecy of the faithful church

Smyrna was the next closest to John geographically in the pattern of a circle that God was drawing. It was also the next nearest to John chronologically. Overlapping the Ephesian church age, Smyrna is the church that most closely mirrors the overall spiritual state of the church as a whole from about A.D. 60 to about A.D. 350. It was during that time period that the church underwent extreme persecution, and many of its faithful members were put to death. The name Smyrna means *crushed*, and they were indeed put under extreme pressure, as was the church as a whole during a very specific time period.

But while the church at Ephesus during some very good times was addressed as the fallen church, the church that had left its first love, the church at Smyrna during the very worst of times was described as the faithful church. Out of all of the seven churches addressed in these seven letters, only this church and the church of Philadelphia have nothing negative at all said of them. All of the other churches found themselves in a position where Christ said, "I have somewhat against you," or in some other way pointed out things that He was not satisfied with.

But not Smyrna. They were going through the fire, but they were faithful in the fire. In fact, I would like you to notice something very pointed and prophetic that God said that many at the church of Smyrna probably did not understand as well looking forward as we do looking back:

Revelation 2:10 *Fear none of those things which thou shalt suffer: behold, the devil shall cast some of you into prison, that ye may be tried; and ye shall have tribulation* **ten days***: be thou faithful unto death, and I will give thee a crown of life.*

What did God mean when He told this church it would have persecution for ten days? This church experienced many more than ten literal days of persecution; they underwent years of persecution.

Remember that the Bible itself is loaded with specific symbolism, especially in reference to time. For instance, Daniel's "seventy weeks" are actually seventy sevens of years, for a total of four hundred ninety.

Here is another one: the *day of the Lord* in Scripture is actually well over a thousand years in length, as you read the description of it. It includes the Tribulation, and the Millennium, and some of what follows the Millennium.

That is the very same type of thing that God is doing here in the letter to Smyrna when he refers to ten *days* of persecution. Here is what we know from a study of history concerning the emperors of Rome.

Nero was on the throne when the church began in earnest. He grew to hate Christians. Tacitus says that he started the fire that burned Rome to the ground. And whether that can be proven or not, one thing that is known for certain is that he blamed the devastating fire on the followers of Christ. He hated Christians with a passion. He crucified them indiscriminately, fed them to the lions in the arena, and others he simply staked up in his garden, covered them in tar, and lit them on fire to light his garden parties. (Public Broadcast Service, 2021)

It was Nero who caused a law to be passed that said this: "If anyone confesses that he is a Christian, he shall be put to death, without further trial, as a convicted enemy of mankind." (Of the Ten. 2021)

Domitian came to the throne in A.D. 93. Thereafter, Antipas was killed, John banished, Urticinus beheaded with an ax, among the thousands of others who were killed just for following Christ.

Trajan came to the throne in A.D. 102. It was because of him that Simon Cleophas was crucified, Ignatius was thrown to the wild beasts, and Onesimus was stoned to death. Countless others were scourged, stoned, and tortured in ways I cannot even describe here.

Marcus Aurelius became the emperor in A.D. 166. He caused people to be burned with red hot plates and others to be torn apart limb from limb like a chicken on a plate. This persecution was so great, a bishop named Irenaeus had more than 19,000 of his members tortured and killed. (Wolff)

Septimius Severus came to the throne in A.D. 201, and his son Alexander carried on what he started. During this day of persecution, tens of thousands of Christians were brought in chains from Egypt and Africa to Alexandria to be put to death. Among those killed were Vivia Perpetua and Felicitas. Vivia Perpetua was a lady of Carthage, about twenty-six years old, well-born, and well-educated. She had a newborn baby boy. She was arrested for her Christianity and sentenced to die. Her father and brother tried to persuade her to recant, but she would not. She was brought before the procurator Hilarianus, who used every emotional tactic to persuade her to forsake Christ. He said, "Spare the grey hairs of your father, and the infancy of your boy, offer sacrifice for the well-being of the emperor." She answered, "I will not do so." The procurator asked, "Are you a Christian?" She freely admitted it. She was then condemned. When they were taken into the amphitheater, they walked in as victors, with radiant faces, singing hymns. A fierce bull was sent to maim and kill Perpetua. When it slammed into her, she fell, and her tunic was torn. This woman, who was about to die, then reached down and pulled the tunic about her; even in such a dire moment, she did not want to be immodest. What an indictment on women of our day! Her companion Felicitas was crushed. Perpetua did not care for her own wounds but went to Felicitas to lift her up. The people were so stunned by these two brave women and by the fact the bull refused to attack again, they recalled them temporarily. A young soldier was then commanded to thrust the condemned Christians through with the sword. When he stabbed Perpetua between the ribs, she could not help but cry out, and the soldier acted as if he could not go on. This would have meant his life, so Vivia Perpetua guided his hand to stab her in such a way that she would be killed. (Vedder, 38) (Foxe, 12)

Maximin became emperor in A.D. 237. He specifically chose to target not Christians in general but preachers of Christ in specific. Is it any surprise that his persecution was the shortest of all since God killed him in only two years?

Decius was next, coming to the throne in A.D. 251. He caused public mandates to go out that if any would not apostatize from Christ, he should be tortured and killed in any way that could be devised.

Valerius and his son, **Gallien**, A.D. 259, was the next day of persecution. He forbade Christians anywhere from assembling together, and when they did so anyway, they were tortured and killed.

Aurelian, A.D. 273. He instituted the ninth day of persecution verbally. But when he picked up a pen to sign the decree, God struck him with paralysis. Shortly thereafter, he himself was killed by a trusted associate.

Diocletian, A.D. 284, was the tenth Roman emperor to institute an official persecution against followers of Christ.

How much of a coincidence is it that God told the church at Smyrna they would have ten days of persecution, and then the church as a whole underwent ten different, specific periods of persecution at the hand of Rome?

None at all.

It is not coincidence; it is prophecy! Every one of these churches was both a literal church and a church chosen by God to illustrate what time periods in the future would be like for the church as a whole. I do not want to jump ahead too far, but knowing that, we can look at our day and see both Philadelphia and Laodicea in our times, and we can know that Jesus is coming soon.

The practice of the faithful church

Each one of these letters is written in the exact same format as if God laid out a template for John to follow. In every one of them, we will see the description of Christ, the discernment of Christ, the direction of Christ, and the delight of Christ.

The description of Christ

Revelation 2:8 *And unto the angel of the church in Smyrna write; These things saith the first and the last, which was dead, and is alive;*

Thirty-five miles north of Ephesus sat a city often called the pride of Asia, the splendid seaport city of Smyrna. It was an extremely wealthy city, made so by the imports and exports that passed through its harbors. It had wide, paved streets, an established monetary system, and schools of science and medicine. If you had been there in A.D. 156, you would have noticed immediately a 20,000-seat theater built high up on mount Pagus. Passing through the streets, you would have come upon a temple built in A.D. 23 in honor of the emperor Tiberius Caesar and his mother, Julia. Further on, you would see the temples of Zeus and Cybele, connected by a street called the Golden Street.

But if you had been in Smyrna on a specific day in A.D. 156, you would have seen more than just a wealthy, beautiful city. You would, on that specific day, also have seen an old man, eighty-six years old in fact, being shoved along the streets by an angry mob. His name was Polycarp, and for many years, he had been the pastor of the church at Smyrna. He was being brought into the theater, where an angry crowd awaited. As he came before the tribunal, his crime was announced: refusal to worship the emperor, Marcus Aurelius. The proconsul looked at this old man and had pity on him. He said to Polycarp, "Consider yourself and have pity on your great age. Reproach Christ, and I will release you." Polycarp answered, "These many years have I served Him, and He never once wronged me. How can I blaspheme my King who saved me?"

The tribunal threatened him with wild beasts and fire, to which Polycarp replied, "What are you waiting for? Do whatever you please." He then voluntarily made his way to the stake to be burned, having been faithful in life and now faithful in death. When the fire was lit, the flames bent away from him on all sides and would not touch him. Finally, a soldier came near and stabbed him with a spear, sending Polycarp into the presence of the Christ he loved so dearly.

With such a pastor as that, it is no wonder that we can read this text and refer to Smyrna as the faithful church.

And with a city like that, so very stuck on itself, believing that it is the end-all-be-all of human civilization, it is no wonder that Christ described Himself to them as the First and the Last, the entire story, the center, the focus, the point of it all. *That is a good reminder.*

But He also described Himself as the one who was dead, and is alive, referencing yet again His death, burial, resurrection, and immortality. This was spoken to a church in the midst of a city that literally believed it would never die. But in 1424, it was invaded and destroyed by the armies of Islam. The city died, but Christ is still alive. That is a great lesson to all of us to affix ourselves to something permanent, and only Christ qualifies in that context!

The discernment of Christ

Revelation 2:9 *I know thy works, and tribulation, and poverty, (but thou art rich) and I know the blasphemy of them which say they are Jews, and are not, but are the synagogue of Satan.*

What was it that Christ said He knew about this church?

To begin with, He knew that they were workers. This was also mentioned as a commendation to the church of Ephesus. God prizes workers!

And then we find that He knew their tribulation. This also should be a comforting thought to us. Whatever we are going through, God knows about it.

Next, we learn that He knew that they were poor. All of their worldly goods had been seized because of their faith, and He did not miss that fact. The God who is in charge of rewarding those who follow Him knows each loss we bear along the way. But as we see that bit of knowledge, we are also given a big truth in a small parenthesis, *"but thou art rich."* Their earthly poverty may have seemed to the world around them to be proof of their failure, but in reality, it was no more than a thin mask veiling their success! Any church and any person who is faithful to God is rich in every way that legitimately matters.

Lastly, He knew that they were encountering people who were not what they claimed to be. Specifically, He said, *"I know the blasphemy of them which say they are Jews, and are not, but are the synagogue of Satan."* Adam Clarke said:

> "There were persons there who professed Judaism, and had a synagogue in the place, and professed to worship the true God; but they had no genuine religion, and they served the devil rather than God." (6: 977)

This would have been a huge hindrance to the church at Smyrna. But Christ knew about it. They did not have to make Him aware of it; He already knew.

This will happen in every church that God is using and in every area in which Christ is using a church. True churches will likely face more opposition from those who are followers of the devil who falsely claim belief in God than from those who claim there is no God!

The direction of Christ

Revelation 2:10 *Fear none of those things which thou shalt suffer: behold, the devil shall cast some of you into prison, that ye may be tried; and ye shall have tribulation ten days: be thou faithful unto death, and I will give thee a crown of life.*

Based on what Christ knew about what was going on in and around the church at Smyrna, what were His directions to that church?

One, do not be afraid of what you are going to suffer.

The word fear in this verse is from the word *phobos,* and we get our word *phobia* from it. If there was ever a church that could have had a giant phobia of what was to come, the church at Smyrna, and the church as a whole from about A.D. 60 to A.D. 350, could have. The devil himself was going to be behind their persecution and imprisonment. Yet God told them not to fear!

Two, be faithful unto death.

It is tempting to throw in the towel when things get hard. No one wants to quit when things are easy, but almost everyone is tempted to quit when things are hard, especially when it is horrific persecution we are talking about. Many Christians today fear this more than anything. And yet, the direction of Christ is that we fear not and that we remain faithful even unto death.

On what basis would He give such instructions?

He could just simply say, "Because I suffered and died for you." But though He could have rightfully said that, He did not say that. Instead, He said, "*be thou faithful unto death, and I will give thee a crown of life.*" The crown of life is one of the tangible rewards we can win by what we do for Christ in this life. God sees and knows when we hurt and suffer for the cause of Christ, and He will make sure the reward we earn for being faithful through all of that will be well worth it!

The delight of Christ

Revelation 2:11 *He that hath an ear, let him hear what the Spirit saith unto the churches; He that overcometh shall not be hurt of the second death.*

What is the delight of Christ for people who are in a Smyrna-like circumstance?

One, it is God's delight that we hear, that we pay attention to what He has said. Nobody likes to be ignored, least of all God

Two, it is God's delight that we overcome. And in this context, overcoming means that we continue to be faithful, no matter what.

Three, it is God's delight that we who overcome will not be hurt of the second death. In other words, real Christians can take pleasure in the fact that there may be pain associated with our first death, but we will be untouched by the second death. We may have to go through the fire here, but we will never feel a flame in eternity.

No matter how bad it gets here, remind yourselves that this is literally the worst it will ever be. The only heaven the lost will ever know is their pitiful version of heaven on earth during their short lifetime, and then they will experience hell for all eternity. But the only hell the saved will ever know is the pitiful torment the devil can put us through here in our lifetimes, and then we will experience heaven for all eternity.

Be faithful!

Chapter Six
Prophecy and Practice in the Fluctuating Church

Revelation 2:12 *And to the angel of the church in Pergamos write; These things saith he which hath the sharp sword with two edges;* **13** *I know thy works, and where thou dwellest, even where Satan's seat is: and thou holdest fast my name, and hast not denied my faith, even in those days wherein Antipas was my faithful martyr, who was slain among you, where Satan dwelleth.* **14** *But I have a few things against thee, because thou hast there them that hold the doctrine of Balaam, who taught Balac to cast a stumblingblock before the children of Israel, to eat things sacrificed unto idols, and to commit fornication.* **15** *So hast thou also them that hold the doctrine of the Nicolaitans, which thing I hate.* **16** *Repent; or else I will come unto thee quickly, and will fight against them with the sword of my mouth.* **17** *He that hath an ear, let him hear what the Spirit saith unto the churches; To him that overcometh will I give to eat of the hidden manna, and will give him a white stone, and in the stone a new name written, which no man knoweth saving he that receiveth it.*

In the last chapter, we looked already at the prophecy and practice of Smyrna, the faithful church. Now we will turn our attention to the city and church of Pergamos, the fluctuating church.

The prophecy of the fluctuating church

Pergamos was the next closest to John along the geographical circle that God was drawing, and it was also the next nearest to him chronologically. Overlapping Smyrna a bit, Pergamos is the church that most closely mirrors the overall state of the church from about A.D. 325 up until about the seventh century. The name *Pergamos* has two primary meanings: high tower and thoroughly married. That is so very significant when you realize that from A.D. 325 until the seventh century, the church, or at least that which called itself the church, began to worship at the high tower of Rome, and the church and the state became thoroughly married through the efforts of a man named Constantine.

The church of Smyrna underwent ten brutal persecutions under the hands of the emperors of Rome. Yet, for all of those persecutions, the church stayed faithful. The devil banked on outward pressure crumbling the church, and it did not work. It never has! Persecution from without strengthens the church that falls on Jesus as its Protector. So instead, the devil took a different approach. Today, we call it "if you can't beat 'em, join 'em." The devil eased off on the pressure and decided to let everybody in on this religion thing! After Diocletian and his successor died, Maxentius and Constantine battled it out for the throne of Rome. In A.D. 325, on the night before a major battle between these two, Constantine supposedly saw a vision of a fiery cross in the sky, with the words "In this sign conquer." So, without faith in Christ, without repentance, without acknowledging his own sinfulness or that of his troops, he just baptized everybody and proclaimed them as Christians. So, as the emperor to be, he became the official head of the church as well as the state. Church and state were now thoroughly married, and the Roman Catholic Church was born. Both the church and state became powerful and inseparable.

A church should be able and willing to confront the state about wickedness, but this one did not because it was thoroughly married to it and worshipping at its high tower.

When we use the term *thoroughly married,* you may think "can a person be **sort of** married?" Yes. Just ask the woman whose husband does not work... trashes the house... never wants to cuddle... ask her if she is married, she will say "I suppose." She is, in her mind, "sort of" married. Ask the man whose wife has completely let herself go since they got married, and is as cold as an ice cube, and makes him keep up the house while she sits in front of the tv and eats bon bons. Ask him if he is married, and he will say, "I guess." He is, in his mind, "sort of" married.

But then think of a couple who has kept themselves in good condition, and he opens her doors, and she keeps a clean house, and he works to bring home the bacon, and he is always sending her flowers, and she always has that "I can't wait till you get home" look in her eyes, those two are "thoroughly married."

That was the condition between the church and state as of the time that Constantine created the basis for the church of Rome.

As always, please understand that there was, even then, a true church, a bunch of believers who still held all of the doctrines of Christ and the apostles just like they always had. But there was also a much more prominent and powerful "church" that deviated wildly from all of that.

The church of Rome did whatever it wanted, no matter how wicked, and the state was there to back it up with the sword.

The state did whatever it wanted, no matter how wicked, and the church was there to back it up by claiming that anyone who disagreed would go to hell.

The three hundred fifty year or so period represented by the literal church at Pergamos was the time when the devil started his own church, which had the full backing of the might of Rome, while the true church had to fight to keep its members faithful to true Christianity. Persecution did not shake true believers, but the popular and acceptable religion of Rome made true believers harder and harder to find. Verse fourteen tells us that Balaam was there, teaching idolatry. Just like the references to Jezebel in these letters, the use of the name Balaam takes us back to a very real and very wicked Old Testament character. There was someone in the church at Pergamos even in John's day who was so leading the church into idolatry, just as Balaam did two thousand years before, that God in so many words labeled him as Balaam.

And this was also a very evident prophecy of Balaam and the Balaams of the Roman Catholic Church who also saw then and see now nothing wrong with their own form of idolatry. In every Catholic Church from that day to this you find idols everywhere, statues and images of saints to be venerated when God commanded against this very kind of thing:

Exodus 20:4 *Thou shalt not make unto thee any graven image, or any likeness of any thing that is in heaven above, or that is in the earth beneath, or that is in the water under the earth:* **5** *Thou shalt not bow down thyself to them, nor serve them: for I the LORD thy God am a jealous God, visiting the iniquity of the fathers upon the children unto the third and fourth generation of them that hate me;*

How have they managed to get seventeen hundred years of Catholics to ignore their obvious disobedience of that command? It was fairly simple, actually: they just leave this out of their Catholic Bibles and split the last one into two to retain ten in number.

The church at Pergamos in John's day also had Nicolaitanism—the idea of the clergy being near God-like status, while the laity was merely there to serve them. That as well very clearly came to full fruition in the Roman Catholic Church. Go to Rome, right now, watch hundreds of thousands looking at a window to try and get a glimpse of the Pope, who supposedly speaks without error. It is Nicolaitanism. But as bad as it is now, it is not nearly as bad as it was from A.D. 325 until the seventh century, when the state made sure that no one openly disagreed with the official church. This church, Pergamos, most closely mirrors that time period. So we have seen Ephesus and the age that it demonstrated, Smryna and the age that it demonstrated, and now the Pergamon age. We have four more to go, and we are now seeing the last two simultaneously in our day. Be ready; Jesus is coming soon.

The practice of the fluctuating church

Each one of these letters is written in the exact same format, as if God laid out a template for John to follow. In every one of them, we will see the description of Christ, the discernment of Christ, the direction of Christ, and the delight of Christ.

The description of Christ

Revelation 2:12 *And to the angel of the church in Pergamos write; These things saith he which hath the sharp sword with two edges;*

Fifteen miles from the Aegean Sea and three miles from the Caicus River was the famed city of Pergamos. The architecture was fabulous, the wealth of the populace was evident everywhere, and the fear of God was almost non-existent. But in this wicked city, God chose to put a church.

One interesting aspect of the city Pergamos that the church was well aware of, as was all of the ancient world, was a library of 200,000 volumes.

You may say, "That's not many books compared to our libraries today!"

But there is one major difference: every single book in those days was copied out by hand. How many books would our libraries have today under those conditions? A handwritten, 200,000 volume library—what a source of pride for a city! People came for miles and miles to see it.

And yet, to this group of people, God addressed Himself as the one who has THE sharp sword with two edges. In verse sixteen and in Revelation 19:5, we see that this is what comes out of His mouth, His word. Pergamos had 200,000 books, and Christ in so many words says to them, "Look at me, I have *one* book..."

And here is how much He thought and thinks of that one book:

Revelation 22:18 *For I testify unto every man that heareth the words of the prophecy of this book, If any man shall add unto these things, God shall add unto him the plagues that are written in this book:* **19** *And if any man shall take away from the words of the book of this prophecy, God shall take away his part out of the book of life, and out of the holy city, and from the things which are written in this book.*

God's book is precious, sacred, not to be tampered with! Any of the 200,000 volumes at Pergamos could be altered wholesale, and humanity would be none the worse. But alter God's book and man's eternal destiny can be altered.

What did Christ, in picture form, tell us about His one book?

He told us that it has two edges. It cuts on either side equally well. In other words, it is utterly perfect. Not one of the 200,000 books in Pergamos could claim this!

Psalm 19:7 *The law of the LORD is perfect, converting the soul: the testimony of the LORD is sure, making wise the simple.*

Do not ever apologize for holding to the perfection of Scripture. Satan started his assault on man with "hath God said..." and he still is using that approach.

He also told us that He has it, meaning that He possesses it, it is His property. The word "hath" comes from *ekown*, it means to have, hold, possess, keep, on occasion it even means to be married to!

If God is this type of a keeper of it, we can trust that He has kept it secure!

For a person to believe that transcribers have filled it with errors, or that time has diminished it, or that the only time it was perfect was in the original documents, they must believe that Christ is not the keeper of His Word, that He is not the one who HAS the sharp sword with two edges!

God still has His word, and it is still perfectly sharp on both edges!

The discernment of Christ

Revelation 2:13 *I know thy works, and where thou dwellest, even where Satan's seat is: and thou holdest fast my name, and hast not denied my faith, even in those days wherein Antipas was my faithful martyr, who was slain among you, where Satan dwelleth.*

In each of these passages, He opens with "I know..." He does not have to wonder or guess; He need not rely on the reports of others; He *knows* what is going on in the church.

Verse thirteen is overwhelmingly positive. He begins by saying that He knows their works. It is instructive to note that they are not even specified for us. It is not necessary for the world to know our works; it is only necessary for Christ to know them!

He then reminds them that He knows their location. Do you think that any of us in America really have a bad location? Compared to Pergamos, none of us have a bad location for a church. They dwelt "where Satan's seat is," "Where Satan dwelleth!" Satan literally lived there!

In Pergamos, there was something they *could* see that pointed to something they *could not* see. One of the wonders of the ancient world was in Pergamos, the altar of Zeus. It was forty feet high, and the base of that altar still exists today. This altar was Zeus's throne, his seat, a monument to a false god.

Satan has his headquarters on Earth. Let this sink in—the church at Pergamos lived in the city that Satan had as his headquarters on Earth. He could not be seen, but you know that his presence could be felt everywhere. Imagine walking by this throne/altar, and Satan unseen is sitting on it, brooding, smiling at the wickedness, seething at the handful of righteousness, turning sulfurous breath and hate filled eyes toward the little church that has come to town. Imagine going on door-to-door visitation in Pergamos. Demons hovering like vultures, an oppressive air of filth and wickedness, and Satan himself opposing your every effort. We know that he did oppose it, because verse thirteen says that one man, Antipas, had already been martyred. Can you just imagine the scene as demon possessed men dragged Antipas to his death?

If there was ever a reason for a church to throw in the towel, this would have been it. But God does not call churches to give up but to go forward. In all of this, they stayed faithful. Antipas' death was not in vain. They held fast to the name of Christ; they kept His faith. Even as the blood of Antipas was staining the streets of Pergamos, the saints of God were holding high the banner of Christ. As Antipas breathed his last earthly breath, he could look up through swollen eyes and see a look of determination on the face of the church, and he could know that the work would continue. What a hot church! But now notice the fluctuation...

He told them that He knew their idolatry.

Revelation 2:14 *But I have a few things against thee, because thou hast there them that hold the doctrine of Balaam, who taught Balac to cast a stumblingblock before the children of Israel, to eat things sacrificed unto idols, and to commit fornication.*

Remember again that Baalam was an Old Testament "prophet for profit." He had tried to put a curse on God's people, but God would not allow it. So instead, he taught Balak, the king of Moab, how to lure God's people into idolatry. For all of its good qualities, the church at Pergamos made the mistake of allowing people into membership and even leadership that taught others about "the joys of idolatry!"

For the most part, modern man is far too sophisticated to worship stone carvings anymore. But even in the church of today, idolatry may still be found. Idolatry is when something becomes more important than God, and it is demonstrated by disobedience to God. If something causes you to disobey God, it has become an idol. It can be sports, hobbies, friends, illicit relationships, money, anything.

Any idolatry of any kind must not be tolerated in the church.

But He was still not done yet. He then told them that He knew of their fornication.

Revelation 2:14 *But I have a few things against thee, because thou hast there them that hold the doctrine of Balaam, who taught Balac to cast a stumblingblock before the children of Israel, to eat things sacrificed unto idols,* ***and to commit fornication***.

Once again God focuses in on the doctrine of Baalam. The church at Pergamos allowed people to teach that fornication was okay. But it was not, it is not, and it never will be. And no amount of smoke machines and huge crowds and sensual music and heretical preaching that fornication is no longer a sin, all slapped with a church label, will ever make it okay:

1 Thessalonians 4:3 *For this is the will of God, even your sanctification, that ye should abstain from fornication:*

Fornication is any type of sexual impurity. It is any sexual contact or behavior outside of marriage. And it will never be okay and should never be labeled as okay by any church.

Lastly, He told them that He knew of their elitism.

Revelation 2:15 *So hast thou also them that hold the doctrine of the Nicolaitans, which thing I hate.*

Nicolaitans is found only twice by name in Scripture, both times in Revelation 2. Pay attention to the fact that the same problem was referenced in the letters to two different churches. Nicolaitanism, the idea that the clergy are to act as lords over the people, is an insidious doctrine that crosses denominational barriers and survives from era to era.

But the doctrine of the Nicolaitans is so abhorrent to God that He said he HATES it. The word He used for hate indicates to *pursue with hatred and anger.* God is a Nicolaitan hunter!

As a man of God, God has invested me with a great deal of authority, but He has also entrusted me with the responsibility to remember that I am a member of the church under Christ along with everyone else! Honor God's men, but never give in to hardnosed, overbearing, members-are-cattle Nicolaitanism. Members are to be vessels, not vassals.

<u>The direction of Christ</u>

Revelation 2:16 *Repent; or else I will come unto thee quickly, and will fight against them with the sword of my mouth.*

The church at Pergamos had idolatry, fornication, and Nicolaitanism in their midst. So what were Christ's directions to that fluctuating church?

Repent! One word of admonition that means to stop fluctuating, do right in all things. Their only other option was to suffer the consequences, namely having God Himself fight against them with the sword of His mouth! What a sobering thought that the mouth we are hoping to hear words of kindness and help from would instead utter words of condemnation.

God's direction to everyone who is fluctuating is to repent.

The delight of Christ

Revelation 2:17 *He that hath an ear, let him hear what the Spirit saith unto the churches; To him that overcometh will I give to eat of the hidden manna, and will give him a white stone, and in the stone a new name written, which no man knoweth saving he that receiveth it.*

It is God's delight that we hear, that we pay attention to what He has said. Nobody likes to be ignored, least of all God.

It is God's delight that we be overcomers. For the fluctuating church, overcoming means to continue being faithful in every persecution and at the same time fix the faulty doctrine and remove the impurities. When we obey God in doing this, the delight, the "revival," if you will, will come. Look at the delight He offers for obedience:

He will give us of the hidden manna. The tradition of the Jews says that king Josiah hid the Ark of the Covenant. The Bible tells us that the Holy of Holies contained the Ark (inside of which were the tables of the commandments, 1 Kings 8:9) Aaron's rod that budded, and a pot of manna collected from the wilderness. No one had seen any of that for a very long time, at least since the days of Josiah.

It would be the desire of every Jew's heart to eat of that hidden manna. God is saying that when we obey God, focus ourselves upon Him, He will give us the desires of our heart.

Psalm 37:4 *Delight thyself also in the LORD; and he shall give thee the desires of thine heart.*

Verse seventeen also tells us that He will give us a white stone with a secret name written in it. Be ready to enjoy this...

The white stone first of all was given in a courtroom to signify a declaration of innocence. Overcomers will not just be declared innocent by the blood of Christ, they will be given outward proof of their innocence, something that the world itself can see.

But the second thing you need to know is that a stone with a name written in it was called a *tessera*. Two people would exchange them, with a name or symbol on them, to show that there was permanent friendship and allegiance between the two. It was an "inside thing." Here, though, only one stone is given, and it is given from Christ to the overcomer, the one who stops fluctuating. It shows that though we are capable of becoming steady, we can never be flawlessly faithful to God, but that does not matter to Him. He will be flawlessly faithful to us. It is not the name of the overcoming Christian that is on the rock, it is a brand-new name of Christ that will only be revealed to the overcoming Christian. There are things that I call my wife that no one else knows about. There is a name of God that God will give to us, for all of eternity, that only we will have access to. This is the height of trust and intimacy! All of this, and all God asks is that we stop fluctuating, that we be faithful...

So many have so much that they are doing so right, and God knows all about those works, but it seems there is nearly always an area or two where an enemy altar exists in our hearts. Do not ever justify those area; repent!

Antipas gave his life for the truth of the gospel and the purity of the believers' lives. If he could walk today in Bergama, the modern city that was once Pergamos, he would find many mosques but little or no gospel witness. I wonder if he would cry bitter tears when he reached the spot where the church of Pergamos once stood. If we could transport ourselves one hundred years into the future, would we weep over what was once the Bible-believing, Christ-exalting church we attend, or would we rejoice that it has been an overcomer? *Repent*—lest He come quickly to fight against us.

Chapter Seven
Prophecy and Practice in the Fornicating Church

Revelation 2:18 *And unto the angel of the church in Thyatira write; These things saith the Son of God, who hath his eyes like unto a flame of fire, and his feet are like fine brass;* **19** *I know thy works, and charity, and service, and faith, and thy patience, and thy works; and the last to be more than the first.* **20** *Notwithstanding I have a few things against thee, because thou sufferest that woman Jezebel, which calleth herself a prophetess, to teach and to seduce my servants to commit fornication, and to eat things sacrificed unto idols.* **21** *And I gave her space to repent of her fornication; and she repented not.* **22** *Behold, I will cast her into a bed, and them that commit adultery with her into great tribulation, except they repent of their deeds.* **23** *And I will kill her children with death; and all the churches shall know that I am he which searcheth the reins and hearts: and I will give unto every one of you according to your works.* **24** *But unto you I say, and unto the rest in Thyatira, as many as have not this doctrine, and which have not known the depths of Satan, as they speak; I will put upon you none other burden.* **25** *But that which ye have already hold fast till I come.* **26** *And he that overcometh, and keepeth my works unto the end, to him will I give power over the nations:* **27** *And he shall rule them with a rod of iron; as the vessels of a potter shall they be broken to shivers: even as I received of my Father.* **28** *And I will give him the morning star.* **29** *He that hath an ear, let him hear what the Spirit saith unto the churches.*

In the last chapter, we looked at the prophecy and practice of Pergamos, the fluctuating church. Now we will turn our attention to the city and church of Thyatira, the fornicating church.

The prophecy of the fornicating church

Thyatira was the next closest to John along the geographical circle that God was drawing, and it was also the next nearest to him chronologically.

Bear in mind, again, that there is not a "hard cut-off" from one church age to the next. These church periods tend to overlap as one fades into another. So, overlapping that of Pergamos a bit, Thyatira is the church that most closely mirrors the overall state of the church from about A.D. 500 up until about A.D. 1500. You may recognize that time period from history as being what is normally called the *Dark Ages*. It was during that thousand-year period that there was more religion and less truth on earth than at any other time in history. The dark ages were not "dark" because they did not have lightbulbs; the dark ages were dark because the common masses of humanity did not have Bibles. The Roman Church forbade anyone to have a copy of the Bible in their language, so wickedness ran amuck. There was fornication, idolatry, and violence; Jezebel would have her way during the Thyatiran age.

The practice of the fornicating church

Each one of these letters is written in the exact same format as if God laid out a template for John to follow. In every one of them, we will see the description of Christ, the discernment of Christ, the direction of Christ, and the delight of Christ.

The description of Christ

Revelation 2:18 *And unto the angel of the church in Thyatira write; These things saith the Son of God, who hath his eyes like unto a flame of fire, and his feet are like fine brass;*

It is interesting to note that above-average wickedness is often found in below-average places. For instance, San Francisco is often looked upon as the capital of Sodomy, but little Asheville, NC, is just as bad or worse. Hollywood is regarded as porn city USA, but the largest pornography ring ever busted was in little Charlotte, NC. The size of a city does not necessarily determine the size of its evil. Churches in Washington, D.C., have a lot of evil to overcome, but so do churches in Mooresboro, NC, population two hundred ninety-seven!

The city of Thyatira was the smallest city mentioned in these seven letters, yet its church received the longest letter and probably the strongest warning about the evil that they were facing.

Situated on the road between Pergamos and Sardis, containing every craftsman's guild imaginable, Thyatira was home to a church that we have already observed can rightly be called "the fornicating church." And in that atmosphere of impurity, notice how Christ the Son of God described Himself in verse eighteen.

He described Himself as the Son of God. Oftentimes, Christ referred to Himself as *the Son of Man.* In fact, that was the title He most commonly gave Himself. It emphasized His condescension in becoming a man for us. It showed His meekness and humility. And there is certainly a time and place for meekness and humility. But when you are rebuking the vilest of sin, it is a time for boldness and authority. So when Jesus dealt with Thyatira, He did not call Himself the Son of Man, but *the Son of God.*

When God comes after your sin, kindly remember Who it is that is so "bothering you." Your problem is not with a pastor; it is with the Son of God. And you need to remember that when a preacher is rebuking sin, he does not need to be soft about it because Jesus Himself was not soft about it.

He also described Himself as having eyes like a flame of fire. Have you ever felt like someone was looking right through you? Jesus actually does it. You cannot hide one thing you are doing, or wishing, or wanting, or planning, or thinking from the eyes of God.

He then described Himself as having feet like fine brass. This was a visual picture everyone in Thyatira understood. With all of the craftsmen's guilds, people in Thyatira knew some things about fine brass. For instance, they knew how pure it is. Jesus' feet, that which on a mere man gets dirty the most and the quickest, are utterly pure. There is no spot, blemish, or stain in or on Him. When God speaks against our sin, He does so as one who is living as pure as He is preaching.

People who preach purity should live pure. People who have purity preached to them from a pure Bible given by a pure God should also live pure! Purity is not just for the one in the pulpit; it is for everyone in the pews as well. It is for every one of every age in the pulpit or in the pews.

The discernment of Christ

Revelation 2:19 *I know thy works, and charity, and service, and faith, and thy patience, and thy works; and the last to be more than the first.* **20** *Notwithstanding I have a few things against thee, because thou sufferest that woman Jezebel, which calleth herself a prophetess, to teach and to seduce my servants to commit fornication, and to eat things sacrificed unto idols.* **21** *And I gave her space to repent of her fornication; and she repented not.* **22** *Behold, I will cast her into a bed, and them that commit adultery with her into great tribulation, except they repent of their deeds.* **23** *And I will kill her children with death; and all the churches shall know that I am he which searcheth the reins and hearts: and I will give unto every one of you according to your works.*

Notice first of all the positive things Christ had to say about the church of Thyatira.

He said, "I know thy works." These were not lazy people, in their jobs, or in their service for God. Has it occurred to you yet how often God mentions this? This is not a small issue to God; it is a big issue to Him!

He also said that He knew their love, their charity. These were people who sacrificed for the good of others and treated others well, whether they earned it or not.

He said, "I know thy service." The word service means ministering to the physical needs of others. They made sure, as best they could, that the family of God was clothed, fed, and warm.

Years earlier, James said:

James 2:15 *If a brother or sister be naked, and destitute of daily food,* **16** *And one of you say unto them, Depart in peace, be ye warmed and filled; notwithstanding ye give them not those things which are needful to the body; what doth it profit?*

Especially in this, actions really do speak louder than words!

He then said, "I know thy faith." The true believers in the church of Thyatira held firmly to the convictions of Scripture and would not budge. They are an example to us not to be swayed by the Jehovah's Witnesses, or the Mormons, or the New Age movement, or any false thing.

And then we come to what at first blush seems to be a redundancy. He said, *"I know thy works"* in verse nineteen. Does that sound familiar? It is mentioned twice in one verse. And both in English and in Greek, it is the exact same word as the first time He told them He knew their works. But He now adds that *"the last is more than the first."* That is a Biblical way of saying that not only did they keep doing the things that were right, but they also kept on increasing and increasing and increasing in doing the things that are right. They spread the gospel more every year, read their Bibles more every year, gave more tithes and offerings every year, spent more time in prayer every year, came to church more every year; they just grew and grew and grew in good works. These are five truly positive things that God said He knew about this church.

But the positive things about them were not the whole story. There was also quite a bit of negative.

He knew that they were involved in fornication and idolatry.

In so many things, the past has the potential to tell us much about the present and the future. Thyatira was actually, in the days of John, a fairly recent name for this city. It had a much more ancient name. It used to be called *Semiramis*. Anyone who has been around Bible teaching for a while might remember that name. It was the name of a woman who was the beginning of the fertility cult of Babylon and began mother and child worship along with her son Tammuz, which we still see the shadows of in the Catholic Church in their joint worship of Mary along with Jesus. It was a cult centered around sexuality.

Never let it be said that the devil is too dumb to know the easiest things to get us to "worship!" And even though the city of Semiramis had since changed its name, that ancient heresy was still alive and well in Thyatira, and it had infected the church. The church in Thyatira had a woman there, and God called her by the name Jezebel. That may or may not have been the name her mother and father gave her, but it was definitely a name that God felt fit her perfectly. She was just as wicked, twisted, and corrupt as the Old Testament Jezebel.

Note that God said she *called* herself a prophetess. In other words, anybody can call themselves a prophet or a prophetess, but that does not make it so. She also actually taught people in the church how wonderful fornication was.

That still goes on even today. Evangelicalism especially has fewer and fewer voices stating that the only non-sinful way to have sex is between a husband and wife, and more and more voices who claim that everything God labeled as fornication, from premarital sex to homosexuality to adultery, is actually "just love."

But even in Biblical churches that do not go that far, another form of this Jezebel doctrine still takes place. Every time some boy and girl who are not married end up with child and the church ignores it like nothing wrong has been done, we are teaching God's people to commit fornication. Every time we celebrate an illegitimate conception in the same way that we celebrate a legitimate conception, we are teaching God's people to commit fornication.

No child born in fornication ought to ever be treated any differently than any child born legitimately. As far as they know, as they grow, they should be on equal ground with everyone else. But no adult who has committed fornication and produced a child through that sinful act should be made to feel as if they have done nothing wrong because they have!

We have to be forgiving, and we have to be helpful. But we also have to be very careful not to send mixed signals about right and wrong because our young people are watching.

When I was a boy of about ten years of age, I was in such a "tolerant" church. They would never dream of offending anybody by calling something a sin!

One day a girl got pregnant out of wedlock. Not one negative word was ever said, **not one**. No apology was required. A church-wide baby shower was held in the fellowship hall. Everyone doted on the young lady like she was a Disney princess. And yet, a little sister was watching all of this attention lavished on her fornicating older sister. Her exact words were, "Well, if she gets treated that good for doing wrong, I guess I can too!" Sadly, she was right, and the next illegitimate baby born was hers.

While a church needs to be a place of restoration and forgiveness, a church also needs to be very careful that neither a Jezebel, nor an Ahab, for that matter, does anything to teach God's people to commit fornication or idolatry.

You say, "But isn't God merciful?" Yes, and that mercy is seen in verse twenty-one. He gave that woman space to repent of the fact that she was seducing people into fornication. She was not just teaching it; she was participating in it. But even with a person that wicked, God gave her a chance to repent—and she would not.

That is the right definition of merciful and compassionate—giving people an opportunity to get right. God did that for this Jezebel, but she would not repent. Because of that, God told the church in verse twenty-two that He was going to drag Jezebel and her lovers out of their pleasure-filled bed of *fornication* and cast them into a bed of *tribulation*.

Understand this. Momma and daddy might not be able to drag you away from your sin, grandma and grandpa might not be able to drag you away from your sin, your spouse might not be able to drag you away from your sin, your Sunday school teacher might not be able to drag you away from your sin, the preacher might not be able to drag you away from your sin, but one day, God Himself will drag you out of that bed of sin, and throw you right into the middle of the consequences of your sin. And it will not stop with just you. Verse twenty-three should be a terrifying warning to any lost or backslidden parent:

Revelation 2:23 *And I will kill her children with death; and all the churches shall know that I am he which searcheth the reins and hearts: and I will give unto every one of you according to your works.*

Your sin left unforsaken may cost your own children their lives, as it did with David. Is such a thing extreme and rare? Yes. But is God still serious enough about sin to do exactly as He said He would do when He feels it is warranted? Yes again.

God is righteous! He is the one who searches the reins and the hearts. He will give to everyone according to their works, whether good or bad, and that may come home to roost in the lives, or even by the deaths of our children. Be sure your sin will find you out.

<u>The direction of Christ</u>

Revelation 2:24 *But unto you I say, and unto the rest in Thyatira, as many as have not this doctrine, and which have not known the depths of Satan, as they speak; I will put upon you none other burden.* **25** *But that which ye have already hold fast till I come.*

This verse is specific, sarcastic, soothing, and scalding! Look at a few things carefully.

Note that God addressed both the righteous members of the church and the unrighteous. When He said, *"unto **you** I say,"* He was talking to the "you" of Jezebel's crowd. But when He spoke of *"the rest in Thyatira, as many as have not this doctrine,"* He was speaking to God's crowd. He was carefully distinguishing between two different groups of people found in the same church.

There usually are two different groups of people in one church, those who are serious about living for the Lord and those who are not.

When God spoke of those who had not known the "depths of Satan," He was using the finest of divine sarcasm. You see, people who held to the beliefs of Jezebel and her crowd in Thyatira told others that they had access to **"*the deep knowledge of God*."** They were living however their flesh wanted to live because they "knew God better than anyone else."

What hypocrisy! What abomination! What filth! God said, in so many words, "You don't have the deep knowledge of God; you have the deep knowledge of Satan."

I do not care how many Bible college degrees you have, I do not care how many big theological books you have read, I do not care how good of a speaker you are, if you are living wickedly and claiming that it is okay because you have some deeper knowledge of God than other people do, you do not know the depths of God, but you do know the depths of Satan!

A godly but illiterate old grandma who could not spell her name if her name actually was X knows more about God than a person who uses ten syllable words to describe how it is okay to live in sin because they have "deep knowledge of God."

Another thing to notice is that when God told both of these crowds that He would not put any other burden on them and that both of those crowds were to hold fast that which they already had till He comes, He was soothing the ones doing right and scalding those doing wrong. He told both right and wrong to keep doing what they were doing.

When that happens to someone doing wrong, trouble is on the way!

When I was fussing at my children in their young years, trying to get them to stop screaming at each other, they were still alright. But when I had enough, when I told them, "Keep screaming. It'll take me a few seconds to get the paddle, so keep screaming till I do," they knew it was over at that point.

Is that mean? No, God gave them space to repent, and they would not. If God always withheld the due reward from those doing right, He would be wrong. Likewise, if God always withheld the due reward from those doing wrong, He would be wrong. Eventually, there must be a payday. And if you have been living in sin and living in sin and living in sin, believe me, payday is coming.

The delight of Christ

Revelation 2:26 *And he that overcometh, and keepeth my works unto the end, to him will I give power over the nations:* **27** *And he shall rule them with a rod of iron; as the vessels of a potter shall they be broken to shivers: even as I received of my Father.* **28** *And I will give him the morning star.* **29** *He that hath an ear, let him hear what the Spirit saith unto the churches.*

These words are directed to the ones doing right. God has nothing left to say to those who still refuse to repent. But those who refuse to follow Jezebel, refuse to fornicate, refuse to idolize anything or anyone, they will rule over those that have cruelly ruled over them.

Believers may get beaten down now; they may be lied about, slandered, laughed at, stolen from, and abused, but one day God is going to make them rule over the very nations of men who have so abused them.

But better still, the overcomers will be given the morning star. You say, "What is the morning star?"

Wrong question. You should ask *who* is the morning star?

Revelation 22:16 *I Jesus have sent mine angel to testify unto you these things in the churches. I am the root and the offspring of David, and the bright and morning star.*

The overcomer will be given Jesus. Not in salvation; he already had Him like that. No, in a new and special way, in a new kind of fellowship, we will be brought closer to Jesus than ever before. The farther we push away from impurity, the closer we pull to Him. He that hath an ear, hear what the Spirit saith unto the churches!

There is one thing that I have not mentioned about Thyatira that I find very interesting as we draw this section to a close. Their problem centered around a woman who was not living right.

Many people say, "But how can I live right when everyone around me seems to be doing wrong?" It can be done, and I have a name to prove it: Lydia. Do you remember godly Lydia, the seller of purple, the first convert in Asia Minor? In case you do not, let me remind you of one verse of Scripture:

Acts 16:14 *And a certain woman named Lydia, a seller of purple, of the city of Thyatira, which worshipped God, heard us: whose* *heart the Lord opened, that she attended unto the things which were spoken of Paul.*

Lydia was from the city of Thyatira. While Jezebel and her crowd were living the low life of sin, Lydia was living the high life of sanctification. No matter where you are or who is around you, the way you live your life is your choice, no one else's. You can be blessed or blistered by a holy God. You can be a Jezebel or a Lydia; the choice is entirely up to you.

Chapter Eight
Prophecy and Practice in the Fake Church

Revelation 3:1 *And unto the angel of the church in Sardis write; These things saith he that hath the seven Spirits of God, and the seven stars; I know thy works, that thou hast a name that thou livest, and art dead.* **2** *Be watchful, and strengthen the things which remain, that are ready to die: for I have not found thy works perfect before God.* **3** *Remember therefore how thou hast received and heard, and hold fast, and repent. If therefore thou shalt not watch, I will come on thee as a thief, and thou shalt not know what hour I will come upon thee.* **4** *Thou hast a few names even in Sardis which have not defiled their garments; and they shall walk with me in white: for they are worthy.* **5** *He that overcometh, the same shall be clothed in white raiment; and I will not blot out his name out of the book of life, but I will confess his name before my Father, and before his angels.* **6** *He that hath an ear, let him hear what the Spirit saith unto the churches.*

In the last chapter, we looked at the prophecy and practice of Thyatira, the fornicating church. Now we will turn our attention to the city and church of Sardis, the fake church.

The prophecy of the fake church

Sardis is the church that most closely mirrors the overall state of the church from about A.D 1500. until about A.D. 1900, with large pockets of it still to be found today. It was during that time period that so much about the church looked so very right but was in reality so very wrong. Although Baptists predate the protestant reformation by some 1,600 years, we can still look at history and thank God for much of what happened at the urging of Martin Luther and many others. Many came out of the wicked and corrupt Roman Church system during that time, and as a result, we have Presbyterians, Methodists, Lutherans, and many others that are not Catholic. So much that happened during that time was right and good. But there was also much that was paper-thin and not quite right. Luther, who railed against the Catholic Church burning heretics, burnt one of his own. Men who parted ways with the Roman Church over the issue of indulgences still made people baptize babies. Many people got themselves out of the Roman Church, but they never got the Roman Church out themselves. As a result, we are now in our day seeing many of those groups beat a path back to the arms of Rome and the pope. Unification movements are taking place all over. Go into any town around Christmas or Easter, and you will find Methodists, Presbyterians,

Lutherans, Episcopalians, and even some Southern Baptists having joint worship services with the Catholic Church. Again, many people have gotten themselves out of the Roman Church, but they have never gotten the Roman Church out of themselves.

It was hypocrisy, just as it was in the days of the literal church of Sardis.

The practice of the fake church

Each one of these letters is written in the exact same format as if God laid out a template for John to follow. In every one of them, we will see the description of Christ, the discernment of Christ, the direction of Christ, and the delight of Christ.

The description of Christ

Revelation 3:1a *And unto the angel of the church in Sardis write; These things saith he that hath the seven Spirits of God, and the seven stars;*

Sardis was one of the oldest and most important cities of Asia Minor. It was located at the slope of Mount Tmolus, and at the base ran the Pactolus River which served as a mote, making the city very secure from attack. According to church history, Sardis was one of the first cities to accept Christianity and also one of the first to abandon it. The church there was widely regarded as the one of the seven with the most vitality, but that was all because of the image they portrayed on the surface. Underneath, though, both this city and this church were corrupt and rotten; it is just that most people could not see through their facade. He described them in verse one this way, "thou hast a name that thou *livest*, and art *dead*."

To this church, God described Himself in two ways. He began by calling Himself the one who has the seven spirits of God. Many times you will hear people teach that this is a reference to the Holy Spirit Himself. This is possible but not provable. Just reading what the text says, I take this as seven literal spirits. Either way, Revelation 5:6 makes it clear that they are His "eyes, sent forth into all the Earth."

Revelation 5:6 *And I beheld, and, lo, in the midst of the throne and of the four beasts, and in the midst of the elders, stood a Lamb as it had been slain, having seven horns and* **seven eyes, which are the seven Spirits of God** *sent forth into all the earth.*

Whether you regard this as the Holy Spirit or seven individual Spirits, what they say about Christ is clear: He sees everything, He misses nothing! Solomon wrote of that fact a thousand years earlier:

Proverbs 15:3 *The eyes of the LORD are in every place, beholding the evil and the good.*

The church of Sardis thought it had pulled the wool over His eyes, but Christ sees right through every veneer of man. He knew that their "lively name" was not deserved. He knew that they were really dead.

It is no wonder the world hates Christ; He keeps on exposing them for what they are, and no one likes to have their hypocrisy exposed.

Consider the Democrat mayor of San Francisco, London Breed. In August of 2021, she issued an order stating, "Residents need to wear masks indoors regardless of their vaccination status." And then on September 16, 2021, she spent the evening at a crowded nightclub with the co-founder of BLM, Alicia Garza, partying maskless.

All. Night. Long.

Not a single mask was in sight on one single person, including her, in the entire crowded nightclub.

Pictures managed to get out, and some folks called her out on it. Her response? Breed said that everyone who came into the club had to show proof of vaccination, which gave her 'a lot of reassurance.' (Reyes, 2021)

It is hypocrisy. It is wicked mankind doing what wicked mankind always does: rules for me but not for thee. It is hollow posturing. It is style over substance.

We can rightly expect that kind of hypocrisy from the world, especially the liberal, left-progressive wing of this world. But when it is called out in a church as Christ did with Sardis, that is a huge issue. And Christ was pointing out that He sees everything to the church at Sardis, not just to the general world around them.

He then described Himself as the one who has hath the seven stars.

Remember that this is a reference to the seven "angels" (messengers, pastors) of the seven churches, as we learned in Revelation 1:20.

Please pay close attention to this: the subject is still that of people who are fake, people who have a name, a reputation that is different from their reality and the fact that God has ways to see through them and expose them. He mentioned that one way He does so is by means of these seven spirits.

The subject has not changed, yet He now moves from talking about spirits to talking about pastors. Why is that? Because just as God gives His spirits ability to discern between the true and the fake, He also uses men of God in much the same manner.

No man of God knows or speaks without error. None are infallible in their estimation of other people. But when God brings a man into the ministry, He does give him abilities in discernment that are far beyond himself. I know that many times in the past, people who seem to be perfect have walked through our own church doors, but there would be something troubling and unsettled in my spirit. Something just "wasn't right." I truly try to pay attention to that because in almost every case, something would be exposed later that let me know that God was warning me so that I could protect the church.

Is it possible that you can be a complete fake and fool a man of God? It is *possible,* but I definitely would not bet the farm on it.

The discernment of Christ

What is it that Christ knew when He looked at this church? To begin with, He knew of the fakes.

Revelation 3:1b *I know thy works, that thou hast a name that thou livest, and art dead.*

These were people who had something that they prized: *a name.* They lived for that name. Their reputation meant everything to them. They would do anything for it, *except for actually living right!* They were concerned about what people thought of them—but they were not concerned about the fact that they were spiritually dead.

This, to me, is amazing and frustrating to behold. It is unbelievable to watch people live one way and demand that people think of them another way!

It is amazing and frustrating when preachers do not sacrifice to make a ministry work, do not show any stability in the place that God puts them, bounce from place to place every couple of years, and then expect to be thought of like Charles Spurgeon. Or, worse still, live like devils, abuse people, fornicate, commit adultery, and then use the words "man of God" as Teflon coating to deflect people rightly pointing out that they have no business behind any pulpit anywhere at any time.

But it is not just preachers. This matter of hypocrisy is an every-pew-of-the-church matter to consider. Singers who are only interested in performing, while taking no pains at all to live holy lives, expecting their good voice to overcome the fact that God is never going to bless the filthy heart they bring onto the platform. Deacons who would never lower themselves to serve even though "servant" is the actual definition of the word deacon. Prominent members who are utterly unfaithful and yet want to be looked to as some sort of ecclesiastical influencers.

God expects every single one of us from the pulpit to the very back pew to have a good name as a Christian, not because we are good actors, but because we are genuinely what we are supposed to be, all day every day, not just at church.

God looked at Sardis, and He knew of the fakes.

But He also knew of the few.

Revelation 3:4a *Thou hast a few names even in Sardis which have not defiled their garments...*

It is tempting to focus on the fakes. We can get all worked up and righteously indignant over those dirty, rotten, filthy, fakes. But God did not just know about the fakes; He also knew about the few. He called them "a few names who have not defiled their garments."

He was not talking about people who work and get their clothes dirty; He was using that phrase as a euphemism for people who actually live right. These people do not just *seem to be* godly; they actually are godly. It is very easy to get so caught up in the hypocrites that we lose sight of something that Christ Himself did not lose sight of: some people are utterly genuine.

For every pastor that pretends for years and then gets caught and exposed as a monster, there are thousands of others who live right and do right from the start of their ministries until they die of old age, having just walked out of the pulpit.

For every golden-voiced gospel singer who lives like some debauched rock star, shacking up and fornicating and popping, snorting, and chugging, there are countless people who love the Lord, live for the Lord, lift up their voices for the Lord.

For every deacon who views himself as a diva to be venerated, there are countless good deacons who would be right beside Christ wrapping a towel around their waist and washing the feet of the disciples.

For every unfaithful "pillar of the church" who thinks of himself like unshakable Joseph when he is really more like unstable Reuben, there are countless people who do not have a forty- or fifty-year "legacy" but who do have present-day faithfulness.

Yes, Christ saw the fakes, and yes, we often do as well. But He also saw the few, and so should we. And notice this also: those few who were living right in Sardis were doing so in the midst of prevailing hypocrisy. They were swimming against the tide.

Do not tell me you cannot live right because everyone around you is a hypocrite. They are them, and you are you. If people in the church of Sardis could walk pure, holy, and undefiled in the midst of the hypocrisy all around them, then you can live right no matter what hypocrisy is raging in your own circle.

There may be young people reading who have hypocritical family members. Ultimately, that does not matter; you be genuine. There may be adults reading who are living with a hypocritical spouse.

Ultimately, that does not matter; you be genuine. Never defile your garments just because others do.

You may say, "But why should I walk right when others are not? Why should I make such efforts to be genuine when others are fakes? Because *God knows and observes those living honestly in the midst of dishonesty around them.* God did not condemn everyone just because they happened to be in the same crowd. *He carefully distinguished between those who were trying and those who were lying.*

Others did not know. He knew.

During the Mexican-American War, an American general named Gideon Pillow had some troops that won a great battle. Gideon Pillow then set about publicizing his own greatness. He wrote to his wife that never in the history of warfare had anyone ever distinguished themselves as much as he did. He was going down in history as one of the greatest military minds ever, and, as one of his devotees put it, others in the military were "mere marionettes" compared to him.

The problem with all of this was that Gideon Pillow won that battle in spite of himself. His followers had the good sense to make the right maneuver while he was giving the wrong orders! Nevertheless, Gideon Pillow's reputation grew until he was the next Alexander the Great in the minds of many. But then came the Civil War. And one man who had a pretty good idea of how much of a fake Gideon Pillow was, was Ulysses S. Grant.

Pillow became a general for the South; Grant became a general for the North. As it turns out, Grant's first battle had him taking a small force against a large force commanded by Pillow. Many people wondered why Grant would engage in such a battle. But he had already written home to his wife his suspicions about Gideon Pillow's lack of military skills.

He was right. At every single point in the battle, Pillow did exactly the opposite of what he should have done. It was a route for the North, with Pillow barely escaping. Three months later, they met again, and Pillow surrendered a huge force that could easily have won the battle under good leadership. Grant knew that Pillow was more likely to lie than to try.

God knows the exact same thing about every hypocrite who puts feet to the floor each morning. If you are fake, He knows it. And if you are genuine, He knows that, too.

<u>The direction of Christ</u>

Revelation 3:2 *Be watchful, and strengthen the things which remain, that are ready to die: for I have not found thy works perfect*

before God. **3** *Remember therefore how thou hast received and heard, and hold fast, and repent. If therefore thou shalt not watch, I will come on thee as a thief, and thou shalt not know what hour I will come upon thee.*

Some in Sardis were already spiritually dead. But some were not there yet. They were trying to do right, but it was so hard with everyone else doing wrong. God looked at them, and He saw weakness developing. He saw that some good things in them were about to die, things that could be saved and continue to live if they listened to Him. That was a strong warning.

Understand this: people who were at least somewhat living right still received a strong warning from God. They needed to become even stronger, for there was weakness beginning to show in their own lives. There were certain good things dying in their own lives, and God addressed that.

There is no logic or sensibility in spending all of our time dealing with those who are already dead. Some people simply will not change. As odd as it sounds, they are dead and happy with that deadness.

None of us have enough time in the day, it seems. And that is true of ministry as much as it is true of construction or factory work. Every moment will either be wasted or invested. And in the context of ministry, in the context of the church, it is a mistake to constantly spend the bulk of our time doing CPR on people who have been spiritually dead for years. It is much more sensible to find those who still have a pulse, even a weak pulse, and minister to them in such a way as to make that weak pulse stronger.

God saw none in Sardis who were perfect, but He did see some who were trying. They still had a spiritual pulse. So He taught them. He told them what they were doing right and how to make it better. He told them what they were doing wrong and how to change it. He then told them to do three things:

The first was, "Remember how you received and heard."

Every word of Scripture is inspired and essential, and there is one small word here that we should pay close attention to: *How*. We would expect at this point for God to tell them to remember *what* they received and heard, but in this case, He did not say that. He told them to remember *how* they received and heard. What was he saying?

That word for *how* is from the word *poce*, and it means "in what way, by what means."

So, how, in what way did people in Sardis "receive and hear" the gospel? Someone showed up and preached it to them:

Romans 10:14 *How then shall they call on him in whom they have not believed? and how shall they believe in him of whom they have not heard? and* **how shall they hear without a preacher?**

There were people in the church of Sardis trying to be genuine but struggling because of all those they saw who were not genuine. So God told them to think back on those who were genuine. Someone was genuine enough to leave their own land to bring the gospel to strangers. Someone was genuine enough to love them and pray for them and win them to God. Someone was genuine enough to do the hard work necessary to get a church up, and running, and flourishing. They heard and received the gospel because of some people who were truly genuine.

What an encouraging thought! Are you struggling to be genuine because you sometimes see people who are fake? Think back on that someone who was genuine enough to bring the gospel to you. Think back on that someone who was genuine enough to drive that bus out to your house and load you up and bring you to church to hear the gospel. Think back on that someone who years ago sacrificed and sweat and labored to start the church you got saved in and your family got right in and your kids grew up in. Remember how you received and heard!

There are very good, godly people out there who got you and others the gospel.

He then told them, "Hold fast." This two-word phrase means to guard, hold, keep, and attend carefully. In modern vernacular, we would say, "Hang in there! Stick to it!" Genuine people hang on to what is right and do not let go.

Lastly, He told them to repent.

Repent of what? Of those things that are not as good as they should be, those things they were letting die off. We always think of sin from the commission side, but it is just as much sin from the omission side. We need to repent of not doing the right things just as thoroughly as we need to repent of doing the wrong things.

Remember, hold fast, repent. Otherwise, Jesus said, He will come on us as a thief, and we will not be ready for it. That is the Bible way of saying *Jesus is coming, and the more you drift and slip, the less prepared you will be at His coming, the more it will catch you off guard, the more regrets you will have at the judgment seat of Christ.* Live like He is coming because He is.

The delight of Christ

Revelation 3:4 *Thou hast a few names even in Sardis which have not defiled their garments; and they shall walk with me in white: for they are worthy.* **5** *He that overcometh, the same shall be clothed in white* *raiment; and I will not blot out his name out of the book of life, but I will confess his name before my Father, and before his angels.* **6** *He that hath an ear, let him hear what the Spirit saith unto the churches.*

Please note three words from verse four: *with, white, worthy.*

What motivation is there to be genuine, honest, strong, and pure? Because people like that will get to walk ***with*** Christ. Forget Moses, Abraham, Elijah, Noah, Daniel; we can get around to them later. If you live genuine, your first stroll through heaven will be with Jesus. We will get to be dressed in ***white.*** People who struggle hard against sin, desperately labor to keep themselves from sin, confess and forsake sin in their lives as soon as they realize it, will one day be dressed in white that they do not have to try and keep white anymore, it will just come naturally. We will have these great privileges, walking with Jesus, in white, and we will be ***worthy*** of it! It will not be a stretch; it will be something we have earned that God Himself proclaims us worthy of. Mind you, we cannot earn salvation: that is always a free gift of grace. But we can earn honors and rewards, and that is what this passage is reminding us of.

I am looking forward to getting to kneel before Jesus and proclaim Him as worthy because He is worthy. But that does not show up in the book of The Revelation until chapter four. Every believer, everyone whose name is not blotted out of the book of life as verse five says, will have a chance to proclaim Jesus as worthy, but the very first time we see anyone being proclaimed as worthy in this book, it is right here in chapter three as Jesus proclaims before the Father as worthy those who have done everything in their power to be genuine, and pure, and undefiled.

Everybody will get to tell Jesus that He is worthy—but I want to get in on having my King tell me that I am worthy! I crave His approval, I want His favor, I desire His recognition, His "Well done" means everything to me, and no one is going to hear "well done" unless they have done well!

Again, being saved is all on Jesus's shoulders; hearing Him tell us we are worthy and have done well is on our shoulders. He that hath an ear, he that understands that our God expects us to be genuine and pure, let us hear what the Spirit saith unto the churches.

Chapter Nine
Prophecy and Practice in the Favored Church

Revelation 3:7 *And to the angel of the church in Philadelphia write; These things saith he that is holy, he that is true, he that hath the key of David, he that openeth, and no man shutteth; and shutteth, and no man openeth;* **8** *I know thy works: behold, I have set before thee an open door, and no man can shut it: for thou hast a little strength, and hast kept my word, and hast not denied my name.* **9** *Behold, I will make them of the synagogue of Satan, which say they are Jews, and are not, but do lie; behold, I will make them to come and worship before thy feet, and to know that I have loved thee.* **10** *Because thou hast kept the word of my patience, I also will keep thee from the hour of temptation, which shall come upon all the world, to try them that dwell upon the earth.* **11** *Behold, I come quickly: hold that fast which thou hast, that no man take thy crown.* **12** *Him that overcometh will I make a pillar in the temple of my God, and he shall go no more out: and I will write upon him the name of my God, and the name of the city of my God, which is new Jerusalem, which cometh down out of heaven from my God: and I will write upon him my new name.* **13** *He that hath an ear, let him hear what the Spirit saith unto the churches.*

In the last chapter, we looked at the prophecy and practice of Sardis, the fake church. Now we will turn our attention to the city and church of Philadelphia, the favored church.

The prophecy of the favored church

Philadelphia was the next closest to John along the geographical circle, and it was also the next nearest to him chronologically. Philadelphia is the church that most closely mirrors the state of the true church from about A.D. 1900 up until the Tribulation Period begins. Here is how we know that last part:

Revelation 3:10 *Because thou hast kept the word of my patience, I also will keep thee from the hour of temptation, which shall come upon all the world, to try them that dwell upon the earth.*

God told the church at Philadelphia that He would keep them from the hour of temptation that would come upon *all the world*. That does not describe anything that occurred during the time the church at Philadelphia that received this letter was in existence. There was no worldwide trial, temptation, that they had to deal with. There were localized persecutions but nothing worldwide. This is a description of the Tribulation Period itself. This is just one more way we know that these churches were not only literal churches but also great representations of the ages and stages of the church.

This Philadelphia time period has been a time where much of the church was on fire for God, living pure, winning souls by the thousands. It has been during this time that great citywide crusades closed down bars and brothels, and missions swept the entire globe from here in America.

But the Philadelphia age is much bigger than just what could be seen in America. It has also been a time where all over the world in places where there is no religious freedom at all, underground churches have thrived and grown into millions of believers who are willing to give their life to be Christians rather than Muslims in Islamic countries and believers rather than unbelievers in atheistic countries. I think we are going to be shocked when we get to heaven to find out that there was far more of the Philadelphia church to be found in the Middle East and the Far East than there was in the West!

The church during these days has not been perfect because Laodicea has moved onto the scene at the same time as Philadelphia, and I contend that in our day, there is much more of Laodicea in the church than there is Philadelphia. But these two do still exist together. In the same town that you can find red hot, favored churches, you can also find lukewarm foul churches. The church age is winding down; you better be ready; Jesus is coming soon.

The practice of the favored church

Each one of these letters is written in the exact same format as if God laid out a template for John to follow. In every one of them, we will see the description of Christ, the discernment of Christ, the direction of Christ, and the delight of Christ.

<u>The description of Christ</u>

Revelation 3:7 *And to the angel of the church in Philadelphia write; These things saith he that is holy, he that is true, he that hath the key of David, he that openeth, and no man shutteth; and shutteth, and no man openeth;*

Many years before God gave John the words for this letter to the church of Philadelphia, He spoke some words to those who would form the very first church:

Matthew 5:14 *Ye are the light of the world. A city that is set on an hill cannot be hid.*

There is no verse that better describes the city of Philadelphia or the church that God planted in it. The city of Philadelphia was situated upon a terrace, six hundred fifty feet above sea level. Its modern name is

Ala Shehir, and it still has, after nearly 2,000 years, some form of a Christian witness! This was a church that did things right, and it was a church that God favored highly. That gives us some insight as to why Christ described Himself the way He did to them *numerically*.

Here is what I mean: Christ gave Himself a two-part description in the letter to Ephesus, a two-part description in the letter to Smyrna, a one-part description in the letter to Pergamos, a three-part description in the letter to Thyatira, a two-part description in the letter to Sardis, and you will see in the next passage a three-part description in the letter to Laodicea. But here, to the favored church of Philadelphia, Christ gives Himself a four-part description. In other words, the church He was most pleased with was given the most information about Him; they were allowed to know Him better than any other church.

That should be the desire of every real Christian's heart, to know Christ as well as possible:

Philippians 3:10 *That I may know him, and the power of his resurrection, and the fellowship of his sufferings, being made conformable unto his death;*

Paul wanted to really know Christ. The church at Philadelphia got to really know Christ. He revealed four things to them about Himself.

He first of all tells them here in verse seven that He is holy.

Holiness, as seen in the Scriptures, is both being apart from evil and being actively opposed to evil. It is much more than just being separated from evil and therefore indifferent to it since you are separate from it; it is so despising it that you actively push back against it wherever it is found. This is the character of Christ, and it is also the character He expects in us:

1 Peter 1:15 *But as he which hath called you is holy, so be ye holy in all manner of conversation;* **16** *Because it is written, Be ye holy; for I am holy.*

Christ is holy, and we are to be as well. This was the first description that He gave of Himself to the church at Philadelphia.

The second part of the description He gave of Himself is that He is true. The fact that He is true not only means that He does not lie, it also means that He *cannot* lie! And this is not the first time in Scripture we have seen this characteristic of God:

Titus 1:2 *In hope of eternal life, which God, that cannot lie, promised before the world began;*

I tell the truth, but I could lie if I wanted to. I tell the truth, but sometimes I really want to lie. I tell the truth, but sometimes I regret telling the truth and wish I had lied just because of how much trouble the truth often causes me! But Christ never lies, never wants to lie, and never regrets not lying.

The third part of the description that He gives of Himself is that He has the key of David. This means that He has the ruling right of the kingdom. During the 1000-year reign of Christ on earth that will begin as soon as the Tribulation Period ends, Jesus will rule the world from Jerusalem. The Jewish nation that has thus far rejected Him will turn to Him with one heart. They have been looking for the Messiah for all these years, and they will one day see Jesus carrying the key of David, and they will bow before Him in reverence and worship.

The final part of the four-part description that Christ gives of Himself to the church of Philadelphia is that He is the one that openeth, and no man shutteth; and shutteth, and no man openeth. No specifics are given of that because we are to understand it of all things that He opens or shuts. In other words, no matter what it is, He is the one who opens things with such authority that no man can shut them and shuts things with such authority that no man can open them.

It means that Christ cannot be overruled in any matter. The United Nations cannot overrule Jesus. The U.S. Congress cannot overrule Jesus. The White House cannot overrule Jesus. The Pentagon cannot overrule Jesus. The Vatican cannot overrule Jesus. CBS, ABC, NBC, CNN, and FOX cannot overrule Jesus. The New York Times cannot overrule Jesus. He is the one who opens things with such authority that no man can shut them and shuts things with such authority that no man can open them.

The discernment of Christ

Revelation 3:8 *I know thy works: behold, I have set before thee an open door, and no man can shut it: for thou hast a little strength, and hast kept my word, and hast not denied my name.*

As we have seen in every one of these letters thus far, we now see again that God did not need to rely on scouting reports or guesswork. He **knew** this church's works. Her works had pleased Christ so much that He who opens and no man shuts and shuts and no man opens had opened a door for them to minister, and would not let anybody shut it, though all the demons and devils of hell would have loved to.

And what were their great works that Christ discerned?

To begin with, He knew this church did all that it did while only having *a little strength.* In other words, this was not a high-powered, consumer mentality, ecumenical, high rolling, doctor/lawyer/politician/banker membership kind of church. Without much money, power, or influence, this church shook the world for God and outlasted all of the rest of them by thousands of years!

From our perspective, it would be nice if God gave us power and money—but we can shake the world for God without those things because if we have Christ, we already have everything we need to do a mighty work for God.

He also knew that this church kept His Word. The word *kept* is from the word *tereo,* and it means to hold fast, to observe, to cling to.

A Philadelphia kind of church clings to the fact that God's Word is inspired:

2 Timothy 3:16 *All scripture is given by inspiration of God, and is profitable for doctrine, for reproof, for correction, for instruction in righteousness:* **17** *That the man of God may be perfect, throughly furnished unto all good works.*

A Philadelphia kind of church clings to the fact that God's Word is preserved:

Matthew 24:35 *Heaven and earth shall pass away, but my words shall not pass away.*

Psalm 119:89 *For ever, O LORD, thy word is settled in heaven.*

A Philadelphia kind of church clings to the fact that God's Word is perfect:

Psalm 19:7 *The law of the LORD is perfect, converting the soul: the testimony of the LORD is sure, making wise the simple.*

A Philadelphia kind of church clings to the fact that God's Word is to be obeyed:

James 1:22 *But be ye doers of the word, and not hearers only, deceiving your own selves.*

We can hold to those first three, inspiration, preservation, and perfection, but if we stop there, it is of no use whatsoever. What good is an inspired and preserved and perfect Word of God if we are not actually reading it and studying it and applying it to our lives and obeying it? By the words that God used here to describe the church of Philadelphia, it is evident that they not only believed right about the Word of God, they also behaved right because of the Word of God.

A church that will not keep the Word is not a Philadelphia Church. It may not even be good enough to qualify as a Laodicea church. If a church expects God's favor, it must keep His Word.

He also knew that they did not deny His name. This would have been the absolute safest thing for those in Philadelphia to do; just deny Christ outwardly but still "keep Him in a very special place in their hearts." That is the world's ideal philosophy concerning Christ, and it is now even the avowed philosophy of the "We don't go to church; we are the church" crowd, but it flies in the face of Scripture:

Luke 9:26 *For whosoever shall be ashamed of me and of my words, of him shall the Son of man be ashamed, when he shall come in his own glory, and in his Father's, and of the holy angels.*

Our forefathers did not deny Christ through the stake and the sword and the drowning chair and confiscation of property and a thousand other injustices. The worst that happens to us today is normally insult. Never, never, never, never deny the name of Christ. Live it, carry it, show it, let the world know it, never deny the name of Christ.

The direction of Christ

Revelation 3:11 *Behold, I come quickly: hold that fast which thou hast, that no man take thy crown.*

Notice how simple the direction of Christ is to this favored church: hold fast that which you have, hold fast to your crown. That is God's way of saying, "Keep doing what you are doing. Just by doing what you are doing, you are earning crowns."

One of the greatest commendations a church or anyone in it could ever have is for Jesus to walk in the midst, observe all that is going on with His holy eyes, and say, "Just keep doing what you are doing!"

How wonderful it would be for God to be able to say that about every area in a church.

"Pastor, I've watched you carefully. You are steady, you labor in the Word of God, you feed the sheep well, keep doing what you are doing."

"Deacons, I've watched you carefully. You serve with all of your heart, never expecting or needing to be noticed. Keep doing what you are doing."

"Members, I've watched you carefully. You attend church faithfully. You tithe. You support missions. You live right. Keep doing what you are doing."

Any church that God cannot say those things to is far more like Laodicea than Philadelphia. Any person in the church that God cannot say those things to is far more like Laodicea than Philadelphia.

"But it is so hard to be steady!" comes the cry of the modern, carnal believer, "It is so hard to be a mature, faithful servant!"

Perhaps it is hard, but God gave this church two very good reasons to do so in verse eleven. The first is that He is coming quickly. Quickly is an adverb of manner. It tells how He is coming. When God blows that trumpet, it is over in the twinkling of an eye, and that trumpet could sound at any moment.

The next time you decide to be unsteady and unfaithful, please remember that Jesus is coming soon.

The next time you decide to think of yourself rather than others, please remember that Jesus is coming soon.

The next time you decide to be easily offended or not to forgive, please remember that Jesus is coming soon.

You that are doing right keep doing right because Jesus is coming soon.

The second reason He gives in verse eleven for the faithful to keep doing what they are doing is because people are out to steal your crown.

Those rewards that you have been earning to cast at Jesus' feet? They can be taken from you. But here is the interesting part: you have to open the door for the thieves. No one can overpower you and steal that which is spiritual. What they can do is lure you into doing wrong, and by so doing, they grab your reward away from you. That is why God told us in verse eleven to *hold fast* that which we have. In other words, grab hold, dig in, wrap yourself around those rewards, and hang on for dear life. When you open yourself up to strike back at people, you are not holding onto your crown. When you open yourself up to get bitter, you are not holding onto your crown. When you open yourself up to start missing church, you are not holding onto your crown. When you open yourself up to let temptation in, you are not holding onto your crown. Keep doing right because the devil wants to steal your crown.

<u>The delight of Christ</u>

To this church, Christ not only revealed more of Himself than to any other church, but He also promised them more than any other. He begins expressing His delight in verse nine, in which He tells them that His delight is first of all that He will make false Jews come and worship Christ before them.

Revelation 3:9 *Behold, I will make them of the synagogue of Satan, which say they are Jews, and are not, but do lie; behold, I will make them to come and worship before thy feet, and to know that I have loved thee.*

This is an amazingly harsh evaluation in verse nine—but it is absolutely necessary. And this was more than just a localized problem for the city and church of Philadelphia. Christ previously mentioned this problem as existing in Smyrna as well:

Revelation 2:8 *And unto the angel of the church in Smyrna write; These things saith the first and the last, which was dead, and is alive;* **9** *I know thy works, and tribulation, and poverty, (but thou art* *rich) and I know the blasphemy of them which say they are Jews, and are not, but are the synagogue of Satan.*

Everywhere this happened, it was for the same purpose and with the same goal. It was to undermine the work of God by infiltration. Think of wicked people calling themselves believers and doing wicked things or calling themselves believers while lying about and attacking others who actually are believers. When this happens, it hurts the credibility of everyone who is a real believer and of every church that is a real church. The churches in both Smyrna and Philadelphia were being battled by people who were on Satan's payroll while posing as religious, observant Jews.

Are there people out there who claim to be believers but are absolutely intentionally lying about it? Yes. But God told the church at Philadelphia, "One day they will come and worship Jesus before your feet." Every crooked thing that people do will be exposed in God's time, and the faithful will have the joy of seeing everyone worship their Christ, even those who spent so long adamantly opposing Him.

The next part shown of the delight of Christ is that He would shield them from the worldwide tribulation to come:

Revelation 3:10 *Because thou hast kept the word of my patience, I also will keep thee from the hour of temptation, which shall come upon all the world, to try them that dwell upon the earth.*

There is in these words a glorious promise to the true church. Again, this goes far beyond anything that happened during the days of the actual church at Philadelphia. There is a worldwide Tribulation coming, and false churches across the world will go headfirst into it. But the true church will be kept from it. This is a strong argument for the Pre-tribulation Rapture. God did not promise to preserve them as they went through it; He promised to keep the favored church from it. That sounds very similar to what Paul said. Speaking about the Tribulation to the church at Thessalonica, he said this:

1 Thessalonians 5:9 *For God hath not appointed us to wrath, but to obtain salvation by our Lord Jesus Christ,*

God has a great deal of delight in the true church. So much so that He has promised to keep it from the worldwide temptation to come.

The next part of the delight of Christ is that He will make them a pillar in the temple:

Revelation 3:12a *Him that overcometh will I make a pillar in the temple of my God...*

The pillars of any temple were there for two reasons: to be beautiful and to support things. In other words, God is saying that He will make people who live right both beautiful and necessary, not just here and now, but in eternity, in His temple. You may not feel very "vital" here and now, but it is God's desire to make you beautiful and necessary for all eternity.

The next part of the delight of Christ concerning Philadelphia Christians and churches is that they will not go out anymore:

Revelation 3:12b... *and he shall go no more out...*

This is not describing some kind of imprisonment. It simply means that we will have a permanent home. We will not lose it for not paying the mortgage; we will not lose it to termites; we will not have it taken away so some state government can build a road through it. When we get there, everything will already be unpacked and in place, and we can stay.

The next part of the delight of Christ is that He will write three names on us:

Revelation 3:12c *...and I will write upon him the name of my God, and the name of the city of my God, which is new Jerusalem, which cometh down out of heaven from my God: and I will write upon him my new name.*

The world is getting ever fonder of being marked, both metaphorically and physically. People are more likely to be tattooed than they are to be natural, it seems. And while there is ample reason both in Scripture and logic not to ever have such a mark on one's body made by man, one day God will write on the faithful, and we will not mind a bit. God, somewhere, somehow, is going to put the name of God the Father, the New Jerusalem, and His own new name upon Philadelphia-type Christians. I cannot begin to understand it all, but I absolutely do want God to mark me; people have been getting marked by the world long enough.

We should be favored. We CAN be favored...

Revelation 3:13 *He that hath an ear, let him hear what the Spirit saith unto the churches.*

God looked at this church and did not have a bad word to say about it. Do you know what that means? It means that it is possible. It is possible for a church to totally please God. It is possible for you to live right. It is possible for God to look at you and be pleased with what He sees, not just positionally but practically.

Chapter Ten
Prophecy and Practice in the Foul Church

Revelation 3:14 *And unto the angel of the church of the Laodiceans write; These things saith the Amen, the faithful and true witness, the beginning of the creation of God;* **15** *I know thy works, that thou art neither cold nor hot: I would thou wert cold or hot.* **16** *So then because thou art lukewarm, and neither cold nor hot, I will spue thee out of my mouth.* **17** *Because thou sayest, I am rich, and increased with goods, and have need of nothing; and knowest not that thou art wretched, and miserable, and poor, and blind, and naked:* **18** *I counsel thee to buy of me gold tried in the fire, that thou mayest be rich; and white raiment, that thou mayest be clothed, and that the shame of thy nakedness do not appear; and anoint thine eyes with eyesalve, that thou mayest see.* **19** *As many as I love, I rebuke and chasten: be zealous therefore, and repent.* **20** *Behold, I stand at the door, and knock: if any man hear my voice, and open the door, I will come in to him, and will sup with him, and he with me.* **21** *To him that overcometh will I grant to sit with me in my throne, even as I also overcame, and am set down with my Father in his throne.* **22** *He that hath an ear, let him hear what the Spirit saith unto the churches.*

In the last chapter, we looked at the prophecy and practice of Philadelphia, the favored church. Now we will turn our attention to the city and church of Laodicea, the foul church.

The prophecy of the foul church

To review, Ephesus is the church that most closely mirrors the overall spiritual state of the church as a whole from the time of the apostles until the apostles and those that learned directly from them died out, and John was the last of the apostles. Smyrna is the church that most closely mirrors the overall spiritual state of the church as a whole from about A.D. 60 to about A.D. 350. Pergamos is the church that most closely mirrors the overall state of the church from about A.D. 325 up until about the seventh century. Thyatira is the church that most closely mirrors the overall state of the church from about A.D. 500 up until about A.D. 1500. Sardis is the church that most closely mirrors the overall state of the church from about A.D 1500. until about A.D. 1900, with large pockets of it still to be found today. Philadelphia is the church that most closely mirrors the state of the true church from about 1900 up until the Tribulation Period begins.

But running parallel to the church of Philadelphia, we see that Laodicea has moved onto the scene at the same time as Philadelphia. Laodicea is the lukewarm church, and it represents much of our lukewarm church age. If you look around at churches all over the place, you will absolutely not be able to miss the fact that apathy is the chief characteristic of churches today.

The church age is winding down; you better be ready; Jesus is coming soon.

The practice of the foul church

Each one of these letters is written in the exact same format as if God laid out a template for John to follow. In every one of them, we will see the description of Christ, the discernment of Christ, the direction of Christ, and the delight of Christ.

The description of Christ

Revelation 3:14 *And unto the angel of the church of the Laodiceans write; These things saith the Amen, the faithful and true witness, the beginning of the creation of God;*

Laodicea was located in the Lycos valley in the province of Phrygia. Here are some important things to remember about it as we go through the text. One, it was famous for fine black wool, out of which exceptionally nice clothing was made. Two, it was famous for medicinal eye powder. Three, it had a world-famous school of medicine. Four, it was an extremely wealthy city with many banks.

In this well-dressed, medically advanced, wealthy city was a church: a warm, filthy, foul church. This church was so disgusting to God that He chose to deliver a scathing, scalding, scorching rebuke. Because of that, He described Himself in terms of absolute righteousness. He wanted everyone to know that He has every right to blister a foul church as strongly as possible. Look then, at how He described Himself:

He begins by saying that He is the Amen. This word means that He is the "so be it." In other words, Jesus is the One that everyone is *obligated* to agree with. You do not have to agree with me. But you do not have an option when it comes to agreeing with Jesus. You are obligated to agree with Him.

He then says that He is the faithful and true witness. This means that He is the one who can be counted on to testify and to do so perfectly. No one will intimidate Him. No mob boss or gang punk will frighten Him into keeping quiet. He can be counted on to testify accurately, and He will not make a single mistake. There will not be a single lawyer cross-examining Him saying, "But isn't it possible that..." No. It is not. Whatever He says is absolutely right every single time, without exception.

He then says that He is the beginning of the creation of God. People who have not studied their Bibles very well use this verse to try and prove that God the Father created Jesus before He created anything else. But that is not what this word means. It is the Greek word *arkay*, and it means the beginning in the sense of the *originator of it all*. He is the beginning because He is the one that began it all:

John 1:1 *In the beginning was the Word, and the Word was with God, and the Word was God.* **2** *The same was in the beginning with God.* **3** *All things were made by him; and without him was not any thing made that was made.*

In the context of these words to the church at Laodicea, this means that Jesus made it all, so He has every right to say who and what is right and wrong. Any judgment He pronounces is right.

The discernment of Christ

Revelation 3:15 *I know thy works, that thou art neither cold nor hot: I would thou wert cold or hot.* **16** *So then because thou art lukewarm, and neither cold nor hot, I will spue thee out of my mouth.* **17** *Because thou sayest, I am rich, and increased with goods, and have need of nothing; and knowest not that thou art wretched, and miserable, and poor, and blind, and naked:*

Here is what Christ knew about this church and its works, and His verdict based on that knowledge.

He first of all knew that they were neither hot nor cold.

Adam Clarke described this beautifully, saying, "Ye are neither heathens nor Christians, neither good nor evil, neither led away by false doctrine nor thoroughly addicted to that which is true." (6: 985)

They were neither hot nor cold!

It is a bit of a shame that this metaphor needs any explanation at all, but in our day, unfortunately, the simple often needs explaining. So here it is:

In our walk with Christ, cold is bad:

Matthew 24:12 *And because iniquity shall abound, the love of many shall wax cold.*

How awful it is for a church or an individual to be cold, wicked, absolutely devoid of any godliness, heathen, rotten to the core. Cold is bad.

By contrast, hot is good. The word for it in verses fifteen and sixteen of our text is the word *zestos*. We get our words *zest* and *zeal* from the root word of this, *zeo*, meaning to boil. It means burning hot and fervor of mind.

In verse nineteen, God instructs this church to be zealous. It comes from the same root word, *zeo*, as the one above for hot. In other words, God expects us to be piping, steaming, boiling hot for Him!

His verdict, based on the knowledge of the fact that they were neither hot nor cold, was that He would spue them out of His mouth. To spue is more than just a little spit; it is a violent ejection from the mouth. It is like when you attend the redneck family reunion, absent-mindedly reach down for your cup, and pick up someone's tobacco spit bottle instead, and take a big swig!

This really is amazing to consider; God would literally rather us be cold, godless heathens than have us be lukewarm.

It is amazing to see that what we commonly refer to as a cold, dead church, is not really cold after all, but something much worse: lukewarm. Most bad churches are not drinking in the sanctuary or fornicating on the altar. They are doing something worse; they are sitting back and being satisfied with themselves while having no zeal for God. They think they have arrived. They are spending their time now resting on their laurels and convincing themselves that they are superior to others.

Look at God's appraisal of a church like this:

Revelation 3:17 *Because thou sayest, I am rich, and increased with goods, and have need of nothing; and knowest not that thou art wretched, and miserable, and poor, and blind, and naked:*

They thought they had need of nothing. They said, "Look at our medical skills!" But God said, "You are wretched and miserable; your medicine hasn't helped."

They said, "Look at our banks and all of our wealth!" But God said, "You are spiritually bankrupt."

They said, "Look at our eye powder!" But God said, "You are blind about spiritual things."

They said, "Look at our fine clothing, made from the nicest black wool!" But God said, "You people are naked."

They had forgotten that only in Christ are we healed, only in Christ have we any wealth, only in Christ can we truly see, and only in His righteousness are we truly clothed.

The direction of Christ

Revelation 3:18 *I counsel thee to buy of me gold tried in the fire, that thou mayest be rich; and white raiment, that thou mayest be clothed, and that the shame of thy nakedness do not appear; and anoint thine eyes* *with eyesalve, that thou mayest see.* **19** *As many as I love, I rebuke and chasten: be zealous therefore, and repent.* **20** *Behold, I stand at the door, and knock: if any man hear my voice, and open the door, I will come in to him, and will sup with him, and he with me.*

Christ directed this church to *buy* some things from Him. But everything they had was worthless in the spiritual realm. How could they buy anything from Him? The last word of verse nineteen tells them the price of what He was offering: repent! Turn away from being satisfied with yourselves, turn away from trusting in yourselves, turn away from your sinful apathy, and become completely dependent upon and addicted to Christ. When you do, here is what you will be buying

The first purchase of repentance is "gold tried in the fire." This is a way of saying to stop trusting in your riches that will one day burn up and perish. Trust and gain the riches of Christ that never can be destroyed.

The second purchase of repentance is "white raiment." This is a way of saying that this city and church was glorying in its fine, black wool clothing, but to God, those things were no more acceptable than the fig leaves in the garden of Eden. Spiritually, God was reminding them that until they were clothed in the righteousness of Christ, they were as nude as a plucked chicken.

The third purchase of repentance is eye salve that they were to anoint their eyes with. They were trusting in their eye powder, and yet, they were still spiritually blind. A person is as blind as Samson post-Delilah until he sees things like Christ sees them.

In His directions thus far, He has covered three out of four of their spiritual problems. But He has not yet dealt with the fact that they are wretched and miserable. To this, He speaks in the first part of verse nineteen:

Revelation 3:19 *As many as I love, I rebuke and chasten: be zealous therefore, and repent.*

They had their great medical centers, and they stayed spiritually sick. True healing and health come as God rebukes and chastens us, and we submit. A person or church not responding to God's correction will be miserable and wretched.

So how does a church or a person get like this? Here is your answer; look at what position they had put Christ in:

Revelation 3:20 *Behold, I stand at the door, and knock: if any man hear my voice, and open the door, I will come in to him, and will sup with him, and he with me.*

What an awful thing, that in His directions to a church, He had to say, *"Oh, by the way, how about letting me in?"*

What an awful thing for a church or a person (this verse applies equally well either way, especially since a church is actually made up of individual people) to have Christ standing on the outside looking in! You could be having sweet fellowship with Him, but you have locked Him out. It is no wonder that you are so lukewarm and disgusting! What is so amazing is that God still loved them and did not want to have to spew them out. He will do it if you do not open up and let Him back in to heat things up, but He does not want to have to do it.

The delight of Christ

Revelation 3:21 *To him that overcometh will I grant to sit with me in my throne, even as I also overcame, and am set down with my Father in his throne.* **22** *He that hath an ear, let him hear what the Spirit saith unto the churches.*

Do you know what delights Christ? He is delighted when a lukewarm church, or a lukewarm person, overcomes that disgusting state. When a person or church goes from lukewarm to hot, they will be allowed to sit with Him in His throne. We are talking about crawling up in the lap of Christ and having Him wrap His loving arms around us like a father would a repentant child. Oh, what a delight!

Lukewarm. This church was lukewarm. Do you know what is so frightening about that? To be blazing hot, it actually takes effort. You have to work at it. To be freezing cold also takes effort. Refrigeration is not a natural thing; it only happens through great effort. If you are on fire for God, it took effort to get you there. If you are a reprobate heathen, sticking your fist in God's face, it took effort to get you there. But to be lukewarm, all you have to do is... nothing. Lukewarmness is just the natural state of things that do not make an effort. Put a cup of water down and walk away; it will be lukewarm soon. Leave a piping hot steak on a plate, walk away, and it will be lukewarm soon. It does not take any effort to become lukewarm; all you have to do is stop making the effort not to be.

Chapter Eleven
The Throne Room of God, 01

Revelation 4:1 *After this I looked, and, behold, a door was opened in heaven: and the first voice which I heard was as it were of a trumpet talking with me; which said, Come up hither, and I will shew thee things which must be hereafter.* **2** *And immediately I was in the spirit: and, behold, a throne was set in heaven, and one sat on the throne.*

There is something remarkable about royalty. Just over two hundred forty years ago, we went to war against England. King George and his forces had been so brutal to America that this country chose to fight for freedom. The battle lasted for years, cost an enormous amount in lives and materials, and ended with a great big win for us, the underdogs. The Union Jack ceased to fly over the USA, and the Stars and Stripes went up instead. We now have Oreos and Sundrop instead of tea and crumpets, Sunday afternoon football instead of a three-day cricket game, and pizza instead of blood pudding. Long Live America!

But here is a funny thing. We independent, stubborn, King-George-whipping Americans are still enthralled at the thought of royalty. We have been independent for two hundred-plus years, but when Prince Charles married lady Diana, we, along with about 4 billion other people, were glued to our televisions watching! We all know that Prince Charles is next in line for the throne and are at least aware of the issues between Prince William and his now thoroughly emasculated brother, Harry.

Most Americans, like most of the rest of the world, think that Queen Elizabeth is what a queen should be. And I guarantee you that if I or any of you were invited to Buckingham Palace to meet the queen, we would put on our Sunday finest and be more respectful than we have ever been in our lives.

And here is what is so amazing about that: the queen has *absolutely no power or authority!* I do not mean just that she has no power or authority over us; I mean she has no power or authority at all. Over the past couple of hundred years, British law has arrived at the point where the parliament and the prime minister have all of the authority in England, and the royal family has basically none. The position of King or Queen is largely just a symbolic position now. As a UK governmental website explains, "Time has reduced the power of the monarchy, and today it is broadly ceremonial." (Parliament and Crown, 2022)

The King or Queen cannot make or throw out a single law. Yet even though everyone knows this, we are still somewhat awed by the thought of royalty. When we see a person sitting on a throne, it makes a sense of reverence come over us. How much more would that be true if we were ever brought into a throne room where a real, all-powerful king sat holding court?

In Revelation 1:19, God gave John the outline for the book of The Revelation:

Revelation 1:19 *Write the things which thou hast seen, and the things which are, and the things which shall be hereafter;*

In chapter one, John followed the first part of the outline, covering the things which he had seen, the events of his past. In chapters two and three, he followed the second part of the outline covering the things which are, the current local churches and the entire church age. In chapter four, that which we normally think of when we think of "The Revelation" will begin to unfold. It is in chapter four that John begins to write about things which will be *hereafter*. All through chapters two and three, our attention is on earth. It is in those two chapters that we see fifty-one straight verses on the local church. Fifty-one verses focused on earth. Eighteen times in those fifty-one verses, we see the word *church* or *churches*. And then our focus, which has been fixated on the earthly, on the church on earth, changes completely.

As we get into chapters four and five, we are no longer fixated on the church; we are now fixated on the throne. We are not gazing on earth anymore; we are gazing on heaven. In chapter four alone, we read the word *throne* twelve times. Chapters two and three had us riveted to the earthly; chapters four and five will take us into *The Throne Room of God*.

As we begin, we will actually spend a great deal of our time looking at other New Testament passages that shed light on these two verses. It is in the next chapter that we will really begin to dig into what we see going on in heaven. In this one, we will deal with the timing of what we see in these two verses.

Revelation 4:1 *After this I looked, and, behold, a door was opened in heaven: and the first voice which I heard was as it were of a trumpet talking with me; which said, Come up hither, and I will shew thee things which must be hereafter.* **2** *And immediately I was in the spirit: and, behold, a throne was set in heaven, and one sat on the throne.*

These verses begin with two important words to consider: *after this*. Your immediate question should be, "After what?"

These words are big and broad in their meaning. Here is a good way to understand them: after everything that has come before, and after every way that they have come before. In other words, it means *after this* in the sense of *after John heard about and wrote to the seven churches*. But it also means *after this* in the sense of *after all of what John wrote about the churches comes to pass.* This *"after this"* happened to John in his day, but it covers events thousands of years after John, after all that God said about the churches has come to pass.

Consider that just in light of what God said to the church at Philadelphia. After God has kept the church from the worldwide Tribulation to come, after that, this scene in heaven will take place. I believe that this teaches fairly clearly that the events that take place after chapter three take place after the church is removed from earth in the event that we call the Rapture. That seems to be the only logical explanation for the fact that the church is mentioned eighteen times in the first three chapters of the book and then is not mentioned again until the very end of the book. Here is what God said is in store for the true church, those of this age who are saved:

John 14:1 *Let not your heart be troubled: ye believe in God, believe also in me.* **2** *In my Father's house are many mansions: if it were not so, I would have told you. I go to prepare a place for you.* **3** *And if I go and prepare a place for you, I will come again, and receive you unto myself; that where I am, there ye may be also.*

Jesus introduced the doctrine of the Rapture by telling His troubled disciples that He was leaving them, but He would also be coming back to get them. Paul followed that up later with this additional information:

1 Thessalonians 4:13 *But I would not have you to be ignorant, brethren, concerning them which are asleep, that ye sorrow not, even as others which have no hope.* **14** *For if we believe that Jesus died and rose again, even so them also which sleep in Jesus will God bring with him.* **15** *For this we say unto you by the word of the Lord, that we which are alive and remain unto the coming of the Lord shall not prevent them which are asleep.* **16** *For the Lord himself shall descend from heaven with a shout, with the voice of the archangel, and with the trump of God: and the dead in Christ shall rise first:* **17** *Then we which are alive and remain shall be caught up together with them in the clouds, to meet the Lord in the air: and so shall we ever be with the Lord.*

As these verses specify, God is going to come for us, and He is not going to hit the ground at that time. When we hear the shout, and when we hear the trumpet of God, we are going to be caught up and meet God in the air. We will be reunited with those who have been saved and died already. Paul went further in 1 Corinthians 15 and gave us this information:

1 Corinthians 15:50 *Now this I say, brethren, that flesh and blood cannot inherit the kingdom of God; neither doth corruption inherit incorruption.* **51** *Behold, I shew you a mystery; We shall not all sleep,* *but we shall all be changed,* **52** *In a moment, in the twinkling of an eye, at the last trump: for the trumpet shall sound, and the dead shall be raised incorruptible, and we shall be changed.* **53** *For this corruptible must put on incorruption, and this mortal must put on immortality.*

When God comes in the Rapture, those who have already died have developed a serious case of "split personalities." Their inner man, the soul and spirit, have already been in heaven, with God, some of them for hundreds of years! But their bodies have been lying in the ground, rotting and decomposing.

People that have died saved are no doubt glad to be in heaven, and they still very clearly have all of their five senses as other portions of Scripture make clear. But still, it has to be kind of awkward to be there while your body is still here. But when Christ comes in the Rapture, He is going to bring all of those dear souls with Him and call their dead bodies out of the grave. Those bodies, no matter how badly they have decomposed, will be remade in an instant into new, perfect, glorified, never-dying bodies. Those dear souls will take up residence in those glorified bodies forevermore.

We who are still alive, though, will never have our bodies separated from our soul and spirit. Our bodies will simply be instantly transformed into the same kind of new, perfect, glorified, never-dying bodies that the dead saints receive.

But let us keep looking for a moment at the question of timing. When does the church arrive before the throne that we see in Revelation 4:1? Here is another passage that deals with the subject:

1 Thessalonians 5:1 *But of the times and the seasons, brethren, ye have no need that I write unto you.* **2** *For yourselves know perfectly that the day of the Lord so cometh as a thief in the night.* **3** *For when they shall say, Peace and safety; then sudden destruction cometh upon them, as travail upon a woman with child; and they shall not escape.* **4** *But ye, brethren, are not in darkness, that that day should overtake you as a thief.* **5** *Ye are all the children of light, and the children of the day: we are not of the night, nor of darkness.* **6** *Therefore let us not sleep, as do others; but let us watch and be sober.* **7** *For they that sleep sleep in the night; and they that be drunken are drunken in the night.* **8** *But let us, who are of the day, be sober, putting on the breastplate of faith and love; and for an helmet, the hope of salvation.* **9** *For God hath not appointed us to wrath, but to obtain salvation by our Lord Jesus Christ,*

At the end of 1 Thessalonians 4, Paul told that church about the Rapture. But as he begins chapter five, he has some additional things to say on another portion of this subject of the last days. In 1 Thessalonians

4:13, Paul indicated that there were some things that they did not know, some things concerning the Rapture:

1 Thessalonians 4:13 *But **I would not have you to be ignorant**, brethren, concerning them which are asleep, that ye sorrow not, even as others which have no hope.*

We see in these words that there were many details of the Rapture about which the church at Thessalonica was ignorant. But look at how Paul opens chapter five:

1 Thessalonians 5:1 *But of the times and the seasons, brethren, ye have no need that I write unto you.* **2** *For **yourselves know perfectly** that the day of the Lord so cometh as a thief in the night.*

The Rapture of chapter four was something that the Church at Thessalonica did not understand very well; Paul said he did not want them to be ignorant about it. But the day of the Lord in chapter five was something they understood very well indeed; Paul said of that event, "yourselves know perfectly."

These two events relate to each other, but they are not the same thing; they are distinct events. The Rapture is when the church is removed from the earth. The Day of the Lord is the judgment that follows the Rapture:

1 Thessalonians 5:3 *For when they shall say, Peace and safety; then sudden destruction cometh upon them, as travail upon a woman with child; and they shall not escape.*

This church knew about that judgment to come. Christ Himself spoke of that judgment over and over again. Here is another indication that they knew all of this:

1 Thessalonians 5:4 *But ye, brethren, are not in darkness, that that day should overtake you as a thief.*

Is there a very serious day of judgment coming? Yes. But children of God will not be overtaken in this judgment. Look at verse nine:

1 Thessalonians 5:9 *For God hath not appointed us to wrath, but to obtain salvation by our Lord Jesus Christ,*

In context, the wrath spoken of here is the wrath associated with the day of the Lord, the Tribulation Period and that which follows. God has not appointed us to that. If He had, He would carry us through it with no worries. But He hasn't. We are not appointed to that.

With some regularity, though, this question arises, "What if you are wrong? Shouldn't you get ready just in case we do have to go through the Tribulation Period?" And the answer is yes. We need to get ready just in case.

"Good thinking preacher!" comes the almost immediate response. "Let's store up buckets of freeze-dried rice, and fill jugs full of water!"

For the record, I am actually all in favor of storing up things like that for disasters of the here and now, common disasters like fires, floods, hurricanes, ice storms, and Democrats getting elected and trying to turn us into a Socialist disaster like Venezuela and the old USSR. But may I ask a question? What good are buckets of freeze-dried rice going to do when the Antichrist rules the earth, and demonic scorpions are stinging people, and war is destroying most of the population? What good are jugs of water going to do when all water on earth, including water in jugs, gets turned to blood? I do not think there are enough MRE's, duct tape, and gas masks on earth to deal with stars falling from the heavens and hail the size of bowling balls raining down from the heavens.

No, that is not what I mean when I say "get ready." Right now, I am getting ready just in case I am wrong, and we have to go through the Tribulation. I am reading my Bible, and praying, and serving Jesus, and drawing as near to God as I can; that is the absolute best way to prepare for anything in the world, and it does not cost me a dime.

But truthfully, I am not at all worried about it. When Paul spoke of the judgment to come and then said we were not appointed to it, I believe that means that we are not appointed to it.

Is this a major issue? Is it something to scream and fight over? Is it something to break fellowship over? No, it is not. Christians can actually disagree over this, and it not be a really big deal. The timing of His coming is not really the main issue; the fact of His coming is the main issue. Nonetheless, based on the text of Scripture, I do not see any possibility at all that any born-again believers are going to be plunged into the Tribulation Period. We will be raptured and gone before it begins.

The Thessalonian church got the message, and as far as we know, did well for a while. Until another letter arrived, with a forged signature, that told a different story. When Paul found out, he had to write them again and settle the issue all over again:

2 Thessalonians 2:1 *Now we beseech you, brethren, by the coming of our Lord Jesus Christ, and by our gathering together unto him,* **2** *That ye be not soon shaken in mind, or be troubled, neither by spirit, nor by word, nor by letter as from us, as that the day of Christ is at hand.* **3** *Let no man deceive you by any means: for that day shall not come, except there come a falling away first, and that man of sin be revealed, the son of perdition;* **4** *Who opposeth and exalteth himself above all that is called God, or that is worshipped; so that he as God* *sitteth in the temple of God, shewing himself that he is God.* **5** *Remember ye not, that, when I was yet with you, I told you these things?* **6** *And now ye know what withholdeth that he might be revealed in his time.* **7** *For the mystery of iniquity doth already work: only he who now letteth will let, until he be taken out of the way.* **8** *And then shall that Wicked be revealed, whom the Lord shall consume with the spirit of his mouth, and shall destroy with the brightness of his coming:* **9** *Even him, whose coming is after the working of Satan with all power and signs and lying wonders,* **10** *And with all deceivableness of unrighteousness in them that perish; because they received not the love of the truth, that they might be saved.* **11** *And for this cause God shall send them strong delusion, that they should believe a lie:* **12** *That they all might be damned who believed not the truth, but had pleasure in unrighteousness.* **13** *But we are bound to give thanks alway to God for you, brethren beloved of the Lord, because God hath from the beginning chosen you to salvation through sanctification of the Spirit and belief of the truth:* **14** *Whereunto he called you by our gospel, to the obtaining of the glory of our Lord Jesus Christ.* **15** *Therefore, brethren, stand fast, and hold the traditions which ye have been taught, whether by word, or our epistle.*

The very first subject Paul mentioned as he began the second chapter of the second letter was the Rapture once again. He called it our *gathering together unto him.* Then we find out in the next verse why he is having to write to them about the same thing he wrote to them about earlier:

2 Thessalonians 2:2 *That ye be not soon shaken in mind, or be troubled, neither by spirit, nor by word,* **nor by letter as from us***, as that the day of Christ is at hand.*

"Fake news" did not start in our day. It has been around for many millennia. Here in our text, we find that in Paul's day, somebody had been writing letters full of heresy and signing the apostle's name to them! The church at Thessalonica got a letter telling them that the day of Christ, the same thing as the day of the lord, was at hand. In other words, this church had heard from Paul that the Rapture was coming, and they would be caught up. After that, the Day of the Lord, the Day of Christ, the Tribulation Period, would fall on this earth.

They breathed a great big sigh of relief... and then another letter showed up. This one, probably in bold print, red lettering, and underlined, basically said:

RUN FOR THE HILLS! THERE IS NO RAPTURE, THE TRIBULATION IS ABOUT TO START! WE'RE ALL GONNA DIE! AGGGHHH!!!!!
Love, Paul.

So Paul had to write again and say, "Look, I don't care who says, or writes, or imagines what. You are not appointed to wrath."

This whole affair had to be frustrating to Paul, and you know it was to the church at Thessalonica. But it is ultimately very good that it happened because Paul used the occasion of the second letter to give even more details concerning all of this. He had previously told them some things verbally that he now put into writing:

2 Thessalonians 2:3 *Let no man deceive you by any means: for that day shall not come, except there come a falling away first, and that man of sin be revealed, the son of perdition;* **4** *Who opposeth and exalteth himself above all that is called God, or that is worshipped; so that he as God sitteth in the temple of God, shewing himself that he is God.* **5** *Remember ye not, that, when I was yet with you, I told you these things?*

That day. What day? The Day of the Lord, the day when the judgment of God falls on earth. The day that happens after the church is removed. According to these verses, that day will not come until certain things happen.

First, there will come a *falling away*. That phrase is from the Greek word *apostasia*. We get our English word *apostasy* from it. So, the Tribulation Period cannot start until an apostasy takes place. But does anything about that statement seem odd?

There has never been a time on earth when there was *not* apostasy. Apostasy means a willful rebellion from God's truth by those who should know better. And that has been happening for 6,000 years now. Adam was an apostate when he ate the fruit. David was an apostate when he committed adultery and murder. Peter was an apostate when he denied Christ three times. Judas was an apostate when he betrayed God for thirty pieces of silver. Every book of the New Testament deals with some individual or group that had gone off into apostasy. So when Paul wrote to the church at Thessalonica that the Tribulation would not begin until a falling away, an apostasy came, he was not just talking about your average, garden variety, apostasy.

He was talking about **APOSTASY**. He was talking about all out, no holds barred, full-fledged wickedness running wild with nothing to hold it back kind of apostasy. He was talking about apostasy with no preacher speaking against it, no newspaper denouncing it, no politician trying to correct it, and no police officer writing tickets over it. He was talking about the kind of wicked, lawless, godless behavior that is only possible when there is no more church to stand up and say THOU SHALT NOT! In fact, even though it was not necessary to translate it into English due to the clear context, there is actually a definite article along with the word apostasy in Greek. This is not just some general apostasy; this is THE APOSTASY. This is apostasy like the world never *has* seen and never *could* see until there is no more Holy Ghost-filled church to stand in its way.

The second thing that this passage teaches us has to happen before the Tribulation takes place is that the man we know as Antichrist will be revealed. Look at verses three and four again:

2 Thessalonians 2:3 *Let no man deceive you by any means: for that day shall not come, except there come a falling away first, and that man of sin be revealed, the son of perdition;* **4** *Who opposeth and exalteth himself above all that is called God, or that is worshipped; so that he as God sitteth in the temple of God, shewing himself that he is God.*

Do you remember the word apocalypse that we said our English word Revelation comes from? That is the same word used here when we are told the Antichrist must be revealed before the Tribulation begins. Antichrist will not just slowly appear on the scene, gradually gaining power and prestige over many years until he takes over. This man will explode onto the scene and be in charge so fast that it will make heads spin.

Notice that he is called <u>the</u> *son of perdition*. The word perdition means *absolute destruction*. It describes what he causes and what is going to happen to him. This phrase "the son of perdition" is found exactly twice in the entire Bible. The other time it is used came when Jesus was thinking about and praying for His disciples in the immediate moments after Judas left to betray Him:

John 17:12 *While I was with them in the world, I kept them in thy name: those that thou gavest me I have kept, and none of them is lost, but the son of perdition; that the scripture might be fulfilled.*

John 17:12 calls Judas <u>the</u>, not <u>a</u>, son of perdition. 2 Thessalonians 2:3 calls Antichrist <u>the</u>, not <u>a</u>, son of perdition.

It would really not be proper, as much as my flesh would like it, for me to be called *the Bo Wagner*. You see, there is actually another Bo Wagner on Earth, and he is a jazz musician. I am *a* Bo Wagner, but I am not *the* Bo Wagner. If I was the only Bo Wagner that ever had been or ever will be on earth, you could rightfully call me *the Bo Wagner*.

This is certainly not a major issue, and it will not change anything eschatologically either way, but I believe that a resurrected Judas Iscariot will be the Antichrist. There is a phrase in Scripture concerning a Judas after he died that is not used of any other deceased person in the entire Bible:

Acts 1:25 *That he may take part of this ministry and apostleship, from which Judas by transgression fell,* **that he might go to his own place.**

Where did Judas go after he died? If you use the general answer of "hell," let me remind you of something:

Matthew 25:41 *Then shall he say also unto them on the left hand, Depart from me, ye cursed, into everlasting fire, prepared for the devil and his angels:*

Hell was not prepared for Judas. Hell is for every devil, demon, and wicked sinner who has ever lived. Judas did not get the privilege of going to what we would call "general population" in Hell. I believe that wherever it is in hell that God sent Judas, whatever torments he has been suffering for the past 2,000 years makes regular Hell seem like a day in the park. You do not betray Christ and get treated like every Joe-blow sinner who has ever lived. I believe that old Judas, newly resurrected Antichrist, will be so tormented and furious and terrified of going back to where he has been that he will fight like a mad dog to beat God and get out of having to go back. That would explain perfectly the desperate, awful, hateful rage of Antichrist! His die has been cast; it is sink or swim, no turning back; in his mind, he cannot afford to lose. How else can a person arrive at the blasphemous point that Antichrist will get to halfway through the Tribulation Period?

2 Thessalonians 2:4 *Who opposeth and exalteth himself above all that is called God, or that is worshipped; so that he as God sitteth in the temple of God, shewing himself that he is God.*

History, especially evil history, has a demonic way of repeating itself. After the death of Alexander the Great and the four-way division of his empire, Ptolemy Lagus, who controlled Egypt, and Seleucus, who controlled Syria, began to war. In between them was Israel, so they caught it from both sides. In 175 B.C., a man by the name of Antiochus Epiphanes became king of Syria. He was determined to make the Jews convert to Hellenism. In 169 B.C., he captured Jerusalem. He killed anyone who had a copy of the law of Moses, crucified 100,000 Jews who refused to worship his false gods, hung all of the young Jewish boys who had been circumcised, mutilated Jewish women, and then on December 15, 169 B.C., set up an idol to a false god and offered a sow upon the altar in the temple.

During the Tribulation Period, history will repeat itself, only worse in every detail. Antichrist will be filled with all of the rage and the hate of Antiochus, plus about 2,000 years more hate on top of it. Anyone who refuses to worship him as God, when they are caught, will be tortured and then die.

In verse five, Paul said, "Don't you remember? I told you all of these things." But then he added more incredible details to the account:

2 Thessalonians 2:6 *And now ye know what withholdeth that he might be revealed in his time.* **7** *For the mystery of iniquity doth already work: only he who now letteth will let, until he be taken out of the way.* **8** *And then shall that Wicked be revealed, whom the Lord shall consume with the spirit of his mouth, and shall destroy with the brightness of his coming:* **9** *Even him, whose coming is after the working of Satan with all power and signs and lying wonders,* **10** *And with all deceivableness of unrighteousness in them that perish; because they received not the love of the truth, that they might be saved.*

Verses eight through ten tell us a bit more about Antichrist. He is called *wicked* in verse eight. Verse nine tells us that his *coming* is after the working of Satan with all power and signs and lying wonders. I personally take this to mean that God allows Satan to perform a demonic miracle and raise Judas from the dead, and then vault him as Antichrist to worldwide power. Verse ten tells us who will follow him: those who received not the love of the truth that they might be saved. In other words, a whole bunch of the world. All people who have the truth of God's Word staring them right in the face and reject it will follow Antichrist hook, line, and sinker.

But why has it not happened yet?

2 Thessalonians 2:7 *For the mystery of iniquity doth already work: only he who now letteth will let, until he be taken out of the way.*

Everything is already in place. It has been since Paul's day. Almost 2,000 years ago, Paul said, "The mystery of iniquity is already at work!" He was talking about this *specific* iniquity, the iniquity that will produce Antichrist. If it was already at work nearly 2,000 years ago, why has it not happened yet? Because someone is *letting,* which is an old English word that means the opposite of what you might think. It actually means to hinder. Someone is *hindering, preventing* the Antichrist from coming to power. Who is that someone?

There is only one possible answer: God, specifically the Holy Spirit, who has been at work since Jesus went back to heaven, has been holding that hound of hell at bay for nearly 2,000 years. Antichrist has banged the bars of his cell, screamed constant obscenities, blasphemed until his throat is raw, but the blessed Holy Ghost has kept him on his leash and in his cage.

But there will come a time on earth, an awful time, a time when God the Father takes the Holy Ghost, not out of the world, that would be impossible, because He is just as omnipresent as the Father Himself, but will take Him out of the *way.* In other words, the Holy Ghost, for two thousand years, has had God the Father's permission to keep the devil from having full sway and appearing. But there will come a time, I believe at the very moment that the church is removed, that God the Father says to the Spirit, "Don't stand in his way anymore. If this world is so intent on serving Satan, so be it. Let them have it their way, and let them reap what they sow."

In fact, it will be even more terrifying than that. Not only will God allow those who have rejected Christ to follow Antichrist, He will actually not leave them any other option:

2 Thessalonians 2:11 *And for this cause God shall send them strong delusion, that they should believe a lie:* **12** *That they all might be damned who believed not the truth, but had pleasure in unrighteousness.*

Every person who has been confronted with the gospel and yet has chosen not to accept Christ before the trumpet sounds will be forever doomed once it does sound. Every person who has been convicted of their sin, and refused to repent, will never be convicted again when the Tribulation begins. God Himself will send them a strong delusion, and they will believe the biggest lie of all time.

If you do not get saved before the Rapture, having had a chance to do so, you will look all around you, you will see millions and millions of people disappear, clothes left lying around, planes falling from the sky, entire churches missing, and you will believe that it was not the Rapture that did it. Even though the Bible describes it so very well, you will look right at it and believe something else. If you were counting on recognizing the Rapture and then getting saved, forget about it, it cannot and will not happen.

Think of this; let it sink into your very soul. There is coming a day, not too very long from now, may even be today, that the last trumpet of the church age will sound. At that very moment, we who are saved will be caught up together to meet Jesus in the air. We will be taken from the earth to the throne room of God. The Rapture does not occur in Revelation 4:1; it occurs sometime after chapter three ends and before chapter four begins. When John gets caught up in Revelation 4:1, He sees the elders of the church already there. The trumpet has already sounded for them; they are delivered, while those who have rejected Christ are condemned forever.

The very same trumpet that takes the saved into the throne room will take the sinner into the Tribulation Period. The very same trumpet that marks the timing of our arrival in heaven marks the timing of the sinner's arrival in hell on earth. The very same trumpet that ensures that we will never have another day of suffering ensures that the sinner who has previously rejected Christ will never have another day when he or she does not suffer. This will be a day of separation like this world has never ever known. Glory to God, we are headed for the throne room! But oh! May God have mercy, for at that very same moment, some sitting and reading this book will be headed for the Tribulation Period, with no hope of escaping it, or the eternity in hell and the lake of fire that follows it.

The trumpet of God may sound at any moment. Our here may in the next two minutes become *hereafter.* Are you ready?

Chapter Twelve
The Throne Room of God, 02

Revelation 4:2 *And immediately I was in the spirit: and, behold, a throne was set in heaven, and one sat on the throne.* **3** *And he that sat was to look upon like a jasper and a sardine stone: and there was a rainbow round about the throne, in sight like unto an emerald.* **4** *And round about the throne were four and twenty seats: and upon the seats I saw four and twenty elders sitting, clothed in white raiment; and they had on their heads crowns of gold.* **5** *And out of the throne proceeded lightnings and thunderings and voices: and there were seven lamps of fire burning before the throne, which are the seven Spirits of God.* **6** *And before the throne there was a sea of glass like unto crystal: and in the midst of the throne, and round about the throne, were four beasts full of eyes before and behind.* **7** *And the first beast was like a lion, and the second beast like a calf, and the third beast had a face as a man, and the fourth beast was like a flying eagle.* **8** *And the four beasts had each of them six wings about him; and they were full of eyes within: and they rest not day and night, saying, Holy, holy, holy, Lord God Almighty, which was, and is, and is to come.* **9** *And when those beasts give glory and honour and thanks to him that sat on the throne, who liveth for ever and ever,* **10** *The four and twenty elders fall down before him that sat on the throne, and worship him that liveth for ever and ever, and cast their crowns before the throne, saying,* **11** *Thou art worthy, O Lord, to receive glory and honour and power: for thou hast created all things, and for thy pleasure they are and were created.*

For years, people have been wondering "what's out there." Is there life anywhere besides earth? Are there little green men on another planet just waiting to invade? Are we the only intelligent life in the universe? There are actually long-running government programs studying this issue to see if indeed there is intelligent life out there somewhere. Billions have been spent on this project! I wish they would have asked me; I could have saved the American taxpayer billions of dollars. There is intelligent life out there. The real question is whether there is much intelligent life on earth!

If you could travel far enough and go to the right place, you would arrive at a destination that John went to nearly two thousand years ago. It is a place that every child of God will go to one day, probably one day soon. It is the throne room of God, it is an actual, literal place, and the King rules the universe from that place.

In the last chapter, we entered the throne room of Almighty God. We found out that one day very soon, all of the saved will be raptured out of this world and taken into that throne room while the world experiences the Tribulation Period, enduring hell on earth.

In this chapter, we will be looking at the throne, the throng, and the testimony.

The throne

Revelation 4:2 *And immediately I was in the spirit: and, behold, a throne was set in heaven, and one sat on the throne.*

I want you to notice first of all that the throne of God is "set" in heaven. It was already there and occupied when John arrived. As John took his first breath in heaven, as he blinked his eyes for the first time in that celestial city, the very first thing that arrested his attention was the throne of God.

Not the street of gold... not the river of life... not the mansions... and not any Old Testament saints. All of those were there, but the first thing his attention was captured by was the throne and the person on it! I do not know if it is like that for everyone; it may be that we end up starting off entering in at the gates and making our way to the throne, the Bible does not specifically say. But one way or the other, I know that the highlight of Heaven is the throne and the One sitting on it!

When the Bible tells us that this throne was "set" in heaven, the word used indicates that this is a done deal, a long-standing established fact, something that is not going to change. Human governments come, and human governments go, but the throne of God remains the same, and the God on the throne remains the same. Immutability is a quality of our God we should be grateful for! It is nice to know there are never any elections in heaven!

This God that John saw on the throne looks like a jasper and sardine stone:

Revelation 4:3a *And he that sat was to look upon like a jasper and a sardine stone:*

This description has nothing to do with shape because rocks come in all different shapes. What is being described is the color of His glory. Look at how awesome a sight just the glory of God on the throne will be:

"The ancient stone once called a jasper is much more beautiful and valuable than our modern jasper. Its base color is pure white, with bright bands of blue, purple, and green." (Linder, Family Bible Notes)

The sardine stone was a bright red. Both of them took a high polish and reflected light brilliantly.

I wonder how long it will take our glorified eyes to adjust to a degree that they can see Him clearly? As John arrived in heaven, all he could make out of God initially was a brilliant glow around Him of white, purple, blue, green, and red!

We then learn that there is an emerald-colored rainbow around the throne:

Revelation 4:3b *...and there was a rainbow round about the throne, in sight like unto an emerald.*

This is utterly remarkable in that it goes against the laws of nature. Nature dictates that a rainbow is produced when light passes through a watery prism separating the light into the very predictable colors of red, orange, yellow, green, blue, indigo, and violet. But this rainbow is all green, defying the laws of nature. I wonder when man will finally grasp the fact that God is not subject to the laws of nature. God made the laws of nature, and He suspends or alters them at His pleasure.

This rainbow also defies the laws of nature by existing without one of its two key ingredients. A rainbow needs light and rain to exist. There is undoubtedly light in heaven, but there is no indication in Scripture that there is ever rain in heaven. This is a rainbow that exists, at all times, in the same location, with no rain to act as a prism for the light.

This rainbow, rather than just being a generally pretty object, exists for a particular purpose, surrounding a particular object, the throne of God.

Then we find that it is made of only one color, green. And not just any green; the most beautiful green in the universe is that found in the finest of emeralds, and that is the color that God chose to make His heavenly, throne-surrounding rainbow out of. You have never seen a rainbow as magnificent as the one out there around the throne of God!

The throng

The God who is and will be sitting on that throne is the entire point of heaven. But He will not be alone. He could have chosen to be alone, but He chose otherwise. There will be a great number of people and creatures on this sea of glass around this throne. Chief among them in this great throng is a group of people simply called "elders."

Revelation 4:4 *And round about the throne were four and twenty seats: and upon the seats I saw four and twenty elders sitting, clothed in white raiment; and they had on their heads crowns of gold.*

John here began to tell of the throng around the throne. He noted that there were twenty-four seats around the throne and twenty-four elders sitting on those twenty-four seats. But who are those twenty-four elders, and what do they mean for us? We have not seen a reference to twenty-four elders before in Scripture, so this bears some examining and investigation.

Notice three things about them, and by the time we get to the third, their identity should be obvious.

<u>We first of all see that they are right.</u>

These twenty-four elders are clothed in white clothing. That is emblematic of purity. These are the righteous, the ones who are washed in the blood of the Lamb, the ones who are clean.

<u>Then we see that they are rewarded.</u>

These twenty-four elders are wearing gold crowns. Where did they get them? They surely did not bring them from earth to heaven! If anyone has a crown in heaven, it is because God has given them a crown in reward for what they have done.

<u>Then we find that they are redeemed.</u>

Jump ahead a bit to a description of them from the next chapter:

Revelation 5:8 *And when he had taken the book, the four beasts and four and twenty elders fell down before the Lamb, having every one of them harps, and golden vials full of odours, which are the prayers of saints.* **9** *And they sung a new song, saying, Thou art worthy to take the book, and to open the seals thereof: for thou wast slain,* **and hast redeemed us to God by thy blood** *out of every kindred, and tongue, and people, and nation;* **10** *And hast made us unto our God kings and priests: and we shall reign on the earth.*

Pay attention to what these twenty-four elders said. Both the elders and the beasts fall down to worship God, but understand that grammatically, though both groups fell down, only one group did the singing at this point, and that is the elders. In their song, they pointed out that God has *redeemed* them. He has bought them back; He has delivered them from sin. They also note that they are a group that was redeemed out of every single nation and ethnic group on earth! That is significant for two reasons. One, it means that they are not just Jews, so this cannot be the apostles and a representative of each tribe of Israel, as some have said. Two, there are far more than twenty-four nationalities and ethnicities on earth. So these twenty-four have to be the representatives of a group much larger than themselves. There is only one group in all of history that matches that description, and that is the church, those who have been saved. That matches perfectly with what they said in verse ten, "You have made us kings and priests," that God said He would do for the church:

Revelation 1:4 *John to the seven churches which are in Asia: Grace be unto you, and peace, from him which is, and which was, and which is to come; and from the seven Spirits which are before his throne;* **5** *And from Jesus Christ, who is the faithful witness, and the first begotten of the dead, and the prince of the kings of the earth. Unto him that loved us, and washed us from our sins in his own blood,* **6 And hath made us kings and priests** *unto God and his Father; to him be glory and dominion for ever and ever. Amen.*

God spoke to the churches and told them He had made them kings and priests unto God. Then in Revelation 5:10, the elders thank God for making them kings and priests unto God. These twenty-four elders are the representatives of a much larger group, the church that has been saved and raptured into the throne room of God.

Why twenty-four, though?

The Jewish priesthood in the days of David had twenty-four courses that ministered. (Clarke, 6: 989). This is just a carryover from that. The church that left earth after chapter three appears before the throne of God in chapter four. We will say more about that later, but for now, just understand that if you have not been redeemed as these elders, you will not appear before this throne, but before the great white throne, and it could be at any moment.

After telling us of the first part of the throng in the throne room, the text then tells us that there are lightnings, thunderings, and voices coming out of the throne.

Revelation 4:5a *And out of the throne proceeded lightnings and thunderings and voices:*

The God that sent thunder and lightning down on Mount Sinai is the God that John saw seated on the throne. When he saw God on the throne, there was no rain, no clouds, no storms, but there was thunder and lightning coming out of the throne. We are talking about one of nature's most violent and powerful forces, and yet the God on the throne is calmly sitting on top of it. This is an indication that He is in complete control even of things that we seem to think cannot be controlled.

But then, just to show that this thunder and lightning was not a random, weather-driven thing, John also said, "I heard voices coming out of the throne along with that thunder and lightning!" Storms may rumble, but they do not talk. The God on the throne is able to have an actual conversation with thunder and lightning. There is nobody like Him.

All of this, the thunder, lightning, voices, showed John the majesty and power of the One sitting on the throne.

We then see the next group making up the great throng before the throne:

Revelation 4:5b *...and there were seven lamps of fire burning before the throne, which are the seven Spirits of God.*

This is now the third time in the book of The Revelation that we have found reference to the seven Spirits of God. Here, again, were the first two:

Revelation 1:4 *John to the seven churches which are in Asia: Grace be unto you, and peace, from him which is, and which was, and which is to come; and from the seven Spirits which are before his throne;*

Revelation 3:1 *And unto the angel of the church in Sardis write; These things saith he that hath the seven Spirits of God, and the seven stars; I know thy works, that thou hast a name that thou livest, and art dead.*

As I explained when we covered Revelation 3:1, many times, you will hear people teach that this is a reference to the Holy Spirit Himself. This is possible but not provable. Just reading what the text says, I take this as seven literal spirits. Either way, Revelation 5:6 makes it clear that they are His "eyes, sent forth into all the Earth." So whether you regard this as the Holy Spirit or seven individual Spirits, what they say about Christ is clear: He sees everything, He misses nothing!

This throng standing in front of the throne is standing on one of the most remarkable things imaginable, a sea of glass like crystal:

Revelation 4:6a *And before the throne there was a sea of glass like unto crystal:*

Try and let your mind wrap around this. When we think of a throne and a king, the very biggest thing we think of is probably Buckingham palace. But you could run completely around Buckingham palace in two- or three-minutes time!

When we enter the throne room of God, every one of us, even though I am going to describe it right now, will be amazed by what we see.

First of all, it will be huge. This is a *sea* of glass. Not a pool, not a pond, not even a great lake, a sea. We are being told about a throne room that stretches for tens of thousands of square miles.

Secondly, it will be water, but water that is glass. Can I explain this scientifically? No, I can only tell you about it; I cannot even begin to explain it. But just think of how amazing this will be. Have you ever wanted to walk on water? If you are saved, you will, every time you enter the throne room. Have you ever wanted to be able to see everything that is in the ocean without getting wet? If you are saved, you will, every time you enter the throne room.

It will be as clear as crystal. We will be able to look down and see miles and miles into this glassy water and see the color of a fish's eyes swimming along the bottom. There is no place anywhere like the throne room of God.

And that brings us to the third group of beings who make up the great throng around the throne in heaven, four amazingly unique beasts:

Revelation 4:6b *...and in the midst of the throne, and round about the throne, were four beasts full of eyes before and behind.* **7** *And the first beast was like a lion, and the second beast like a calf, and the third beast had a face as a man, and the fourth beast was like a flying eagle.* **8** *And the four beasts had each of them six wings about him; and they were full of eyes within: and they rest not day and night, saying, Holy, holy, holy, Lord God Almighty, which was, and is, and is to come.*

As you let the words of this passage paint a mental picture in your mind, the first thing you see is a group of beasts opening their mouths and praising God. There is nothing in all of nature that could prepare you for a sight like the sight of these beasts! In the middle of the throne room area and around the throne room area itself, John saw four beasts.

But what exactly are they?

They have some similarities to the Seraphim of Isaiah chapter six. For instance, they each have six wings:

Revelation 4:8a *And the four beasts had each of them six wings about him;*

Isaiah 6:2 *Above it stood the seraphims: each one had six wings; with twain he covered his face, and with twain he covered his feet, and with twain he did fly.*

But they also have some similarities to the Cherubim described in Ezekiel 1 and Ezekiel 10. Those creatures only had four wings apiece, but they each, individually, had all of the faces described on the beasts here in Revelation 4, if we can assume that a cherub looked like a calf, which I think is safe:

Revelation 4:7 *And the first beast was like a lion, and the second beast like a calf, and the third beast had a face as a man, and the fourth beast was like a flying eagle.*

Ezekiel 10:14 *And every one had four faces: the first face was the face of a cherub, and the second face was the face of a man, and the third the face of a lion, and the fourth the face of an eagle.* **15** *And the cherubims were lifted up. This is the living creature that I saw by the river of Chebar.*

The cherubim were also described as being full of eyes, like the creatures here in Revelation 4:

Revelation 4:6 *And before the throne there was a sea of glass like unto crystal: and in the midst of the throne, and round about the throne, were four beasts full of eyes before and behind.*

Ezekiel 10:12 *And their whole body, and their backs, and their hands, and their wings, and the wheels, were full of eyes round about, even the wheels that they four had.*

But what these creatures are saying in Revelation 4 is almost identical to what the Seraphim spoke in Isaiah 6:

Revelation 4:8 *And the four beasts had each of them six wings about him; and they were full of eyes within: and they rest not day and night, saying, Holy, holy, holy, Lord God Almighty, which was, and is, and is to come.*

Isaiah 6:3 *And one cried unto another, and said, Holy, holy, holy, is the LORD of hosts: the whole earth is full of his glory.*

But there were four cherubs described in Ezekiel, just like there are four of them described here:

Revelation 4:6 *And before the throne there was a sea of glass like unto crystal: and in the midst of the throne, and round about the throne, were four beasts full of eyes before and behind.*

Ezekiel 10:10 *And as for their appearances, they four had one likeness, as if a wheel had been in the midst of a wheel.*

I think it is safe to say that all of these creatures, in Isaiah 6, Ezekiel 1, and Revelation 4, are angels of God. The creatures in Isaiah 6 are specifically called Seraphim. The creatures in Ezekiel 10 are specifically called Cherubim. But these creatures in Revelation 4 are not specifically called either, and they have an intriguing mixture of the characteristics of both. So, in other words, we do not know exactly what they are, there seems to be nothing else at all in the universe precisely like them, but we do know that they are awesome! Not only have there never been creatures like this in the ranks of nature, it does not seem like there have ever even been creatures exactly like this in the ranks of commonly known angels! When you come across creatures this fantastic, and those creatures start testifying of the greatness of God, it seems that it would be very wise to listen to what they have to say. And what they say, and what the elders say as well, brings us to our next point for examination.

The testimony

As we begin to hear these majestic beasts testify of the greatness of the God on the throne, they begin with a word of testimony about His purity.

Revelation 4:8b *...and they rest not day and night, saying, Holy, holy, holy, Lord God Almighty, which was, and is, and is to come.*

There are very few examples in the Bible of a word being repeated three times in a row in a sentence. The fact that this word "holy" here and in Isaiah 6 is repeated three times lets us know that we better pay attention to it.

God is love, but never is He described in Scripture as "love, love, love."

God is merciful, but never is He described in Scripture as "merciful, merciful, merciful."

This is why we call God the "thrice-holy God." God is holy; He is utterly pure and in open opposition to anything that is impure.

If I look long enough with my two frail human eyes at your life, I will eventually find something wrong somewhere. But these creatures, whose entire bodies are covered with eyes, look at God night and day for all eternity and never find a single flaw. No wonder God has the right to say, "*Be ye holy, for I am holy!*" (1 Peter 1:16)

I hear people say, "God doesn't have a right to tell me not to sin." No, the truth is that because He is holy, we do not have a right to sin!

This holiness of God is not just about His behavior. It is about His essence. In other words, I can behave holy, but I cannot be holy in and of myself. But God behaves in a holy manner because He is holy in His essence! Holiness is not an effort for Him; holiness is who He is.

But not only do they testify of His purity, they also testify of His power. We find them in verse eight calling Him, "Lord God Almighty."

The words chosen here by these beasts are absolutely perfect for the situation at hand. They could have truthfully said, "Lord God Forgiving." They could have truthfully said, "Lord God Everlasting." But this is the book of The Revelation. This is the book that is about to show us the final battle between God and Satan, good and evil. This is the book in which the enemy pulls out all the stops. This is the book in which all the armies of the earth, with all of their weapons and bombs, will join together to fight against God. At such a time, what more appropriate description could these creatures give than Lord God Almighty!

When I think of what is coming, I am glad He is Lord God Almighty. When I think of Antichrist and the mark of the beast, I am glad He is Lord God Almighty. When I think of the Beast and the False Prophet and the spirits of demons working miracles, I am glad He is Lord God Almighty.

But even when I simply think of what we have to go through right now from day to day, I am glad He is Lord God Almighty. It is not that humanity will one day need Him; it is that even now, there is never a day when humanity does not need Him.

Having testified of His purity and His power, these four beasts will now testify of His presence, calling Him the One "Which was, and is, and is to come."

It is often said that the only thing you can count on not changing is the fact that things change. If you do not believe things change, get anyone over forty years of age to show you their high school yearbook pictures. A hundred years ago, we were riding in horse-drawn buggies. Look at what we drive now! Things change quickly and drastically. Human views of morality change. It used to be that a man would never curse in front of a woman. Now women themselves will curse bad enough to make a sailor blush! In such a changing world, especially in a world where views of morality are constantly changing for the worse, it is nice to know that one thing will never change:

Hebrews 13:8 *Jesus Christ the same yesterday, and to day, and for ever.*

That is essentially what these beasts are saying. Jesus was, and is, and is to come. That is why Jesus is able to promise in Hebrews 13:5 that He will never leave you nor forsake you.

These beasts have set the table pretty well! It is hard to imagine a better litany of praise than what they have given. But there are only four of those beasts. Around about them, there are twenty-four elders who have just been listening.

As well as they did in their testimony, these beasts have never been redeemed. These beasts did not have God die for them. These twenty-four elders have experienced more of the goodness of God than these beasts ever will. So after just listening to all of this glorious testimony, these elders have to jump in and add their praise to the mix. The beasts have testified about His purity, His power, and His presence.

The elders then testify of His pleasure:

Revelation 4:9 *And when those beasts give glory and honour and thanks to him that sat on the throne, who liveth for ever and ever,* **10** *The four and twenty elders fall down before him that sat on the throne, and worship him that liveth for ever and ever, and cast their crowns before the throne, saying,* **11** *Thou art worthy, O Lord, to receive glory and honour and power: for thou hast created all things, and for thy pleasure they are and were created.*

What you just saw from the elders would be considered "indecent and out of order" by the modern pharisees. These elders fell down voluntarily (they were not "slain in the Spirit") before the throne. They threw their crowns at the feet of God. Then they said, "Lord, you are worthy of glory and honor and power." Why? "Because you have created all things, and you did so for your pleasure."

In other words, all of the New Agers and secular humanists can quit asking, "Why am I here?" You are here because God felt like making you, and your purpose in life is to please Him.

There is not a human being on earth who deserves to be pleased at all times. But the God who made every human being and gave them an earth to live on deserves to be pleased at all times!

He deserves to be pleased when it comes to being faithful. He deserves to be pleased in any relationship matter. He deserves to be pleased in our entertainment choices. He deserves to be pleased when the plates are passed. He deserves to be pleased in the way we sing as a congregation.

He is God. He made all things, including the air that we are breathing and the blood that is coursing through our veins; He deserves to be pleased in all things.

As glorious as this passage is, there is one thing about it that troubles me a bit. All of it is something that John saw in heaven, after the Rapture. Why shouldn't this be something we see now on earth? Why should we not be just as free in testifying of God's greatness as the beasts and elders were? Why should we not agree that in all things, God deserves to be pleased? And why should beasts, even as glorious as these beasts are, be better at glorifying God than we are? Calvary was not for them; it was for us.

Chapter Thirteen
Tears and Triumph

Revelation 5:1 *And I saw in the right hand of him that sat on the throne a book written within and on the backside, sealed with seven seals.* **2** *And I saw a strong angel proclaiming with a loud voice, Who is worthy to open the book, and to loose the seals thereof?* **3** *And no man in heaven, nor in earth, neither under the earth, was able to open the book, neither to look thereon.* **4** *And I wept much, because no man was found worthy to open and to read the book, neither to look thereon.* **5** *And one of the elders saith unto me, Weep not: behold, the Lion of the tribe of Juda, the Root of David, hath prevailed to open the book, and to loose the seven seals thereof.* **6** *And I beheld, and, lo, in the midst of the throne and of the four beasts, and in the midst of the elders, stood a Lamb as it had been slain, having seven horns and seven eyes, which are the seven Spirits of God sent forth into all the earth.* **7** *And he came and took the book out of the right hand of him that sat upon the throne.* **8** *And when he had taken the book, the four beasts and four and twenty elders fell down before the Lamb, having every one of them harps, and golden vials full of odours, which are the prayers of saints.* **9** *And they sung a new song, saying, Thou art worthy to take the book, and to open the seals thereof: for thou wast slain, and hast redeemed us to God by thy blood out of every kindred, and tongue, and people, and nation;* **10** *And hast made us unto our God kings and priests: and we shall reign on the earth.* **11** *And I beheld, and I heard the voice of many angels round about the throne and the beasts and the elders: and the number of them was ten thousand times ten thousand, and thousands of thousands;* **12** *Saying with a loud voice, Worthy is the Lamb that was slain to receive power, and riches, and wisdom, and strength, and honour, and glory, and blessing.* **13** *And every creature which is in heaven, and on the earth, and under the earth, and such as are in the sea, and all that are in them, heard I saying, Blessing, and honour, and glory, and power, be unto him that sitteth upon the throne, and unto the Lamb for ever and ever.* **14** *And the four beasts said, Amen. And the four and twenty elders fell down and worshipped him that liveth for ever and ever.*

Let me briefly remind you of where we have been and where we are now in our study of the book of The Revelation. In chapter one, we observed an old man named John, on the Isle of Patmos, coming face to face once more with Jesus. John saw Jesus as the one walking in the midst of the churches. He was then given the outline for the book of The

Revelation that he was to write; he would write about the things of the past, the present, and then the future.

Chapter one covered the past. In chapters two and three, John covered the present age, that which we call the church age. He did so by writing letters to seven literal churches that convey spiritual truths to the church in every age.

Between the end of chapter three and the beginning of chapter four, we covered what Paul spoke of over and over again, the Rapture of the church. When John arrived in the throne room of heaven in chapter four, verse one, the church was already there, praising God for how He had redeemed them out of every single nation and ethnic group on earth. We looked at the throne itself and the throng of elders and creatures around it.

We are still viewing the throne and throne room of God as we begin to examine chapter five.

Tears in the throne room

Revelation 5:1 *And I saw in the right hand of him that sat on the throne a book written within and on the backside, sealed with seven seals.* **2** *And I saw a strong angel proclaiming with a loud voice, Who is worthy to open the book, and to loose the seals thereof?* **3** *And no man in heaven, nor in earth, neither under the earth, was able to open the book, neither to look thereon.* **4** *And I wept much, because no man was found worthy to open and to read the book, neither to look thereon.*

As we look at the scene in heaven presented to us throughout the book of The Revelation, we will sometimes see Jesus sitting on the throne. In chapter five, though, our eyes, along with John's, settle on God the Father sitting on the throne. Verse one tells us that He is holding in His omnipotent right hand a book, or what we would today call a scroll, a long piece of parchment written on both sides and rolled up into a roll. It is such a small, simple thing. It just does not seem like something so small could cause any tears of sorrow to flow in heaven.

But as our eyes look on God the Father, and the book in His right hand, a second sense kicks in. Our eyes have seen, and now our ears will hear. In verse two, we are told that a strong angel steps forward. This is the only place in the Bible that descriptive phrase is used. Every angel is a strong, powerful, being, so for this one to be the only one actually called a strong angel, you know that he was and is something amazingly impressive, not a being to be tangled with.

That strong angel steps forward, and we, along with John, hear him utter a challenge: *Who is worthy to open the book?* Just a moment earlier, beasts were glorifying God, elders were shouting and praising, but now, all of heaven falls deathly silent. Verse three tells us that "... *no man in heaven, nor in earth, neither under the earth, was able to open the book, neither to look thereon.*"

And then, a moment later, in verse four, we hear it: a wail, a loud sobbing from the person that is recording all of this for us. John is bawling like a baby, and you just cannot help crying along with him. It has taken no time at all for John to realize that no one in all of glorious heaven is able to open the book. And so John weeps.

And he weeps, first of all, because of <u>*the description of the book*</u>.

John had been brought into heaven to write about the future. He was supposed to be recording the things that would happen to mankind in the last days. He was supposed to be putting on paper things that will most likely begin happening in our days! That book that God the Father was holding in his hand contained the details about man's final destiny. That book contained Revelation 6-16. There were seven seals on the book, and those seals were to be opened, revealing seven judgments of God on man. The seventh seal opened and contained seven trumpets, revealing seven more judgments of God on man. The seven trumpets were part of the seventh seal. The seventh trumpet sounded and revealed seven vial judgments of God on man. The seven vials were part of the seventh trumpet, and the seven trumpets were part of the seventh seal. All twenty-one of those judgments are recorded for us in Revelation 6-16.

Those eleven chapters of the most awesome judgment that will ever hit this world were already written in that book that God the Father held in His hand. That book showed God finally cleaning house. That is what every real child of God desires as we look at the wickedness and filth of this world! We hate it when people mock God and practically spit in His face from day to day. How often have we wished for God to rain fire from heaven on those who wreck and ruin everything that is good and beautiful in this world? How often have we wished that God was not so nice and was not so patient with those who hate Him?

The book that God the Father held in His hand shows God finally doing what we, and John, have wished that He would do all along! God had been promising to judge this wicked world for thousands of years. John knew that it would happen in the last days. He knew that he was being asked to record those last days.

But when it finally came time for John to see how God was going to clean house, everything ground to a halt because no one was worthy to open the book. John knew the wickedness that was going on on earth in his own day. He knew from the writings of Peter and Paul that it was going to get even worse still in our day. He knew this world desperately needed to have God show up in awesome judgment and power to clean up the entire mess. He knew that book contained the judgment that he sought; he knew that the judgment could not fall until the book was open. And so John wept because of the description of the book.

He also wept because of *the deficiency in heaven and earth.*

When we read that no one was worthy, that is a general statement. But it is when we begin to apply it in specific ways that the general statement begins to take our breath away, as it did for John. Do you understand who is included in that "no one" that John writes of?

None of the Old Testament heroes of the faith were worthy to open the book.

Think of who was already there! Abraham... Enoch... Moses... Noah... Job... Daniel... David... Elijah... Isaiah... Jeremiah... Yet all of heaven was silent, and none of those great men were worthy to step forward and open the book.

The twenty-four elders were not worthy to open the book.

These are men, representatives of the blood-bought church, who have been hand-picked by God to sit with Him in the throne room. But twenty-four heads hung in shame, and they represent all of our heads that must likewise hang in shame, for none of them were worthy to open the book.

None of the apostles, all of whom had been in heaven for years now, were worthy to open the book.

Peter was there, the great preacher of Pentecost, unworthy to open the book. Stephen was there. He was the first Christian martyr. Jesus even stood up off of His throne for him to receive him home. But he was unworthy to open the book. Matthew was there. And James, and even John the Baptist, who personally baptized Jesus. And they were one and all unworthy to open the book. Paul the apostle was there. Just think of that great man, that greatest among all the servants of God! He could say he had finished his course. He could say that he had kept the faith. He could say that there was a crown of righteousness laid up for Him. But he could not say that he was worthy to open the book because even he was not worthy.

None of the great saints of the young church, right then walking the earth, were worthy to open the book. God did not just look throughout heaven and find all unworthy; verse three says that no man in heaven, or earth, or even <u>under</u> the earth, even those who were right then buried, none were worthy. But I do not think that even scratches the surface of what made John weep and wail and moan. Consider this:

John himself, who loved Jesus and whom Jesus loved, was not worthy to open the book. John who leaned on Jesus' breast, John who stayed with Jesus all the way to Calvary, John who took care of Mary for the rest of her life, John who wrote one gospel, three epistles, and was now writing the last book of God ever to be given to man, John himself was not worthy. John, in anguish, considered himself a failure when he faced this question in the throne room of who was worthy to open the book.

Triumph in the throne room

Revelation 5:5 *And one of the elders saith unto me, Weep not: behold, the Lion of the tribe of Juda, the Root of David, hath prevailed to open the book, and to loose the seven seals thereof.* **6** *And I beheld, and, lo, in the midst of the throne and of the four beasts, and in the midst of the elders, stood a Lamb as it had been slain, having seven horns and seven eyes, which are the seven Spirits of God sent forth into all the earth.* **7** *And he came and took the book out of the right hand of him that sat upon the throne.* **8** *And when he had taken the book, the four beasts and four and twenty elders fell down before the Lamb, having every one of them harps, and golden vials full of odours, which are the prayers of saints.* **9** *And they sung a new song, saying, Thou art worthy to take the book, and to open the seals thereof: for thou wast slain, and hast redeemed us to God by thy blood out of every kindred, and tongue, and people, and nation;* **10** *And hast made us unto our God kings and priests: and we shall reign on the earth.* **11** *And I beheld, and I heard the voice of many angels round about the throne and the beasts and the elders: and the number of them was ten thousand times ten thousand, and thousands of thousands;* **12** *Saying with a loud voice, Worthy is the Lamb that was slain to receive power, and riches, and wisdom, and strength, and honour, and glory, and blessing.* **13** *And every creature which is in heaven, and on the earth, and under the earth, and such as are in the sea, and all that are in them, heard I saying, Blessing, and honour, and glory, and power, be unto him that sitteth upon the throne, and unto the Lamb for ever and ever.* **14** *And the four beasts said, Amen. And the four and twenty elders fell down and worshipped him that liveth for ever and ever.*

Oh, pay attention to this! When verse four ended, John was weeping and crying because no one, including himself, could open that book. He was crying so hard that he did not notice what had happened, and somebody had to tell him! John was still crying like a baby, but while he was wailing, Christ was winning, and the elders were watching. While John cried, Jesus stepped up to the throne, took the book, and loosed the seals, getting ready to fully open it. While John was in anguish over how unworthy he was, the only really worthy person in heaven or earth had stepped onto the scene, and one of those twenty-four elders had to tell John, "John, stop crying, the book is being opened right now! The Lion of the tribe of Judah has prevailed to loose the seals."

John, all teary-eyed, and snotty-nosed, and gasping for air because he had been crying so hard, looked up to see that great lion... and instead, he saw the Lion who is also the Lamb. He saw the one that John the Baptist called the Lamb of God who taketh away the sins of the world. He saw the Lamb who had been slain, right before his very eyes, some sixty years earlier, on a hill called Calvary. But oh, what an unusual Lamb he saw! Verse six says, *"And I beheld, and, lo, in the midst of the throne and of the four beasts, and in the midst of the elders, stood a Lamb as it had been slain, having seven horns and seven eyes, which are the seven Spirits of God sent forth into all the earth."*

He had, past tense, been slain; but as John looked, He was standing right there, very much alive.

Horns in the Bible generally symbolize power. And most creatures who have horns have two of them. But this lamb had seven horns. There is no lamb in nature like that. But this is not a lamb that was created by nature; this is the Lamb who created nature. And this Lamb does not have some power, He has all power, and therefore He has seven horns since seven is normally used to symbolize perfection or completion. And, as we have seen previously in the book of the Revelation, He also has seven eyes, meaning that He never misses anything; nothing ever escapes His notice.

In verse four, that Lamb had loosed the seals of the book that the Father still held in His hands. But now, in verse seven, the Father opened His omnipotent hand and let Jesus take the book fully into His own hands. That was the Father's way of saying, "All of this depends on my Son. It is His right to do as He will." Everybody in heaven knew what a moment that was:

Revelation 5:8 *And when he had taken the book, the four beasts and four and twenty elders fell down before the Lamb, having every one of them harps, and golden vials full of odours, which are the prayers of saints.* **9** *And they sung a new song, saying, Thou art worthy to take the book, and to open the seals thereof: for thou wast slain, and hast redeemed us to God by thy blood out of every kindred, and tongue, and people, and nation;* **10** *And hast made us unto our God kings and priests: and we shall reign on the earth.*

In response to the Lamb prevailing to open and to receive the book, the elders, the representatives of the church, fell down to worship with music and with prayer, which John saw as golden vials full of odors, sweet-smelling scents to God.

They prayed, and they sang. And the song they sang in verse nine was a new song that was their way of saying, "God, are you ready to judge the world? You are worthy to do so, Lord, because you died to save them, and if they have chosen to reject you, you have every right to condemn and judge them. We accepted you out of every people group on earth. You made us kings and priests, and we will literally get to reign on this earth. You would have done the same for them if they had let you. Do you want to judge the world, Lord? Go ahead, for you are worthy."

John's weeping had stopped and been replaced by the sound of twenty-four elders and four beasts praising God. But then the choir grew. Oh my, did it grow. Suddenly, John realized that every creature in all of heaven had crowded into the throne room. No wonder it had to be the size of a sea! There were so many that John could not even put an exact number on it:

Revelation 5:11 *And I beheld, and I heard the voice of many angels round about the throne and the beasts and the elders: and the number of them was ten thousand times ten thousand, and thousands of thousands;*

All of those innumerable voices, in unison, were shouting the exact same thing as loud as they possibly could:

Revelation 5:12 *Saying with a loud voice, Worthy is the Lamb that was slain to receive power, and riches, and wisdom, and strength, and honour, and glory, and blessing.*

All of this scene in the throne room has centered around the word "worthy." In verse two, there was a challenge shouted throughout heaven and earth as to whether anyone was worthy to open the book. In verse four, John wept because no one was found worthy. In verse nine, the Lamb was declared to be worthy to take and open the book. And now in verse twelve, He is proclaimed worthy not just of that, but also of receiving power and riches and wisdom and strength and honor and glory. That is a huge list! Could something like that ever even remotely be a unanimous choice, or would it, like all of our human "elections," be no more than a split decision with one side gaining a small majority?

We do not have to wonder because the next two verses tell us:

Revelation 5:13 *And every creature which is in heaven, and on the earth, and under the earth, and such as are in the sea, and all that are in them, heard I saying, Blessing, and honour, and glory, and power, be unto him that sitteth upon the throne, and unto the Lamb for ever and ever.* **14** *And the four beasts said, Amen. And the four and twenty elders fell down and worshipped him that liveth for ever and ever.*

Dear reader, try and wrap your mind around something that most commentators dodge, ignore, or make out to be only symbolic. John said that he heard, with his own two ears, every creature in the entire universe, animal, man, bug, bird, praise God, with their mouths, saying the exact same words, "Blessing, and honour, and glory, and power, be unto him that sitteth upon the throne, and unto the Lamb for ever and ever." I cannot decide which is more amazing; the fact that every kind of creature in the universe suddenly speaks at the same time in the same language, or that a world filled to the brim with wicked, evil men, a world that the church has already been pulled out of, suddenly stops and praises God! Again, most commentators say that we should not take this literally, but look again at verse fourteen:

Revelation 5:14 *And the four beasts said, Amen...*

They said amen to what? Something that did not really happen? Words that were not said? What kind of ridiculous nonsense is that? No, they said amen to the same thing that John heard; they said amen to all of creation verbally praising the Creator. I cannot even begin to explain it, but somehow, after the Rapture, God is going to arrest the entire focus of the universe for just a moment, and every voice will praise Him at once! It obviously does not change them much because God still has to judge them. They may not even remember it a moment later. It may be completely wiped from their memory by a sovereign God who has determined that they have already rejected Him for the last time, and the day of judgment has finally arrived. But all creation will, at that very moment, have one verdict resounding from their lips:

Blessing... and honour... and glory... and power... be unto him that sitteth upon the throne, and unto the Lamb for ever and ever, amen!

If you could be watching heaven at that moment, let me tell you what you would see. You would see an old man, stooped and bent, with tears running down his wrinkled old cheeks. Not tears of sorrow anymore, though. That was for a moment ago when he realized how unworthy he was. Now he is crying tears of joy because something has dawned on him that he seemed to have forgotten for a moment: his *lack* of worthiness gave way to Jesus' *limitless* worthiness! It was not until John realized how unworthy he was that he truly realized how much he needed Jesus.

And that reminds us of exactly why people do not get saved. They still somehow think they are worthy! But if Moses was not worthy, if David was not worthy, if Abraham was not worthy, if Enoch was not worthy, if Elijah was not worthy, if John the Baptist was not worthy, if Paul the apostle was not worthy, then neither are we. We need Jesus! If John the apostle had to weep over his own deficiency, then how foolish is any man, woman, boy, or girl that thinks they can get to heaven without falling on their face as an unworthy sinner and begging God for the mercy that can only be found in Jesus? He alone is worthy!

Chapter Fourteen
The Four Horsemen of the Apocalypse

Revelation 6:1 *And I saw when the Lamb opened one of the seals, and I heard, as it were the noise of thunder, one of the four beasts saying, Come and see.* **2** *And I saw, and behold a white horse: and he that sat on him had a bow; and a crown was given unto him: and he went forth conquering, and to conquer.* **3** *And when he had opened the second seal, I heard the second beast say, Come and see.* **4** *And there went out another horse that was red: and power was given to him that sat thereon to take peace from the earth, and that they should kill one another: and there was given unto him a great sword.* **5** *And when he had opened the third seal, I heard the third beast say, Come and see. And I beheld, and lo a black horse; and he that sat on him had a pair of balances in his hand.* **6** *And I heard a voice in the midst of the four beasts say, A measure of wheat for a penny, and three measures of barley for a penny; and see thou hurt not the oil and the wine.* **7** *And when he had opened the fourth seal, I heard the voice of the fourth beast say, Come and see.* **8** *And I looked, and behold a pale horse: and his name that sat on him was Death, and Hell followed with him. And power was given unto them over the fourth part of the earth, to kill with sword, and with hunger, and with death, and with the beasts of the earth.*

In chapter one of the book of The Revelation, we observed an old man named John, on the Isle of Patmos, coming face to face once more with Jesus. John saw Jesus as the One walking in the midst of the churches. He was then given the outline for the book of The Revelation that he was to write; he would write about the things of the past, the present, and then the future. Chapter one covered the past. In chapters two and three, John covered the present age, that which we call the church age. He did so by writing letters to seven literal churches that convey spiritual truths to the church in every age.

Between the end of chapter three and the beginning of chapter four, we covered what Paul spoke of over and over again, the Rapture of the church. When John arrived in the throne room of heaven in chapter four, verse one, the church was already there, praising God for how He had redeemed them out of every single nation and ethnic group on earth. We looked at the throne itself and the throng of elders around it, and we saw the mighty God in His glory being praised as He deserves. We heard the testimony in the throne room, the things that the beasts and elders had to say about Jesus. And then, in chapter five, we saw a challenge issued in heaven. A powerful angel stood forth and shouted out *who is worthy to take the book and open it up?* That book contained all of Revelation 6-16, the unleashing of God's judgment on earth. John the old man, John the faithful and loving apostle, wept bitter tears as he realized that neither he nor anyone else was worthy to open that book. But then Jesus Christ, the darling Lamb of God, stepped up to the throne, took the book, loosed the seals, and all of the universe shouted in adoration. But throughout all of the shouting, John was still watching the Lamb and the book very carefully:

Revelation 6:1 *And I saw when the Lamb opened one of the seals, and I heard, as it were the noise of thunder, one of the four beasts saying, Come and see.*

John, while crying, had missed Jesus loosing the seals of the book. He was not about to miss anything else. He watched intently, from a distance, as Jesus opened the first seal, and when that seal was cracked open, there was a noise like thunder. What an ominous sound to open an ominous book to! It was then that one of the four beasts before the throne spoke and specifically called John in for a closer look. And when he came closer, he did not just see words written on a page; he actually saw a vision, a mental movie of those words. He could see it, smell it, feel it, and hear it as the sound of galloping hooves raced out of the book and into the halls of human future to come. John saw a rider on a white horse, a rider on a red horse, a rider on a black horse, and a rider on a pale (the word means greenish yellow) horse. We are going to use this chapter to look at these four horsemen.

The duration of the four riders

When you study the book of The Revelation, it is necessary to remember that there are often a great deal of things going on at the exact same time. During this seven-year time period called the Tribulation, it is not normally true that one judgment falls and then stops, and then another falls and then stops, and then another falls and then stops. Quite the contrary. Normally, a judgment will fall and just keep on having effects while other judgments pile up on top of it.

As we begin to consider these riders, let me teach you something: we see their ride having a definite beginning point in Revelation 6. But there is no specified ending point to their ride! The four horsemen of the apocalypse will begin their ride on day one of the Tribulation Period, and they will continue to ride for all seven years. The world will not see them as riders on horses, but that is how God sees them, and their seven-year ride will devastate the world.

The destruction of the three riders

I am going to start in an unusual place. It may seem normal to start at the first seal, then go to the second, and so on. But I am going to start by covering riders two, three, and four at the very outset, and then we will come back to verse two and examine rider number one, the most significant of these four horsemen for the rest of this chapter.

The red rider

Revelation 6:3 *And when he had opened the second seal, I heard the second beast say, Come and see.* **4** *And there went out another horse that was red: and power was given to him that sat thereon to take peace from the earth, and that they should kill one another: and there was given unto him a great sword.*

In verse three, the second seal of the book, the second judgment of the Tribulation Period, is opened and unleashed on the world.

As John looked at the second rider, he observed that he was riding a horse that was red. This was symbolic of great bloodshed. And this rider will fulfill that symbolism. Verse four says that he will be given power to take peace from the earth and to make people kill each other. He will do his job abundantly well because verse four says that he is given not a knife, not a dagger, but a great sword.

Consider this carefully, and you will see an amazing irony. For years and years, religious "fundamentalists," especially Christians, have been blamed for all of the hate on the planet earth. If we would just go away, the world is convinced that everyone could all get along. But here in Revelation 6:3, we find that in a world with no preacher preaching against sodomy, no preacher preaching against drunkenness, no preacher preaching against drugs, no preacher preaching against laziness, no preacher preaching against pornography, no preacher preaching against liberalism, no preacher preaching against fornication, peace is absolutely removed from peoples' individual lives.

The red rider is often referred to as war, but that is not fully correct. The red rider is the one who gets individuals living down to their lowest potential, gets every individual to hate other individuals, and then delights in a world filled with murder. The Tribulation Period will see the murder rate skyrocket beyond any police officer's wildest dream. Yes, he will also cause wars, especially during the last half of the Tribulation, but the red rider, the second seal judgment, will wreak a havoc in murder like this world has never seen.

The black rider

In verse five, the third seal of the book, the third judgment of the Tribulation Period, is opened and unleashed on the world.

Revelation 6:5 *And when he had opened the third seal, I heard the third beast say, Come and see. And I beheld, and lo a black horse; and he that sat on him had a pair of balances in his hand.* **6** *And I heard a voice in the midst of the four beasts say, A measure of wheat for a penny, and three measures of barley for a penny; and see thou hurt not the oil and the wine.*

As John looked at the third rider, he observed that he was riding a horse that was black. This was symbolic of great disaster and mourning, specifically caused by famine.

God does all things well, including leveling judgments. While the red rider is causing murders to be on every hand, those who somehow are not victimized may tend to think everything is fine. But then, when God allows this third rider to come galloping across this world, everyone, young and old, will be affected. How greatly this world will be affected by the famine during the Tribulation Period is seen by what this rider has in his hands. He is holding a pair of balances with which to weigh out food. The famine during the Tribulation Period will be so great, every person on earth will be under food rationing. They will not be able to simply go out and buy what they want and what they can afford; they will have a worldwide governing body telling them how much they are allowed to eat each day. This famine will be bad. As John was considering it, he heard a voice from the midst of the four beasts, and from the location, we know that it is the voice of God speaking, and the voice says:

Revelation 6:6b *...A measure of wheat for a penny, and three measures of barley for a penny; and see thou hurt not the oil and the wine.*

A "measure" of wheat was enough dry bread for a man to eat in a day if he did not overdo it. A penny was a day's full wage for a laborer. In other words, during the Tribulation Period, not only will food be rationed, but it will cost a man everything he can make at work in a day just to feed himself. Or if he wants to try and feed his family, he can buy enough barley bread, which is of far lower quality, to feed himself, his wife, and a child for his day's wages.

Someone may reason, "Well, that doesn't sound so bad; people will be able to survive." But anyone who thinks that is not even beginning to grasp the severity of the situation. Everything a man makes at work will go for food. But people will still have house payments to make. People will still have car payments to make. People will still have insurance payments to make. People will still have medical payments to make. People will still have power bills to pay. People will still have water bills to pay. People will still have credit card payments to make.

How is any family going to stay afloat, even a two-income family, when the husband's entire paycheck has to be used just to feed to the family, and there is not a single dime left over?

As John considered this awful famine, a giant irony was thrown into the mix. Look at the last instruction that God gave this black rider:

...and see thou hurt not the oil and the wine.

Food will be almost impossible to come by, but if you would like some oil to cook with, you will be able to get that. Food will be almost impossible to come by, but if you want to give up and waste the family food money on booze, you will be able to do that. And you will not have to worry about any annoying preachers telling you that it is wrong because preachers like that will all be gone.

<u>The pale rider</u>

In verse seven, the fourth seal of the book, the fourth judgment of the Tribulation Period, is opened and unleashed on the world.

Revelation 6:7 *And when he had opened the fourth seal, I heard the voice of the fourth beast say, Come and see.* **8** *And I looked, and behold a pale horse: and his name that sat on him was Death, and Hell followed with him. And power was given unto them over the fourth part of the earth, to kill with sword, and with hunger, and with death, and with the beasts of the earth.*

As John looked at the fourth rider, he observed that he was riding a horse that was pale, meaning yellowish green. This was symbolic of death. The horse was the color that a person turns as they are dying after having been consumed by a long illness.

This horseman, unlike the others, is riding with a henchman. Hell is following him like a vulture follows a lion to the kill. After all of these years, after all the billions who have died from Adam until the trumpet sounded, why is hell, personified as if he is a living, breathing being, now following death instead of simply waiting for his prey to be handed to him? Very simply because the Christians have been removed at the Rapture. Many people will get saved during the Tribulation Period, but most will not. During those seven years, just about everybody who dies will be headed for hell, not heaven.

This pale rider, death, and hell with him, are given power to kill people by weapons, by starvation, by any kind of death in general, and even by attacks from wild animals. This rider will be so very devastating that he personally will destroy a quarter of the world's population during the Tribulation Period. Assuming that even after the Rapture, there will probably be at least six billion people on earth, that means that one and a half billion people will fall by the hand of the pale rider. That does not even include all of the specific judgments that also take billions of lives during this time period. These three riders are amazingly destructive.

But now, we need to go back to verse two and examine, in-depth, the most significant of these horsemen.

The deception of the one rider

As the book of The Revelation progresses, the three horsemen that we have already looked at will be riding in the background. But the first rider, the first seal judgment, will be front and center the entire way, and he will be in human form. He is not merely personified; he is a person.

Revelation 6:2 *And I saw, and behold a white horse: and he that sat on him had a bow; and a crown was given unto him: and he went forth conquering, and to conquer.*

When we think of the book of The Revelation, we usually think of Jesus coming back riding on a white horse, and that is exactly what He does in Revelation 19:

Revelation 19:11 *And I saw heaven opened, and behold a white horse; and he that sat upon him was called Faithful and True, and in righteousness he doth judge and make war.* **12** *His eyes were as a flame of fire, and on his head were many crowns; and he had a name written, that no man knew, but he himself.* **13** *And he was clothed with a vesture dipped in blood: and his name is called The Word of God.* **14** *And the armies which were in heaven followed him upon white horses, clothed in fine linen, white and clean.* **15** *And out of his mouth goeth a sharp sword, that with it he should smite the nations: and he shall rule them with a rod of iron: and he treadeth the winepress of the fierceness and wrath of Almighty God.* **16** *And he hath on his vesture and on his thigh a name written, KING OF KINGS, AND LORD OF LORDS.*

That rider on the white horse is the King. That rider on the white horse is Jesus. That rider on the white horse is coming in openness and honesty and cleaning house. That rider on the white horse is <u>not</u> the same as the rider on the white horse in Revelation 6.

The rider in white of Revelation 6 is the man we know as Antichrist. He is the first part of the judgment that will fall on earth during the Tribulation Period. We will see him and deal with him over and over in detail throughout the rest of the book of The Revelation. But for now, I want to show you his deception and then show you what he really is and really will be.

Notice with me that this deceiver is riding the same color horse as Jesus, he is wearing a crown like Jesus, and he has a weapon, as does Jesus. The Antichrist will convince the world that he is the Messiah, the savior that they have needed for so long. Earth will fall under his spell and worship at his feet. But everything he does is deception, he cannot be trusted, and he will destroy everything he touches. He wants the world to think he is the savior, but he is a snake. Let me tell you what the Bible says about this man, who is probably alive and on earth right now in our day.

He is a diplomat

Nothing in Scripture is accidental. This rider is described as having a bow, but nothing is said about arrows. That fits perfectly with something Daniel said about Antichrist many years before John was even born:

Daniel 8:25a *And through his **policy** also he shall cause craft to prosper in his hand; and he shall magnify himself in his heart, and by **peace** shall destroy many...*

This man is going to be, quite simply, the greatest politician that ever lives. He is intent on taking over the world, and he will do so simply by making speeches and negotiating treaties. Take Colin Powell, Condoleezza Rice, Henry Kissinger, and every other great diplomat of history, roll them into one, and they will not begin to scratch the surface of how skilled a diplomat this man will be. He will be more charismatic than Hitler, more charming than JFK; he will be a bigger superstar than Elvis ever thought of being. This man will do the impossible:

Daniel 9:27a *And he shall confirm the covenant with many for one week...*

When Daniel spoke of Antichrist, the "prince that is to come," he mentioned that this man would confirm THE covenant for one week. When Daniel referred in his prophecies to a week, that week represented not seven days but seven years. That one week, seven years spoken of here, is the seven years of Daniel's seventieth prophetic week, otherwise known as the Tribulation Period. At the very beginning of the Tribulation Period, the Antichrist will get the world to sign onto the greatest peace treaty of all time. It is so great that it is called THE covenant. If you go on into the next verse, you find that Antichrist makes a covenant that even includes the Jewish people. It allows their temple to be restored, it allows the Old Testament form of worship to be re-instated, it promises them safety from their enemies, and somehow, amazingly, in the heart of the Arab-run Middle East, he gets everybody to go along with it. No American president, no British Prime Minister, no secretary of state has ever come close to this, even though every single one of them has tried! Every world leader of a free country wants to be remembered as the man who brought complete peace to the Middle East. But it has never happened, and never will happen, until the greatest diplomat this world has ever known, Antichrist, comes on the scene. But not only is he a diplomat, we also find that:

He is disgusting

Antichrist has some very big personal issues to deal with. And when you see what they are, you will see why it will be so easy for him to come to power in our day as opposed to earlier, more godly times:

Daniel 11:37a *Neither shall he regard the God of his fathers, nor the desire of women...*

The word *regard* in this verse means to understand. Simply put, the Antichrist will not understand what is so desirable about women and why other men like them.

So many politicians are tripped up by an affair with a woman; perhaps a secretary or an intern. That will not be a problem for Antichrist, at all.

Antichrist is a diplomat, and he is disgusting. But we also see that:

He is defiling

This man, Antichrist, will be spiritually defiling. Let me show you from another passage of Scripture what I mean when I say that:

2 Thessalonians 2:3 *Let no man deceive you by any means: for that day shall not come, except there come a falling away first, and that man of sin be revealed, the son of perdition;* **4** *Who opposeth and exalteth himself above all that is called God, or that is worshipped;* **so that he as God sitteth in the temple of God, shewing himself that he is God**.

In Jerusalem today, there is no temple. The last time they had a temple was in A.D. 70. That temple was destroyed by Rome and has never been rebuilt. But it will be rebuilt. And for the first half of the Tribulation Period, the Jews will be able to worship in it peacefully, even though their sacrifices will mean nothing since their Messiah has already come and gone, and the last sacrifice ever needed was made on Calvary. But at the mid-way point of the Tribulation, Antichrist will walk into the temple, stop Judaistic worship, proclaim himself as God, and demand to be worshipped.

Antichrist is a diplomat, he is disgusting, and he is defiling. We see lastly that:

He is dangerous

We have already observed how this man will break the covenant with Israel. He will hate and persecute them. But he will not just be dangerous to the Jews. He will also be dangerous to his own political allies:

Daniel 7:7 *After this I saw in the night visions, and behold a fourth beast, dreadful and terrible, and strong exceedingly; and it had great iron teeth: it devoured and brake in pieces, and stamped the residue with the feet of it: and it was diverse from all the beasts that were before it; and it had ten horns.* **8** *I considered the horns, and, behold, there came up among them another little horn, before whom there were three of the first horns plucked up by the roots: and, behold, in this horn were eyes like the eyes of man, and a mouth speaking great things.*

This fourth beast spoken of by Daniel is the revived Roman empire that the Antichrist will arise from. The Bible is so very specific; there is no other book on earth like it. Look at this quickly:

Daniel 9:25 *Know therefore and understand, that from the going forth of the commandment to restore and to build Jerusalem unto the Messiah the Prince shall be seven weeks, and threescore and two weeks: the street shall be built again, and the wall, even in troublous times.* **26** *And after threescore and two weeks shall Messiah be cut off* [calvary], *but not for himself: and the people of the prince that shall come shall destroy the city and the sanctuary;* [that happened in A.D. 70] *and the end thereof shall be with a flood, and unto the end of the war desolations are determined.*

Notice this: Jesus the Prince with a capital P in verse twenty-five was cut off at Calvary. Then the people of the prince, little p, the Antichrist that shall come, destroyed the sanctuary in A.D. 70. Antichrist is going to arise from one of the ten nations that will make up the revived Roman Empire. He may not be of fully Roman blood; in fact, I suspect he will at least partially be of Jewish descent, but he will definitely arise from the area of the revived Roman Empire. And when he does, Daniel 7:8 tells us that he will destroy three of the leaders of the nations that were allied with him and helped bring him to power in the first place. We do not know who the ten nations of the new Roman Empire will be, we do not know which one he will come from, we do not know which three leaders he will destroy, but we do know that this man is dangerous, even to his political allies.

He will also be dangerous to Christians.

It must be awful to be the leader of the world and still find yourself getting irritated by things you did not expect. You would think that when you are in charge of everything, nothing would ever be allowed to get under your skin. But alas, shed a sympathetic tear for the Antichrist, for the poor dear ends up with a problem.

When he starts his reign, every Christian on earth is gone, and he likes it that way. But in just a short period of time, people from all over the globe who had not been convicted of their lost estate before the Rapture, are getting saved by the tens of thousands. Antichrist's nice, evil, self-glorifying world is being re-filled with Bible-believing Christians. They are handing out tracts, and holding revivals, and going on visitation, and preaching on the streets, and sending out missionaries. And Antichrist, the white rider, this most dangerous of men, determines to put a stop to it once and for all:

Daniel 7:25 *And he shall speak great words against the most High, and **shall wear out the saints of the most High**, and think to change times and laws: and they shall be given into his hand until a time and times and the dividing of time.*

A "time" in Daniel's prophecy is a year. So for three and a half years, the last half of the Tribulation, Christians will not only be suffering the calamities falling on earth through God's judgment like everybody else, they will also have Antichrist chasing them to the ends of the earth to torture and kill them, and we will see some specific details of that as we go further in the book of The Revelation. Just know for now that Antichrist is a diplomat, he is disgusting, he is defiling, and he is dangerous.

He is the rider on the white horse of Revelation 6. But his ride will only last for seven years. The rider on the white horse of Revelation 19 will ride forever, and you can ride with Him if you receive Him.

Chapter Fifteen
The Fifth and Sixth Seal

Revelation 6:9 *And when he had opened the fifth seal, I saw under the altar the souls of them that were slain for the word of God, and for the testimony which they held:* **10** *And they cried with a loud voice, saying, How long, O Lord, holy and true, dost thou not judge and avenge our blood on them that dwell on the earth?* **11** *And white robes were given unto every one of them; and it was said unto them, that they should rest yet for a little season, until their fellowservants also and their brethren, that should be killed as they were, should be fulfilled.* **12** *And I beheld when he had opened the sixth seal, and, lo, there was a great earthquake; and the sun became black as sackcloth of hair, and the moon became as blood;* **13** *And the stars of heaven fell unto the earth, even as a fig tree casteth her untimely figs, when she is shaken of a mighty wind.* **14** *And the heaven departed as a scroll when it is rolled together; and every mountain and island were moved out of their places.* **15** *And the kings of the earth, and the great men, and the rich men, and the chief captains, and the mighty men, and every bondman, and every free man, hid themselves in the dens and in the rocks of the mountains;* **16** *And said to the mountains and rocks, Fall on us, and hide us from the face of him that sitteth on the throne, and from the wrath of the Lamb:* **17** *For the great day of his wrath is come; and who shall be able to stand?*

In chapter six of the book of The Revelation, the judgment of God on earth begins to unfold. In verses one through eight, we looked at the opening of the first four of the seven seals, which will unleash the four horsemen of the apocalypse on the world. The red rider represented great bloodshed, the black rider represented famine, and the pale rider represented death. Between them, more than twenty-five percent of the world's population will die at their hand.

But we also looked at the white rider, the son of perdition, the Antichrist. During the Tribulation Period, he will dominate the earth, taking over by peace and diplomacy but resorting to unheard of violence. We will see much more of him as we continue our study of this book. In this chapter, though, we are going to observe the opening of the next two seals, the fifth and sixth out of seven. It is unique in that it initially does not seem like much of a judgment. But trust me on this one, it is.

The altar

Revelation 6:9 *And when he had opened the fifth seal, I saw under the altar the souls of them that were slain for the word of God, and for the testimony which they held:*

Do you think of heaven from time to time? Those of us who are saved are going to spend all eternity there, so it is normal to think about it. But is not the picture in your mind when you do a little fuzzy? We are given so very few details about heaven; it is no wonder we seem to have a hard time getting a grip on it. In fact, if we were able to take ten Christians and have them all draw a picture of what shows up in their minds when they think of heaven, we would end up looking at some very different pictures! Some of the *major* details would be the same, the street of gold, the emerald-colored rainbow, notable things like that. But the millions of little details that make up the scenery would be very different because we do not know much about them.

One little detail that often goes overlooked is found here in Revelation 6:9; there is an altar in heaven.

When we think of an altar, we think of what is at the front of a church, a place for people to come and pray. But that is not what an altar primarily was in Bible times. An altar in the Bible was normally a sacred piece of furniture on which the blood of sacrifices was poured. That blood would flow through the grate and collect in the bottom of the altar.

As John continued to observe the scene in heaven at the opening of the seals, he saw an altar in that holy place. When he was allowed to look under the altar, the place where the blood of sacrifices was collected, he saw the souls of those who had become sacrificial lambs for Christ. These people will be killed during the Tribulation Period for the Word of God, the Bible, and for the testimony they hold, their faith in Jesus Christ.

This is an amazing thing to consider. Jesus is precious to Christians because He was sacrificed for us. These particular Christians will be precious to Jesus because they were sacrificed for Him. He died so that they could believe in Him, and they died because they did believe in Him.

Jesus holds every Christian as precious in His sight, but those who lose their lives for Him are especially precious. He stood up to receive Stephen home, and I believe He does that for every martyr of the faith. These Christians are so special to Him that they are, at least for a time, given a special place in heaven in the Holy of Holies, very near to Him. I do not know how all of this works. I do not know exactly how these Tribulation martyrs are under the altar. But I do know that as you look at this altar, you can see how much God cares for anyone who stands for Him even unto death.

The asking

Revelation 6:10 *And they cried with a loud voice, saying, How long, O Lord, holy and true, dost thou not judge and avenge our blood on them that dwell on the earth?*

Again, as we look at heaven, we may often get some unrealistic pictures in our minds. We may have a picture of peaceful people in a glowing haze of white, meandering through a field of flowers, softly singing Kum-bay-yah. We may get that picture, but it does not bear much resemblance to the reality of heaven we see in this verse. There may not be any sin in heaven, but there are some pretty angry souls crying out for justice! Just going to heaven does not mean that you are not able to remember and recognize when wrong has been done. Just going to heaven does not mean that you cease to desire righteous judgment to fall. These martyred souls have a request of God. And they are not asking in a hushed, library-whisper type of voice. We have, thus far in heaven, heard the loud shouts of angels, beasts, and elders. Now, we hear more loud shouts from these martyrs under the altar. They are letting it ring at the top of their lungs.

Look at some particulars of their asking:

They are asking for judgment to fall on people still living on the earth, specifically the people who have caused their persecution and death.

They are asking for God to judge Antichrist. They are asking for God to judge neighbors who turned them in for refusing to take the mark of the beast. They are asking for God to judge the government officials who carried out their death sentence. They are asking for God to judge the mobs who killed many of them in the street. Every single person who in any way contributes to the martyrdom of a child of God will face the sure judgment of God.

They are asking for this judgment to come from the hand of the holy and true God.

This is very significant. It lets us know that a holy and true God will not let wicked men kill His servants and get away with it. It also lets us know that it is not satisfying to God or man for killers of Christians to die some generic, normal death. It is only satisfying, it only really "fits" when God steps in and lowers the hammer. It is a frightening thing to assault a servant of God.

They are not asking IF God is going to judge their killers; they are asking WHEN He is going to do it. They did not say *will you*... They said *how long will it be TILL YOU.*

Do not ever think for a moment that the death of even one child of God who was killed for following Christ will go unpunished. It is not a matter of if God will do it; it is only a matter of when.

The assurance

Revelation 6:11a *And white robes were given unto every one of them; and it was said unto them, that they should rest yet for a little season...*

Mob speak is a frightening thing, and it has an impact whether we like it or not. As all of America observed in 2020 and 2021, a seventeen-year-old kid was incessantly called a racist, white supremacist, and murderer. Even President Biden said those things about him. And yet, when a jury looked at all of the evidence, he was unanimously found not guilty.

But let me tell you how frightening mob speak is. I posted about his acquittal, and then I posted the pictures of the three men he shot. One was a convicted child molester, one a convicted wife abuser, and one a convicted thief. And all were very, very white. And when I posted their pictures, immediately someone commented, "Seriously? Were the people he shot really white? I heard he shot three black people, killing two of them."

That's what mob speak does. Many members of the media actually started that lie, and it spread like wildfire from there.

But as bad as all of that was for an innocent kid, that is not even a tiny taste of what these martyrs will go through during the Tribulation Period. The entire world will be screaming at them, lying about them, mocking them, making them feel as dirty as possible, drumming up excuses to kill them.

But when this fifth seal is open, God will give to each of these tortured souls a white robe. That is an outward declaration of their innocence and purity, and this time, the mob around them will be a mob of angels and elders cheering for them! Then God will tell them not to be uptight, their labors are over, and they need to just rest for a while.

Here is what I love about that. Hard workers often feel guilty about taking time to rest. And no one will have ever worked harder for God and been under worse circumstances than these martyrs of the Tribulation Period. They are so used to working and slaving for God. A thousand preachers could tell them to slow down and rest, and they probably would not do it. Moses and Paul and Elijah could form a committee and tell them to rest, and they probably would not do it. But when they hear the voice of the God they spoke to in verse ten answering them in verse eleven and telling them to rest, a thousand pounds will lift off of them, and they will rest. This is, after all, the God who said, *"Come unto me, all ye that labor and are heavy laden, and I will give you rest..."* Matthew 11:28.

The answer

Revelation 6:11b *...until their fellowservants also and their brethren, that should be killed as they were, should be fulfilled.*

God has arrayed these souls in white robes. He has given them rest. But He has not answered their question yet. Now, He will do so.

There will come a specific time that God will avenge those who lose their lives for Him during the Tribulation Period. There is a definite, exact number of martyrs who will fall during the Tribulation Period. God alone knows exactly how many there will be. God knows the exact date and time that the last one will die. He knows the exact manner in which he or she will be killed. He knows the name of that person. And when that last martyr dies, all of God's wrath will be poured out without measure on every single killer of a Christian. God could judge them each individually at the moment they take the life of a child of God. Instead, in addition to any earthly judgment He may choose to bring down on them, He will also judge them all together at the very moment that their last victim dies.

That makes this fifth seal judgment something like a time bomb. When it is unveiled, the people it is directed at do not have any idea when it is going to go off. The first four seals unleash violent judgment, but the fifth seal is opened, and nothing happens. And while that may seem so anticlimactic, it really is not, because what God alludes to in the fifth seal, He unleashes in the sixth:

Revelation 6:12 *And I beheld when he had opened the sixth seal, and, lo, there was a great earthquake; and the sun became black as sackcloth of hair, and the moon became as blood;* **13** *And the stars of heaven fell unto the earth, even as a fig tree casteth her untimely figs, when she is shaken of a mighty wind.* **14** *And the heaven departed as a scroll when it is rolled together; and every mountain and island were moved out of their places.* **15** *And the kings of the earth, and the great men, and the rich men, and the chief captains, and the mighty men, and every bondman, and every free man, hid themselves in the dens and in the rocks of the mountains;* **16** *And said to the mountains and rocks, Fall on us, and hide us from the face of him that sitteth on the throne, and* *from the wrath of the Lamb:* **17** *For the great day of his wrath is come; and who shall be able to stand?*

Here is one way we know that the fifth and sixth seals go together: the first four seals happen at the beginning of the Tribulation Period. The fifth seal happens a little way into the Tribulation Period. But what is described in the sixth seal happens at the very end of the Tribulation Period, which will be after the last martyr dies. Remember that the book of the Revelation does not always follow a chronological order. Much of what you see in the chapters to follow will actually happen before what you see in the sixth seal. God spoke of this timing in Matthew 24. Notice carefully how what He described there matches the details of the sixth seal:

Matthew 24:29 *Immediately after the tribulation of those days shall* **the sun be darkened***, and* **the moon shall not give her light***, and* **the stars shall fall from heaven***, and the powers of the heavens shall be* **shaken***:* **30** *And then shall appear the sign of the Son of man in heaven: and then shall all the tribes of the earth mourn,* **and they shall see the Son of man** *coming in the clouds of heaven with power and great glory.*

This is the same series of events. Jesus, in Matthew 24, was preaching about the sixth seal of Revelation 6. Those souls under the altar asked when God would avenge them. That is exactly what He will do at the unveiling of the sixth seal. Look at what an awesome and awful judgment it will be, and remember that it is brought about in large measure because wicked men dared to kill children of God.

We first of all find that there will be a great earthquake. You say, "Earth has already had great earthquakes." True, but this one will be great even in comparison to all of those. This one will make all that came before it seem tame. This one will cause the powers of the heavens to shake! This will not be a part of the ground on earth shaking; this will be the *earth* shaking!

We then see that the sun will go black. I do not mean an eclipse; I mean that for at least a time, it will go out. That has never ever happened before, but God is going to throw the switch on it.

Then we learn that the moon will turn as red as blood. Think this through! The moon is merely a reflective body. When the sun goes out, it should go dark. But instead, it will give off an eerie, blood-like glow.

Then we are informed that the stars will fall from heaven. There will be a meteor shower of proportions that man has never seen, leaving holes in the ground, toppling what few buildings are left, obliterating mountains.

Then we find that the atmosphere vanishes, and it is therefore only God's choice that allows men to keep on breathing.

And lastly, we learn that every mountain and island is violently relocated. Cuba perhaps slams into Florida, many of the Caribbean Islands sink, mount Everest falls.

And that is when men finally get it. That is when they finally realize, too late, what they have done:

Revelation 6:15 *And the kings of the earth, and the great men, and the rich men, and the chief captains, and the mighty men, and every bondman, and every free man, hid themselves in the dens and in the rocks of the mountains;* **16** *And said to the mountains and rocks, Fall on us, and hide us from the face of him that sitteth on the throne, and from the wrath of the Lamb:* **17** *For the great day of his wrath is come; and who shall be able to stand?*

Absolute pandemonium takes over what is left of the earth. Big-shot political leaders are screaming like kids, begging what is left of the mountains to fall on them, as are the nobodies from nowhere of earth. They are forsaking their decimated estates and hiding in caves and holes. For there, clearly visible, coming back toward the earth that has scorned Him, is the Lamb of God in His wrath and anger. All of the sudden, that the promise of the fifth seal that is unleashed by the sixth does not seem so tame anymore. All of the sudden, when people realize that God is coming to avenge those souls under the altar, men would give anything on earth if they could have one more chance to accept Christ and one more chance to treat His people well, but it is too late.

And the Christian says, "But preacher, that doesn't apply to me!" In a way, I beg to differ. The same God who will hold wicked men responsible for what they do to His people is also going to hold His people responsible for what they do to His people. We sometimes seem to think that because we are saved, we get a pass when we get in the flesh and give brothers and sisters in Christ a fit. Not so. I love my children, but when they were young if one of them intentionally hurt the other, I spanked the one that did the wrong deed. Brethren, it is to our benefit to treat each other very, very well.

Chapter Sixteen
The Calm That Is a Storm

Revelation 7:1 *And after these things I saw four angels standing on the four corners of the earth, holding the four winds of the earth, that the wind should not blow on the earth, nor on the sea, nor on any tree.* **2** *And I saw another angel ascending from the east, having the seal of the living God: and he cried with a loud voice to the four angels, to whom it was given to hurt the earth and the sea,* **3** *Saying, Hurt not the earth, neither the sea, nor the trees, till we have sealed the servants of our God in their foreheads.* **4** *And I heard the number of them which were sealed: and there were sealed an hundred and forty and four thousand of all the tribes of the children of Israel.* **5** *Of the tribe of Juda were sealed twelve thousand. Of the tribe of Reuben were sealed twelve thousand. Of the tribe of Gad were sealed twelve thousand.* **6** *Of the tribe of Aser were sealed twelve thousand. Of the tribe of Nepthalim were sealed twelve thousand. Of the tribe of Manasses were sealed twelve thousand.* **7** *Of the tribe of Simeon were sealed twelve thousand. Of the tribe of Levi were sealed twelve thousand. Of the tribe of Issachar were sealed twelve thousand.* **8** *Of the tribe of Zabulon were sealed twelve thousand. Of the tribe of Joseph were sealed twelve thousand. Of the tribe of Benjamin were sealed twelve thousand.* **9** *After this I beheld, and, lo, a great multitude, which no man could number, of all nations, and kindreds, and people, and tongues, stood before the throne, and before the Lamb, clothed with white robes, and palms in their hands;* **10** *And cried with a loud voice, saying, Salvation to our God which sitteth upon the throne, and unto the Lamb.* **11** *And all the angels stood round about the throne, and about the elders and the four beasts, and fell before the throne on their faces, and worshipped God,* **12** *Saying, Amen: Blessing, and glory, and wisdom, and thanksgiving, and honour, and power, and might, be unto our God for ever and ever. Amen.* **13** *And one of the elders answered, saying unto me, What are these which are arrayed in white robes? and whence came they?* **14** *And I said unto him, Sir, thou knowest. And he said to me, These are they which came out of great tribulation, and have washed their robes, and made them white in the blood of the Lamb.* **15** *Therefore are they before the throne of God, and serve him day and night in his temple: and he that sitteth on the throne shall dwell among them.* **16** *They shall hunger no more, neither thirst any more; neither shall the sun light on them, nor any heat.* **17** *For the Lamb which is in the midst of the throne shall feed them, and shall lead them unto* *living fountains of waters: and God shall wipe away all tears from their eyes.*

In chapter six of the book of The Revelation, the judgment of God on earth begins to unfold. In verses one through eight, we looked at the opening of the first four of the seven seals, which will unleash the four horsemen of the apocalypse on the world. The red rider represented great bloodshed, the black rider represented famine, the pale rider represented death, and the white rider represented the son of perdition, the Antichrist. We then observed the opening of the fifth seal, the souls under the altar crying out for judgment against the ones who caused their deaths. That caused the opening of the sixth seal, which chronologically vaulted us all the way to the end of the Tribulation Period and showed us the final, cataclysmic judgment of God on earth. We read there of the sun going out, the moon turning to blood, stars falling from heaven, and an earthquake like no other.

In chapter eight, we will see what we have not seen yet, the opening of the seventh seal. But in chapter seven, we head right back into the Tribulation Period itself, before the events of the sixth seal take place and before we are allowed to read about the opening of the seventh seal. That seventh seal will unleash a fresh storm of judgment on the earth. But before we get there, Revelation 7 will allow us to see certain events that I have titled *The Calm That Is a Storm*.

The stopping of the wind

Revelation 7:1 *And after these things I saw four angels standing on the four corners of the earth, holding the four winds of the earth, that the wind should not blow on the earth, nor on the sea, nor on any tree.* **2** *And I saw another angel ascending from the east, having the seal of the living God: and he cried with a loud voice to the four angels, to whom it was given to hurt the earth and the sea,* **3** *Saying, Hurt not the earth, neither the sea, nor the trees, till we have sealed the servants of our God in their foreheads.*

Every one of you felt something on the very first day of your life that you ventured outside the hospital. You have felt it every single day since then. Some days it was very noticeable; some days it was so light that you did not even give it a thought; that something is wind. Did you realize that there has never been a single day since the world began that there was no wind? Yet there will come a day that the wind stops completely. Around the globe, in every city, country, and county, in the rich sections and the poor sections, there will be no wind at all.

You say, "But that does not sound like much of a judgment. That sounds like a great calm!" Yes, it is a great calm. It is a "calm that is a storm." Let me show you two things.

First of all, consider the effects of the wind stopping.

Wind is a blessing from God that does a great deal more important things than just keeping kites in the air. Wind spreads out pollution and then helps to spread rain to purify the air of that pollution. Without wind, certain areas of earth, especially industrialized areas, would soon become uninhabitable. Wind also evens out temperature. Without it, temperatures would become wildly unstable. It could be thirty degrees below zero in one neighborhood and one hundred fifty degrees in the next neighborhood over.

Wind moves clouds. Without wind, evaporation would still occur over bodies of water, seas, lakes, etc. But the clouds would remain right over those bodies of water and rain right back down into them. The ground would get drier and drier; crops would become difficult if not impossible to grow.

Wind blows oxygen into the water. Without wind, seas and lakes would become stale, fish would suffer and die, and useable water would become scarce. Wind helps to control insects. Without wind, flies and locusts and mosquitos and other insects would run rampant. Wind makes flight possible. The jet stream in particular is counted on by commercial flights. Without wind, flight will be much more difficult, probably to the point of being impossible.

When God has the angels hold the wind, it is not a good thing. It does not represent "a time of peace" in the Tribulation Period as many people have said over the years. This will be one of the most devastating judgments of the Tribulation Period. We are not told how long this judgment will last, but it is so bad that one angel tells the four angels in charge of this task to give him a bit of time to protect God's children before they stop the winds and hurt the earth, sea, and plant life in the process.

Consider secondly the effort needed to stop the wind.

When I was trying to really grasp the effect of this stopping of the wind, I took a wild chance and sent an email to Eric Thomas, the meteorologist at channel three news in Charlotte, NC. I told him who I was and why I was studying the subject. I asked him what the effect on earth would be, and the response he so graciously took his time to send back was absolutely jaw-dropping. Here was his response:

> "Interesting question. In order for wind to stop blowing, the atmospheric pressure would have to be equal at all points on the earth. The only way for that to

happen is for the temperature to be equal at all points on the earth. About the only way that could happen is if the sun was snuffed out and the earth turned into a hyper-frozen rock. So I would say the conditions leading up to that situation are far more important and provocative than what happens after the wind stops."

Did you understand that? From a natural perspective, the only way the wind could ever stop blowing is if the sun went completely out, and the earth completely froze over down to its very core. Here is why that is so important: that is not what happens during the Tribulation Period! The sun will go out for a brief time at the end of the Tribulation Period, but the earth will never freeze over.

Yet, when this happens, with the sun still shining in the sky, when the wind stops blowing across the earth, wicked man will look up and scream, "This is a natural occurrence! This isn't the hand of God. Do not go getting all religious on us and say that God is judging us. This is the result of global warming and climate change caused by Republicans, and SUVs, and American factories; we just need to drive electric cars and all work in basket weaving factories and the wind will start blowing again!"

No matter what judgment God levels, until they see His face, they will try to explain it away. Men hate the very idea of God because they do not want to be accountable to anyone.

The sealing of the 144,000

Revelation 7:4 *And I heard the number of them which were sealed: and there were sealed an hundred and forty and four thousand of all the tribes of the children of Israel.* **5** *Of the tribe of Juda were sealed twelve thousand. Of the tribe of Reuben were sealed twelve thousand. Of the tribe of Gad were sealed twelve thousand.* **6** *Of the tribe of Aser were sealed twelve thousand. Of the tribe of Nepthalim were sealed twelve thousand. Of the tribe of Manasses were sealed twelve thousand.* **7** *Of the tribe of Simeon were sealed twelve thousand. Of the tribe of Levi were sealed twelve thousand. Of the tribe of Issachar were sealed twelve thousand.* **8** *Of the tribe of Zabulon were sealed twelve thousand. Of the tribe of Joseph were sealed twelve thousand. Of the tribe of Benjamin were sealed twelve thousand.*

Revelation 7:4 reintroduces us to a group of people we may have forgotten about by now in our study, the nation of Israel. This is the first time Israel is mentioned during the Tribulation Period, but you will see her a great deal from here on out. The Tribulation Period, though a worldwide event, will center around and major on Israel. The last half of it is called the time of Jacob's trouble by the prophet Jeremiah. Isaiah 4, only six verses long, uses seven references to Israel to describe the Tribulation Period. God has a national plan for His people, Israel, and that plan leads them right through the Tribulation Period, where they will finally come to know Him as they should.

As we look at these verses, there are some things we absolutely need to notice. First of all, the identity of the 144,000 is so perfectly clear that only those who have chosen to establish and/or participate in cults can miss it. The 144,000 are 12,000 literal Jews from each of the twelve tribes of Israel.

The second thing to notice is that God will protect His people. While hell is breaking loose on earth, God will seal 144,000 of His people, and though the Antichrist will persecute them, the judgments of God will not touch them. It is comforting to realize that even now, though the devil may assault and assail us, the judgment of God will not touch us! God's judgment against us fell on Christ while He was hanging on Calvary.

The third thing to notice about these tribes is who is mentioned and who is not mentioned. There are three significant things here:

Levi is mentioned in verse seven. Levi was one of the sons of Israel, but Levi was the tribe of the priests and was not a landholding tribe. Joseph had two sons, Manasseh and Ephraim, and they became two tribes of their own, making for twelve landholding tribes and the tribe of the priests. But here, Levi is given full blessing and full protection along with the other eleven tribes.

That is God's way, I think, of blessing His ministers. In general, preachers tend not to be wealthy. They tend not to be famous. They tend to sacrifice a great deal. They tend to give a lot of time, effort, and money to help others. Most preachers live in a home that the church owns, a parsonage. So even though this is literally descendants of Levi, by extension it assures me that God will bless His men right along with the tribes who were not "in the ministry."

Ephraim is not mentioned, though Manasseh is in verse six. Ephraim is included in this list, but he is called by his father's name, Joseph, in verse eight. Why is that?

Ephraim was the largest and strongest of the tribes, but he was also the quickest to go off into idolatry whenever the opportunity arose. Ephraim also received this condemnation from the psalmist:

Psalm 78:9 *The children of Ephraim, being armed, and carrying bows, turned back in the day of battle.*

The fact that he is among the sealed in Revelation seven, but without God even using his name, indicates that God was still very displeased by Ephraim's unfaithfulness. God expects our absolute loyalty, our absolute faithfulness. Do not ever vainly imagine that you can be unfaithful and get by with it; it is required in stewards that a man be found faithful!

This, to me, is the most interesting of all. There is one tribe that is missing from the list altogether. There are still twelve here because Joseph's two sons have become two tribes. But one of the original twelve tribes is just gone! Look at the list and see if you know who is missing. If you do not remember who the twelve tribes were, Genesis 49 has the entire list.

The answer is Dan. Dan, the fifth son of Jacob, born to him by Bilhah, Dan, the second-largest tribe when Israel came out of Egypt, Dan, the tribe of Samson, is missing completely from the list of tribes sealed during the Tribulation Period. In fact, Dan is never mentioned after Amos 8! It is possible that they were simply so diminished in number that they were absorbed into another tribe, but not at all likely. Dan as a tribe disappears completely from Scripture, and possibly even from human history, and as far as I can see, never arises again. From what I see of Scripture, it is my contention that either through complete assimilation with foreign people or through extinction, the tribe of Dan has already, or will soon, cease to exist. If it has not happened already, there will come a day when there is not one more living member of the tribe of Dan on earth.

But why? Look back at what Jacob said of Dan his son, so many years ago:

Genesis 49:17 *Dan shall be a serpent by the way, an adder in the path, that biteth the horse heels, so that his rider shall fall backward.* **18** *I have waited for thy salvation, O LORD.*

Jacob called his own son a snake! The lowest, vilest, most cursed of all creatures. It is also the creature that is used over and over to represent the devil himself. And in the middle of talking about his son being a snake, in the middle of talking about that snake trying to destroy someone, Jacob says, *"I have waited for thy salvation, O LORD."*

Has Jacob gotten off subject? Not at all. When he spoke of waiting for God's salvation, he meant the same thing every Jew meant by it. He was waiting for the Messiah that had been prophesied way back in Genesis 3:15 after the snake had caused man to fall into sin. His son Dan was going to be an enemy to Messiah. He was going to be a sneaky, low-life traitor to the Lamb of God. I personally surmise from this that Judas Iscariot was from the already greatly diminished tribe of Dan. That is about the only thing that can explain why an entire tribe of Israel eventually disappears from the face of the earth rather than being restored at some point to its former privilege.

Be warned. What you do not only affects you, it will affect your children, and their children, and their children's children.

The soothing of the great multitude

Revelation 7:9 *After this I beheld, and, lo, a great multitude, which no man could number, of all nations, and kindreds, and people, and tongues, stood before the throne, and before the Lamb, clothed with white robes, and palms in their hands;* **10** *And cried with a loud voice, saying, Salvation to our God which sitteth upon the throne, and unto the Lamb.* **11** *And all the angels stood round about the throne, and about the elders and the four beasts, and fell before the throne on their faces, and worshipped God,* **12** *Saying, Amen: Blessing, and glory, and wisdom, and thanksgiving, and honour, and power, and might, be unto our God for ever and ever. Amen.* **13** *And one of the elders answered, saying unto me, What are these which are arrayed in white robes? and whence came they?* **14** *And I said unto him, Sir, thou knowest. And he said to me, These are they which came out of great tribulation, and have washed their robes, and made them white in the blood of the Lamb.*

This is the second enormous praise session that we see happening in heaven after the Rapture. The first one was in chapters four and five, where four beasts, twenty-four elders, and an innumerable company of angels are glorifying God for all He has done. Now, a few years into the Tribulation Period, another group has arrived.

The Antichrist, by this point, has done everything he can to eliminate any worship of the one true God. Bibles are forbidden. No one can evangelize openly. People can be killed for even whispering the name of Jesus. And in the midst of such a time as that, millions and millions who have never been convicted before are getting saved and spreading the gospel. That makes Antichrist very, very unhappy. The poor little world dictator is having himself a very bad day.

Antichrist strikes back with all of the fury of hell behind him, and the blood of the saints flows in the streets like never before. Men, women, children, no Bible-believing Christian that is caught is spared. Thousands at a time, they are executed, and thousands at a time, they arrive in the throne room of God, where the church, the beasts, the angels, and God Himself have been waiting for them. And when they arrive, they start to shout, "Salvation to our God!" That is a Greek phrase that means that whatever is included in salvation is due to God alone; He gets the glory for it. And then the angels, having heard something they agree with, feed off the praise of the saints and start to praise God again themselves:

Revelation 7:11 *And all the angels stood round about the throne, and about the elders and the four beasts, and fell before the throne on their faces, and worshipped God,* **12** *Saying, Amen: Blessing, and glory, and wisdom, and thanksgiving, and honour, and power, and might, be unto our God for ever and ever. Amen.*

Notice that the praise of one group led to another group joining in. Praising God is and should be contagious. I am amazed that people want to go to a good restaurant other people have told them about, they want to know where the cheapest gas is so they can go get their own gas there, but they do not want to praise God when others are doing so for fear of "getting too emotional."

Psssst. I have a secret: the angels of glory did not care a bit about whether they were getting too emotional. They just knew that if people were praising God, they wanted to join in!

One of the twenty-four elders asked John a question, and then he answered the question for John. The question was where this big crowd of people came from. The answer was that they came of the Great Tribulation. They were martyrs for Christ during that awful time yet to come. They had been made white and clean by the blood of the Lamb, and because of that, their own blood had been shed, in the most torturous ways possible, by Antichrist. This man will show no mercy. He will make Islamic terrorists seem like nursery kids; he will make people wish they were dead before he kills them. But what will make him the angriest is that those that he is killing are glad to die for Christ and refuse to deny His name. They lose their lives in awful ways for Christ, and that is why verse fifteen starts with a therefore:

Revelation 7:15 *Therefore are they before the throne of God, and serve him day and night in his temple: and he that sitteth on the throne shall dwell among them.* **16** *They shall hunger no more, neither thirst any more; neither shall the sun light on them, nor any heat.* **17** *For the Lamb which is in the midst of the throne shall feed them, and shall lead them unto living fountains of waters: and God shall wipe away all tears from their eyes.*

There is an intimacy in these verses that is truly beautiful. Because these martyrs lost their lives on earth, they are allowed to spend day and night in heaven before the throne and in the temple. They get to live with God. But God also chooses to live with them. Verse fifteen says that God Himself will dwell among them.

Think of this. While they were losing their lives, no doubt their killers were mocking them and asking where their God was. God was there; they knew that by faith, so they held fast even unto death. But in heaven, the God that they knew was there but could not see will be right there in plain sight for them at all times.

On earth, many of them were starved to death and deprived of water, dying of dehydration. But in heaven, they will never be hungry or thirsty again. In fact, verse seventeen says that Jesus Christ Himself, the Lamb of God, will personally feed them. He Himself will lead them to fountains of cool, clear water.

On earth, many of them were burned to death. Many were tied down to the ground out in the hot sun until the heat from the sun simply burned their bodies into shock and then death. But in heaven, there will be no sun to burn them, no heat to scorch them.

On earth, imagine the tears that they shed. Tears when their loved ones were carried away to death. Tears as they were tortured. Tears as these new, baby Christians experienced agony that many old veteran Christians have never known. Amazingly, when they get to heaven, they will still be crying. The memories are still fresh.

So Jesus greets them, and He kneels down to them, and takes His nail-scarred hands, and wipes away their tears, hugs them close, and all of those hurts and memories just drift away.

This means something, not just to those Tribulation saints; it means something to you. God sees your tears... God hurts when you hurt... He is there every time a bad report comes back from the doctor. He is there every time a layoff comes. He is there every time a home falls apart. He is there every time a heart gets broken. He is there every time a dream falls through. And there will come a day when you stand in His presence, and you look up and see Him smile, and the next thing you know, you will feel His nail-scarred hand touch your cheek, you will feel Him wipe away your tears, you will hear His heartbeat as He hugs you to His chest, and you will feel His soothing, warming love wash over you. He knows; He cares. There is not one tear that you have ever shed that He somehow missed.

In northern Chile, between the Andes Mountains and the Pacific Ocean, lies a narrow strip of land where the sun shines every day. Clouds gather so seldom over the valley that one can say, "It almost never rains here!" Morning after morning, the sun rises brilliantly over the tall mountains to the east. Each noon it shines brightly overhead, and every evening it brings a gorgeous sunset. Although storms are often seen rising high in the mountains, and heavy fog banks drift far over the sea, the sun continues to shine upon this place. One might imagine this area to be an earthly paradise, but it is far from that! It is a sterile and desolate wilderness! There are no streams of water, and nothing grows there.

We do not like it when the storms come, but they must come. We do not like it when tears fall, but they must fall. But there will come a day when those tears are no longer necessary, So Jesus will simply wipe them all away.

Chapter Seventeen
The Seventh Seal

Revelation 8:1 *And when he had opened the seventh seal, there was silence in heaven about the space of half an hour.* **2** *And I saw the seven angels which stood before God; and to them were given seven trumpets.* **3** *And another angel came and stood at the altar, having a golden censer; and there was given unto him much incense, that he should offer it with the prayers of all saints upon the golden altar which was before the throne.* **4** *And the smoke of the incense, which came with the prayers of the saints, ascended up before God out of the angel's hand.* **5** *And the angel took the censer, and filled it with fire of the altar, and cast it into the earth: and there were voices, and thunderings, and lightnings, and an earthquake.*

Six seals have now been opened as we watch the judgment of God fall on a rebellious world, and we now come to chapter eight of the book of The Revelation, which shows us the opening of the seventh seal.

Silence in Heaven

Revelation 8:1 *And when he had opened the seventh seal, there was silence in heaven about the space of half an hour.*

There are a great many places where silence is the normal thing and would not catch us at all by surprise, places like libraries, funeral homes, and very formal churches. But what we have seen in the book of The Revelation thus far makes it abundantly clear that silence is not at all normal in heaven. In heaven, in the place where God is, in the place where the heroes of the faith are, in the place where angels and the redeemed of the ages are, silence is not normal in the least.

In heaven, the angels are not silent.

They rejoice when someone gets saved:

Luke 15:10 *Likewise, I say unto you, there is joy in the presence of the angels of God over one sinner that repenteth.*

They constantly shout the praises of God:

Isaiah 6:1 *In the year that king Uzziah died I saw also the Lord sitting upon a throne, high and lifted up, and his train filled the temple.* **2** *Above it stood the seraphims: each one had six wings; with twain he covered his face, and with twain he covered his feet, and with twain he did fly.* **3** *And one cried unto another, and said, Holy, holy, holy, is the LORD of hosts: the whole earth is full of his glory.*

In heaven, the elders are not silent. They are constantly shouting about all of the wonderful things God did for them. They are constantly shouting about the character of God:

Revelation 4:10 *The four and twenty elders fall down before him that sat on the throne, and worship him that liveth for ever and ever, and cast their crowns before the throne, saying,* **11** *Thou art worthy, O Lord, to receive glory and honour and power: for thou hast created all things, and for thy pleasure they are and were created.*

In heaven, the beasts are not silent. They are always engaged in lifting up their voices in praise to their creator:

Revelation 4:8 *And the four beasts had each of them six wings about him; and they were full of eyes within: and they rest not day and night, saying, Holy, holy, holy, Lord God Almighty, which was, and is, and is to come.*

In heaven, the souls under the altar are not silent. They are crying out for vengeance over their slaying:

Revelation 6:10 *And they cried with a loud voice, saying, How long, O Lord, holy and true, dost thou not judge and avenge our blood on them that dwell on the earth?*

In heaven, God Himself is not silent. He is shown over and over in Scripture as thundering from heaven:

2 Samuel 22:14 *The LORD thundered from heaven, and the most High uttered his voice.*

If things are loud in heaven, if there is vocal praise of God in heaven, if God approves of things being vocal there, it is ludicrous to believe that He is somehow offended when we lift up our voices and shout His praises now. There is no logical or Scriptural basis for imagining that what is decent and in order in heaven is somehow indecent and out of order on earth.

Heaven is not normally a place of silence. In fact, it is so consistently ringing with the praise of God that when it does finally get silent even for half an hour, Scripture takes time to record it as a highly unusual thing! If the average church were silent for half an hour, it would not be an odd thing; it would not make Scripture. But for heaven to be silent is so odd that it makes Scripture.

This silence in heaven goes from the top to the bottom. It is not silent in "part of heaven," it is silent "in heaven." Everyone in heaven takes their cue from God. This silence is not God reacting to His creation, it is His creation reacting to God. This silence starts at the throne. For half an hour, God says nothing. For half an hour, He does not so much as whisper. As far as we know, this is the first time this has ever happened. Scripture does not record another time in history or eternity that God has been silent for half an hour. So when God gets silent, every elder, every servant, every angel, every animal, every beast, everything that has breath, holds it. The leaves on the trees in heaven do not rustle. The birds do not chirp. People breathe very lightly. This is the most complete and profound silence the universe has ever seen.

This silence is in response to the opening of the seventh seal.

Revelation 8:1 *And when he had opened the seventh seal, there was silence in heaven about the space of half an hour.*

It is amazing how often God judges man, and man continues to flap his gums and mouth off at God. Be warned; no matter how hard God has dropped the hammer on you, it can get much, much worse.

A pastor friend of mine had a man visiting his church, but the man never joined. The pastor went to see him, and the subject of joining came up. The man told him that he could not join a church. The pastor asked why. The man said, "I am under the judgment of God, and I am afraid that any church that I join would end up under His judgment as well." Years before that, the man was dating a woman he had no business being with. He actually prayed and said, "God, I know I'm not supposed to be with her, and I know you're going to judge me, but bring it on, I can take it." This man looked at my pastor friend and said, "I wish I had never said that. My life has been a living hell for the past thirty years. God has done everything but kill me, and truthfully, I wish He would."

Be careful what you think about the judgment of God. God can make it bad enough that all heaven and earth will drop their jaws and go totally silent for half an hour.

Seven more judgments

Revelation 8:2 *And I saw the seven angels which stood before God; and to them were given seven trumpets.*

The judgment of God on earth began when the Lamb of God took the book and began to open the seals in Revelation 6:1. After seven seals were opened, seven trumpets were produced out of the seventh seal.

In Revelation 1:4, we were introduced to the seven angels before the throne. They are there to minister, to serve God. Now God gives them each a trumpet. Because they have served faithfully before God, God is going to increase their usefulness. If you want God to give you more and more to do, do well at what He has already given you to do:

Matthew 25:23 *His lord said unto him, Well done, good and faithful servant; thou hast been faithful over a few things, I will make thee ruler over many things: enter thou into the joy of thy lord.*

So many want the glory of a big position. But if you simply faithfully serve Him in all things, He Himself will advance you and increase your usefulness. Everyone wants to wield the scepter, but few want to wield the sweeper. But if you will not wield the sweeper, you are not fit for the scepter.

These angels are given seven trumpets, and every one of them will unleash another judgment of God on earth. I am fascinated by this thought: trumpets were used by God and His people for a variety of reasons, and most of them were positive! Oftentimes when people heard the trumpet sound, they were being called to come together and celebrate a feast day. Oftentimes when people heard the trumpet sound, they were being called together to worship. Sometimes when people heard the trumpet sound, they were being called to the year of jubilee, when all debts were forgiven, and every servant was allowed to go free.

So many times when God had a trumpet blown, the sound was something that would bring joy to the hearers. When these trumpets sound, the sound will make men tremble in fear as God lowers the hammer time after time, after time, after time, after time, after time.

You and I can be the recipients of sounds from God that make us rejoice, or we can be the recipients of sounds from God that make us cringe in fear. Think of your parents' voices. How often did you rejoice as those voices called you to dinner, or to the Christmas tree, or to get loaded up for vacation? But when that very same set of voices called us in for a lecture or into the room for a spanking, our reaction to those voices was completely different!

It is up to us. It is up to us whether or not we enjoy what we hear from the throne of God.

Smoke from the altar

Revelation 8:3 *And another angel came and stood at the altar, having a golden censer; and there was given unto him much incense, that he should offer it with the prayers of all saints upon the golden altar which was before the throne.* **4** *And the smoke of the incense, which came with the prayers of the saints, ascended up before God out of the angel's hand.*

On ordinary days in ancient Israel, incense was offered on the golden altar in a silver censer, and a censer was sort of like a shallow pan. But on the day of atonement, once a year, the incense was offered in a golden censer. This was a very, very special day.

The tabernacle on earth was merely a model of the tabernacle in heaven. And now, in heaven, God breaks out the golden censer again for a very special day. On earth, the use of the golden censer signaled forgiveness. But now, in heaven, we will see in verse five that the golden censer is about to signal God's judgment on the earth.

Again, the choice belongs to man. God can offer us the golden censer of forgiveness through the blood of His son, or He can offer us the golden censer of judgment through the wrath of His Son.

The angel had the golden censer in hand, and he was given an enormous amount of sweet-smelling incense to offer before the throne of God. When the golden censer was used on earth, the people were gathered outside the tabernacle praying. Again, this was just a model of what takes place in heaven. We see here in heaven that while incense is being offered, prayers are being offered up as well. The angel is holding this golden pan in his hand, and there is a mixture of smoke coming up from it. There is the smoke of the sweet-smelling incense, and it is mixed with the prayers of the saints.

That is an indication of what God thinks of our prayers. We go before God in prayer, and we stumble in our words, and our minds wander, and we have to fight to keep evil thoughts from intruding, and when we are done, we think, "Well, if that's praying, the woods are full of it. I bet God is in heaven groaning over that." And truthfully, that is the impression that a lot of preachers will leave you with:

"If you aren't getting up at 4:00 a.m. and spending three hours of uninterrupted time praying, starting with praising God, following that with repentance, being sure you cry and groan, then God will not hear your prayers!"

But the truth is, the Holy Spirit makes intercession for us with groanings which cannot be uttered (Romans 8:26). The truth is, even when we stumble, and mumble, and struggle in our prayers, God is in heaven going *Mmmmm. What a sweet smell. It reminds me of the finest of incense.*

There is smoke coming off of the altar in heaven, and God loves it.

Scattering coals

Revelation 8:5 *And the angel took the censer, and filled it with fire of the altar, and cast it into the earth: and there were voices, and thunderings, and lightnings, and an earthquake.*

Year after year, generation after generation, the priests would offer up incense before God. They took fiery coals from the altar, put incense on it, and offered up that sweet-smelling smoke before God. But let me tell you what they never did. They never took that pan of fiery coals and threw it on the people! That would have been unheard of. That would have been a sign of the worst kind of anger and wrath.

But in Revelation 8:5, that is exactly what happens. From the very altar that sends up the sweet smoke of incense and prayers before

God, the angel takes hot, burning coals and scatters those coals out into the earth. That will be a heavenly meteor shower like never before.

Imagine those coals hitting buildings, and houses, and power plants. And as they are being scattered across the world, they are producing voices out of thin air. They are producing thunder loud enough to wake the dead and scare the deaf. They are producing the most violent lightning the world has ever known. They cause an earthquake for the record books. All of this is produced by the coals off of the altar, those things which help to produce a sweet smell before God.

But wicked men have never helped to produce that sweet smell before God. They have scoffed at offering God anything, much less giving Him their lives, bodies, time, talents, tithes, and offerings. Those things are foolishness to wicked man. Wicked man has ignored the coals of the altar, scoffed at the coals of the altar, and denied the existence of the altar for the coals. So God will take those hated, despised, denied coals, and cast them out upon the earth by the hand of a mighty angel.

Is it not ironic that God uses the things that man despises and disbelieves to bring judgment on him? God uses the things that could have blessed man and instead blisters him with it.

All of Revelation 8:1-5 points out that man makes choices, and they reap what they sow. Before the Tribulation, during the Tribulation, after the Tribulation, you will reap what you sow. And it may be bad enough to make all of heaven fall silent.

Chapter Eighteen
Four Trumpets and Fatal Thirds

Revelation 8:6 *And the seven angels which had the seven trumpets prepared themselves to sound.* **7** *The first angel sounded, and there followed hail and fire mingled with blood, and they were cast upon the earth: and the third part of trees was burnt up, and all green grass was burnt up.* **8** *And the second angel sounded, and as it were a great mountain burning with fire was cast into the sea: and the third part of the sea became blood;* **9** *And the third part of the creatures which were in the sea, and had life, died; and the third part of the ships were destroyed.* **10** *And the third angel sounded, and there fell a great star from heaven, burning as it were a lamp, and it fell upon the third part of the rivers, and upon the fountains of waters;* **11** *And the name of the star is called Wormwood: and the third part of the waters became wormwood; and many men died of the waters, because they were made bitter.* **12** *And the fourth angel sounded, and the third part of the sun was smitten, and the third part of the moon, and the third part of the stars; so as the third part of them was darkened, and the day shone not for a third part of it, and the night likewise.* **13** *And I beheld, and heard an angel flying through the midst of heaven, saying with a loud voice, Woe, woe, woe, to the inhabiters of the earth by reason of the other voices of the trumpet of the three angels, which are yet to sound!*

It is God's desire that men realize He exists, and that after they realize He exists, they respond to His calling them, and that after they realize He exists and respond to His calling, that they have a real, personal relationship with Him. The problem is, no matter how often things happen that should convince men that God is real, they still deny that He even exists, much less respond to His calling or develop a relationship with Him. But as hard-headed as men are now, they will be even worse during the Tribulation Period.

When John saw Jesus take the book, or scroll, out of God the Father's hands, he observed that it was sealed with seven seals. Each of those seals, when opened, unleashed a cataclysmic judgment of God on earth.

But when the seventh seal was opened, it produced seven more judgments, each one introduced by a trumpet blow from an angel. There is nothing at all random about these trumpet judgments. The first four of them go together, and each one of them destroys exactly a third of the major things that they fall on. That is so exact that there is no possible explanation other than this: there is a sovereign God in heaven, and He rules over the world of men, and people better wise up and admit that He does exist and that they owe Him their allegiance.

The storm like no other

Revelation 8:6 *And the seven angels which had the seven trumpets prepared themselves to sound. 7 The first angel sounded, and there followed hail and fire mingled with blood, and they were cast upon the earth: and the third part of trees was burnt up, and all green grass was burnt up.*

Whenever a huge hurricane or tornado comes through, it is usually billed as the greatest natural disaster anyone has ever seen. But I wonder what it is going to be like for weathermen during the Tribulation Period. How are they going to cover this particular storm of actual hail, fire, and blood? When a hurricane hits now, every station sends some intrepid reporter right out into the middle of it to get the obligatory tv shot of the reporter hanging onto a pole to keep from being blown away. I dare any of them to try that stunt with the storm of Revelation 8:6-7. There will never be a storm quite like this one.

In each thing that we see in this passage, we will be given both the details and the damage.

The details

This is a storm made up of three falling elements: hail, fire, and blood.

If you want to know how amazing this is, go buy an expensive set of commentaries. You can always tell how amazing something is by how hard an expensive set of commentaries tries to explain it away. But there is no explaining this away. It means exactly what it says, and it means it literally. Across the entire earth, there will be a raging storm, shorting out every Doppler radar, stunning every weatherman. This storm will literally be a storm of hail, fire, and blood.

Of those three elements, hail is the only one that naturally falls from the sky. Fire does not naturally fall from the sky. Blood certainly does not naturally fall from the sky. The hail will beat men down, the fire will burn men up, and the blood will scare them out of their wits. There has never been a horror movie more terrifying than this! Imagine the sheer terror that would be caused just by the blood aspect! How badly would you be shaken if you went out for a walk, storms clouds gathered overhead, and all of a sudden driving sheets of blood came raining down on you out of the sky? Imagine the smell, the awful taste as it gets into your mouth, the burning as it gets in your eyes. Then add the hail and the fire to it. There has never, never been a storm with details like this.

The damage

Please take your Bible literally, as God designed it. This storm will burn up exactly one-third of the trees on earth, not one tree more, not one tree less. As a smaller matter, all of the green grass will also be burned up.

Think through the ramifications of this. Trees are used to make wood, so housing costs have just gone totally out of control. Trees are used to make paper, so there goes the supply of everything from the local paper to Charmin bathroom tissue. But worse still, the plant life on earth is what produces our oxygen supply. Trees and grass take in carbon dioxide and give off oxygen. When this storm hits, the oxygen supply on earth is going to get very thin. People already living in high-altitude cities will die in droves.

The sea under attack

Revelation 8:8 *And the second angel sounded, and as it were a great mountain burning with fire was cast into the sea: and the third part of the sea became blood;* **9** *And the third part of the creatures which were in the sea, and had life, died; and the third part of the ships were destroyed.*

Ted Danson once made the statement that we were polluting the oceans so badly, there would not be any sea life left on earth inside of ten years' time, a statement that the late, flamboyant Rush Limbaugh had a field day with. By the way, Ted the would-be-climate-scientist said that way back in 1988. Please remember that when you go out deep sea fishing and take in your bountiful haul all of these many decades later. "Cheers," Ted. (Limbaugh, 2007)

I am not in favor of polluting the oceans, but the truth is that the oceans are far more durable than pseudo-scientists like Ted Danson or Greenpeace or the Sierra Club want you to believe.

But there is an assault on the seas that is coming, not from the hand of man, but from the hand of God.

The details

The Bible is very specific in its wording. Please note that it does not say that a great mountain burning with fire was cast into the sea. It says, "as it were" a great mountain burning with fire was cast into the sea. This will not be a natural object, like a mountain. This will be something else entirely, something from the very hand of God, something that looks like a great mountain. This something will be burning, smoking, flaming its way through the air, and it will be cast into the sea. It will not be caused by fossil-fuel burning cars, or aerosol cans, or evil corporations. It will be a direct, divine, destructive assault on the sea straight from the hand of God.

Even something the size of a small mountain being cast into the sea is going to cause a tidal wave like you could not imagine. But that is not the worst part.

<u>The damage</u>

...and the third part of the sea became blood; **9** *And the third part of the creatures which were in the sea, and had life, died; and the third part of the ships were destroyed.*

Again, notice how exact God is. To the molecule, one-third of the water in the oceans of earth will become blood. This planet will stink all the way to Jupiter. Down to the smallest piece of plankton, exactly one-third of the living creatures in the sea will die. The main source of much of the food on earth will be devastated.

Down to the smallest sailboat, one-third of the ships on earth will be destroyed. The word for ship in the Bible is the exact same word as the word for boat. Destroyers will take just as bad of a hit as canoes, aircraft carriers will sink as quickly as pontoon boats, and submarines will be no safer than kayaks. This will cripple much of the world's commerce, much of the world's travel, and much of the defenses of industrialized nations.

The star called Wormwood

Revelation 8:10 *And the third angel sounded, and there fell a great star from heaven, burning as it were a lamp, and it fell upon the third part of the rivers, and upon the fountains of waters;* **11** *And the name of the star is called Wormwood: and the third part of the waters became wormwood; and many men died of the waters, because they were made bitter.*

As the third destructive trumpet sounds, it causes a star to fall. We are not told what galaxy it comes from or how it gets here so quickly, but the hand of God is clearly at work in it.

<u>The details</u>

This star, when it falls through earth's atmosphere, will not be at all like the little meteors we see in our "spectacular" meteor showers. Did you know that when you see a meteor light up the sky for a few brief seconds, that you are normally seeing a piece of space rock about the size of a grain of sand? Something so small looks so impressive, if only for a few seconds.

But when this star, whatever is left of it, hits earth's atmosphere, it is described as a great star falling from heaven. And it will not just light up for a few seconds and then be gone; it will literally fall through our sky like a burning torch. As it does, it fragments, and every piece of it lands on a river or some other fountain of water. Every fragment of this falling star is guided like a missile from the hand of God.

<u>The damage</u>

Men are in the habit of naming things, even things they cannot reach. We have named Jupiter, Pluto, Saturn, and Alpha Centauri, even though we likely will never set foot on any of them. But every heavenly body has a name that has been given to it by God, and that is its real name.

Somewhere out there, there is a star that has been named by God. Its name is Wormwood. It was designed by God from the foundation of the world for one reason, and that reason is to fall on the running waters of earth during the Tribulation Period and destroy them. Just think of it. While Noah was building an ark in anticipation of the first worldwide judgment, Wormwood was already overhead in anticipation of the second worldwide judgment. While David was fighting Goliath, Wormwood was in the sky, ready to explode and head for the earth. While the star of Bethlehem was showing the Wise Men the way to Jesus, Wormwood was waiting for Jesus to command it to fall on the waters of earth. For 6,000 years now, Wormwood has been held in store, waiting to die, explode, and fall through earth's atmosphere.

When this star lands on the waters, it will have an awful effect. They will be made bitter, not just to the taste but to the body chemistry. This fallen star will literally poison exactly one-third of the running waters of earth, not one molecule more or less, and many men will die from drinking this water.

Perhaps you wonder how, when the waters are made disgustingly bitter, men will still drink it and die from its poison. Let me tell you something else that shows how awesome this judgment will be.

Wormwood is not just the name of a star; it is also the name of a plant well-known to those in the eastern world for many years. Its scientific name is Absinthe. It has been used for everything from medicinal purposes to witches' brews. But Wormwood, Absinthe, especially without the high levels of natural thujone artificially removed, can cause seizures, muscle breakdown (rhabdomyolysis), kidney failure, restlessness, difficulty sleeping, nightmares, vomiting, stomach cramps, dizziness, tremors, changes in heart rate, urine retention, thirst, numbness of arms and legs, paralysis, and death. When used on the skin, wormwood can reportedly cause severe skin redness and burning. (Web.MD)

Yet it is as highly addictive as it is dangerous.

This star will poison the waters, yet men will still be thirsty. They will give in and have just a small drink of water, and they will be hooked like they were on crack cocaine. They will go back for more and more. They will be under its bondage. They will go into convulsions and have seizures, and their nervous systems will fall apart, they will become psychotic, they will have violent nightmares, and many men will die horrible deaths because of this wormwood water.

This will not be an accident, nor will it be something that should catch men by surprise. This was prophesied way back in the days of Jeremiah:

Jeremiah 9:15 *Therefore thus saith the LORD of hosts, the God of Israel; Behold, I will feed them, even this people, with wormwood, and give them water of gall to drink.*

Jeremiah 23:15 *Therefore thus saith the LORD of hosts concerning the prophets; Behold, I will feed them with wormwood, and make them drink the water of gall: for from the prophets of Jerusalem is profaneness gone forth into all the land.*

This is direct, specific, and sent straight from the hands of an angry God.

The sun, stars, and moon darkened

Revelation 8:12 *And the fourth angel sounded, and the third part of the sun was smitten, and the third part of the moon, and the third part of the stars; so as the third part of them was darkened, and the day shone not for a third part of it, and the night likewise.* **13** *And I beheld, and heard an angel flying through the midst of heaven, saying with a loud voice, Woe, woe, woe, to the inhabiters of the earth by reason of the other voices of the trumpet of the three angels, which are yet to sound!*

People are used to the bright light of day; they can deal with it. To a certain extent, they are even used to the pitch black of night. They know it is coming, so they sleep through it, or they turn on more lights. But there will be something tremendously ominous about this fourth trumpet judgment.

<u>The details</u>

Exactly one-third of the sun will be smitten, and will not shine during the day. Exactly one-third of the moon will be smitten, and will not shine at night. Exactly one-third of the stars will simply go out and not give off any light.

The damage

Because of the damage to the sun, moon, and stars, when there is light, it will be an eerie, two-thirds light. Imagine the weird feeling when there is only two-thirds the normal light, day and night. Additionally, there will be no light at all for a third of normal daylight hours or for a third of normal nighttime hours. Again, this is a fulfillment of ancient prophecy:

Amos 8:9 *And it shall come to pass in that day, saith the Lord GOD, that I will cause the sun to go down at noon, and I will darken the earth in the clear day:*

By the time the Tribulation comes, imagine how much of our power on earth will be solar power. God is going to shut the power down without even sending a disconnect notice. One-third of the light is gone, one-third of the solar power is gone as well. Additionally, the crops will have a third less light to grow by.

All of these judgments are ultra-specific, all of them are clearly divine, all of them clearly the product of the God that men refuse to acknowledge even exists.

How stubborn is mankind! How much easier it would be to acknowledge Him, love Him, and serve Him voluntarily, especially since He loved us and gave Himself for us.

The London Observer told the story of a family of mice who lived all their lives in a large piano. To them in their piano-world came the music of the instrument, filling all the dark spaces with sound and harmony. At first, the mice were impressed by it. They drew comfort and wonder from the thought that there was Someone who made the music--though invisible to them--above, yet close to them. They loved to think of the Great Player whom they could not see. Then one day, a daring mouse climbed up part of the piano and returned very thoughtful. He had found out how the music was made. Wires were the secret; tightly stretched wires of graduated lengths which trembled and vibrated. They must revise all their old beliefs: none but the most conservative could any longer believe in the Unseen Player. Later, another explorer carried the explanation further. Hammers were now the secret, numbers of hammers dancing and leaping on the wires. This was a more complicated theory, but it all went to show that they lived in a purely mechanical and mathematical world. The Unseen Player came to be thought of as a myth. But the pianist continued to play, while the mice inside the piano denied his very existence... (Webster, 2020)

There is a God; He loves you; please be ready to meet Him.

Chapter Nineteen
The Opening of the Pit

Revelation 9:1 *And the fifth angel sounded, and I saw a star fall from heaven unto the earth: and to him was given the key of the bottomless pit.* **2** *And he opened the bottomless pit; and there arose a smoke out of the pit, as the smoke of a great furnace; and the sun and the air were darkened by reason of the smoke of the pit.* **3** *And there came out of the smoke locusts upon the earth: and unto them was given power, as the scorpions of the earth have power.* **4** *And it was commanded them that they should not hurt the grass of the earth, neither any green thing, neither any tree; but only those men which have not the seal of God in their foreheads.* **5** *And to them it was given that they should not kill them, but that they should be tormented five months: and their torment was as the torment of a scorpion, when he striketh a man.* **6** *And in those days shall men seek death, and shall not find it; and shall desire to die, and death shall flee from them.* **7** *And the shapes of the locusts were like unto horses prepared unto battle; and on their heads were as it were crowns like gold, and their faces were as the faces of men.* **8** *And they had hair as the hair of women, and their teeth were as the teeth of lions.* **9** *And they had breastplates, as it were breastplates of iron; and the sound of their wings was as the sound of chariots of many horses running to battle.* **10** *And they had tails like unto scorpions, and there were stings in their tails: and their power was to hurt men five months.* **11** *And they had a king over them, which is the angel of the bottomless pit, whose name in the Hebrew tongue is Abaddon, but in the Greek tongue hath his name Apollyon.* **12** *One woe is past; and, behold, there come two woes more hereafter.*

There is something powerful built into every human being. It is called the "will to live." A soldier trapped behind enemy lines will fight like a cornered rat to get back to his unit because he has a will to live. A person dying of an illness will still struggle for breath because they have a will to live. A person who is driving down the highway and sees a truck veer into his lane and come straight for him will instinctively jerk the wheel, or slam on the brakes, or do something to try and avoid the collision because he has a will to live. This is so universal that every suicide shocks people because it is very odd for a person to give up that will to live. But there will come a day when people by the billions will give anything to be allowed to die, and they will not be able to do so.

When John saw Jesus take the book, or scroll, out of God the Father's hands, he observed that it was sealed with seven seals. Each of those seals, when opened, unleashed a cataclysmic judgment of God on earth.

But when the seventh seal was opened, it produced seven more judgments, each one introduced by a trumpet blow from an angel. There was nothing at all random about these judgments. The first four of them went together, and each one of them destroyed exactly a third of the major things that they fell on. A third of the sea was destroyed, along with a third of the sea life and a third of all ships. A third of the trees were burned up. A third of the sun, a third of the moon, and a third of the stars were smitten. A third of all the rivers and other sources of fresh water became poisoned with addictive wormwood, and many men died. Yet as bad as these judgments were, the next thing that happened was an angel flying through the heavens saying:

...Woe, woe, woe, to the inhabiters of the earth by reason of the other voices of the trumpet of the three angels, which are yet to sound!

Imagine basically a third of earth destroyed and then hearing that the next three judgments would make the first four pale by comparison. We will look at these last three trumpet judgments individually, and this chapter dealing with the sounding of the fifth trumpet is called *The Opening of the Pit*.

The pit

Revelation 9:1 *And the fifth angel sounded, and I saw a star fall from heaven unto the earth: and to him was given the key of the bottomless pit.* **2** *And he opened the bottomless pit; and there arose a smoke out of the pit, as the smoke of a great furnace; and the sun and the air were darkened by reason of the smoke of the pit.*

By the time the first four trumpets sounded and did their damage, men will have probably gotten into the habit of looking up to see what is coming down next. And sure enough, when the fifth trumpet sounds, something else will fall from the heavens. Man, who has spent hundreds of years convincing himself that there is no God up there, will have God dropping things on him left and right.

When the fifth trumpet sounds, something incredibly unique will happen. A star is going to fall to earth. But this star is not an "it," but a "him."* Speaking of this star, verse one says that to "him" was given the

---

* Both Clarke and Barnes, among others, rightly regard this star as an angelic being and the one to whom the key was handed. Clark: "An angel encompassed with light suddenly descended, and seemed like a star falling from heaven." Barnes: "And I saw a star fall from heaven unto the earth. This denotes... a leader, a military chieftain, a warrior."

key to the bottomless pit. So what him is this? Look ahead to Revelation 20:1, and you will see him again:

Revelation 20:1 *And I saw an angel come down from heaven, having the key of the bottomless pit and a great chain in his hand.*

The star still has the key. The star is an angel. But he was also a star! There is no need at all to try and make this symbolic or figurative. In the sky above your head tonight, there is a star that is also an angel. We have no idea which one it is. I doubt if we would know it if we saw it. But it, he, is there, waiting for the command from God to leave his space in the sky, fall to earth, assume angelic form along the way, and pick up a key from God that will literally unleash part of hell on earth.

This star, this angel, is going to unlock and open the bottomless pit.

Now here is an interesting thing to look at. Is there, can there be, such a thing as a bottomless pit on earth? The answer is yes. Not just biblically, but scientifically, the answer is yes.

Pay attention to this paragraph from Live Science:

"Biblical views of the center of the Earth as a hellish pit raging with fire and brimstone have some support from new research. Scientists have found that the vast majority of brimstone — reverently referred to in biblical times as "burning stone," but now known more commonly as sulfur — dwells deep in the Earth's core.

"'In a way, we can also say that we have life imitating art,' study lead author Paul Savage, a research scientist in the Department of Earth Sciences at Durham University in the United Kingdom, said in a statement. 'For millennia, tales have been told of the underworld being awash with fire and brimstone. Now at least, we can be sure of the brimstone.'" (Goldbaum, 2015)

That is not from a Bible college: it is from secular scientists who do not even believe the Bible. He called it, the Bible, "art." And yet somehow the Bible got it right thousands of years before scientists ever managed to figure it out...

The very center of the earth, filled with fire and lava, is rotating at a high speed and is high in its gravitational pull.

If you put something, or someone, in a constantly rotating circle where they are always being pulled toward the center, they will fall and fall and fall and never hit any type of a bottom. There is a bottomless pit; it is a portion of hell itself. And even if the center of the earth had been made of iron itself, the God of all power could easily have produced and provided a rotating and bottomless pit within it.

When this angel opens the bottomless pit, this will be like a volcano times ten thousand. A normal volcano will spew up ash from dozens or hundreds of miles deep, but the opening of the pit will let out filth and ash from the very center of the earth, thousands of miles deep. The amount of black soot and smoke released into the air will totally block out the light of the sun for a time. People will die from struggling to breathe. People will not be able to drive. Radio and cellular signals will be blocked out. Television and satellite as well. The pit is real, it is right now below your feet, and there will come a day when an angel from heaven opens the door to it up for a time, not to let men in, but to let some things out.

The pestilence

Revelation 9:3 *And there came out of the smoke locusts upon the earth: and unto them was given power, as the scorpions of the earth have power.*

It is incredible to think just how ominous things will be during the Tribulation Period, especially in this instance. The door to the bottomless pit has been physically opened. I wonder how big it is? I wonder how many times people have walked right over it, not even knowing it. I wonder if it is an open field, or a mountainside, or a patch in the desert, or maybe an ice cap on the north or south pole?

The door will be opened. Smoke will pour out. The sun will be blocked out. And then there will be a noise, a terrible, droning, angry noise, like trillions and trillions of angry bees. Mighty locusts, deformed and demon possessed, having lived in hell for who knows how many thousands of years, will suddenly be turned loose on earth.

Revelation 9:4 *And it was commanded them that they should not hurt the grass of the earth, neither any green thing, neither any tree; but only those men which have not the seal of God in their foreheads.*

These locusts will not bother to nibble from a single leaf or even a blade of grass. These creatures, which would normally devour every green thing in sight, will bypass every plant on earth and focus instead on hurting men. And they will be very good at their job:

Revelation 9:5 *And to them it was given that they should not kill them, but that they should be tormented five months: and their torment was as the torment of a scorpion, when he striketh a man. 6 And in those days shall men seek death, and shall not find it; and shall desire to die, and death shall flee from them.*

These locusts will have stings that feel exactly like the sting of a scorpion. The sting of a scorpion is not like many other types of bites or stings. This sting is immediately and intensely painful. The sting of the bark scorpion is highly toxic. These demon locusts, by the millions, will be stinging and harassing and tormenting men for five months.

How bad will it be? It will be so bad that people will give up the will to live. Men and women will decide to commit suicide and end it all, but they will not be able to. For five months, men will try to die, and God will make them go on living and getting stung, and living and getting stung, and living and getting stung.

A man will be getting stung over and over; he will put a gun up to his temple, pull the trigger, and live through the blast missing most of his head and continuing to get stung. People will be covered in locusts, getting stung, they will jump out of buildings and off of bridges. They will hit the ground with a thud and live through the fall, continuing to get stung. People will overdose, and hang themselves, and slit their wrists. But they will live through it all, for five months, getting stung and stung and stung. Death, which has been chasing men down for 6,000 years, will run away from them for five months. For five months, there will not be a single funeral on earth. For five months, men will live in torments, the hospitals will be full, but the mortuaries will be absolutely empty. For five months, men will want to die, but not one backhoe or shovel will so much as disturb a blade of grass in the cemetery. There has never ever been anything at any time on earth like this. This is a taste of hell unleashed on earth, but only a small taste. If you are not saved, all you have to look forward to is an eternity of this. All you have to look forward to is an eternity of wishing you could die and realizing that you will live forever in hell, falling and burning and being stung and weeping and wailing and choking and not being able to die. And what is awful to consider is the men at the end of these five months. Men will have been begging to die, and after five months, many of them will finally get to die. And then they will wake up in hell and realize that they were better off living with demon locusts on earth than they are in hell for all eternity.

Revelation 9:7 *And the shapes of the locusts were like unto horses prepared unto battle; and on their heads were as it were crowns like gold, and their faces were as the faces of men.* **8** *And they had hair as the hair of women, and their teeth were as the teeth of lions.* **9** *And they had breastplates, as it were breastplates of iron; and the sound of their wings was as the sound of chariots of many horses running to battle.* **10a** *And they had tails like unto scorpions...*

These creatures are locusts. But they do not look like locusts. If God had not told men that they were locusts, no one would have ever known.

The locust is roughly twice the size of a grasshopper. These giant bugs from the pit, though probably the same in size as the average locust, are definitely different in their shape. They are actually shaped like horses, and they are dressed like horses prepared for battle. They look like they are wearing golden crowns on their heads, and they have faces like men, adult males, and long hair like women. These horse-shaped, man-faced, woman-haired, crown-wearing bugs also have teeth like lions, and they have on breastplates that appear like iron. Worse still, they have tails shaped like scorpions, and we will see the damage they can do in just a few moments.

Like all locusts, these deformed creatures have wings, and they do fly. Men will be watching the awful, thick cloud from the pit, and they will hear an awful sound coming out of it, the sound of millions of wings beating so loudly that they sound like horses running towards a battle.

Revelation 9:10b *...and there were stings in their tails: and their power was to hurt men five months.*

These demonic locusts will be able to use those stings in their tails. In fact, the ability to sting will not be a secondary thing to them; it will be their primary purpose. As we saw in verse four, they will simply ignore the vegetation and will specifically have as their focus the torment of mankind.

Revelation 9:11 *And they had a king over them, which is the angel of the bottomless pit, whose name in the Hebrew tongue is Abaddon, but in the Greek tongue hath his name Apollyon.*

These demonic locusts are not random, wandering bugs. They are an orderly, organized, ordered assembly. They have a king over them. He is a fallen angel whose Hebrew name is Abbadon and whose Greek name is Apollyon. Both of those names mean "the Destroyer."

This is an angel near in power to Satan himself and just as hateful. He will, in a satanic fury, direct and drive on these demon locusts, not giving them as much as a second to rest. They are only going to live for a short five months, and Apollyon will make sure that they spend every moment of those five months doing their destructive job.

Revelation 9:12 *One woe is past; and, behold, there come two woes more hereafter.*

Five months... for five months this "woe," this horrible judgment will plague the earth making men wish for a death that will not come. But its end will not be a relief, merely an invitation for the next two woes to come.

Chapter Twenty
The Army Like No Other

Revelation 9:13 *And the sixth angel sounded, and I heard a voice from the four horns of the golden altar which is before God,* **14** *Saying to the sixth angel which had the trumpet, Loose the four angels which are bound in the great river Euphrates.* **15** *And the four angels were loosed, which were prepared for an hour, and a day, and a month, and a year, for to slay the third part of men.* **16** *And the number of the army of the horsemen were two hundred thousand thousand: and I heard the number of them.* **17** *And thus I saw the horses in the vision, and them that sat on them, having breastplates of fire, and of jacinth, and brimstone: and the heads of the horses were as the heads of lions; and out of their mouths issued fire and smoke and brimstone.* **18** *By these three was the third part of men killed, by the fire, and by the smoke, and by the brimstone, which issued out of their mouths.* **19** *For their power is in their mouth, and in their tails: for their tails were like unto serpents, and had heads, and with them they do hurt.* **20** *And the rest of the men which were not killed by these plagues yet repented not of the works of their hands, that they should not worship devils, and idols of gold, and silver, and brass, and stone, and of wood: which neither can see, nor hear, nor walk:* **21** *Neither repented they of their murders, nor of their sorceries, nor of their fornication, nor of their thefts.*

The world has seen some incredible military might in its history. The armies of Babylon were precise, organized, and moved in straight lines with brute force. The army of Alexander the Great of Greece moved with incredible speed and simply beat its enemies from point to point, outmaneuvered, outflanked, and destroyed them with fury. The air force of Hitler's Germany was cutting edge in technology and boasted numbers that all of the allies together could not match. The United States of America has, for about the past fifty years, had a military like the world has never seen. The U.S. Military has about 1.3 million soldiers. We have snipers that can kill with a single shot from nearly two miles away. We have stealth bombers that are virtually undetectable. We have special forces, SEALs, and Delta Forces that are nearly superhuman in their abilities. We can drop a bomb down a chimney from ten miles up. We have submarines that can fire missiles from the bottom of the ocean, up into the sky, hundreds of miles inland.

But there will come a day when all of the world's military might, including the awesome forces of the USA, will seem like just a few kids on a school ground with sticks and rocks. There is coming a day when this world will be exposed to an army like no other...

Ever since the first seal was opened, we have been viewing the miraculous judgments of God falling on earth. The seven seals were opened, and the seventh one produced seven trumpets. The first four trumpets went together, each one destroying a third of what it aimed at. The last three trumpets are called woes and make the first four pale in comparison. The fifth trumpet caused the opening of the bottomless pit, which unleashed the demonic horde of locusts on earth for five months. That brings us to the next judgment, the sounding of the sixth trumpet that we read about in our text, and that sixth trumpet will usher in what I have just been referring to, the army like no other.

This is the army like no other because of its demonic leaders

Revelation 9:13 *And the sixth angel sounded, and I heard a voice from the four horns of the golden altar which is before God,* **14** *Saying to the sixth angel which had the trumpet, Loose the four angels which are bound in the great river Euphrates.*

The book of Hebrews lets us know that the tabernacle on earth was merely a shadow, just a pattern of the true tabernacle in heaven. Everything that was in the earthly tabernacle is also in the heavenly tabernacle, including the golden altar of incense.

Way back in Exodus 30, God gave Moses the instructions concerning the building and use of the altar of incense. As the priest moved toward the temple every day, he would pass, outside, the brazen altar of sacrifice. That altar painted the picture of Christ dying on earth for us. As the priest went into the Holy of Holies once a year, behind the veil, in the very back of the tabernacle, he would find the mercy seat, the altar that represented Christ's sacrifice applied to the altar in heaven. So in effect, the altar outside was earth, and man. The altar in the Holy of Holies was heaven, and God the father. But in between those two altars, there was another altar, the golden altar of incense.

That altar was a go-between between the outer altar and the altar in the Holy of Holies. That golden altar represented Christ, the God-man, interceding for us, being our mediator between God and man:

1 Timothy 2:5 *For there is one God, and one mediator between God and men, the man Christ Jesus;*

That altar, just like Christ's mediation on our behalf, was incomprehensibly sweet. Every day, twice a day, the priest would offer sweet-smelling incense upon it. He did it in the morning when he came into the tabernacle, and the fragrance lasted all day. He did it again when he came out of the tabernacle, and the fragrance lasted all night. Exodus

30:8 described it as a perpetual incense. That altar was easily the sweetest thing in the entire tabernacle.

But that golden altar had even more significance than that. Once a year, on the Day of Atonement, the high priest would enter the Holy of Holies, and make atonement for the people. On his way back out, having shed the blood and sprinkled it on the mercy seat, he would stop by the altar of incense again and put some of the blood on each of the four horns of the golden altar of incense. That was to bring mercy to the man of God himself, the priest who had offered the sacrifice.

The golden altar also did something else. The incense that rose up off of it represented the prayers of the saints gathered outside the tabernacle. As the smoke rose up and wafted through the overhead curtains out into the open air, the people got a visual reminder that their prayers were going up before God.

All the way around, the golden altar of incense was sweet. It spoke of Christ's intercession on our behalf, it spoke of the fact that God remembers and has mercy on His men, even though they are sinful creatures of flesh, and it spoke of the fact that God hears our prayers. This was a piece of furniture that seemed to cry out one word, every minute of its existence: MERCY!

But as we come to Revelation 9:13-14, the message coming from that altar has radically changed:

Revelation 9:13 *And the sixth angel sounded, and I heard a voice from the four horns of the golden altar which is before God,* **14** *Saying to the sixth angel which had the trumpet, Loose the four angels which are bound in the great river Euphrates.*

The Lord's angels are not bound; but some of the devil's angels are. These four demonic powers are another judgment of God on this wicked world. But notice who, or rather what, calls for that judgment to be released: it is literally the four horns of the altar that are speaking with one voice, crying out for judgment. That little preposition *from* in verse thirteen is a Greek word that indicates source. Those four horns are the source of the voice. That altar that had been crying "MERCY!" for so long is now crying out for judgment.

This voice from the altar cries out for the release of four mighty angels. May I give you a geographical fact that you have never gotten in any school geography class?

In Eastern Turkey, a river begins. It is 1,780 miles long and flows through Turkey, Syria, and Iraq. It is one of the four great rivers that originally flowed from the garden of Eden, and it is one of the few landmarks that survived Noah's flood. That river eventually empties out into the Persian Gulf. At its widest point, the Euphrates is more than four hundred yards wide. That river is used for drinking water, for business, and for recreation. All of that you can find in a geography book. But a fact that you will not find in a geography book is this: somewhere in that 1,780 mile long, four-hundred-yard-wide river, there are four demonic generals imprisoned. We do not know how long they have been there or what their particular rebellion was that landed them there, but God Himself has literally chained four angels up somewhere in that river, and those four angels are going to be the military leaders of the army like no other. They are powerful, they are ruthless, they are called horsemen, and they are furious over their chains. When they are released, they are going to go on a killing spree, and they will have an army with them.

This is the army like no other because of its dramatic size

Revelation 9:15 And the four angels were loosed, which were prepared for an hour, and a day, and a month, and a year, for to slay the third part of men. 16 And the number of the army of the horsemen were two hundred thousand thousand: and I heard the number of them.

This army that is like no other is given an exact timetable, by God, in which they can run free and do their damage. The Bible here starts from the smallest unit of time and goes to the largest. We are used to doing it the other way. So for ease of understanding, here is what you need to know. For exactly one year, one month, one day, and one hour, this army will be moving, confronting, and killing. We are actually going to see some details of a great battle they are in later on in the book of The Revelation. I do not want to give that away here, but I do want to point out the dramatic size of this army.

John looked out at an army that there was no possible way for him to count. But he did not have to count it. By revelation, he was given the number of soldiers in this army like no other. These four demonic leaders, these horsemen, are going to have an army of two hundred million soldiers! There has never, ever, in all of human history, been an army like this to take the field in battle. It will be nearly a hundred times bigger than any current military on earth. This may be a demonic army, or it may be an army made up of men, or a combination of both, but either way, it will be an overwhelming, devastating force.

This is the army like no other because of its devastating effect

Revelation 9:17 And thus I saw the horses in the vision, and them that sat on them, having breastplates of fire, and of jacinth, and brimstone: and the heads of the horses were as the heads of lions; and out of their mouths issued fire and smoke and brimstone. 18 By these three was the third part of men killed, by the fire, and by the smoke, and by the brimstone, which issued out of their mouths. **19** *For their power is in their mouth, and in their tails: for their tails were like unto serpents, and had heads, and with them they do hurt.*

As John continued gazing at the army whose size has never been matched, the four demonic warlords suited up for battle, picked their horses, strapped on the saddle, put a foot into the stirrup, and swung up onto their horse to ride. Their horses are demonically deformed, having heads that look like lion's heads. The horsemen have on breastplates made up of three elements and three colors. The ingredients of the breastplates are fire, jacinth stone, and brimstone, which means sulfur. Those elements produce red, blue, and yellow colors. These horsemen are awesome to behold, but they are deadly to the core. Let this terrible thought sink in—these four demons, according to verses fifteen and eighteen, are going to kill a third of the men on earth all by themselves, separate from the damage that their 200,000,000-man army does!

Look at how they achieve this devastating effect. The horses of the horsemen are literally breathing out fire, smoke, and brimstone. Many years ago, modern armies stopped using horses. What good are horses against tanks? But for one year, one month, one day, and one hour, people will be asking, "What good are tanks against these horses?"

No doubt, some military genius will figure out a way to stop these horses. The plan will go something like "attack them from behind!" All of the smoke and fire and brimstone is coming out of their mouths!"

The only problem is verse nineteen lets us know that their awesome power is also in their tails. No one ever died from a long, swishy, horse's tail. But the army like no other with demonic leaders like no other also has horses like no other. These horses have unusual tails. They are not like hairs, they are like snakes, and each strand has the biting head of a snake. As these horsemen are mowing down army after army, when they have won each victory, the horsemen will stroll across the field of battle, listening to the moans of those who have been wounded. And while the horse is walking by, one of its serpent heads on the tail will sink its fangs into those wounded, unleashing devastating and demonic poison into those dying bodies. The Bible says that these serpent heads will "hurt." I think that is the nicest way it could be put. This hurt will be unspeakable agony. This army, led by these demonic horsemen, is devastating in its effect. But look at what the text says next:

Revelation 9:20 *And the rest of the men which were not killed by these plagues yet repented not of the works of their hands, that they should not worship devils, and idols of gold, and silver, and brass, and stone, and of wood: which neither can see, nor hear, nor walk:* **21**

Neither repented they of their murders, nor of their sorceries, nor of their fornication, nor of their thefts.

There will be many who heard the gospel and were convicted of their sins yet refused to get saved before the Rapture. 2 Thessalonians 2:11-12 makes it clear that those people will not be given a chance to get saved after the Rapture. God will send them a "strong delusion," and they will believe a lie and not get saved. But there will be many others on earth who could get saved. Multitudes of them will, and most of them will be murdered by the Antichrist and his forces. But the vast majority of them will not. The vast majority of them will be just like these we read about in Revelation 9:20-21. They will see Scripture unfolding before their very eyes, and they will not repent. Friends will be consumed by fire from these horses' mouths, and they will not repent. Entire towns full of people will die in an instant; they will see it, and know it, and will not repent. They are so fixed on material things, gold, silver, brass; they are so idolatrous, worshipping things that they themselves have made, that they refuse to worship the living God of heaven.

They are murderers and will not repent. They kill old men, little kids, and even babies in the womb, but they will not repent.

They are sorcerers and will not repent. This word for sorcery is a word that indicates both dabbling in the occult and the use of drugs. It is the word *pharmakia*, and we get our word pharmaceuticals from it. Men will be high on weed, hooked on crack, cooking up meth, strung out on PCP, and will not repent. They will justify their behavior; they will say that it is alright because the government has legalized it, and everyone is doing it, and they do not care a bit what the Bible says.

They are fornicators and will not repent. They are sexually impure. They do not care a bit about the God who gave us the gift of sex and also gave us clear guidelines for sex. They are open Sodomites and will not repent. They are open lesbians and thumb their noses at God. They are pornographers and consumers of pornography and defy anyone to tell them it is wrong. They are pedophiles and have no mercy in their hearts for the children they are destroying. They abhor marriage and instead just live together, shacking up, not caring a bit about their testimony or the fact that they are living in immorality. They are teens engaging in pre-marital sex and laughing about any notion of old-fashioned morality. They are sleeping around with anybody they want, anytime they want, any way they want, and people are dying by the millions at the judgment of the army and the horsemen, and they will not repent.

They are thieves and they will not repent. The concept of respecting the property of others is out the window. They do not even wait for the cover of darkness. They band together and take whatever they want from anyone who cannot stop them. While a 200,000,000-soldier army is running wild, while the four demonic generals and their horses are consuming a third of the population, those who are not being killed are so hardened, so wicked, so past hope, that they refuse to repent, even though God wants them to, even though He loves them, even though He died for them.

This year, and month, and day, and hour are basically the last year, month, day, and hour of the Tribulation Period. This army will be seen again in Revelation 16 and Revelation 19. They are running wild across the earth, but they are headed for a last-second showdown with the King of kings. They will lose. But so will everyone, then or now, who refuses to repent of their sin and get right with God.

Chapter Twenty-One
The Final Countdown

Revelation 10:1 *And I saw another mighty angel come down from heaven, clothed with a cloud: and a rainbow was upon his head, and his face was as it were the sun, and his feet as pillars of fire:* **2** *And he had in his hand a little book open: and he set his right foot upon the sea, and his left foot on the earth,* **3** *And cried with a loud voice, as when a lion roareth: and when he had cried, seven thunders uttered their voices.* **4** *And when the seven thunders had uttered their voices, I was about to write: and I heard a voice from heaven saying unto me, Seal up those things which the seven thunders uttered, and write them not.* **5** *And the angel which I saw stand upon the sea and upon the earth lifted up his hand to heaven,* **6** *And sware by him that liveth for ever and ever, who created heaven, and the things that therein are, and the earth, and the things that therein are, and the sea, and the things which are therein, that there should be time no longer:* **7** *But in the days of the voice of the seventh angel, when he shall begin to sound, the mystery of God should be finished, as he hath declared to his servants the prophets.* **8** *And the voice which I heard from heaven spake unto me again, and said, Go and take the little book which is open in the hand of the angel which standeth upon the sea and upon the earth.* **9** *And I went unto the angel, and said unto him, Give me the little book. And he said unto me, Take it, and eat it up; and it shall make thy belly bitter, but it shall be in thy mouth sweet as honey.* **10** *And I took the little book out of the angel's hand, and ate it up; and it was in my mouth sweet as honey: and as soon as I had eaten it, my belly was bitter.* **11** *And he said unto me, Thou must prophesy again before many peoples, and nations, and tongues, and kings.*

As we have been progressing through the book of The Revelation, we have noted that the events described do not always come in chronological order. They go back and forth, and sometimes the flow is interrupted completely by what we call a "parenthesis" in the book. Chapter ten is one of those parenthetical portions. It is not specifically spelled out in Scripture exactly what time these events will take place. What is specifically spelled out is that these events will impact an aspect of time itself.

The invasion of the angel

Revelation 10:1 *And I saw another mighty angel come down from heaven, clothed with a cloud: and a rainbow was upon his head, and his face was as it were the sun, and his feet as pillars of fire:* **2** *And* *he had in his hand a little book open: and he set his right foot upon the sea, and his left foot on the earth,* **3a** *And cried with a loud voice, as when a lion roareth...*

John, the old man, had seen a lot in his lifetime. He had seen Jesus walk on water; he had seen the feeding of the five thousand, and so much more. But we are never specifically told that John ever saw angels until he became an old man on the Isle of Patmos. But once he got there, he saw angel, after angel, after angel. Angels praising God, angels sealing servants, angels holding back the wind, angels opening the bottomless pit, angels blowing trumpets. That is why in Revelation 10:1, John said that he saw another mighty angel. Angels in our day have been mostly hidden, invisible, anonymous. During the Tribulation Period, these heavenly messengers are going to be busy and, at least to the saints, very noticeable.

As John looked around at the future in Revelation 10:1, he saw that earth itself was being invaded by a mighty angel. This angel will not be worried about warplanes, surface-to-air missiles, rail guns, or lasers. John saw this angel come down from heaven, and he is clothed with an actual cloud. That is an impossibility of nature. But this is not the natural we are talking about; it is the supernatural. There is a rainbow sitting on his head, his face is as bright as the sun, and his feet look like they are on fire. I do not think the world will be able to miss this. Even if you argue that the angel is normally an invisible creature, let me remind you that clouds and rainbows are not. If they can be seen, I rather suspect that the world will be able to see him as well. They may not remember it a second later; they may choose to block it out of their minds, the devil may steal the thought from them, but this world will be visibly invaded by a mighty angel from glory.

This angel has a little book in his hand. As we have seen so many times, there is in Scripture and in the life of Christ and in examples from heaven and in the lives of all of the apostles a very heavy emphasis on writings, especially on the written Word of God. As we will see in a few moments, this particular little book is not the Bible, but it is something that God wrote for John, and as such, it is another good example of the fact that God prizes the written word. And all of Scripture makes it very clear that He especially prizes the written word called Scripture, the Bible. It is getting very fashionable even among incredibly popular evangelical preachers to say very pious sounding yet heretical things like, "It isn't necessary for us to believe all of the Bible and teach it and preach it to people as if all of it is actually true; it is only necessary for us to point out to people that Jesus rose from the dead."

But this angel was holding a book. And Jesus told John to write all of this in a book. And that same Jesus told people not to add to or subtract from the book. And years earlier, that same Jesus, when confronted by the devil himself, rather than saying, "Do you know who I am?" instead quoted Scripture three times.

Do not allow anyone to minimize the importance of the Bible to you, and do not allow anyone to sow doubts in your mind about the Bible. This angel was not just speaking and hoping John would remember; he was holding a little *book*.

Here is another thing about this angel. He is massive. John saw him stand with his right foot on the sea and his left foot on the land. Not on the edge of the beach, and in the surf that comes and goes: one huge foot is all the way out, who knows how far into the ocean, and one huge foot is all the way in, who knows how far, onto the land. He is standing like that to let the entire world know that his God has absolute authority over every puddle, pond, lake, sea, continent, nation, state, and town on the planet and that what he is about to say will apply to the whole world.

As the angel touches down, he has what some might call an "inappropriate emotional outburst." The Bible says he cried with a loud voice, as when a lion roars. In other words, it was not "words" that he said when he first hit the earth and sea. It was a deafening cry, a roar. This angel will not get Time Magazine's person of the year award, he will not get an Emmy or an Oscar, but he will get everybody's attention.

The intrigue of the voices

Revelation 10:3b *...and when he had cried, seven thunders uttered their voices.* **4** *And when the seven thunders had uttered their voices, I was about to write: and I heard a voice from heaven saying unto me, Seal up those things which the seven thunders uttered, and write them not.*

If you like a bit of mystery and intrigue, here it is. The mighty angel shouts like a lion, and in response, seven thunders speak audible, understandable words in the voice of thunder. John hears the seven thunders speak, and he clearly understands what they said. He quickly grabs pen and parchment and starts to write down what they said—and then God tells him not to.

Do you know what those seven thunders said? No, you do not. And neither do I! We have this incredible, inspired, preserved book, but there is not one verse in it anywhere that tells us what these thunders/voices said. Here are some things we should notice concerning this.

<u>The raw emotion of the angel caused things to happen</u>

I do not believe in being controlled by our emotions. But I do believe in being emotional. In fact, the Bible is quite clear that every great figure, from Moses to Elijah to David to Jesus Himself, was very emotional! And people that actually *use* the emotions that God has given them tend to get much more done for God than those who do not. If you are not passionate about the things of God, why should anyone ever listen to you?

If it does not move you, it will not likely move anyone else, either.

<u>God does not owe us any more information than He has already given us, nor does He owe us any explanations of anything</u>

Are you, like me, curious enough that you really would like to know what those voices said? If you found out that there was a note in the back of your Bible telling you what they said, would you be tempted to sneak a peek?

We may be curious, it may eat us alive like a kid waiting to unwrap that big package on Christmas morning, but God does not owe us any information or explanation of anything:

Proverbs 25:2a *It is the glory of God to conceal a thing...*

Deuteronomy 29:29a *The secret things belong unto the LORD our God...*

Some years ago, we got a message on our church answering machine from a "prophetess" wanting me to call her and get a word of prophecy. If she is a prophetess, why did she call when I was not in? It seems like she would know when I am in and when I am not.

She cannot help me with this. I could call her and ask her what the voices said, and she would not know that either. Nor would any other human being except for John himself. God does not owe us any information or explanation of anything.

That is very helpful to remember when we question why the doctor's report came back bad. It is very helpful to remember when the pink slip comes. We may desperately want to know what is going on. But if God does not tell us, if He seals up that information, it is enough that we know that He is God, and that He is good, and that He is working all things out for His glory and our benefit because He loves us.

The institution of the final countdown

Revelation 10:5 *And the angel which I saw stand upon the sea and upon the earth lifted up his hand to heaven,* **6** *And sware by him that liveth for ever and ever, who created heaven, and the things that therein* *are, and the earth, and the things that therein are, and the sea, and the things which are therein, that there should be time no longer:* **7** *But in the days of the voice of the seventh angel, when he shall begin to sound, the mystery of God should be finished, as he hath declared to his servants the prophets.*

Revelation 10:5-7 is three verses, but only one sentence. Verse five ends with a comma, verse six ends with a colon, and we do not come across the period until the end of verse seven. These three verses, this one sentence, speaks of the beginning of God's final countdown.

For thousands of years, God has been dealing with man, trying to get man to believe in Him and do right. And all the while, God would set deadlines for man, but those deadlines were usually extendable. For instance, in Daniel 4, God was getting ready to judge Nebuchadnezzar. But when Daniel brought this message to him, look at what he said.

Daniel 4:27 *Wherefore, O king, let my counsel be acceptable unto thee, and break off thy sins by righteousness, and thine iniquities by shewing mercy to the poor; if it may be a lengthening of thy tranquillity.*

Daniel told the king that if he would do right, there was a possibility that God would give him more time. Here is another example of that. In I Kings 21, God was going to judge Ahab. But look at what happened:

1 Kings 21:27 *And it came to pass, when Ahab heard those words, that he rent his clothes, and put sackcloth upon his flesh, and fasted, and lay in sackcloth, and went softly.* **28** *And the word of the LORD came to Elijah the Tishbite, saying,* **29** *Seest thou how Ahab humbleth himself before me? because he humbleth himself before me, I will not bring the evil in his days: but in his son's days will I bring the evil upon his house.*

God determined to judge Ahab, and then Ahab humbled himself before God. So God then pushed back the judgment, and it did not happen in Ahab's lifetime; God gave him more time.

That kind of thing happened over and over again in Scripture. God in mercy gave man opportunity after opportunity to believe in Him and do right. But when this mighty angel steps down from glory and plants one foot on the sea and another on the land, he will shout loud enough for all the world to hear, "No more time! This world's opportunity is over. You had every chance you were ever going to have; you can repent if you want, you can beg for mercy if you want, but nothing is going to change; the final countdown has begun."

We do not know at exactly what point during the Tribulation Period this happens. We do know that it will happen and that from that point on, the entire world could seek to get right, and it would not stop or delay a thing.

When the seventh angel begins to blow the trumpet, which happens in Revelation 11:15, everything that God spoke of by the prophets, everything spoken by everyone from Moses to Elijah to Isaiah to Amos and every other prophet, all of it that has not yet been fulfilled will begin to do so. Every judgment, every promise, every threat, not one thing will be left undone. Revelation 10:7 speaks of all of those prophecies, collectively, as the mystery of God. So much of God and His plan for us have been unknown, not because He has not told us, but because we just have not grasped it. But when it all actually happens, nobody will be able to miss it. When the Tribulation Period begins to wind down, and the earth itself is practically falling apart, and Jesus comes back in open glory and power, none of God's plan will be a mystery anymore.

The instructions to follow before the countdown begins

Revelation 10:8 *And the voice which I heard from heaven spake unto me again, and said, Go and take the little book which is open in the hand of the angel which standeth upon the sea and upon the earth.* **9** *And I went unto the angel, and said unto him, Give me the little book. And he said unto me, Take it, and eat it up; and it shall make thy belly bitter, but it shall be in thy mouth sweet as honey.* **10** *And I took the little book out of the angel's hand, and ate it up; and it was in my mouth sweet as honey: and as soon as I had eaten it, my belly was bitter.* **11** *And he said unto me, Thou must prophesy again before many peoples, and nations, and tongues, and kings.*

In verse four, a voice from heaven had spoken to John and told him not to publish what the seven thunders said. Now, that same voice speaks to him again. The voice told him to go and take the book out of the hand of the angel. This book is the subject of the rest of the chapter. But what is it?

Notice first of all that this book is described four times in this chapter as a little book. That phrase does not occur any other place in the entire Bible. Even here in the book of The Revelation, we find the book of God's judgment on earth in Revelation 5, a large book firmly held in God's hands, we find the book of life mentioned seven times, a large book in God's hands, and we find the books, plural, containing the record of man's works in Revelation 20:12-13. But this little book is different from all of those other books.

Here is another thing to notice. The word used here for little book is not *biblon*, that we get our word Bible from, but *biblaridion*. Again, that Greek word does not occur anywhere else in the entire Bible. So here is what we can conclusively say this book is not: it is not the Bible itself, it is not the Book of Life, it is not the book of God's judgment on the earth, and it is not the books containing the record of man's works. This book is different from any other book mentioned in the entire Bible.

So what is it? Let's start moving toward the answer. The voice from heaven told John to go and take the book. And when he demanded the book from the angel, the angel freely gave it to him. Then the angel told John to take that book and eat it! And John did. He took that book, that parchment, and he ate it.

Could I walk down the street, take a book out of someone's hand, and do that? No, but why? Because it is not my book. The reason John could eat that book is because it belonged to him. Look at verse eleven again for more explanation:

Revelation 10:11 *And he said unto me, Thou must prophesy again before many peoples, and nations, and tongues, and kings.*

That book, John did not read it, he did not memorize it, he did not even write it. That book was the rest of the preaching, teaching, and prophesying that John was going to do in the last few years of his life. This was God putting into John every message he was going to preach for the rest of his life. And there are several things very significant about this.

First of all, the man was already somewhere around ninety-five years old. That explains why it was a little book! Even though he would preach before many people, he did not have many years left to do it in. The older we get, the more we need to be aware of the fact that we need to be busy for God. Our book may be "littler" than we think, so let's get busy!

Secondly, the book that John ate, the things he was going to preach, was sweet in his mouth and bitter in his stomach. It was both sweet and sour. It was positive and negative. You who listen to preaching, please understand that it cannot be all sweet, even though some would like it to be, and even though many modern churches are making sure that all of their messages are sweet. Some of the most popular speakers and writers in the Christian world today openly espouse this philosophy. They make no apology for the fact that all of their messages and writings are positive, even though much of the Bible is clearly negative.

On the other hand, many truly odd people actually wish that every message ever preached would be a scalding, mean, sheep-skinning message. If there is not blood on the floor when the service is over, the preacher is a weak compromiser!

But if the Bible teaches anything, it teaches balance. Nine times in the Bible, we are instructed to avoid declining to the right hand or the left. Balance. Right down the middle. Preaching that is directed by man will usually be either all positive or all negative. Preaching that is directed by God will be positive and negative, sweet and sour.

Thirdly, notice that John saw that the final countdown for the world had begun. But in the meantime, he was given a job to do. Go preach. Go witness. Go win as many people to God as you possibly can. That is the exact same task that God has given us. Next door, across the street, in the next town, one state over, across the country, overseas, people are dying without Jesus and going to Hell. Every one of them reaches a point in their lives where there is no more opportunity, a place where God says "Enough! The final countdown has started." Before they get there individually, it is our job to witness, preach, hand out tracts, get on radio waves, send missionaries. It is our job to get to them before they go too far, before God looks down from heaven and says, "Enough; no more; time's up."

Chapter Twenty-Two
The Measuring Day

Revelation 11:1 *And there was given me a reed like unto a rod: and the angel stood, saying, Rise, and measure the temple of God, and the altar, and them that worship therein.* **2** *But the court which is without the temple leave out, and measure it not; for it is given unto the Gentiles: and the holy city shall they tread under foot forty and two months.*

Imagine yourself in a long line of people. You look around you, and you see some people that look pretty good and some people that look pretty bad. They are all ages, all heights, all weights, all races, they are men, and they are women.

Now, I want you to imagine another detail to this scene. A man is coming by. He has a measuring tape in his hands. He is coming down the line, and he is measuring people to see if they are tall enough, thick enough, strong enough, and a dozen other things. But every person that he gets to, he takes several measurements, looks at them, and says, "You're not good enough. You will never do." This happens over, and over, and over. With no exceptions, everyone is getting measured, no one is good enough, and you are in the same line that they are. You start to think, "I know good and well that I will not measure up either. Man, this is going to feel really bad to be measured and found wanting."

But then, something happens that you never expected, something that makes you feel even worse than if you got the same treatment as everyone else. What is the one thing that could happen that would be even worse than being measured and being told you did not measure up?

How about this: as the man measuring everyone comes down the line, when he gets to you, he just looks at you and says, "You're not even worth measuring!" And then he goes on down the line and continues to measure others...

As we have been progressing through the book of The Revelation, we have noted that the events described do not always come in chronological order. They go back and forth, and sometimes the flow is interrupted completely by what we call a "parenthesis" in the book. Chapter ten was one of those parenthetical portions. In it, an enormous angel stood with a foot on the land, and a foot on the sea, and declared that time would be no more, meaning that from that moment onward, even if mankind as a whole had repented, it was too late to stop the final judgment of God.

After that ominous message, John was told to go and take a little book out of the angel's hand and eat it. That book would contain everything that John was to preach and teach for the rest of his life. John did so, and that is where we leave the parenthesis of chapter ten and resume the narrative of the book in chapter eleven. It is in the first two verses of this chapter that we see an unusual and significant scene take place, centered in and around the newly built temple in Jerusalem.

The measured

Revelation 11:1 *And there was given me a reed like unto a rod: and the angel stood, saying, Rise, and measure the temple of God, and the altar, and them that worship therein.*

As chapter eleven begins, aged John is given a reed with which to measure. There were no tape measures in those days, so measurements were commonly done by means of rods of a specified length.

John has been watching the judgments of God unfold on earth, but all of this very much switches the view to religious and political affairs during the Tribulation Period. That view is going to take up a significant portion of the rest of the book of the Revelation as we look at the beast, and the alliances of kingdoms and nations, and the economy, and political machinations. And it is all going to start with John measuring the most important structure that will then be standing on earth, a structure that will be the object of both religious and political attention on earth, the rebuilt temple in Jerusalem.

Before we begin to look at the things that are measured in this verse, let's look at some of the preliminary facts we are given. Notice first of all that the rod for measurement was given by God Himself. This is a reminder that God's standards are all that really matter, not just in this issue but in every issue.

Everyone has opinions—lots of them. But let me give you a news story that pretty effectively illustrates how ridiculous it is to use human opinions and beliefs as any kind of a measuring rod of right and wrong, or even of sanity.

The headline is, "Woman mourns after her dolphin husband dies and says she will never remarry."

"A woman has said she will never marry again, describing herself as a 'one dolphin woman', when her aquatic lover passed away after suffering stomach problems, despite being aged around 40. Many of us struggle in relationships, but with Sharon Tendler she knew it was love at first sight when she met her partner, named Cindy.

"As reported in the Daily Star, Sharon says it was clear right away that she felt an instant bond with Cindy, despite the fact he was a 39-year-old common dolphin.

"The pair were wed in a lavish ceremony, with millionaire Sharon dazzling in a white dress with pink flowers in her hair, but it all came to a sudden and dramatic end as Cindy the dolphin sadly died within months.

"Sharon loved Cindy, but sadly he died less than a year after their wedding. Sharon, aged 26 at the time, and Cindy dated for a while - with the clothes importer and band manager making countless expensive trips visiting Israel to see her alpha male heartthrob.

"Eventually, they wed at Dolphin Reef in the Israeli port of Eilat, 15 years later, and the union was sealed with a chaste kiss as Sharon whispered 'I love you,' and Cindy presumably clicked in agreement. Speaking after the wedding, Sharon told local reporters: 'It's not a perverted thing. I do love this dolphin. He's the love of my life. It's not a bad thing. It's just something that we did because I love him, but not in the way that you love a man. It's just a pure love that I have for this animal.'

"On hearing the news of her 'husband's' death, Sharon ruled out finding another lover, telling the Star: 'I am a one dolphin woman.'" (Bett, 2021)

This woman "married" a dolphin. And the "cultured world" valued her opinion just fine, thank you very much, and how dare anyone suggest that God is not in favor of such insanity! There were serious news stories of this all over the world. I am talking about actual news stories that made it sound as if this were a legitimate wedding and marriage.

But God Himself gave us an easy-to-read measuring rod on everything, the Word of God. And His opinion is the only one that really counts. So when God told John to measure the temple and the altar, and even the worshippers, He Himself gave him the rod with which to measure.

Notice also that after the angel gave John the measuring reed, the angel had to stand back up, and John had to stand back up also. What does that mean? It is easy to see why the angel was stooped down; this is the same huge angel from the end of chapter ten. In order for him to give this measuring reed to John, he had to stoop way down to do so. But the interesting question is why John had to stand back up. It seems that since he was so much smaller than the angel, he would have been standing on his tiptoes to reach up and grab the rod as the angel stooped to give it to him. But John was far too humble for that. He knew enough to realize that he was unworthy; he learned that lesson way back in Revelation 5.

Whenever a real man of God has to evaluate anyone or anything, whenever he has to declare that someone or something is not quite up to par in any area, he is not excited about having to do it. He knows what an awesome responsibility it is. Yet this text reminds us that certain things must be measured.

The house of God must be measured.

The house of God measured here is not even standing yet. Right now, there is no temple in Jerusalem. But count on this; there will be. Every devout Jew desires to have the temple worship re-established, and it will be established before or during the Tribulation Period. We are not told how big it will be. God had John measure it, but He did not have him tell us what the square footage is. For us, the size is not the important thing that God wants us to know; the important thing that He wants us to know is that He is aware of it and measuring it.

This is both a future prophecy and a present-day warning. Whatever calls itself the house of God will be measured by God!

Churches with pulpit prosperity pimps pushing people to give more and more with the promise that if they do, God will make them wealthy in this life, will be measured by God.

Churches that abandoned Scripture years ago and have instead adopted a social gospel, worshipping at the altar of the LGBTQ movement and Critical Race Theory and Neo-Marxist politics, will be measured by God.

Even churches that are sound and solid in doctrine and belief yet have a hard, cold, haughty attitude will be measured by God.

In Revelation 2-3, we saw seven radically different churches, some good, some mediocre, and some downright horrible. And yet Christ was walking in the midst of each and every one making evaluation of them, taking their "measurements."

The altar must be measured.

The temple is not standing yet; therefore there is no altar yet. But there will be a temple, and there will be an altar. The altar mentioned here is the altar of sacrifice, where burnt offerings will be slain and offered. Every so-called sacrifice to God, every act of worship, is something that will be measured and evaluated by God. God expects to be worshipped according to His Word.

When David tried to carry the ark his way, it was a disaster.

When Cain tried to offer the offering he liked rather than the one God required it was a disaster.

God has been very good to us in allowing us to worship, and He has also told us what He likes in the way of worship. And it does not include making God into our image; it requires that we be conformed to His.

The worshippers must be measured.

During the Tribulation Period, there will be millions of worshippers crowding in and around the temple. God will measure them all. Not to see how tall they are, but to evaluate their spiritual "height." Even in our day, every person who claims to be a worshipper of God is going to be measured by God. Every one of us is "under review" every day.

Concerning all of these things, the temple, the altar, and the worshippers during the Tribulation, let me tell you something about the measurement that will be taken. Every one of them will be measured and found wanting. How do we know? Because everything they have built, and everything they are doing, is unnecessary. The one sacrifice for sins has already been made. Yes, there will be a rebuilt temple and the blood of animals flowing on the altar, but the need for all of that has already been passed for nearly two thousand years now.

The unmeasured

As bad as it would be to be measured and found wanting, it will be even worse to not be worthy of being measured at all:

Revelation 11:2 *But the court which is without the temple leave out, and measure it not; for it is given unto the Gentiles: and the holy city shall they tread under foot forty and two months.*

Outside of Herod's temple, there was a court called the Court of the Gentiles. Inside of the temple was regarded as a holy place, and Gentiles were not allowed inside. We could stay outside in the court and worship but never could come inside. I am so glad that Christ broke down the middle wall of partition between us! Nonetheless, during the Tribulation Period, and in the Tribulation Era Temple, there will again be a Court of the Gentiles.

When God declares measuring day, He will measure the temple, the altar, and the individual worshippers. But He will not even bother to measure the outer court, the Court of the Gentiles. Their "spot" is not even worthy of the effort. Why is that?

Gentiles are, during the Tribulation Period, going to dominate and decimate the holy city, Jerusalem, for three and a half years. If you think anti-Semitism is bad now, wait until the church is gone. Wait until the wrath of Antichrist is unleashed. The Gentile world powers will run roughshod over Jerusalem. And here is what you need to know: even when the Jews do not believe in Jesus their Messiah, even when they are offering lambs and ignoring the Lamb, they are still the absolute apple of His eye as far as nations go. They can be absolute reprobates, but you better keep your hands off of them! God loves the Jews, and He is not done with them. And any nation or individual that forgets this is in trouble. When you lay your hands to the Jews, you are in trouble.

This one thing, coming against the Jews, will make God so angry that He says, in so many words, "You aren't worthy of me even pulling out the tape measure; I can see from here that you are coming up very short of my expectations."

Chapter Twenty-Three
The Two Witnesses

Revelation 11:3 *And I will give power unto my two witnesses, and they shall prophesy a thousand two hundred and threescore days, clothed in sackcloth.* **4** *These are the two olive trees, and the two candlesticks standing before the God of the earth.* **5** *And if any man will hurt them, fire proceedeth out of their mouth, and devoureth their enemies: and if any man will hurt them, he must in this manner be killed.* **6** *These have power to shut heaven, that it rain not in the days of their prophecy: and have power over waters to turn them to blood, and to smite the earth with all plagues, as often as they will.* **7** *And when they shall have finished their testimony, the beast that ascendeth out of the bottomless pit shall make war against them, and shall overcome them, and kill them.* **8** *And their dead bodies shall lie in the street of the great city, which spiritually is called Sodom and Egypt, where also our Lord was crucified.* **9** *And they of the people and kindreds and tongues and nations shall see their dead bodies three days and an half, and shall not suffer their dead bodies to be put in graves.* **10** *And they that dwell upon the earth shall rejoice over them, and make merry, and shall send gifts one to another; because these two prophets tormented them that dwelt on the earth.* **11** *And after three days and an half the Spirit of life from God entered into them, and they stood upon their feet; and great fear fell upon them which saw them.* **12** *And they heard a great voice from heaven saying unto them, Come up hither. And they ascended up to heaven in a cloud; and their enemies beheld them.* **13** *And the same hour was there a great earthquake, and the tenth part of the city fell, and in the earthquake were slain of men seven thousand: and the remnant were affrighted, and gave glory to the God of heaven.* **14** *The second woe is past; and, behold, the third woe cometh quickly.*

As we learned earlier in the book, the Antichrist comes to power at the beginning of the Tribulation Period. And he does so by means of peace and diplomacy. He gets the world to sign not just **a** covenant but **the** covenant. He does something that no one has ever been able to do; he brings peace to the world as a whole, but to the Middle East in particular. He gets Jews and Arabs to put their names on the same piece of paper. And for three and a half years, forty-two months, the world is outwardly at peace. But even during those forty-two months of outward peace, Jerusalem is still being trodden down of the Gentiles, as we saw in the first two verses of Revelation 11. It does not take long at all for the Jews to realize that their deal with the Antichrist probably is not going to work out very well. But for forty-two months, they bear with it. For forty-two months, the world has a semblance of peace, even while undergoing the judgment of God as nature itself seems to be coming unraveled. Fire is falling from the sky, the wind is being stopped, waters are turning to blood, but the world is happy. Why? Because all those annoying, Bible-believing Christians are gone. They can sin as much as they want, and no one is there to tell them differently, other than 144,000 Jews that have just gotten saved. But millions of veteran, Bible-believing Christians are gone, so the Antichrist and his crowd pretty much have their way.

But not entirely. Millions of preachers are gone. Millions of Christian witnesses are gone. The Antichrist and the wicked world should not have anything at all to bother them. They look around and see empty churches. The airwaves are void of any real gospel preachers. But then, four feet, two sets of sandals, shuffle into Jerusalem. Two men of God, and from God, two men with a heart for God and a fire in their eyes, walk into the middle of hell on earth and start preaching.

Their preaching

Revelation 11:3a *And I will give power unto my two witnesses, and they shall prophesy a thousand two hundred and threescore days...*

Let's begin by reviewing for certain what we know and what we do not know, and then I will tell you the position I hold and why.

What we absolutely know, because it is very clearly stated here, is that during the Tribulation Period, there will be two witnesses, two prophets, and they will have a ministry that lasts for 1,260 days, three and a half prophetical years. We have already seen that same time period just one verse earlier in relation to the fact that the Gentiles will be trodding down, stomping all over the holy city of Jerusalem. The fact that these two verses are back-to-back, tied together with the word "and," pretty well assures us that it is the same three-and-a-half-year period of time. In other words, there will be a three-and-a-half-year period of time when Jerusalem is trodden down by the Gentiles, and two witnesses are uncompromisingly preaching in that exact same city.

That there will be such a three-and-a-half-year period of time, and that there will be these two witnesses prophesying, that much we know absolutely for certain.

Now let me tell you what we do not know for certain. The Tribulation Period lasts for seven years, the first three and a half of which is a time of relative peace as the Antichrist spreads his influence over the globe, and the last half of which is a time when the Antichrist shows his true colors, a time that is so bad that Jeremiah 30:7 calls it *"the time of*

Jacob's trouble." And we do not know with one hundred percent certainty which of those two three-and-a-half-year periods the events of Revelation 11 take place within.

Reputable commentators have been divided on this for years. The majority of them written recently believe this to be about the last half of the Tribulation Period. But I hold the minority position on this; I believe that what you see in Revelation 11 takes place during the first half of the Tribulation Period, not the last.

In fairness, let me show you a passage where Jesus spoke of this time period, a passage that those holding the other position use to say that it is the last half of the Tribulation Period being spoken of.

Luke 21:24 *And they shall fall by the edge of the sword, and shall be led away captive into all nations:* ***and Jerusalem shall be trodden down of the Gentiles****, until the times of the Gentiles be fulfilled.* ***25*** *And there shall be signs in the sun, and in the moon, and in the stars; and upon the earth distress of nations, with perplexity; the sea and the waves roaring;* ***26*** *Men's hearts failing them for fear, and for looking after those things which are coming on the earth: for the powers of heaven shall be shaken.* ***27*** *And then shall they see the Son of man coming in a cloud with power and great glory.*

That phrase in verse twenty-four is clearly the same wording and the same event being spoken of in Revelation 11:1-2. And in seeing that, those who believe that this refers to the last half of the Tribulation Period point out that this will be *"until the times of the Gentiles be fulfilled."*

When they point that out, they say that it means the end of the Tribulation Period, the end of the time of the Gentiles. But that is not necessarily the case. For starters, there will still be Gentiles after the Tribulation Period, all the way through the Millennial Reign, and even after the Millennial Reign. So this clearly does not refer to their existence being fulfilled, but their "times" being fulfilled.

But what does that mean? It means very much the same thing it means when we use it today. When a sports team is winning championship after championship, and we say, "This is just their time," we mean that they are at the height of their influence, and no one can stop them.

The question is, when does God regard the "times of the Gentiles" as being fulfilled? Is it midway through the Tribulation Period, or is it at the end of the Tribulation Period?

We can go back to a very recent verse we studied in the book of Revelation to find out how He is in the habit of handling these things.

Revelation 10:5 *And the angel which I saw stand upon the sea and upon the earth lifted up his hand to heaven,* **6** *And sware by him that* *liveth for ever and ever, who created heaven, and the things that therein are, and the earth, and the things that therein are, and the sea, and the things which are therein, that **there should be time no longer**: **7** But in the days of the voice of the seventh angel, when he shall begin to sound, the mystery of God should be finished, as he hath declared to his servants the prophets.*

This was the massive angel sent down from God to earth to proclaim that there should be time no longer. In other words, the world's opportunity was up. Final judgment was going to fall, no matter what. And yet, judgment did not then immediately fall. There would still be a few years left of tribulation and massive judgment and upheaval and battle on earth. In other words, the world will most certainly not believe that their time is up, but their time is up.

This is, I believe, the exact same thing that we see from the text in Revelation 11 and in Luke 24. The times of the Gentiles will be fulfilled halfway through the Tribulation Period. That will be the absolute height of world power for the Gentiles; it will never get any better or any more thorough than that. But from that point on, it is a downward spiral heading for the judgment that waits for them three and a half years later.

When I point that out, those who hold the opposite position will respond by pointing out something else from Luke 24:

Luke 21:24 *And they shall fall by the edge of the sword, and shall be led away captive into all nations: **and Jerusalem shall be trodden down of the Gentiles**, until the times of the Gentiles be fulfilled.* **25** *And there shall be signs in the sun, and in the moon, and in the stars; and upon the earth distress of nations, with perplexity; the sea and the waves roaring;* **26** *Men's hearts failing them for fear, and for looking after those things which are coming on the earth: for the powers of heaven shall be shaken.* **27 *And then shall they see the Son of man coming in a cloud with power and great glory.***

People who hold the view that the events of Revelation 11 take place during the last half of the Tribulation Period will tie verses twenty-four and twenty-seven together and point out that verse twenty-seven very clearly is the ending of the Tribulation Period. And they are correct. But they miss two enormous things.

The first thing they miss is the content of verses twenty-five and twenty-six, including that part about "upon the earth distress of nations," which was Jesus taking just a handful of words to summarize several chapters of the book of The Revelation that are sandwiched in between chapter eleven that we are studying and chapter nineteen where the Son of Man comes in that cloud with power and great glory.

But the second massive thing that they miss is that in Revelation 11, after this three-and-a-half-year period takes place, when heaven opens and people look up to see, it is not the Son of Man coming back in that cloud with power and great glory that they see. It is something radically different that they see:

Revelation 11:19 *And the temple of God was opened in heaven, and there was seen in his temple the ark of his testament: and there were lightnings, and voices, and thunderings, and an earthquake, and great hail.*

Because this is what we see after this three-and-a-half-year period, and not Jesus coming again, and because there is still so much that has yet to happen by way of judgments by this point in the narrative, I do not see any clear way to regard this as being the last half of the Tribulation Period. It seems to me that it absolutely has to be the first half of it instead.

But whether the events of Revelation 11 take place during the last half or the first half of the Tribulation Period is really irrelevant to us. This is something we can actually afford to disagree on. It is not a cardinal doctrine of the faith. Prophecy is something that we should tend to approach humbly and cordially; it is not a part of salvation, and we will likely all one day in heaven realize ways in which we got some things about it wrong.

So then, concerning the timing, we know that there will be a three-and-a-half-year period of time in which the Gentiles will be stomping all over Jerusalem. We know that God will have two witnesses to stand up during that time and have their say. And we believe that will be the first half of the Tribulation Period during which all this will take place.

So now, let's begin to look at the preaching of the two witnesses.

Revelation 11:3a *And I will give power unto my two witnesses, and they shall prophesy a thousand two hundred and threescore days...*

Notice that these witnesses know exactly how long they are going to be allowed to preach, 1,260 days. What a luxury that would be! Can you imagine what your last message could be like if you were chafed from years of putting up with obstinate church folks? "You know, most of you are just buzzards. You, you're a gossip. And you, you sing terrible!" In seriousness, though, these men will be on the clock. They will not have forever to do a work for God; they will not even have a long time; they will have just three and a half years. None of us really have a long time, so we all need to be busy about the Master's business.

Notice also that in a day when what preachers there are will all be on the payroll of the Antichrist, these two are empowered by God. In any age, real preachers better be empowered by God but especially during times of trial and tribulation.

Their presentation

Revelation 11:3b *...clothed in sackcloth.*

Sackcloth was a rough, coarse, itchy fabric that people wore during times of great mourning. These two men will not be wearing Dolce suits, Rolex watches, and Louis Vuitton Shoes. They will wear clothing that indicates their anguish over what the world has become by rejecting God.

They will not be responsible for the world's behavior, but they will be broken-hearted over it nonetheless because the things that hurt God hurt them also. Christians in general and preachers in particular should never give the appearance of tolerating evil. Everything about us should indicate our disapproval of it. These two preachers, just by the clothes they wear, will irritate the wicked world to no end.

Their procession

Revelation 11:4 *These are the two olive trees, and the two candlesticks standing before the God of the earth.*

Thus far, everything that we have read in chapter eleven is very literal, with no symbolism whatsoever. But as we arrive in verse four, we find a very clear example of symbolism being used. Two very literal men are now being described as olive trees and candlesticks. And there is a very good reason why God chooses to utilize that symbolism of these men. I will show you that in just a moment.

Where did these two come from? For years, people have speculated as to their identity. There are two main views that commonly come up. Many people hold that these two are Elijah and Enoch, since those two never died, and Hebrews 9:27 says that it is appointed unto men once to die. Others say that these two are Moses and Elijah since the miracles they do are similar to the miracles of Moses and Elijah. The truth is, we have no way of knowing for sure who they are. I believe that they are Moses and Elijah since their miracles match so perfectly.

But they may not be Moses, Enoch, or Elijah. We do not know. But though we do not know their identity, we do know their procession. In other words, we know where they came from because they have been mentioned in Scripture before:

Zechariah 4:11 *Then answered I, and said unto him, What are these* **two olive trees** *upon* **the right side of the candlestick and upon the left side** *thereof?* **12** *And I answered again, and said unto him, What be these two olive branches which through the two golden pipes empty the golden oil out of themselves?* **13** *And he answered me and said, Knowest* *thou not what these be? And I said, No, my lord.* **14** *Then said he, These are the two anointed ones, that stand by the Lord of the whole earth.*

These two witnesses, these olive trees and candlesticks, are messengers from God that have spent a lot of time in heaven standing near God. That is all the explanation we need as to how these two men are able to do what they do, standing against the Antichrist, doing miracles, preaching with amazing power. They have been spending a lot of time with God.

I am in favor of working, and I am in favor of serving God with all the strength we have. But truthfully, we can work for the King with every ounce of strength we have, and if we have not been spending time with Him, our efforts will come to nothing.

Think of this: even if these two witnesses have only been standing near God since the days of Zechariah, that means they have already been standing near God for more than 2,500 years now, and the Tribulation Period has not even started yet! Fight the devil with every ounce of strength you have. But you will have a lot more success fighting him if you proceed from the presence of God to do it.

Their protection

Revelation 11:5 *And if any man will hurt them, fire proceedeth out of their mouth, and devoureth their enemies: and if any man will hurt them, he must in this manner be killed.*

There is no reason whatsoever not to take this literally. These two witnesses will not have a church to protect them. They will not have the first or second amendment to protect them. They will not have the police to protect them. Humanly speaking, they are defenseless. I wonder who will be the first person to try and take them out? Who will be the first person who says, "You know what? Go live with this on Facebook; I'm gonna walk right up and smack those preachers right in the mouth..."

It will happen. People will try to hurt and kill them, and their last thought will be, "They can breathe fire!"

God gives this power to them. God protects His men.

Throughout the years, God has sometimes allowed His men to die for the cause of Christ, and He has sometimes protected them by taking the lives of those who come against them. There is no way to tell what choice God is going to make on this at any given time. You might be able to come against a true man of God and live through it. Or you might come against the man of God and find yourself somehow being destroyed by God. This seems like a very foolish choice, then, and better avoided.

Their power

Revelation 11:6 *These have power to shut heaven, that it rain not in the days of their prophecy: and have power over waters to turn them to blood, and to smite the earth with all plagues, as often as they will.*

This also is absolutely literal. These two preachers, in between messages, are wrecking the Antichrist's little utopia. Every time he talks about how wonderful his world is, these two make the rain stop or turn the waters to blood. During the "Antichrist is great" parade, they turn the dust to lice and make people run screaming for the hills. They can do whatever they want, whenever they want to do it.

Their pain

Revelation 11:7 *And when they shall have finished their testimony, the beast that ascendeth out of the bottomless pit shall make war against them, and shall overcome them, and kill them.* **8** *And their dead bodies shall lie in the street of the great city, which spiritually is called Sodom and Egypt, where also our Lord was crucified.* **9** *And they of the people and kindreds and tongues and nations shall see their dead bodies three days and an half, and shall not suffer their dead bodies to be put in graves.* **10** *And they that dwell upon the earth shall rejoice over them, and make merry, and shall send gifts one to another; because these two prophets tormented them that dwelt on the earth.*

At the midpoint of the Tribulation Period, after these men have preached for forty-two months, we are told that "the beast" that comes up out of the bottomless pit will come against them.

There are several different creatures, individuals, and entities in the book of the Revelation referred to as beasts. We have already seen that word used four times in chapter four and three times in chapter six, referring to the beasts before the throne in heaven. But there is something very interesting you should know at this point. The word for those beasts was *zo-on*; we get our word zoology from it. It indicates a living creature, part of God's organized, special order.

But after those first seven mentions of the word beast in the book of The Revelation, the word beast will be mentioned thirty-seven more times, and not one of them comes from that word. All of them come from a very different word, the word *thayrion*. And that word for beast means a wild animal.

The beasts we saw in heaven are "domesticated to God." They always do His bidding. All the other beasts in the book of Revelation are wild animals; they are rabid and mangy and vicious curs who only do their own bidding.

This particular beast that comes against the two witnesses is the Antichrist. Once they are finished with their ministry and preaching, but not one second before, the Antichrist will be allowed to kill the two witnesses. They will center their preaching in Jerusalem, and then they will die in Jerusalem.

Look again in verse eight at what God calls this city that He has loved so dearly. He calls it Sodom, and Egypt. That is very literally as low as you can go in God's sight. But it is a deserved epithet. Once more prophets are being sent to Jerusalem, and once more, prophets are dying in Jerusalem. They did not hesitate to kill Jesus; they will not hesitate to help the Antichrist kill these two prophets.

For three and a half years, the entire world will watch and hate these two preachers. The entire world will watch and celebrate as these two lay dead and decaying for three and a half days, unburied, in the streets of Jerusalem. Scripture makes that abundantly clear. And for a very long time, people mocked and scoffed at Scripture because of this, regarding it as an absolute impossibility.

And as you are reading this book, you have proof in your hand or pocket or pocketbook that they were wrong.

Everyone everywhere across the world will be able to pull their smartphones out and watch every bit of this happening in real time. And God knew that thousands of years before it even became a possibility. This murder of the two witnesses will be on NBC and CNN, and CBS and Fox, and ABC and Al Jazeera. This will be the tv event of the century. Every ounce of pain for these two men will be covered up close, telephoto lens, as the world streams it live. Antichrist will celebrate, the devil will laugh, the world will cheer. They will not even give these two men the dignity of being buried, they will simply let their bodies lay in the street and rot for three and a half days, and across the world, people will send friends and family members gifts like this is some kind of a satanic Christmas that they are all celebrating.

Their prevailing

Revelation 11:11 *And after three days and an half the Spirit of life from God entered into them, and they stood upon their feet; and great fear fell upon them which saw them.* **12** *And they heard a great voice from heaven saying unto them, Come up hither. And they ascended up to heaven in a cloud; and their enemies beheld them.* **13** *And the same hour was there a great earthquake, and the tenth part of the city fell, and in the earthquake were slain of men seven thousand: and the remnant were affrighted, and gave glory to the God of heaven.* **14** *The second woe is past; and, behold, the third woe cometh quickly.*

This is going to be one of the most remarkable miracles of all time. There will be no chance of this being staged, and the world will know it. These witnesses will be dead and rotting in the streets for three and a half days and then simply come back to life, stand up, and brush themselves off. And then the world hears, and the cameras' mics record, a great voice from heaven calling them home. The world then watches as they ascend up into heaven in a cloud.

And at that very moment, because God's timing is always perfect, there is a great earthquake. A tenth of Jerusalem is destroyed, 7,000 men die, and the rest are scared into giving lip-service praise to God. The second woe, the sounding of the sixth angel, has past, and one more angel is about to sound very quickly.

Yes, this all takes place during the Tribulation Period. But it is not just prophecy; it is also valuable teaching for today. It reminds us that there is nothing better you can ever be than a witness for God, even if the world hates and persecutes you for it. Remember, the world will not even be around to persecute you for very long, but God will be around to reward you for all eternity.

Chapter Twenty-Four
Capital G

Revelation 11:15 *And the seventh angel sounded; and there were great voices in heaven, saying, The kingdoms of this world are become the kingdoms of our Lord, and of his Christ; and he shall reign for ever and ever.* **16** *And the four and twenty elders, which sat before God on their seats, fell upon their faces, and worshipped God,* **17** *Saying, We give thee thanks, O Lord God Almighty, which art, and wast, and art to come; because thou hast taken to thee thy great power, and hast reigned.* **18** *And the nations were angry, and thy wrath is come, and the time of the dead, that they should be judged, and that thou shouldest give reward unto thy servants the prophets, and to the saints, and them that fear thy name, small and great; and shouldest destroy them which destroy the earth.* **19** *And the temple of God was opened in heaven, and there was seen in his temple the ark of his testament: and there were lightnings, and voices, and thunderings, and an earthquake, and great hail.*

In the last section of verses, we looked at the two witnesses who will drive the Antichrist insane for three and a half years during the Tribulation Period. These two men will preach, strike the earth with plagues, and breathe fire on anyone who comes against them. But when their ministry is done, the devil will be allowed to kill them. The wicked world will watch it, live on tv and on their devices, and party like crazy. They will even send each other gifts to celebrate the death of these two preachers! But after three and a half days, the world will see them come back to life and be called up into heaven. God will then strike Jerusalem with an earthquake, and seven thousand men will die.

That point in time marks something very unique. It marks the time that the devil's reign as the god of this world, little g, will begin to come to an end. We will see that in verses fifteen through nineteen. You see, this world does have a "god" right now:

2 Corinthians 4:4 *In whom the god of this world hath blinded the minds of them which believe not, lest the light of the glorious gospel of Christ, who is the image of God, should shine unto them.*

The devil has been the god of this world, little g, for nearly six thousand years. He has, at least in a measure, had the right to do as he has pleased with the world of men, even right down to keeping it or giving it away. He said so, and the Lord did not disagree with him:

Matthew 4:8 *Again, the devil taketh him up into an exceeding high mountain, and sheweth him all the kingdoms of the world, and the* *glory of them;* **9** *And saith unto him, All these things will I give thee, if thou wilt fall down and worship me.*

Jesus disagreed with Satan on most everything he said, except for this. As the god of this world, little g, the devil has had this world for the most part in the grip of evil. When men get saved, they are released from that bondage. But most of the world is lost and, therefore, in the grip of the devil himself. But there will come a day Capital G grabs little g by the wrist and one by one pries all of his filthy fingers off of the world.

A ruling promise

Revelation 11:15 *And the seventh angel sounded; and there were great voices in heaven, saying, The kingdoms of this world are become the kingdoms of our Lord, and of his Christ; and he shall reign for ever and ever.*

By this point in the book of The Revelation, seven seals have been opened, each one unleashing a judgment of God on earth. Six trumpets have been sounded, each one unleashing a judgment of God on earth. In chapter 10, we saw a mighty angel come down from heaven and put a foot on the land and a foot on the sea. That angel declared that the seventh trumpet would be sounding soon and that when it did, time would begin to come to an end. Here in Revelation 11, that trumpet actually sounds, and it unleashes a judgment of God also. The judgment, in this case, is that the world of wicked men is about to be ruled over by God, and in very short order, there will not be any wickedness anymore.

When this seventh angel sounds, it is followed by another sound. Great voices, loud and powerful, ring out through heaven in unison. Notice what those voices say together:

...The kingdoms of this world are become the kingdoms of our Lord, and of his Christ; and he shall reign for ever and ever.

Notice what facts these voices give testimony to.

<u>The kingdoms of this world have not been, before this point, the kingdoms of Christ.</u>

This should not come as a surprise to anyone who actually pays attention to the kingdoms of this world. The kingdoms of this world murder babies under the banner of choice, express pride in what God calls abomination, hate the nuclear family that God so prizes, loathes the Bible because of the truth it tells, and would crucify Jesus all over again if they could.

This world will, when the seventh trumpet sounds, become the kingdoms of God the Father and God the Son.

The devil can read as well as we can. He has doubtless read God's Word many times. He knows that when the trumpets begin to sound, his time in charge is coming to an end. He knows that when the seventh trumpet sounds, he will lose his grip, and even though there will still be wicked men on earth, Capital G will be in charge.

I am very much looking forward to little g losing his grip.

The devil's reign has been temporary, but God's reign will be forever.

Have you ever stopped to think that God created the earth about 6,000 years ago and that for probably 5,999 of those years, little g has been exercising power in the world of men? He must be very proud to be the god of this world, little g. He must be very proud that he has had nearly 6,000 years of power. But his reign is only temporary. When the kingdoms of this world become the kingdoms of Christ, they will never ever go back!

A regal praise

Revelation 11:16 *And the four and twenty elders, which sat before God on their seats, fell upon their faces, and worshipped God,* **17** *Saying, We give thee thanks, O Lord God Almighty, which art, and wast, and art to come; because thou hast taken to thee thy great power, and hast reigned.*

The elders that we have seen since early in the book fall down on their faces to worship God. This is the fifth time in the book that they do this, and they will do it for a sixth time in chapter nineteen. There is something to be said for worship!

In their worship, these elders are giving thanks. Worship and thanks are inseparable. And they are specifically thanking the one who is, and was, and is to come, Jesus.

Notice what they are giving thanks for. They are giving God thanks because he has *taken* His power to Him. That word is a word of power, and it means to take by force! Little g has no intentions of letting go. But capital G does not care about how hard the devil holds on. He is going to take the kingdoms of the world to Himself, and there is not one thing little g can do about it! The elders say that He, Jesus, "has reigned." And that is said in such a way as to indicate a done deal, something that was never really in doubt.

We may sometimes doubt it, but there has never really been a doubt about it.

The elders see this, and they cannot help but praise their King for it. There is something so nice about praising a winner!

In our world, we try to be so nice; we even praise losers because they "tried hard." People today praise winners, losers, everyone. And I do understand and appreciate the concept of kindness and graciousness. But it is going to be very nice to be a part of the scene in heaven when the elders praise God for beating the stuffing out of the devil.

A righteous pronouncement

Revelation 11:18 *And the nations were angry, and thy wrath is come, and the time of the dead, that they should be judged, and that thou shouldest give reward unto thy servants the prophets, and to the saints, and them that fear thy name, small and great; and shouldest destroy them which destroy the earth.*

The elders are still speaking here. They are still talking about Capital G ripping the world away from little g. This entire verse is one sentence, and it is a multi-part righteous pronouncement about what is happening as God takes control of the world.

<u>The nations were angry about it.</u>

Here is the wonderful part. They are angry about it, but that does not change one thing! The world can hate the idea all they want. The world would rather have the devil in charge than to have God in charge. They would rather the world be filled with sin than filled with righteousness. They hate the very thought of Capital G being in charge instead of little g, but there is nothing they can do about it!

<u>The time of God's wrath is come.</u>

If you think God has poured out His anger before this time, you have not seen anything yet. When God has finally had enough, His anger will be enough to make the devil bow in fear.

<u>The time that God will hand out rewards to His own is come.</u>

God is in the habit of rewarding His own, and that is not just limited to the judgment seat of Christ. When God takes charge of the world, He is going to reward those who have been faithful to Him even while the god of this world, little g, has been exercising power.

It is easy to do right when you are in the majority, and your side is winning. But the greatest rewards are for those who do right even when they are in the minority, and it seems like their side is losing! When you look around today, you will see quickly that we are swimming against the tide. Keep swimming; reward day is coming.

<u>The time that God will destroy those who are destroying the earth is come.</u>

I know radical environmentalists love the sound of this. They are convinced that evil capitalists and industrialized nations and big corporations are destroying the earth. I hate to break it to them, but those things do not even show up on God's radar. Those things are not what or who destroys the earth. Ever since the garden of Eden, it has been sin that has destroyed the earth. Man's sin makes the creation groan. This world is waiting for God to redeem it from the curse of sin that we have subjected it to.

When God rips the world away from the devil, He is going to clean house. Every pervert, every child molester, every thief, every abortionist, every pornographer, every adulterer, every wicked man will face the very wrath of God. God will destroy them because they are destroying the earth. That was the righteous pronouncement of the twenty-four elders.

A revealed power

Revelation 11:19 *And the temple of God was opened in heaven, and there was seen in his temple the ark of his testament: and there were lightnings, and voices, and thunderings, and an earthquake, and great hail.*

According to Hebrews 8:1-5, the earthly tabernacle and furniture that the children of Israel made was simply a pattern of the real tabernacle and furniture in heaven. It has been in heaven, veiled and unrevealed, from eternity past. But as God begins to rip the world away from the devil, he will open that heavenly tabernacle to give us a glimpse. He does so to let us notice at least two things:

The real Ark of the Covenant is there.

If there was any one thing on earth that symbolized the authority of God, it was the Ark of the Covenant. When the children of Israel took it into battle, the Philistines were scared to death because they knew what it was and the power associated with it.

When Capital G rips the world away from little g, He will show us again the symbol of His absolute authority and power. This will not be a coup; it will be God taking back what is rightfully His. That Ark is a reminder that He is absolutely in charge and that even while the devil has been the god of this world, he has done so only because God has allowed it! The devil has no Ark of the Covenant, he has no inherent authority, God has allowed him to roam, but he has always been on a leash. He has roared like a lion, but he is a mouse compared to the Lion of the tribe of Judah!

<u>The authority of God in heaven has effects on earth.</u>

When the heavenly tabernacle is opened, earth hears voices and thunder, sees lightnings, and experiences great hail and an earthquake. The authority of God unveiled to a wicked world, will shake earth to its foundation and will shake the devil like a leaf in the wind.

For 6,000 years, the devil has been parading around like a pompous peacock, strutting and clucking and laying rotten eggs all over the place. He has worn his paper crown, lorded over his pathetic domain, and wrecked the lives of his own servants. He has pretended to be God of all when he is nothing but a little g. But when God gets good and ready, when that seventh trumpet sounds, He will grab the devil by his scrawny neck and shake him like a chicken. He will rip the world from his slimy fingers and cast the devil aside like a cheap rag doll. I'm glad that of the two g's I could have followed, I have gotten to follow Capital G instead of little g. Which g are you following?

Chapter Twenty-Five
The Devil's Tale

Revelation 12:1 *And there appeared a great wonder in heaven; a woman clothed with the sun, and the moon under her feet, and upon her head a crown of twelve stars:* **2** *And she being with child cried, travailing in birth, and pained to be delivered.* **3** *And there appeared another wonder in heaven; and behold a great red dragon, having seven heads and ten horns, and seven crowns upon his heads.* **4** *And his tail drew the third part of the stars of heaven, and did cast them to the earth: and the dragon stood before the woman which was ready to be delivered, for to devour her child as soon as it was born.* **5** *And she brought forth a man child, who was to rule all nations with a rod of iron: and her child was caught up unto God, and to his throne.* **6** *And the woman fled into the wilderness, where she hath a place prepared of God, that they should feed her there a thousand two hundred and threescore days.* **7** *And there was war in heaven: Michael and his angels fought against the dragon; and the dragon fought and his angels,* **8** *And prevailed not; neither was their place found any more in heaven.* **9** *And the great dragon was cast out, that old serpent, called the Devil, and Satan, which deceiveth the whole world: he was cast out into the earth, and his angels were cast out with him.*

In 2001, the name Osama bin Laden became famous. And in just the few short years since then, almost everyone learned a great deal about him. We learned that he was 6'5". We learned that he was a billionaire. We learned that he was kicked out of Saudi Arabia. We learned that two years before 9-11, President Clinton had a chance to take him out and decided not to. We learned that he had a beard, walked with a cane, and was hiding somewhere in Afghanistan. We learned that his second in command was a man named Ayman-Al-Zawahiri. We learned that he headed a group named Al-Qaeda. He had only been in the public consciousness for a few short years, and we already knew all this about him.

Now, contrast that with the devil. He has been around for at least six thousand years. He has killed far more people and done far more damage than Osama bin Laden could have ever hoped to do. Yet despite that, most people in the world know far more about Osama bin Laden than they do about the devil. I may not be able to change that around the world, but I certainly hope I can change that for you, my readers. You know Osama bin Laden's tale, but I want to take the chapter and tell you what this portion of scripture talks about, and we will call this section of verses *The Devil's Tale*, T A L E, not tail. His fictitious red pointy tail is not anything for us to concern ourselves with, but his very real tale of thousands of years of rebellion and destruction most certainly is.

Through the first eleven chapters of the book of The Revelation, most of what we have seen has been miraculous and spectacular, but very much literal. But as chapter twelve begins, we are getting into a section of the book that contains a great deal of symbolism. This section is God painting a picture for John to give to us, and it will deal with the far distant past all the way up into the not-so-distant future.

The setting

Revelation 12:1 *And there appeared a great wonder in heaven; a woman clothed with the sun, and the moon under her feet, and upon her head a crown of twelve stars:* **2** *And she being with child cried, travailing in birth, and pained to be delivered.*

As God began to reveal the devil's tale to John, He started by showing John a vision of a woman. That word "wonder" lets us know that we are viewing something symbolic; it means "a sign." As John looked on, the sky itself became the backdrop for a vision of a woman clothed with the sun, with the moon under her feet, and wearing a crown of twelve stars. Even without the word "wonder," it would be pretty easy just from the description to figure out that God is laying out a dose of symbolism for us.

So what does all of this mean?

This woman represents God's chosen people, the nation of Israel.

Always let Scripture interpret Scripture. These symbols have been seen once before in Scripture when a young man named Joseph was having some dreams that got his family pretty upset:

Genesis 37:5 *And Joseph dreamed a dream, and he told it his brethren: and they hated him yet the more.* **6** *And he said unto them, Hear, I pray you, this dream which I have dreamed:* **7** *For, behold, we were binding sheaves in the field, and, lo, my sheaf arose, and also stood upright; and, behold, your sheaves stood round about, and made obeisance to my sheaf.* **8** *And his brethren said to him, Shalt thou indeed reign over us? or shalt thou indeed have dominion over us? And they hated him yet the more for his dreams, and for his words.* **9** *And he dreamed yet another dream, and told it his brethren, and said, Behold, I have dreamed a dream more; and, behold, the sun and the moon and the eleven stars made obeisance to me.* **10** *And he told it to his father, and to his brethren: and his father rebuked him, and said unto him, What is this dream that thou hast dreamed? Shall I* **(The sun)** *and thy mother* **(The**

moon) *and thy brethren* **(along with Joseph, the twelve stars)** *indeed come to bow down ourselves to thee to the earth?*

This family was the beginning of the nation of Israel. Abraham had Isaac, but one child does not really start a nation. Isaac had Jacob, but one child does not start a nation. But Jacob had twelve boys, and those twelve boys started a nation of twelve tribes. Daddy Jacob is the sun of Genesis 37 and Revelation 12. Mama Rachel, Joseph and Benjamin's mother, and Jacob's favorite wife, is the moon of Genesis 37 and Revelation 12, although Leah and the two handmaids, Bilhah and Zilpah, can also conceivably be included since they also gave birth to some of those boys and tribes, and the twelve boys are the twelve stars of Genesis 37 and Revelation 12. So as God began to tell the devil's tale, He started by telling us about the nation of Israel. You see, the Savior of the world, the devil's greatest enemy, Jesus the Son of God, was going to be born into the nation of Israel. Because of that, the devil and the devil's people have always hated the Jews. In fact, that is a pretty good way to tell the devil's people. No matter how piously and polished they talk, if they hate the Jews, they are marking themselves as the devil's crowd. That takes in a great deal of the Middle East and a great deal of the political and academic class in America.

But this woman, this nation, is precious to God. If you are against her, you are against Him!

The second thing we find in the vision concerning this woman is that she gave birth to an important child:

Revelation 12:2 *And she being with child cried, travailing in birth, and pained to be delivered.*

Remember that the "she" here represents a nation, not a single person. Yes, a single person, Mary, gave birth to Jesus. But this was not just a birth to a person; it was a birth to a nation. Jesus did not just come for His mother; He came for His people, Israel:

Matthew 15:24 *But he answered and said, I am not sent but unto the lost sheep of the house of Israel.*

Jesus died for all the world, Jew and Gentile. But the first people He offered Himself to was His own people, the Jews. It was the Jewish nation that gave Him birth, He loved them, and because He loved and loves them, the devil hates them.

Before we go on to the next point, I want to point out that these first two verses are in chronological order. Israel came into being, and then she produced a child, Jesus. That these verses and the following related verses in this chapter are in chronological order will become important as we look at a matter of timing in the next few verses.

The sin

Revelation 12:3 *And there appeared another wonder in heaven; and behold a great red dragon, having seven heads and ten horns, and seven crowns upon his heads.* **4a** *And his tail drew the third part of the stars of heaven, and did cast them to the earth...*

John saw the first wonder, a woman clothed with the sun, the moon under her feet, a crown of twelve stars on her head, Israel. But then God showed him a second wonder, a great red dragon. The dragon represents God's bitter enemy, the devil himself.

What you saw concerning the vision of the woman will help guide your understanding concerning what you see here. The description of the woman began with how she was a long time ago when she first became a nation. What you see here concerning the dragon shows you how he was a long time ago, when he first became the enemy of God. When you read books or commentaries about this text, you will almost always see them compare this passage to a couple of others in the book of The Revelation. But if you will look at those passages, though there are some similarities, you will also notice some very clear differences:

Revelation 13:1 *And I stood upon the sand of the sea, and saw a beast rise up out of the sea, having seven heads and ten horns, and upon his horns ten crowns, and upon his heads the name of blasphemy.*

Revelation 12:3 and 13:1 sound like they might be talking about the same thing. Many reference works say that they are. But look carefully at some of the details that undermine that view.

Revelation 12:3 and 13:1 both have a creature with seven heads. Both also have a creature with ten horns. But there are seven crowns on the head of the creature in Revelation 12:3, but ten on the head of the creature in Revelation 13:1. That is close, but not the same!

Now look at the second passage that 12:3 is often compared to:

Revelation 17:3 *So he carried me away in the spirit into the wilderness: and I saw a woman sit upon a scarlet coloured beast, full of names of blasphemy, having seven heads and ten horns.*

Revelation 17:12 *And the ten horns which thou sawest are ten kings, which have received no kingdom as yet; but receive power as kings one hour with the beast.*

Revelation 12 and 17 both have their creature with seven heads. Both have their creature with ten horns. But the creature of Revelation 12 has ten crowns, and the creature of Revelation 17 is never mentioned as having any crowns. So again, all of these are similar, but the creature of Revelation 12 does not deal with the devil in recorded history on earth or even with his Antichrist. It deals with him, the devil, in a rebellion in heaven not too long after time began.

When the devil rebelled against God, we are shown clearly his motives and behavior from Isaiah 14 and Ezekiel 28. But we are not given very many details as to those he seduced to rebel along with him. Those details are given to us here in Revelation 12:

Revelation 12:3 *And there appeared another wonder in heaven; and behold a great red dragon, having seven heads and ten horns, and seven crowns upon his heads.* **4a** *And his tail drew the third part of the stars of heaven, and did cast them to the earth...*

All through Scripture, and especially here in the book of The Revelation, heads and horns and crowns are symbols of powerful rulers. The devil was the greatest, most powerful of all beings that God created. He had great ruling authority. And when he rebelled against God, he was so persuasive that he apparently managed to lure at least twenty-four powerful angels from three different ranks to go along with him. Seven heads, ten horns, seven crowns, twenty-four in all. Some of them are actually named and shown in Scripture. For instance:

Daniel 10:13 *But the prince of the kingdom of Persia withstood me one and twenty days: but, lo, Michael, one of the chief princes, came to help me; and I remained there with the kings of Persia.*

Daniel 10:20 *Then said he, Knowest thou wherefore I come unto thee? and now will I return to fight with the prince of Persia: and when I am gone forth, lo, the prince of Grecia shall come.* **21** *But I will shew thee that which is noted in the scripture of truth: and there is none that holdeth with me in these things, but Michael your prince.*

This was an angel talking to Daniel. When Daniel prayed, this angel set out to bring an answer to him, and a demonic power, the prince of Persia, tried to stop him. Michael the archangel had to come in to help the first angel get through. And the prince of Persia had a buddy, another demon, the prince of Grecia.

Notice that these "big boys" were not concerned with small fries. They were over powerful nations, pushing them toward evil. So often, we act as if the greatest demons of hell are fighting against us. I doubt it. The greatest demons of hell are demonic lords over America, Russia, Germany, China, etc. We probably do not even rate Henry the god of hemorrhoids, if we are to be honest.

When the devil rebelled, these mighty angels rebelled with him. But in verse four, we find that his tail also drew a third of the stars of heaven with him. In Job 38:7, we find the term stars used to describe the angels of heaven. So when the devil sinned, he did not just convince twenty-four mighty angels to come along with him; he also seduced a third of all of the rank-and-file angels of God! Demons used to be angels:

Matthew 25:41 *Then shall he say also unto them on the left hand, Depart from me, ye cursed, into everlasting fire, prepared for the devil and his angels:*

All angels used to be God's angels, but now a third of them are the devil's angels.

Just think of this. Think of the magnitude of this sin. The devil had everything he ever deserved and more. He was created beautiful. He was powerful, respected, musical, and he got to live in heaven. He was near to the throne of God. And yet all of that was not enough. He just could not be satisfied with what God had given him. He just could not resist getting all puffed up in pride and deciding he deserved more.

How wicked! How wicked to receive God's very best and decide that it is not enough!

But isn't that what we do? God has given us His Son... He has given us the Bible... He has given us life... He has given us family... He has allowed us to be born in the land of the free... and yet it never seems to be enough. It seems like we are always looking up at God and complaining that He is not being good to us. We are rebelling in our hearts, we are making aggressive moves toward the throne, and when we do this, when we get dissatisfied, our rebellion will draw away a few very big people, and a whole lot of everyday people, into a rebellion against God. Do not ever forget how good God has been to you, and do not ever forget how many people are going to be hurt when you develop and nurture an ungrateful attitude.

The second attempt

Revelation 12:4b *...and the dragon stood before the woman which was ready to be delivered, for to devour her child as soon as it was born.* **5** *And she brought forth a man child, who was to rule all nations with a rod of iron: and her child was caught up unto God, and to his throne.* **6** *And the woman fled into the wilderness, where she hath a place prepared of God, that they should feed her there a thousand two hundred and threescore days.* **7** *And there was war in heaven: Michael and his angels fought against the dragon; and the dragon fought and his angels,* **8** *And prevailed not; neither was their place found any more in heaven.* **9** *And the great dragon was cast out, that old serpent, called the Devil, and Satan, which deceiveth the whole world: he was cast out into the earth, and his angels were cast out with him.*

We see from the first few verses in this chapter and from Isaiah 14 and Ezekiel 28 that the devil lost his first battle against God, and he lost big. He got kicked out of heaven. His twenty-four big-shot demons got kicked out of heaven. His multitude, the one-third of God's angels who rebelled with him, got kicked out of heaven. That should have been enough. That should have had him waving the white flag. But unfortunately, he was far too stubborn to do that. And from the moment his clawed feet hit the ground until the end of time as recorded here in the book of the Revelation, he has been engaged in one long second attempt to defeat God.

He tried to destroy Jesus when He was born in the flesh:

Revelation 12:4b *...and the dragon stood before the woman which was ready to be delivered, for to devour her child as soon as it was born.*

The devil was right there waiting, lurking, hoping to destroy Jesus as soon as he was born. Does that sound familiar? Does the name Herod ring a bell? If you have ever wondered how Herod could possibly be so brutal, so heartless, so cold, so violent as to kill babies en-mass just to make sure he killed Jesus in with all the others, now you know. Herod was literally possessed by the devil himself. Every time he breathed, the sulfur of hell was coming out of his mouth. He was crazed, maddened, insane from having Satan himself living in his body. If Herod could have gotten to baby Jesus, he would have strangled Him with his own hands because the talons of the devil were inside the skin of his fingers.

The devil should have known better. He lost once, and his losing streak was going to continue.

Revelation 12:5 *And she brought forth a man child, who was to rule all nations with a rod of iron: and her child was caught up unto God, and to his throne.*

In thirty words, this one verse summarizes the entire thirty-three-year life and ministry of Jesus and more. The devil was waiting right there to destroy Jesus upon His birth, yet Jesus was born, lived, died, was resurrected, ascended into heaven, and will return one day to rule the world as King of kings.

He will try to destroy God's people, Israel, during the Tribulation Period:

Revelation 12:6 *And the woman fled into the wilderness, where she hath a place prepared of God, that they should feed her there a thousand two hundred and threescore days.*

Please notice that there is already nearly a 2,000-year gap between verses five and six. Verse five ended with Jesus ascending into heaven, and verse six begins with Israel having to flee to the wilderness from the wrath of the devil during the Tribulation, where she will be protected and fed. The devil is many things, but he is not a quitter. He hates God, he hates the church, and he hates Israel. For nearly two thousand years, while Israel has been just a persecuted remnant, he has focused his hatred on the church. But when the church leaves via the Rapture, he will turn his attention to Israel again.

Please remember that our calendar has three hundred sixty-five days. But much of the ancient world used a calendar of only three hundred sixty days. In Genesis 7-8, the account of Noah's flood, a period of exactly five months, starting and ending on the same day of the month, was one hundred fifty days, or five months of thirty days. Prophecy in the Bible is based on that three hundred sixty-day view of the year. So, this 1,260 days that keeps popping up in the book of the Revelation equals three and a half years on their calendar. For three and a half years, the first half of the Tribulation Period, even while the worldwide peace treaty is in place, even while the world media talks about how wonderfully Antichrist is treating Israel, he will be coming after them, and many of them will have to flee into the wilderness to survive. The outcome to this attack is given later on in the book, and this part of the devil's second attempt will fail just like the first.

And now, let me deal with that matter of timing I alluded to earlier. When I say that this particular three-and-a-half-year period is the first three and a half years of the Tribulation Period, I do so because of the consistent chronological order of this chapter. Just like the verses concerning Israel and Jesus were clearly chronological, the verses about the dragon and Israel are too. In verses three and the beginning of verse four, we see his rebellion in heaven at the very beginning of time. At the end of verse four, we see his attempt to destroy Jesus at His birth. In verse five, we see Jesus' birth and then His ascension back into heaven. In verse six, we see what we are currently examining, the three-and-a-half-year period during the Tribulation when Israel will have to flee into the wilderness because of Satan trying to destroy her. In verses seven and eight, we find Satan's second attempt to overthrow God as he and his forces charge heaven again. In verse nine, we find him losing that battle and being cast out of heaven yet again. And then, in verse thirteen, we see that because he has been cast out, he is angry and goes after Israel yet again. And then, in verse fourteen, we find that once more she has to flee to the wilderness to escape. All of that is clearly in chronological order.

In other words, both at the beginning of the first half of the Tribulation Period and at the beginning of the second half of the Tribulation period, there will be a concerted effort by Satan to destroy the Jews. Both times they will run into the wilderness for safety. These two similar events are two distinct events, not two descriptions of the same event.

He will invade heaven for one more celestial battle:

Revelation 12:7 *And there was war in heaven: Michael and his angels fought against the dragon; and the dragon fought and his angels,* **8** *And prevailed not; neither was their place found any more in heaven.* **9** *And the great dragon was cast out, that old serpent, called the Devil, and Satan, which deceiveth the whole world: he was cast out into the earth, and his angels were cast out with him.*

This is the culmination of the second attempt Lucifer, Satan, makes to overthrow God. Just imagine this, let your mind wrap around it. Six thousand years before this time, the devil was an unsatisfied angel, lifted up in pride. He led a rebellion against God and lost. For 6,000 years, he has been merely an occasional, invited, enemy guest in heaven. He has been allowed access into heaven just to give account of himself and accuse the brethren. But there will come a day, not too long from now, when the devil gathers his forces again. For all these centuries, there have been demons running around everywhere, doing what to them are insignificant little things. They have been pushing pornography, brewing beer, causing men to lust after other men and women to lust after women. They have been stirring up gossip and working to split churches and giving clothing designers ideas for more and more immodest clothing as the years go by. These things are so huge to us but so insignificant by their standards. They have simply been biding their time, waiting for the summons to come from their leader, the devil. They have been gnashing their teeth for another all-out assault on the throne room of God, and at the mid-way point of the Tribulation Period, when the devil's Antichrist is at the height of his power, the call for the assault will come. Demonic wings will drone, sulfurous breath will fill the air, satanic screams will pierce the ears, and untold millions of fallen angels will rocket towards heaven.

Their coming will be expected. Michael the archangel, Michael who used to be second in command to Lucifer among the ranks of angels, will be waiting at the gates. Behind him will be stretched out all of the ranks of the unfallen angels.

This is fascinating to consider: if He wanted to, God could simply speak the word, the devil would be defeated, and there would not have to be a fight in heaven. But God will actually let this battle take place. He will allow war to take place in heaven. Angels and demons will collide. Wings and talons will be severed. There will be screaming, rage, swords clashing, flashes of light, black clouds of sulfur. Somewhere through it all, you know that the two commanders will meet. Imagine when Michael and Satan spin to face their next opponent—and find themselves staring at each other. They used to worship God together.

They used to be so close. And now they find themselves on totally opposite sides—Michael leading the forces of light and Satan leading the forces of darkness. Imagine the power, the very ground of heaven shaking as their swords meet. There has never, ever, been a battle like this one. Maybe everything around them continues to rage, but I doubt it. I have to believe that when these two finally meet, everyone around them steps back to watch...

One way or the other, the devil and his demons soon find themselves looking at a very familiar outcome:

Revelation 12:8 *And prevailed not; neither was their place found any more in heaven.* **9** *And the great dragon was cast out, that old serpent, called the Devil, and Satan, which deceiveth the whole world: he was cast out into the earth, and his angels were cast out with him.*

He is a great dragon. He is the serpent. He is the devil. He is Satan. He is the deceiver of the whole world. But he is, above all, a loser. He cannot win because of the opponent he has chosen! Our God is greater, the angels of our God are greater, the blood of our God is greater, the word of our God is greater, the Son of our God is greater, Jesus wins! If you want to know the end of the devil's tale, it is found in those two words, Jesus wins.

For those who are lost, I have a question. The devil is going to lose, Jesus is going to win, why would you continue to pick the wrong side?

For the saved, I also have a question. Why so glum? Why so dreary? Our side wins!

Chapter Twenty-Six
History's Biggest Failure

Revelation 12:10 *And I heard a loud voice saying in heaven, Now is come salvation, and strength, and the kingdom of our God, and the power of his Christ: for the accuser of our brethren is cast down, which accused them before our God day and night.* **11** *And they overcame him by the blood of the Lamb, and by the word of their testimony; and they loved not their lives unto the death.* **12** *Therefore rejoice, ye heavens, and ye that dwell in them. Woe to the inhabiters of the earth and of the sea! for the devil is come down unto you, having great wrath, because he knoweth that he hath but a short time.* **13** *And when the dragon saw that he was cast unto the earth, he persecuted the woman which brought forth the man child.* **14** *And to the woman were given two wings of a great eagle, that she might fly into the wilderness, into her place, where she is nourished for a time, and times, and half a time, from the face of the serpent.* **15** *And the serpent cast out of his mouth water as a flood after the woman, that he might cause her to be carried away of the flood.* **16** *And the earth helped the woman, and the earth opened her mouth, and swallowed up the flood which the dragon cast out of his mouth.* **17** *And the dragon was wroth with the woman, and went to make war with the remnant of her seed, which keep the commandments of God, and have the testimony of Jesus Christ.*

In the previous chapter, we looked at "The Devil's Tale." We examined verses one through nine, and we saw first of all the setting of the devil's tale in verses one and two of that. That setting dealt with Israel, God's love for her, and the devil's hatred for her.

We saw, secondly, in verses three through the first part of verse four, the sin of the devil's tale. Those verses reminded us of the devil's first rebellion against God, when he led one-third of the angels of glory in a rebellion against God Himself and was cast out of heaven.

The end of verse four through verse nine let us see the second attempt of the devil, the 6,000-year battle he has been waging against God on so many fronts, which will end as we read in verse nine with him being kicked out of heaven for the second time.

Up until this point, even though he is thoroughly wicked, Satan has also been subtle, skilled, brilliant, and highly successful. He has taken billions to hell riding on lies. He has convinced countless fools to actually worship him. He has even managed to lead not one but two assaults on heaven itself. He has been quite successful at much of what he has attempted! Because of that, people throughout the ages have often tended to be in awe of him, and I believe have even given him far too much credit. Yes, he is a powerful being. But he is not all-powerful. He is not God. And he will not even end up as a winner. You need to know that Satan is going to end up as History's Biggest Failure.

He will fail in his accusations against the brethren

Revelation 12:9 *And the great dragon was cast out, that old serpent, called the Devil, and Satan, which deceiveth the whole world: he was cast out into the earth, and his angels were cast out with him.* **10** *And I heard a loud voice saying in heaven, Now is come salvation, and strength, and the kingdom of our God, and the power of his Christ: for the accuser of our brethren is cast down, which accused them before our God day and night.* **11** *And they overcame him by the blood of the Lamb, and by the word of their testimony; and they loved not their lives unto the death.* **12** *Therefore rejoice, ye heavens, and ye that dwell in them. Woe to the inhabiters of the earth and of the sea! for the devil is come down unto you, having great wrath, because he knoweth that he hath but a short time.*

We have already looked at the devil's second battle against God in heaven and how he and his angels lost and got kicked out again. Verse ten, though, introduces something new at that point. After Satan and company get kicked out of heaven, a voice will be heard. It is a loud voice, and it is ringing in power throughout heaven:

Revelation 12:10 *And I heard a loud voice saying in heaven, Now is come salvation, and strength, and the kingdom of our God, and the power of his Christ: for the accuser of our brethren is cast down, which accused them before our God day and night.*

There is something tremendously unique that we are made privy to in verse ten. There is a loud voice speaking, and it is neither divine nor angelic; it is human. This voice talks about God the Father and God the Son as if viewing them from a distance. This voice then refers to believers as "our brethren." This is the voice of someone who came to saving faith in God while on this earth.

We are not told who this believer is, but whoever he is, he has been watching all the trials that Christians on earth have been going through, and he comes a bit unglued when he sees the devil finally wrecked. This old saint actually starts to shout about it! He has had quite enough of the devil. He knows some things about the devil that he spells out for us in verse ten.

He knows that the devil is the "accuser of the brethren."

The devil, or at least whatever of his servants he has assigned to you, knows all about you. And if he cannot think of anything bad to say truthfully, he will lie and make something up.

This believer shouting in heaven knows something else as well, according to verse ten:

He knows that being the accuser of the brethren is not a part-time job for the devil; it is his full-time job! He does it day and night.

Sometimes Christians get mopey and whine, "Nobody even knows I exist." Au contraire. The devil knows you very well. And when he takes his reporting trips to heaven, he spends day and night spouting off to God about how rotten you are.

He spends all day and night telling God every time you lose your temper. He spends all day and night telling God every time you are dishonest. He spends all day and night telling God every time you are unfaithful. He spends all day and night telling God and every time you even overeat.

The devil has been doing this for so long. And saints of God who have died and gone on to glory have literally had to sit back and listen to it for ages! Just think of this: if this old saint who is shouting for joy was one of the first people who ever came to believe in God, perhaps someone like Enoch, then imagine all he has heard!

He would have heard the devil jump all over Job for his accusations that God has been unfair.

He would have heard the devil smart off about David and his adultery and murder.

He would have heard the devil speak sarcastically about depressed Elijah, the man who brought fire down from God out of heaven and then ran from a woman.

He would have heard the devil spout off about Peter and his three denials of Christ.

He would have heard while the devil laid into Paul and Barnabas about their disagreement over Mark.

Can you imagine having to listen to the devil do that for thousands of years? Can you imagine listening to that much tattling? I wonder if, whoever he was, he ever thought that the devil was going to be successful at this? I wonder how many of us have ever been nervous that he was going to be successful in accusing us?

But here is the good news; Jesus has paid for every one of our sins, even the ones we have not committed yet:

Colossians 2:13 *And you, being dead in your sins and the uncircumcision of your flesh, hath he quickened together with him, having forgiven you all trespasses;*

Here is more good news, Jesus is constantly pleading our case:

1 John 2:1 *My little children, these things write I unto you, that ye sin not. And if any man sin, we have an advocate with the Father, Jesus Christ the righteous:*

And He is the best kind of advocate: not only is he pleading our case, but He has literally made our case His case. We do not even have a case anymore because He has given us His righteousness and taken our sin upon Himself:

2 Corinthians 5:21 *For he hath made him to be sin for us, who knew no sin; that we might be made the righteousness of God in him.*

You need to grasp this, especially if you are desperately trying to "hold on" to salvation: God took every ounce of your sin debt on Himself and paid it in full on Calvary. Then He took every ounce of His righteousness and placed it on you when you got saved. When the devil goes to accuse us before God, he keeps running into the same problem: our sins do not exist anymore. They were punished, paid for, and put away by Jesus's sacrifice on Calvary! He can accuse all he likes, and in his stubbornness, he will keep accusing, but he will fail every time because he keeps on running right into the nail-scarred hands of our advocate, Jesus Christ!

And then one day, after never having won a single case, he will find himself picked up by the back of the neck and thrown out of heaven for the last time. And whoever this old saint is, he will be there to see it and shout about it.

But here is the best part; that saint could actually be one of us! You, dear reader, could possibly be the shouting saint that John the Beloved saw and heard in heaven, since that day has not yet even come, and we will already be in heaven when it does!

This saint that shouts in verse ten points out that this is the point when something special happens. He shouts, *"Now is come salvation, and strength, and the kingdom of our God, and the power of his Christ."* This means that salvation in the sense of deliverance from our enemy, the devil, has come. Strength, *dunamis*, practical power is come since the one who always tried to weaken us is now broken. The kingdom of our God and of His Christ is come. This is the vestibule to the Millennial Reign of Christ that we are seeing.

The brethren win! But how? We know Jesus' part, paying for our sins and being our advocate. But what is our part in this victory? The voice from the old saint tells us that too:

Revelation 12:11a *And they overcame him by the blood of the Lamb...*

That is the part we have already been examining. We win because of the blood of Jesus shed on Calvary. But here are a couple of more things that go into our win:

Revelation 12:11b *...and by the word of their testimony; and they loved not their lives unto the death.*

The blood of Christ has given Christians a testimony that we do not mind sharing with anybody. The blood of Christ has given Christians throughout the ages the courage not just to live for Christ but to die for Him. Christians have been burned and beheaded, shot and stabbed, dragged and drowned but have willingly given up their lives rather than renounce Christ!

Seeing that and hearing the devil accuse us anyway, God will snatch his rebellious tail up and throw him out of heaven like the reprobate spirit he is!

He will fail in his assaults against Israel

Revelation 12:12 *Therefore rejoice, ye heavens, and ye that dwell in them. Woe to the inhabiters of the earth and of the sea! for the devil is come down unto you, having great wrath, because he knoweth that he hath but a short time.* **13** *And when the dragon saw that he was cast unto the earth, he persecuted the woman which brought forth the man child.* **14** *And to the woman were given two wings of a great eagle, that she might fly into the wilderness, into her place, where she is nourished for a time, and times, and half a time, from the face of the serpent.* **15** *And the serpent cast out of his mouth water as a flood after the woman, that he might cause her to be carried away of the flood.* **16** *And the earth helped the woman, and the earth opened her mouth, and swallowed up the flood which the dragon cast out of his mouth.*

The good news for heaven is that the devil has lost and been cast to the earth. The bad news for earth is that the devil has lost and been cast to the earth. Not only that, but it has now finally dawned on him that he is living on borrowed time, and that time is almost up, so he is madder than he has ever been and out for blood. That is when he turns his attention once more to the woman.

Remember from the first part of this chapter that the woman spoken of here is the nation of Israel herself. The devil will always hate what God loves, and God loves Israel. When the devil realizes again that he cannot defeat God, he will turn his attention once again to the nation that brought God into the world in flesh.

For three and a half years, Israel has had it bad, but not as bad as it could be. The peace treaty with Antichrist is still in effect, and even though Jerusalem is still trodden down of the Gentiles, there is at least a small measure of peace that Israel enjoys, shallow though it is. But at the mid-way point of the Tribulation, when the devil gets kicked out of heaven and lands on earth in rage, Antichrist will break his deal with Israel, and the devil will come after her in fury.

It is at that point that verse fourteen says that she will be given "two wings of a great eagle" to fly into the wilderness with and flee from the wrath of the devil and Antichrist. If, and this is a big if, if there is any mention of America in prophecy, this has to be it. Even though her Christians were Raptured out three and a half years earlier, it is possible (though in my opinion not very likely) that America will still honor her alliance with Israel. It is possible that she will help Israel survive. I hope this is the case; I truly do.

But regardless of whether or not these two wings have anything to do with America, they do tell us clearly that God will still be honoring His promises to Israel. He has promised that they will always survive as a nation, He has promised that they will possess the land, He has promised that there will always be a remnant, and all of those promises will hold true.

In verse fifteen, the devil sees Israel fleeing for the wilderness, and he unleashes a flood after her. But not a flood of literal water. Notice that the verse says he unleashes water *as* a flood, not *of* a flood. That word as lets us know we are dealing with a metaphor. So what is this flood? Isaiah told us what this flood will be a long, long time ago:

Isaiah 59:19 *So shall they fear the name of the LORD from the west, and his glory from the rising of the sun. When the enemy shall come in like a flood, the Spirit of the LORD shall lift up a standard against him.*

That prophecy of Isaiah is fulfilled here in Revelation 12:15. The devil will see Israel running for the wilderness for her life, and he will whip his demonic armies into a frenzy to chase her. He already has some that will be more than willing. It will not take much prodding from the dragon to get the armies of Syria and Iraq and Iran and Jordan and Turkey and a dozen other Arab states to tear out after Israel.

They will think they are doing their own thing. They think that even today. Every time they send out a suicide bomber, every time they lob a missile, every time they shoot a Jew, they think they are doing their own bidding, or worse, God's bidding.

But this verse tells a different story. Notice that the dragon will send them out of his mouth after Israel. That is where every Jew-hating country is at this very day, right in the forked tongue mouth of Satan himself. That is where you can find Hamas and Al Qaeda and Isis, and even most of the "respectable governments" of the Middle East. It is where Hitler was in his day, and it is where Haman was in Esther's day. The devil has always carried around antisemites in his mouth, ready to do his bidding at a moment's notice.

The devil in Revelation 12:15 sends out this Jew-hating flood, trying to destroy Israel. He has failed in his accusations against the brethren, so now he turns his attention to an assault against Israel. He just knows he is going to win this time; he just knows it. Israel is running; the demonic armies are in hot pursuit; there is no one in sight to help. And then:

Revelation 12:16 *And the earth helped the woman, and the earth opened her mouth, and swallowed up the flood which the dragon cast out of his mouth.*

Just when the devil thinks he has won, God does something He has already done once before. In Numbers 16, God made the earth open up and swallow Korah, Dathan, and Abiram straight into hell. Here in Revelation 12:16, just when it seems like the devil is going to win, God will do it again. This time the ground will open up and swallow every Jew-hating, demon-possessed soldier and terrorist chasing after Israel into the pit.

He will fail in his attempts to stamp out Christianity

Revelation 12:17 *And the dragon was wroth with the woman, and went to make war with the remnant of her seed, which keep the commandments of God, and have the testimony of Jesus Christ.*

This has got to be a bummer for the devil. He starts out trying to overthrow God. Then as a second option, he determines to destroy Israel. And when that does not work, he has to turn his attention to wiping out the few remaining Christians on earth. Everything he tries is failing, his days are dwindling, and this third attempt will not be any more successful than the first two. He will fight, but read the rest of the book of The Revelation, and you find that he loses again.

Sometimes it is helpful to be reminded of something: the big bad devil, the dragon himself, the guy that horror film writers are always glamorizing as unstoppable, is not going to win! In fact, the next time you feel like all is lost, the next time you look around at the wicked culture and start to sink into a depression, you need to remember this:

the devil is not going to go down as the being who almost beat God, he is going to go down as History's Biggest Failure.

Chapter Twenty-Seven
The Rise of the Beast

Revelation 13:1 *And I stood upon the sand of the sea, and saw a beast rise up out of the sea, having seven heads and ten horns, and upon his horns ten crowns, and upon his heads the name of blasphemy.* **2** *And the beast which I saw was like unto a leopard, and his feet were as the feet of a bear, and his mouth as the mouth of a lion: and the dragon gave him his power, and his seat, and great authority.* **3** *And I saw one of his heads as it were wounded to death; and his deadly wound was healed: and all the world wondered after the beast.* **4** *And they worshipped the dragon which gave power unto the beast: and they worshipped the beast, saying, Who is like unto the beast? who is able to make war with him?* **5** *And there was given unto him a mouth speaking great things and blasphemies; and power was given unto him to continue forty and two months.* **6** *And he opened his mouth in blasphemy against God, to blaspheme his name, and his tabernacle, and them that dwell in heaven.* **7** *And it was given unto him to make war with the saints, and to overcome them: and power was given him over all kindreds, and tongues, and nations.* **8** *And all that dwell upon the earth shall worship him, whose names are not written in the book of life of the Lamb slain from the foundation of the world.* **9** *If any man have an ear, let him hear.* **10** *He that leadeth into captivity shall go into captivity: he that killeth with the sword must be killed with the sword. Here is the patience and the faith of the saints.*

Way back in Revelation 6, we were introduced to the four horsemen of the apocalypse. The first rider, the rider on the white horse, will be the man known as the Antichrist. In that passage, we learned some things about him. Comparing the passages in Revelation with other passages about him from Daniel, we saw that he will be a diplomat, disgusting, defiling, and the most dangerous man who has ever lived.

After we saw all of those things in Revelation 6, the book of The Revelation grows a bit quieter about Antichrist for a few chapters while it deals with other things going on in heaven and earth. But as we arrive in Revelation 13, Antichrist comes to the front and center again. God uses much of this chapter to give us more details about the arrival and workings of the Antichrist.

His presentation

Revelation 13:1 *And I stood upon the sand of the sea, and saw a beast rise up out of the sea, having seven heads and ten horns, and upon his horns ten crowns, and upon his heads the name of blasphemy.*

There are many times in the book of The Revelation where the word sea is to be taken literally as the ocean. When a third of the sea is turned to blood, etc., take those things literally as the ocean itself. But as we come to Revelation 13:1, we are reading something that has been mentioned before in Scripture, and that other passage lets us know that God is using symbolism here:

Daniel 7:1 *In the first year of Belshazzar king of Babylon Daniel had a dream and visions of his head upon his bed: then he wrote the dream, and told the sum of the matters.* **2** *Daniel spake and said, I saw in my vision by night, and, behold, the four winds of the heaven strove upon the great sea.* **3** *And four great beasts came up from the sea, diverse one from another.*

In Daniel's vision, and please remember that Daniel and Revelation go hand-in-hand, Daniel saw and wrote about beasts coming up out of "the sea." But the rest of Daniel's prophecy spells out for us that those beasts were four different kingdoms of men, the Babylonians, the Medo-Persians, the Greeks, and the Romans. And those kingdoms, which have already existed, did not come out of the ocean; they came out of the troubled, wicked world of men. Isaiah used the term that exact same way:

Isaiah 57:20 *But the wicked are like the troubled sea, when it cannot rest, whose waters cast up mire and dirt.*

Another passage in the book of The Revelation spells it out even more clearly:

Revelation 17:15 *And he saith unto me, The waters which thou sawest, where the whore sitteth, are peoples, and multitudes, and nations, and tongues.*

So when you compare the two passages in Revelation with Daniel and Isaiah, you understand pretty quickly that the beast will come out of the troubled, wicked, turmoil-filled world of men.

When this passage speaks of the beast, it is going to tell you about two things at once; there is a double reference to it. It is going to tell you about the Antichrist, and it is going to tell you about his kingdom. Many Scriptures have a double reference like that, just like when God referred to a human named the Prince of Tyrus while He was also speaking about the devil at the exact same time in Ezekiel 28. This beast in Revelation 13 is the Antichrist, and it is the kingdom of the Antichrist.

With that understanding, look at verse one again.

Revelation 13:1 *And I stood upon the sand of the sea, and saw a beast rise up out of the sea, having seven heads and ten horns, and upon his horns ten crowns, and upon his heads the name of blasphemy.*

We are going to see something else called the beast later on in the book of The Revelation, in chapter seventeen, something that sounds very similar to this. It will be the beast, but it will be a different side of the beast. The beast is not just going to be a political world leader but also the one and only religious world leader. The beast that we see here deals with Antichrist as the world political leader; the beast as we see him in Revelation seventeen will deal with him as the religious world leader.

In this text dealing with him as the political leader of the world, we see him described as having seven heads, ten horns, and ten crowns. We have already discussed the fact that horns, heads, and crowns in the Bible speak of powers and leaders. That is what we see here. These ten crowns are the same thing as the ten toes described in the book of Daniel.

Let's go back to Daniel 2 for a reminder of that. Nebuchadnezzar has had a dream of a giant statue with a gold head, a silver torso, a brass lower body, a set of iron legs, a set of feet with a mixture of iron and clay toes, and Daniel is telling him what it means:

Daniel 2:36 *This is the dream; and we will tell the interpretation thereof before the king.* **37** *Thou, O king, art a king of kings: for the God of heaven hath given thee a kingdom, power, and strength, and glory.* **38** *And wheresoever the children of men dwell, the beasts of the field and the fowls of the heaven hath he given into thine hand, and hath made thee ruler over them all. Thou art this head of gold.* **39** *And after thee shall arise another kingdom inferior to thee, and another third kingdom of brass, which shall bear rule over all the earth.* **40** *And the fourth kingdom shall be strong as iron: forasmuch as iron breaketh in pieces and subdueth all things: and as iron that breaketh all these, shall it break in pieces and bruise.* **41** *And whereas thou sawest the feet and toes, part of potters' clay, and part of iron, the kingdom shall be divided; but there shall be in it of the strength of the iron, forasmuch as thou sawest the iron mixed with miry clay.* **42** *And as the toes of the feet were part of iron, and part of clay, so the kingdom shall be partly strong, and partly broken.* **43** *And whereas thou sawest iron mixed with miry clay, they shall mingle themselves with the seed of men: but they shall not cleave one to another, even as iron is not mixed with clay.* **44** *And in the days of these kings shall the God of heaven set up a kingdom, which shall never be destroyed: and the kingdom shall not be left to other people, but it shall break in pieces and consume all these kingdoms, and it shall stand for ever.* **45** *Forasmuch as thou sawest that the stone was cut out* *of the mountain without hands, and that it brake in pieces the iron, the brass, the clay, the silver, and the gold; the great God hath made known to the king what shall come to pass hereafter: and the dream is certain, and the interpretation thereof sure.*

We have been through four Gentile world kingdoms so far. The Babylonians were first. The Medo-Persian was second. The Greek was third. The Roman Empire was fourth. What we are waiting for now is what is known as the revived Roman Empire. It will be a federation of ten nations, some strong, some weak, mixed together. Those kingdoms are the ten toes of Daniel 2 and the ten crowns of Revelation 13. The ten crowns are sitting on ten horns. These are the ten leaders of the ten nations. The ten horns are sitting on seven heads, which will be seven regional leaders for Antichrist that the ten leaders of the ten nations answer to. And all of them, the ten national leaders and seven regional leaders, will answer to the Antichrist himself.

Each of the heads, leaders of nations, have "the name of blasphemy" on them. That name is the name of the Antichrist. In other words, these national leaders will have sworn allegiance to him. They will be his power base that allows him to rule the world. We do not know which ten nations these will be. We do know that it will include some of the nations that sprang out of the Roman Empire because they still have some of the old Roman iron of Daniel 2. But it will also include other nations, according to Daniel 2:43. There is no way to pin down which nations to watch for as they unite together.

The presentation of this man, Antichrist, screams of organization, power, and lethal danger.

His parts

Revelation 13:2a *And the beast which I saw was like unto a leopard, and his feet were as the feet of a bear, and his mouth as the mouth of a lion...*

The Antichrist and his kingdom are going to have some definite and terrifying characteristics that are seen in these animal parts.

The leopard speaks, among other things, of his camouflage. The spots of a leopard help it blend in with its surroundings, keeping its prey oblivious until it is too late for them to be saved. Antichrist is going to fool the world. He will have insanely high approval ratings, he will be loved almost universally, he will have earth eating out of his hands, but the image he will portray is like the spots of a leopard, designed to hide what he really is.

The feet of the bear speak, among other things, of his awesome power. A bear can knock down almost any animal on earth. Antichrist is going to be drunk with power, and the amount of power he possesses will be staggering.

The mouth of a lion speaks of his intimidation. The roar of a lion is legendary for its ability to terrify any man or animal within miles. Antichrist, for all of his popularity, will end up intimidating almost the entire world. He will eventually have people scared to death to move or breathe in any way that might displease him. Earth will walk on eggshells and will jump every time he roars.

His power

Revelation 13:2b... *and the dragon gave him his power, and his seat, and great authority. 3 And I saw one of his heads as it were wounded to death; and his deadly wound was healed: and all the world wondered after the beast.*

All through chapter twelve, we were looking at the devil, who eight times there was called the dragon. That is still who is being spoken of here in verse two when we read that the dragon gave him, the beast, the Antichrist, his power and seat and great authority. Just like God the Father has committed all judgment to the Son (John 5:22) the dragon commits all judgment to the Antichrist. The Father made the Son the part of the Trinity that was visible and focused on by the world, and the devil will make the Antichrist the part of his trinity that is visible and focused on by the world

When Antichrist rises to power and forms his federation, all the world will be watching it like it is some addictive soap opera. Everyone on earth will have committed to memory the nations of Antichrist, the rulers of those nations, and the regional rulers. This will be the devil's "dream team."

Nothing makes people famous like a good drama. Antichrist is going to have his very own drama that will solidify his fame. One of his national leaders is going to be wounded. This wound is going to be one that should be fatal. Now again, we are not talking about a national leader that gets sick, but a national leader that gets wounded. This is almost surely going to be an assassination attempt.

Just as God the Father gave the Son miracle-working power, the devil himself has given Antichrist his own amazing, miraculous power. Antichrist is ruling in his name and on his behalf. So when one of the Antichrist's national leaders undergoes this assassination attempt, Antichrist is going to step in.

Picture the scene: people hear a news flash that president so-and-so has been shot. Everyone rushes to get to a television screen somewhere. All across the world, people are flipping on CNN, Fox

News, ABC, NBC, CBS, Al-Jazeera, every news channel imaginable. Every one of them is showing the same scene. Cameras are trained on doctors in the emergency room, feverishly fighting a losing battle to save this man's life. They finally slump over, dejected, look at the cameras, and say, "We've done what we can, but there's just no way we can save him."

About that time, though, there is a commotion off to the side. The cameras swing around, and Antichrist has stormed into the operating room. The doctors start to object, but when they see who it is, they fall silent. Antichrist storms over to the operating table with a look of fury and determination on his face. He looks down at the dying man, then up at the camera, and says, "I will not allow this man to die, not today." He then reaches down, places his hands over the wound, groans and trembles, and a moment later releases him. At that moment, the man sits up, looks around in shock, and then falls down on worldwide television and worships his lord, the Antichrist, just as those Jesus healed fell down and worshipped him. This is the power that Antichrist will have, and it is little wonder that a world that does not know God's Word will fall all over themselves to follow after him.

His praise

Revelation 13:4 *And they worshipped the dragon which gave power unto the beast: and they worshipped the beast, saying, Who is like unto the beast? who is able to make war with him?*

You surely know by now that the devil wants everything that belongs to God. And during the Tribulation Period, he is going to have many of those things, including the worship of man. When the world sees this miracle of healing, they are going to worship the devil, they are going to worship the Antichrist, and they are going to come to the conclusion that the entire world may as well follow him, because how can you win a war with a man who can keep his soldiers from dying?

His perversion

Revelation 13:5 *And there was given unto him a mouth speaking great things and blasphemies; and power was given unto him to continue forty and two months. 6 And he opened his mouth in blasphemy against God, to blaspheme his name, and his tabernacle, and them that dwell in heaven.*

The sweet-as-honey routine that brings the Antichrist to power will have a dark and filthy side to it. When this man becomes famous after healing his dying lieutenant, he is going to use his platform of popularity to curse God to the entire world. He is going to blaspheme God, the name of God, the house of God, and the people of God that are already in heaven. Basically, if there is any good thing anywhere in the universe, Antichrist will cuss it like a sailor! For forth-two months, the last half of the Tribulation Period, he will be empowered to blaspheme and defame God and all that is good.

His persecution

Revelation 13:7 *And it was given unto him to make war with the saints, and to overcome them: and power was given him over all kindreds, and tongues, and nations.* **8** *And all that dwell upon the earth shall worship him, whose names are not written in the book of life of the Lamb slain from the foundation of the world.*

Here is something that we have mentioned previously in the book of The Revelation. Even though Christians will be removed from earth through the Rapture just before the Tribulation begins, the world and the Antichrist will quickly have a new crop to contend with. 144,000 Jewish evangelists will go across the globe spreading the gospel, the two witnesses will preach from Jerusalem, and people who have never yet been convicted of their sins previously will accept Christ by the millions. This is going to set Antichrist off like coming home to find a million roaches in your kitchen a week after the exterminator has been there! He is going to immediately start stomping. And this man who has power over every group, dialect, and nation on earth will have the power to put these new saints to death in droves.

When this takes place, there will only be two kinds of people on earth: every single saved person, none of which will worship him, and every single lost person, all of which will worship him.

In our day, it is sometimes hard to tell who the real Christians are. Christians like to see how well they can fit in with the world, and the world loves to pretend that they are Christians. It makes for a fuzzy picture. By the way, it is not supposed to be like that.

But during the Tribulation Period, everyone may as well be wearing jerseys because every person will be either clearly and openly for God, or clearly and openly for Antichrist. Every single lost person will be worshipping Antichrist, and every single saved person will be defying him.

That is what persecution does! It separates the professors from the possessors. And this persecution will be severe enough to get everyone out in the open for what they truly are.

Verse eight does not just tell us of the saints, though; it also gives us an incomparable treasure concerning the Savior. We learn here that He, the Lamb, was slain *"from the foundation of the world."* That preposition "from," *apo*, in Greek, is a word of separation. We would, therefore, rightly view it as "back from before." From our perspective, Christ died on Calvary. But before there ever was a Mount Calvary or an earth on which there could be a Mount Calvary or even a universe in which there could be an earth on which there could be a Mount Calvary, God the Father had already determined to send His Son to die for us, and the Son had already fully set His heart to doing so. And since God is unchanging, redemption's drama was thus fully settled before the stage had even been built on which it could begin.

His problem

Revelation 13:9 *If any man have an ear, let him hear.* **10** *He that leadeth into captivity shall go into captivity: he that killeth with the sword must be killed with the sword. Here is the patience and the faith of the saints.*

Have you ever wondered how in the world people can live for God when all hell is breaking loose, and they are being tortured and killed in droves? One reason people can live for God even in those circumstances is found in these verses. John really wanted us to pay attention to this, so he used the *"if any man have an ear, let him hear"* clause that he used seven times in chapters two and three of this book. Here is what he wanted us to know:

...He that leadeth into captivity shall go into captivity: he that killeth with the sword must be killed with the sword

In other words, everything that Antichrist will dish out, he will get back. This is the patience and faith of the saints! We know that Antichrist will get what is coming to him. He will have his time of fun, he will kill millions, he will exalt himself against God, but all of that will be very short-lived. The beast will rise—but the beast will also fall. Every Tribulation saint that defies the Antichrist and refuses the mark of the beast will do so in part because they know that he is on a collision course with Almighty God, and he is going to lose!

Dear saint, no matter what the devil is putting you through, even if he is running you through the ringer of Job, you just need to hang in there and remember that his time is almost up.

Dear sinner friend, if you are having your fun time with the devil right now, you need to remember something; his time is almost up, and so is yours. And if you find yourself one second into eternity without having repented of your sins and trusted Christ as your Lord and Savior, it will be an eternity too late. The devil rose, and he will fall. The beast rose, and he will fall. Every sinner rises, and everyone who does not get saved falls as well, into the very pit of hell from which there is no escape. You better run to Jesus while you still can.

Chapter Twenty-Eight
The Unholy Spirit

Revelation 13:11 *And I beheld another beast coming up out of the earth; and he had two horns like a lamb, and he spake as a dragon.* **12** *And he exerciseth all the power of the first beast before him, and causeth the earth and them which dwell therein to worship the first beast, whose deadly wound was healed.* **13** *And he doeth great wonders, so that he maketh fire come down from heaven on the earth in the sight of men,* **14** *And deceiveth them that dwell on the earth by the means of those miracles which he had power to do in the sight of the beast; saying to them that dwell on the earth, that they should make an image to the beast, which had the wound by a sword, and did live.* **15** *And he had power to give life unto the image of the beast, that the image of the beast should both speak, and cause that as many as would not worship the image of the beast should be killed.*

In the last section of verses, we looked again in detail at the man of sin, the son of perdition, the Antichrist. Verses one through ten of this chapter of the book of The Revelation dealt with him. The rest of this chapter deals with him also, but in the verses we just looked at, it deals with him in regard to a helper he is going to have in his evil work. People tend to think of the Antichrist as a loner, but he is actually part of a gang of three. You see, the devil is forever a counterfeiter of God. Whatever God does, the devil will try to produce a twisted, duplicate version of it. And during the Tribulation Period, the devil is going to have his very own counterfeit trinity. The real Trinity is made up of God the Father, God the Son, and God the Holy Ghost. The Satanic trinity will be made up of the devil, who is trying to play the role of God the Father, the Antichrist, who is trying to play the role of Jesus the Son of God, and then there will be the person we read of in this passage. One verse of Scripture lists them all together:

Revelation 20:10 *And the devil that deceived them was cast into the lake of fire and brimstone, where the beast and the false prophet are, and shall be tormented day and night for ever and ever.*

This individual is the man I call the unholy spirit. Revelation 20:10 calls him the false prophet. He will play much the same role for the Antichrist that the Holy Spirit fulfills for Christ. He will be a vital part of everything Antichrist tries to do during the Tribulation Period.

The contradiction of the unholy spirit

Revelation 13:11 *And I beheld another beast coming up out of the earth; and he had two horns like a lamb, and he spake as a dragon.*

When we start in this verse looking at the Antichrist's helper, the unholy spirit, God does as He did with the Antichrist and gives us a bunch of symbolism to describe him. Remember that Antichrist comes up *"out of the sea,"* meaning he will come up out of the troubled world of men. Here we see that the unholy spirit comes up *"out of the earth."*

Right away, you get the idea that the Antichrist is point, and the unholy spirit is counterpoint. They are opposite sides of the same evil coin. Antichrist will come from part of the world that is troubled, unsettled, tossed like the waves of the sea. But the unholy spirit will come out of part of the world that is much more stable. But even being from different sides of the track, these two will hit it off and become fast friends.

These two do have one thing in common: they are absolute fakes. They hide what they really are. Notice again what verse eleven says about him:

... and he had two horns like a lamb...

The unholy spirit has two horns like a lamb. This guy is a regular sweetheart! Why, he's kind and soft, and practically cuddly. What could be sweeter and softer than a lamb? And the world will watch as this sweet, cuddly, warm fuzzy wooly lamb looks out and smiles and then opens his mouth and says:

"You worthless fools! I am going to kill you all in the most horrible ways! I will make you beg for death, and then I will deliver it!"

Here is how the text puts it, *"and he spake as a dragon."*

It does not seem to fit, does it? It just seems odd to have a cuddly little lamb-type person roar like a dragon and then threaten to kill people. There is a contradiction between his image and his reality. But this again should tell you something about the unholy spirit: his carefully polished image is a lie, and he cannot be trusted. His mouth will give him away for what he really is.

And that, dear reader, is worth parking for a few moments to make application. May I point out what should be obvious, but sadly, usually is not? It is amazing how often, even today, people have an image that they put forth, but their mouth gives them away for what they really are.

You can play godly, teenage, youth choir member all you like, but if your mouth is spouting filthy rap and hip-hop music the rest of the week, then it is giving you away for the inconsistent, unspiritual person you are.

You can develop an image of mature, older, steady, pillar of the church kind of member all you like, but if church is the only place you do not curse, your mouth is giving you away as being either lost or grievously backslidden and unspiritual.

You can carefully cultivate the image of being pure and respectable, but if you use sexual innuendos and suggestive remarks, your mouth is giving you away as a person with a dark and filthy heart.

Your speech is deadly serious! Look how Jesus put it:

Matthew 12:37 *For by thy words thou shalt be justified, and by thy words thou shalt be condemned.*

God sees right past our image into our reality. And unfortunately, He sees a lot of people who look like lambs but talk like dragons.

The cause of the unholy spirit

Revelation 13:12 *And he exerciseth all the power of the first beast before him, and causeth the earth and them which dwell therein to worship the first beast, whose deadly wound was healed.* **13** *And he doeth great wonders, so that he maketh fire come down from heaven on the earth in the sight of men,* **14** *And deceiveth them that dwell on the earth by the means of those miracles which he had power to do in the sight of the beast; saying to them that dwell on the earth, that they should make an image to the beast, which had the wound by a sword, and did live.*

As the text continues describing the man who will act as the unholy spirit, you see that he will be demonically empowered to do miracles, just as Antichrist is. This is one reason why it is foolish to seek after miracles and believe that they will infallibly lead you to the truth. God did verify His Word with miracles while it was being written, but if a "miracle" goes contrary to the Word of God, it is not coming from above; it is coming from below because the devil very clearly has miracle-working power and will not be shy about using it when God allows him to do so.

Verse thirteen says that not only will this man do wonders, he will do great wonders. He will even call down fire from the sky while people are watching! And all of these miracles have a purpose to them. They are not random or pointless. The cause of the unholy spirit, according to verses twelve and fourteen, is to get people to worship the Antichrist.

Now follow this. Do you remember when I said that the devil has made himself a satanic trinity, a copy of the real Trinity? If you pay attention to what you read in this chapter, you will get confirmation of how the real Trinity works by watching the false trinity. Satan is acting as God the Father, running the show, but not being seen. Look at what the Bible says of God the Father:

John 1:18 *No man hath seen God at any time; the only begotten Son, which is in the bosom of the Father, he hath declared him.*

God the Father, the first member of the real Trinity, operates unseen; no human has yet laid eyes on Him in this world. The devil, the first member of the satanic trinity, mimics that.

What about the second members of each trinity? The Antichrist, the second member of the satanic trinity, is out front and center; he is the one made visible; he is the focus of what men see in the world. He is mimicking Jesus:

John 14:9 *Jesus saith unto him, Have I been so long time with you, and yet hast thou not known me, Philip? he that hath seen me hath seen the Father; and how sayest thou then, Shew us the Father?*

Jesus, the second member of the real Trinity, is out front and center, and the Antichrist, the second member of the satanic trinity, mimics Him.

And that brings us to the third member of each trinity. The unholy spirit, the false prophet, will mimic the ministry of the Holy Spirit. Please notice that this man does not draw glory or attention to himself; he does everything he does to get people to worship the Antichrist. He is absolutely consumed with glorifying his version of "Jesus."

What is he doing? He is perfectly mimicking the ministry of the real Holy Spirit. Look at this:

John 16:13 *Howbeit when he, the Spirit of truth, is come, he will guide you into all truth: for he shall not speak of himself; but whatsoever he shall hear, that shall he speak: and he will shew you things to come.* **14** *He shall glorify me: for he shall receive of mine, and shall shew it unto you.*

John 15:26 *But when the Comforter is come, whom I will send unto you from the Father, even the Spirit of truth, which proceedeth from the Father, he shall testify of me:*

Notice those three important phrases concerning the Holy Spirit. He shall not speak of himself. He shall glorify me. He shall testify of me. The Holy Spirit is consumed night and day with pointing people to Jesus, speaking of Jesus, glorifying Jesus, and teaching about Jesus. It is never about the Holy Spirit; it is always about Jesus. That is why, whenever you see a man or a movement that says or infers that the Holy Spirit points you to the Holy Spirit, you know that they have missed it and are not to be followed. The second man to the Antichrist understands this principle quite well! The devil, his demons, and all of their human helpers know that it is the second member of their trinity that is to be in primary focus, and we should certainly understand that about the second member of the real Trinity.

Look at verse fourteen again, and notice what this man does to bring glory to Antichrist:

Revelation 13:14 *And deceiveth them that dwell on the earth by the means of those miracles which he had power to do in the sight of the beast; saying to them that dwell on the earth, that they should make an image to the beast, which had the wound by a sword, and did live.*

This man will remind the world of what Antichrist did, healing one of his "heads," one of his rulers, which had the deadly wound. And then he will suggest to them (and his suggestion will be "an offer they can't refuse") that they make an image, a bust, of the Antichrist. Antichrist will get his own statue! All of this will be done to get the world to worship Antichrist, and that is the entire cause of the false prophet, the man we call the unholy spirit.

The crest of the unholy spirit

Revelation 13:15 *And he had power to give life unto the image of the beast, that the image of the beast should both speak, and cause that as many as would not worship the image of the beast should be killed.*

In every career, good or evil, there is a point at which a person reaches the very top of his game. I may not know when it is, but there will be a point at which I am the best pastor and author I will ever be. There will come a point in your life when you will be the best "whatever you are" that you will ever be. Everyone will reach their own crest at some moment.

For the third member of the satanic trinity, the man we call the unholy spirit, his crest, his greatest moment, will come right here in Revelation 13:15. In verse fourteen, this man will tell the people still alive on earth that they need to make an image, a statue of the Antichrist. They will do just that. This statue will be the most famous piece of sculpture on earth. It will be more recognizable than the Statue of Liberty, more notable than Mount Rushmore, more glowingly regarded than Michelangelo's David.

Knowing what the Bible shows about the pride of the devil and the Antichrist, you can safely assume that it will probably be the biggest statue on earth as well. It is certainly not going to be any figurine.

The worldwide media will surely be covering the unveiling of this statue. They will be there in droves, cameras rolling, commentators commentating. They will be telling the world how tall it is, how much it weighs, what it is made of, everything. But on that day, the media and the world will get the shock of their lives. The sidekick of Antichrist, the unholy spirit, the man who commissioned the statue to be built, will be in attendance at the ceremony. And somewhere after the unveiling, at some point in the festivities, he will interrupt the proceedings. He will doubtless tell all the world how happy he is to work for Antichrist, and how pleased he is with the statue. But he will also tell them that the statue is not quite right yet. How can any statue to the world's greatest man be truly complete while it stands there without life? This statue cannot be like other dead works of stone or iron. This statue needs to be alive. And it will be. This man will perform one of the greatest miracles of the devil's career. He will literally bring this image to life. While cameras are rolling and flashes are popping, this statue will begin to breathe and speak. As if the Antichrist himself is not bad enough, he is going to have a giant statue, just as alive and just as wicked and just as foul-mouthed as he himself is! And the false prophet will then command, just as Nebuchadnezzar of old, that whoever will not worship the image will be killed.

And while someone not worshipping in ancient Babylon from day to day might have been able to slip by unnoticed if there were no tattletales in attendance as there were for Shadrach, Meshach, and Abednego, that will not be a possibility with this image. Remember, this image is alive. It can see, and it can talk.

Imagine as a follower of Christ walks by, trying not to be noticed. He has a hat over his forehead and his hands in his pocket, hiding the fact that he has not taken the mark. Maybe he is out trying to find a way to get food for his family. And as he walks by, unnoticed by the followers of the beast, the statue locks eyes on him. He shouts out, "You! Why didn't you take time to bow before me? Why didn't you worship me? Kneel, subject." The Christian now has a choice to make. And he makes the choice that every follower of the Lamb will make during the Tribulation Period. He lifts his head, locks eyes on the statue, and says, "I bow only to Jesus, the King of kings and Lord of lords." And when he does, the face of that statue twists in demonic rage, and it shouts, "Kill him! Kill the follower of Jesus! Kill him now!"

This statue that has been brought to life by the unholy spirit will be the oracle of the world, a violent, living, breathing image made by the hand of man. People who could never gain an audience with the Antichrist now will not need to. All of them will flock to this statue, and the statue of Antichrist will tell them what he expects of them. Mecca and Salt Lake City and Vatican City will be like ghost towns as the world comes to wherever this idol is for their pilgrimages and bows before this new, hellish idol.

This moment is when the world will have a new center of religious activity to supersede all that ever came before it, and the new icon of this twisted faith will be the image of the Antichrist. This will be the crest, the greatest moment in the career of the unholy spirit.

Dear reader, you do not want to be there when this happens. If you are sitting there reading this book, lost and undone with Christ, you better get saved while you can, so you can avoid this coming, awful time.

I trust that as we have gone through this section of verses, you have been able to spot the differences between the unholy spirit and the Holy Spirit. In case you have missed or just need a reminder, here goes.

The unholy spirit is cruel and will destroy people. The Holy Spirit is the Comforter and loves people.

The unholy spirit is contradictory, presenting an image that his mouth contradicts. The Holy Spirit is consistent, never changing.

The unholy spirit is corrupt and will tell lost men they are fine while helping to send them to hell. The Holy Spirit is a convictor, telling lost men they are not fine so they can get saved and go to heaven.

Listen to the Holy Spirit!

Chapter Twenty-Nine
The Mark of the Beast

Revelation 13:16 *And he causeth all, both small and great, rich and poor, free and bond, to receive a mark in their right hand, or in their foreheads:* **17** *And that no man might buy or sell, save he that had the mark, or the name of the beast, or the number of his name.* **18** *Here is wisdom. Let him that hath understanding count the number of the beast: for it is the number of a man; and his number is Six hundred threescore and six.*

There are some things in the book of The Revelation that come as a surprise to people when they hear it. Most people out in the world and even a great many inside today's churches do not know that this book of The Revelation was first written and sent to seven literal churches. A great many people are unaware of the twenty-one specific judgments of God that fall on earth via the seven seals, seven trumpets, and seven vials. Many do not know that anyone who has had the prompting and the chance to get saved before the Tribulation begins will not be given the opportunity to be saved after it has begun. The great whore of the book generally makes people scratch their heads when a preacher speaks of it. A great deal of the book of The Revelation simply catches people by surprise when they hear of it.

But the subject matter of Revelation 13:16-18 does not catch anyone by surprise. This text deals with 666, the mark of the beast. Every lost drunk in the gutter knows about 666. People who do not know church from Cheerios will give an extra penny at the drive-through window if their total comes up to $6.66. You could walk into a crowded mall and shout, "Somebody finish this phrase for me: the mark of the _____" and ninety-nine out of one hundred of them would shout "beast!" Everybody has some familiarity with 666, the mark of the beast.

When I first preached through the book of the Revelation in 2006, that year obviously had a June 6, 2006, or 6-6-6 as the date. And people everywhere were panicking. Pregnant ladies were literally begging doctors to induce them early so their babies would not be born on 6-6-6. People know that this number has something to do with the final and greatest evil that this world will face.

On FOX News, a day before June 6, 2006, a lady was interviewed about the significance of this date and of this number. She openly mocked any notion that this number has any real significance. She said, "Only fanatics actually take 666, or anything in the Bible literally anymore."

Do you realize how dumb she made herself look with that statement? If someone put a gun to her head, she would surely take "Thou shalt not kill" literally. If someone tried to heist her car, she would take "Thou shalt not steal" literally. If someone told her she was living in sin, she would take "judge not" literally. When someone she loves dies, she will, whether they were actually saved or not, take heaven literally. So what is she, a fanatic?

The truth is, the end times will have a very significant man at the forefront of human events, and he will have a very significant number attached to his name, and he will have a very significant mark that goes along with it. And after all of the warnings that God and men of God have given through the years, only a fool would ignore or minimize the mark of the beast, 666.

The compulsion of the mark

Throughout history, there have been people who have worshipped the devil in the shadows. There have also been people who worshipped God in the shadows. Believe me on this, neither God nor the devil like this arrangement.

God desires and deserves to be worshipped openly.

The devil does not deserve it, but he, too, desires to be worshipped openly.

In this regard, this thing that will happen during the Tribulation, the mark of the beast, will be pleasing to both God and the devil himself. This mark is going to be a universal demand of Antichrist. No one is going to be exempt from it. Anyone who is not a follower of Christ will ultimately be wearing this mark. Verse sixteen says that small and great, rich and poor, free and bond will be made to take the mark. Small and great refer both to size and age. Rich and poor deal with finances. From princes to paupers, money will not matter; everyone will be required to take the mark. Free and bond are mentioned also. Though slavery in America ended a very long time ago, slavery still exists to this day in many areas of the world. Sharia law, the binding law of Islam, still speaks of it in the present tense. (Keller & Ibn-al-Naqib, 34, 286, 476, 604)

And during the Tribulation Period, at least for the last half of it, perhaps even for all of it, both slaveholders and slaves will be equal in that they will be required to take the mark of the beast. No one on earth will get a pass on this; it will be the demand of the Antichrist that everyone take the mark.

The mark itself is interesting and, I believe, often misunderstood. For years old commentaries have decided that it will not be a literal mark but the practice of Roman Catholicism. But while following the beliefs and doctrines of the church of Rome is foolish in light of Scripture, it is not the mark of the beast.

In our modern age of technology, people have now decided that the mark of the beast is a computer chip, a way that technology will handle all financial transactions. I believe that is much closer, and I think it will be part of it, but that is still not the whole story. The Bible uses a very descriptive word for mark when it refers to the mark of the beast. In every case, it is the word *charagma*, and it literally means an imprinted mark, an engraving, something that is visible. An invisible micro-chip alone will not give the devil the attention that he desires. I *believe* that the mark of the beast will be accompanied by some microchip technology that allows cashless buying and selling. The world economy will pretty much have to go cashless to force everyone into taking the mark. There will not be any underground economy at all, no yard sales, no flea markets, no nothing. So yes, I *believe* that the mark of the beast will be accompanied by some microchip technology that allows cashless buying and selling. But I *know* that the mark will be an actual mark, a *charagma*, something that openly and visibly identifies people as followers of Antichrist.

Remember that this is all about worship. The devil and Antichrist want the open attention and adoration that only belongs to God. This mark will be something that the devil can see, love, and smile at, and billions upon billions of people, small and great, rich and poor, bond and free will line up to be visibly imprinted with it.

The control of the mark

Revelation 13:17a *And that no man might buy or sell, save he that had the mark...*

Sometimes the most complicated plans are utter failures, while the simplest of the simple get the job done. Dictators throughout the ages have tried to control the world by stealing all of the world's wealth. That is a hard, complicated, almost impossible thing to do. But Antichrist will come up with the simplest, most brilliantly wicked plan of the ages. He will not bother to try stealing all of the world's wealth to control the world. He will simply control all of the financial transactions on earth, and in so doing, he will control the world. It will not matter how wealthy a person is. If Bill Gates is still alive during the Tribulation Period, he will be just as much under the control of the Antichrist as the minimum wage worker at McDonald's. Neither of them will be able to buy or sell anything unless they take the exact same mark.

In our age, wealth gives a measure of freedom. But not during the Tribulation Period. You could have a million dollars sitting under your mattress, but you will not be able to go on vacation without the mark. You could have a fortune in your bank account, but you will not be able to buy so much as a cotton ball with it unless you have the mark.

    I truly suspect that being the independent, self-reliant people that they often are, many wealthy people will at first refuse the mark. Rich people just do not like to answer to anybody. But after a few weeks, all the food in the mansion will be gone. Within a day or so after that, the stomach will begin to rumble and grumble. So Mr. Rich man will do what he has always done. He will try to use his wealth to get groceries. But Wal-Mart will not let him use any of that electronic money unless he can flash the mark, wave the hand over the scanner, and give allegiance to Antichrist.

    So the next logical option is to sell or trade some things to get groceries. But he cannot even buy so much as an apple with a Ferrari. No mark, no deal, no way. So Mr. Rich man will humble himself down, swallow his pride, and line up downtown in the same line as the school janitor and the illegal immigrant squash picker and the high school fast-food worker. People who have a billion dollars and people who are so far in debt they cannot even look up and see bottom will be in the same line. An old woman will go in with a splotchy, wrinkled forehead, and she will come out with an imprint on top of her furrowed brow. A middle-aged, hard-working farmer with hands as strong as steel will go in with callouses on his palms and come out with a mark on the back of his right hand. A high school girl with skin as smooth as silk, not so much as a blemish on her face, will come out on the other end of that line with the devil's mark on her previously spotless face. Small and great, rich and poor, free and bond, black and white, man and woman, boy and girl, no one on earth will be able to buy or sell so much as a green bean without taking the mark of the beast.

    Just think with me for a second. How many of you are planning on going out to eat after service on Sunday? What kind of a sinking feeling would you get in your gut if, before the service was out, you found out that you would not be able to go out and sit down for your Sunday afternoon dinner unless you first took the mark of the beast?

    But if the trumpet sounds during that service and you are sitting there lost, that is exactly what will happen, if not that day, by the midway point of the Tribulation for sure. Believe me; the devil has been preparing for this for centuries. The technology is already in place to make it happen. Permanent markings have been available for years, and now micro-chip technology is also already in place that can control every transaction you ever make for the rest of your life.

The content of the mark

Revelation 13:17b*... save he that had the mark, or the name of the beast, or the number of his name.* **18** *Here is wisdom. Let him that hath understanding count the number of the beast: for it is the number of a man; and his number is Six hundred threescore and six.*

Here in verse seventeen, we are given the content of the mark of the beast; we learn what exactly it is. The name and the number in verse seventeen both refer to the mark. In other words, the mark of the beast can actually be one of two things; it can either be the name of the Antichrist or the number of the Antichrist. We do not yet know what his name is. It could be Carlos or Achmed or Bob or Eugene. But whatever his name is, when he bursts onto the scene, billions of people will have his name imprinted on their foreheads. Why? Why would the devil desire this? Here is your answer:

Revelation 14:1 *And I looked, and, lo, a Lamb stood on the mount Sion, and with him an hundred forty and four thousand, having his Father's name written in their foreheads.*

Revelation 22:3 *And there shall be no more curse: but the throne of God and of the Lamb shall be in it; and his servants shall serve him:* **4** *And they shall see his face; and his name shall be in their foreheads.*

At least the 144,00 sealed and chosen Jews, and maybe all of us who are saved, will literally have the name of God written on the forehead. The devil knows this, and he wants every bit of the same adoration that is given to God. The name of Jesus, the second member of the Trinity, will be seen visibly on the forehead of His servants, so the name of Antichrist, the second member of the satanic trinity, will also be seen on the foreheads of his servants. This is just another way that Satan will try to steal the attention and devotion that should belong only to God.

But in addition to being able to take the name of Antichrist, a second option will be that people can simply take his number.

Throughout the years, people have speculated endlessly as to how 666 ties in with Antichrist. The guesses range from complicated to completely ridiculous. One of the things that people have done most often through the years is to find people whose first, middle, and last names each have six letters and proclaim them to be the Antichrist on that basis. For instance, at the height of his popularity, President Ronald Wilson Reagan was proclaimed by some to be the Antichrist. But does the fact that a person has six letters in each of their names mean they are the Antichrist? Robert Arthur Wagner (me!) definitely hopes not!

There must be half a billion people on earth who have six letters in each of their names; that is a ridiculous way to try and determine who the Antichrist will be.

The truth is, we do not know yet how this number ties in with his name, all we can do is guess. But what we do know is this: when he arrives on the scene, every time the number 666 shows up on a cash register, or a scale, or a forehead, or a license plate, everyone who sees it will identify it with one specific person.

However it ties in with him, 666 will be the number of a man, the number of the Antichrist. And there will be people by the billions walking the face of this earth, with 666 forever marked visibly onto their foreheads. Yes, I do believe that there will be a computer chip underneath it, but I know that there will be a literal mark of 666 that stains the foreheads of teeming multitudes that have turned their souls over to Satan and sold out for a morsel of bread. Just imagine what it will be like walking into downtown New York City and seeing 666 at eye level everywhere you look, stamped on the foreheads of the doomed.

The cost of the mark

Let's skip ahead in the book a little to see the cost of the mark. We will cover these verses in detail when we get to them, but I want to pull a couple of things out of them now that tie in with the verses we are examining.

Revelation 14:9 *And the third angel followed them, saying with a loud voice, If any man worship the beast and his image, and receive his mark in his forehead, or in his hand,* **10** *The same shall drink of the wine of the wrath of God, which is poured out without mixture into the cup of his indignation; and he shall be tormented with fire and brimstone in the presence of the holy angels, and in the presence of the Lamb:* **11** *And the smoke of their torment ascendeth up for ever and ever: and they have no rest day nor night, who worship the beast and his image, and whosoever receiveth the mark of his name.*

In Revelation 14, three actual angels are flying through the earth's atmosphere, shouting at the top of their lungs. One is demanding that people fear God and worship Him. Another is shouting out that Babylon has fallen. The third, though, is shouting out a message for all those people lined up to receive the mark. Just imagine what it will be like as thousands upon thousands of people are lined up in Chicago, New York, Los Angeles, Paris, and Berlin, waiting to take the mark. All of a sudden, there is a sonic boom as an angel breaks the sound barrier. He is racing through the air, giving a final warning. He is screaming at the top of his angelic lungs for people not to take the mark. His message is *Don't take the mark! Don't take the mark! You'll die and go to hell if you take the mark. You'd be better off to accept Christ and starve to death than to take the mark. If you take that mark, all hope is lost, don't take the mark!*

An old woman who has been bitter at God for years will look up and shake her fist at the angel and say, "Shut up! I'll take the mark if I want to."

A young man whose girlfriend took the mark the day before will mumble under his breath, "I'd rather die and go to hell than lose my girl." And he will stick his right hand out for the mark.

A liberal preacher, lost as a goat, who has been preaching nothing but a social gospel for years, will sneer and say, "I'm a preacher; God would not dare condemn me, if there even is a God." And he will leave with the devil's mark on his forehead, just above his eyes.

Even an angel of God flying through heaven will not be able to keep people from taking the mark because they want what they want when they want it, and they refuse to ever do without.

We are there. Our world is ready for this! The entitlement mentality has consumed our land; everyone already thinks that people owe them everything from health care to housing to clothing and food to having their student loans paid off. People by the billions are already conditioned to take the mark like a bunch of sheep led to the slaughter. People by the billions would rather live for the moment, even though their unforgiven sin will cost them heaven and send them to hell for all eternity.

Chapter Thirty
Purity on Display

Revelation 14:1 *And I looked, and, lo, a Lamb stood on the mount Sion, and with him an hundred forty and four thousand, having his Father's name written in their foreheads.* **2** *And I heard a voice from heaven, as the voice of many waters, and as the voice of a great thunder: and I heard the voice of harpers harping with their harps:* **3** *And they sung as it were a new song before the throne, and before the four beasts, and the elders: and no man could learn that song but the hundred and forty and four thousand, which were redeemed from the earth.* **4** *These are they which were not defiled with women; for they are virgins. These are they which follow the Lamb whithersoever he goeth. These were redeemed from among men, being the firstfruits unto God and to the Lamb.* **5** *And in their mouth was found no guile: for they are without fault before the throne of God.*

In 1864, a man named James N. Gamble, a chemist, made this notation in his diary: "I made floating soap today. I think we'll make all our soap that way." (Smallwood, 2015)

Fifteen years later, in October of 1879, the first bar of Ivory Soap rolled off of the production line. Consumers were snagged by this new "floating soap" that would not get lost in the bath water. By the way, the name for the soap came from Psalm 45:8, which says, "*All thy garments smell of myrrh, and aloes, and cassia, out of the ivory palaces, whereby they have made thee glad.*" (Broussard-Simmons & Hunt, 2001)

In 1891, the soap's slogan officially became "it floats." But in that same time period, the soap was given another slogan, one that has lasted to this day. Do you remember what it is, the slogan that can still be found on bars of Ivory?

99.44% pure.

You see, Proctor and Gamble decided to have a laboratory exam performed on their soap. A chemist's analysis of the "pure soap" revealed that 56/100 of the soap was actually "other ingredients." So, by subtracting the 56/100, they arrived at the conclusion that they had soap that was 99.44% pure. The 56/100 did not and does not bother them in the least; they are perfectly willing to call Ivory "pure soap," and it almost is. Almost...

There is something forever compelling about purity. Every godly guy wants to marry a pure virgin girl. Gold coin makers want every coin to be 24-karat. Water filters want to eliminate bacteria down to as small as .03 microns. People know instinctively that the more pure something is, the more valuable it is. And that is nowhere more true than in a Christian's walk with God. He does not want us to be striving for 99.44 percent purity; He expects us to be striving to eliminate even that last little 56/100 of impurity! God expects holiness from all of us who are His:

1 Peter 1:15 *But as he which hath called you is holy, so be ye holy in all manner of conversation;* **16** *Because it is written, Be ye holy; for I am holy.*

1 Thessalonians 4:3 *For this is the will of God, even your sanctification, that ye should abstain from fornication:*

2 Timothy 2:22 *Flee also youthful lusts: but follow righteousness, faith, charity, peace, with them that call on the Lord out of a pure heart.*

During the Tribulation Period, the world is finally going to see something that I believe it has never seen yet: a large group of people who actually live pure, holy, undefiled lives. These are people who are not just satisfied to rest in positional justification; they also live in practical sanctification.

Back in Revelation 7, as another judgment of God was about to fall on earth, we were introduced to a group of men, 144,000 strong. They are 12,000 Jews from each of the twelve tribes of Israel who have come to recognize and accept Jesus as their Messiah and Lord. These 144,000 are sealed in their foreheads, openly identifying them as followers of Christ.

Remember, please, that Antichrist thinks he is rid of all these "Jesus freaks." He knows about the Rapture; he is tickled to death that his world is now "Jesus free," and he is enjoying life. But then, seemingly out of nowhere, 144,000 Bible-believing, preaching/praying/praising Christians show up. They will not back up or slack up, and all 144,000 have their bony fingers pointed at Antichrist, telling him he is going to rot in hell.

What a scene! So Antichrist unleashes all of the fury of hell against them. He is out to exterminate them all, and by the time we arrive in Revelation fourteen, he has done it. All of these have become martyrs for Christ; their lives have been taken, they are now on Mount Zion with Jesus, they have won it all.

You say, "Pardon me, don't you mean to say they have lost it all?" No, I mean to say they have won it all. They are victors over the worst enemies the world will ever see, and in the midst of the vilest and fullest filth ever, they are nothing less than purity on display.

Purity is preferable

Revelation 14:1 *And I looked, and, lo, a Lamb stood on the mount Sion, and with him an hundred forty and four thousand, having his Father's name written in their foreheads.* **2** *And I heard a voice from heaven, as the voice of many waters, and as the voice of a great thunder: and I heard the voice of harpers harping with their harps:* **3** *And they sung as it were a new song before the throne, and before the four beasts, and the elders: and no man could learn that song but the hundred and forty and four thousand, which were redeemed from the earth.*

All of Revelation 13 was a foul chapter; it was about the Dragon, the Antichrist, and the false prophet. But the first five verses of chapter fourteen are going to be as fair as chapter thirteen was foul. This portion of Scripture is about the Lamb and this very special group of 144,000 who choose to follow Him under the most dire of circumstances.

This is about people who realize how preferable purity is.

As this chapter begins, it begins not with the Lamb being with His men, but His men being with the Lamb. There is, in fact, a difference.

Revelation 14:1 *And I looked, and, lo, a Lamb stood on the mount Sion, and with him an hundred forty and four thousand, having his Father's name written in their foreheads.*

In these first few verses, we see the veil of the spiritual world pulled back a bit; heaven and earth seem to become one as the grammar of the text unfolds.

John saw Jesus standing on Mount Zion in Jerusalem. We do not know if this was merely something that only he saw or if everyone else saw it as well. One way or the other, these 144,000 pure witnesses found that a very good reason to be pure is that it identified them publicly with their dear Christ and with God the Father, whose name was written on their foreheads. For all eternity, it will be known that they were peculiarly His.

On behalf of humanity, which to be charitable is often "not very bright," I am grateful for some things that will not make it into heaven. Tattoos, for example. If you were the guy who got saved with a tattoo of his ex- ex- ex-girlfriend on his posterior, would you not be overjoyed to realize that when you go to heaven, you can finally lose the Sally on your seat? That would be wonderful! But it will not be half as wonderful as realizing that when we get marked for a pure life here, it will still last into eternity.

Revelation 14:2 *And I heard a voice from heaven, as the voice of many waters, and as the voice of a great thunder: and I heard the voice of harpers harping with their harps:*

John saw the 144,00 standing on Mount Zion, which is in Jerusalem. He heard a voice *from heaven* coming down to earth. Keep those details in mind; they will become important in a moment.

In the very context of the purity of these followers of Christ, we find a great voice sounding out from heaven and musicians beginning to play their harps. Purity is to be preferred because it is recognized and celebrated from heaven, and the celebration makes it all the way down to earth.

This music that started will be known to the 144,000 martyrs for Christ:

Revelation 14:3 *And they sung as it were a new song before the throne, and before the four beasts, and the elders: and no man could learn that song but the hundred and forty and four thousand, which were redeemed from the earth.*

Now is the moment at which we find all that I told you to remember becoming important. John saw the 144,00 standing on Mount Zion, which is in Jerusalem. He heard a voice *from heaven* coming down to earth. But as the 144,000-voice choir begins to sing, they are singing their song *"before the throne, and before the four beasts, and the elders."* In the spiritual world, there is no temporal barrier between heaven and earth. The praise of earth is at once the praise of heaven. Since God is omnipresent and yet seated on His throne, His throne is everywhere present. How radically different from the tiny, insignificant thrones of man!

The song they sing is described as a new song, one which only they can learn. Their purity has caused God to reward them by giving them their own song of praise to sing to Him.

Purity is possible

Revelation 14:4a *These are they which were **not defiled** with women; for they are **virgins**. These are they which follow the Lamb whithersoever he goeth...*

Pay attention, please, to those two words and phrases I emphasized: not defiled, virgins. They will be followed up in the last half of the verse by the descriptives "no guile, and without fault." All four of these terms are terms of absolute purity. Purity is possible! And when we "follow the Lamb wherever He goes," as is said of these men in verse four, it will be a certainty. One never engages in impurity while following the Lamb since the Lamb never leads that way.

So yes, even in this wicked world, purity is possible.

Purity is possible even when you are in the extreme minority, which they will be.

Purity is possible even when your life is on the line, and their lives definitely will be.

Purity is also possible both individually and as a group. One hundred forty-four thousand *individuals* will be absolutely pure. But a *group* of 144,000 will also be pure. You, as individuals, can be pure. A church youth group can also be pure. An entire church can be pure. It is possible, and we should be striving for that very thing!

Purity is possible even in the face of our strongest desires to do wrong. Notice that it says they were not defiled with women; they were virgins. In other words, God sealed 144,00 unmarried men to do his bidding. None of them will have the privilege of getting married, and none of them will give away their virginity.

Sex is one of the strongest desires God ever placed in human beings. But it is a desire that can only be righteously fulfilled between a man and his wife. Anyone who is unmarried needs to understand that God's expectation is that you not be sexually active.

Especially in regard to young people, the lost world hears this and says, "That's impossible; kids are going to have sex; they just need to do so safely." That is a lie from hell. They do not have to give up their virginity; they are not supposed to give up their virginity, purity is possible, and impurity is never safe!

Purity is powerful

Revelation 14:4b *...These were redeemed from among men, being the firstfruits unto God and to the Lamb.* **5** *And in their mouth was found no guile: for they are without fault before the throne of God.*

I love plums. A few days ago, as I write this, I planted two plum trees by my house. And here is what I know about them at this stage of their development. If they produce any plums at all this year, it will be just a few very small ones. But that does not worry me a bit because I knew that those few plums will be followed up by a great many more plums in later years. Those first few will just be "the firstfruits;" the real harvest is yet to come.

In verse four, these 144,000, just a small handful compared to the billions on earth, not much more than the population of Cleveland County, NC, are redeemed from among men. They are born again, and they live a life that proves it.

As a "reward," Antichrist hunts them down and kills them. But not before they demonstrate the true power of purity. That power of purity is shown by the fact that even though they will be hunted down and killed, even though the whole world will know they will not survive long, they will still manage to win countless millions to Christ.

When you can win souls to God while living a life that God is blessing with good health and good fortune, that is wonderful. But try being chased and persecuted and reviled and marked for death, and see how easy it is to win souls then! Try saying, "If you accept my Jesus, you will get to be murdered too, like all of us will be!" Try saying that and still winning souls. How in the world can they do it? Simple, that is the power of purity.

I have people come to me pretty regularly and ask, "How can I win mom/dad/brother/sister/friend to Jesus? My answer always includes this: live pure at all times. Let them hear purity in your music; let them see purity in the clothes you wear; let them see purity in your financial dealings; let them hear purity in your speech.

If you truly care about your loved ones and want them to get saved, your clothes will show it, and your movie selections will show it, and your money matters will show it, and your vocabulary will show it.

In verse five, we find that these 144,000 are pure in their speech; their lips have "no guile." Purity is possible even with our most uncontrollable body part, the tongue!

In other words, we can tell the truth even when we want to lie.

We can keep our mouth shut even when we want to curse, even when someone may, in our estimation, deeply deserve that cursing.

We can bless someone when we want to bless them out. Purity is possible!

Verse five also shows us that purity is possible even under the piercing gaze of God. We read of these 144,00 that *"they are without fault before the throne of God."* You may be able to fool a parent or a pastor, but you cannot fool God. God knows if you are a Sunday Christian or an every day Christian. God knows if you drink the water of life in church and the alcoholic brew of hell out in the world. God knows if you smile in church and smoke pot at home. God knows if you click on Bible verses in church and click on pornography on your phone. You simply cannot fool God! God demands purity, and purity is possible:

John 1:12 *But as many as received him, to them gave he power to become the sons of God, even to them that believe on his name:*

If you are saved, you have the power, the *exousia*, the authority to live like a child of God! Before you got saved, you did not. You could pretend, you could put on a moral front, you could act the part for a while, but deep inside you, that old sin nature still reigned. That is why so many people cannot seem to get victory over sin; the Giver of victory has never taken up residence in their hearts.

But if 144,000 men can live pure and holy lives right under the nose of the devil himself, we who are saved can do the same here and now.

Chapter Thirty-One
Three More Preachers

Revelation 14:6 *And I saw another angel fly in the midst of heaven, having the everlasting gospel to preach unto them that dwell on the earth, and to every nation, and kindred, and tongue, and people,* **7** *Saying with a loud voice, Fear God, and give glory to him; for the hour of his judgment is come: and worship him that made heaven, and earth, and the sea, and the fountains of waters.* **8** *And there followed another angel, saying, Babylon is fallen, is fallen, that great city, because she made all nations drink of the wine of the wrath of her fornication.* **9** *And the third angel followed them, saying with a loud voice, If any man worship the beast and his image, and receive his mark in his forehead, or in his hand,* **10** *The same shall drink of the wine of the wrath of God, which is poured out without mixture into the cup of his indignation; and he shall be tormented with fire and brimstone in the presence of the holy angels, and in the presence of the Lamb:* **11** *And the smoke of their torment ascendeth up for ever and ever: and they have no rest day nor night, who worship the beast and his image, and whosoever receiveth the mark of his name.* **12** *Here is the patience of the saints: here are they that keep the commandments of God, and the faith of Jesus.* **13** *And I heard a voice from heaven saying unto me, Write, Blessed are the dead which die in the Lord from henceforth: Yea, saith the Spirit, that they may rest from their labours; and their works do follow them.*

There is kind of a funny yet sad phenomenon here in the Bible belt. Buildings do not stay vacant for very long. If an empty building gets noticed, it is usually only a matter of time until some group of people who have split from another church rent it and start a new one. We go from Hope Baptist Church to New Hope Baptist Church to No Hope Baptist Church. And then No Hope splits off and starts a non-Denominational church, and then some of their folks who think that church is an offensive term split off and start a "fellowship." We go from churches the size of oak trees and split them down to 4x4s and then shave them down to furring strips and then bust them up into toothpicks for the devil to chew up and spit out.

And each of those churches, at some point, has a pastor. For better or for worse, in our day and in our area, preachers are as plentiful as kudzu! It used to be that a few dedicated, godly, skilled, effective men were the preachers in any given area. There was a day that, if a man bore the title of preacher or pastor, there was something special about him. That man could preach, he could explain the Word, he could hold people's attention, and the power of God was on him. He was respectable, hard-working, well-trained, and a good shepherd.

But these days, with the proliferation of splinter churches and the lure of prosperity gospel churches, preachers are multiplying like rabbits whether they meet the qualifications of 1 Timothy 3 or not. It is generally easier to find a preacher these days, good or bad, than a used car salesman or a burger flipper.

But there will come a day when that is not true. There will come a time when preachers are rare, almost non-existent. The bad ones will have stopped preaching to save their sorry hides, and the good ones will have all been killed. Pulpits will be empty; churches will be vacant. Radio waves will be void of any real gospel message. There will be an absolute drought of Bible preaching.

But the sovereign God has determined that while the world stands, there will be preaching. And if that preaching cannot be done on the ground, it will be done in the air. If it will not be done by men, it will be done by angels. Three of them, in fact. Three heavenly messengers, with three more sermons the world needs to hear.

A message of redemption

Revelation 14:6 *And I saw another angel fly in the midst of heaven, having the everlasting gospel to preach unto them that dwell on the earth, and to every nation, and kindred, and tongue, and people,* **7** *Saying with a loud voice, Fear God, and give glory to him; for the hour of his judgment is come: and worship him that made heaven, and earth, and the sea, and the fountains of waters.*

Throughout the book of The Revelation, John has been seeing angels fly through the heavens, shouting and dropping judgments. Now he sees another one. He watches him fly and then hears him shouting, preaching at the top of his angelic lungs.

The substance of the message

Revelation 14:6a *And I saw another angel fly in the midst of heaven, having the everlasting gospel to preach...*

This angel is preaching the everlasting gospel. Even during the last of the last days, even during the judgment of God on earth, God is still desirous that people be saved. He still wants them to be redeemed, to have their sins forgiven.

Oh the wonder of wonders, that God loves man!

John 3:16 *For God so loved the world, that he gave his only begotten Son, that whosoever believeth in him should not perish, but have everlasting life.*

Romans 5:8 *But God commendeth his love toward us, in that, while we were yet sinners, Christ died for us.*

1 John 4:19 *We love him, because he first loved us.*

Even during this, the Tribulation Period, the time when mankind is being judged and deserving every bit of it, God still loves man and sends an angel to preach the gospel to them. There is just nothing in the universe like the love of God!

The scope of the message

Revelation 14:6b *...unto them that dwell on the earth, and to every nation, and kindred, and tongue, and people,*

This angel is preaching the gospel to every nation, kindred, tongue, and people on earth. God is concerned with sin, not skin. Whiteness does not make you anything special before God. Blackness does not make you anything special before God. Red and yellow, black and white, they are all EQUALLY precious in His sight! All of us have been altogether born in sin, we have chosen to do wrong, we are incapable of getting ourselves out of the mess we are in, and we desperately need a Savior to rescue us. The truth is that God wants to save blacks just as desperately as He wants to save whites, and He wants to save whites just as desperately as He wants to save Orientals, and He wants to save Orientals just as desperately as He wants to save Latinos and Eskimos and Islanders and Aborigines. And He is equally able to save any of those people! There is no race that is farther from or nearer to God than any other race. And in that pursuit of souls, God has commanded us to do what this angel is doing:

Matthew 28:19 *Go ye therefore, and teach all nations, baptizing them in the name of the Father, and of the Son, and of the Holy Ghost:* **20** *Teaching them to observe all things whatsoever I have commanded you: and, lo, I am with you alway, even unto the end of the world. Amen.*

It is our job to evangelize every race of people on earth. The scope of the gospel is universal! It reaches from the uttermost to the guttermost, from the whitest to the blackest; it goes out to every nation and kindred and tongue and people.

The specifics of the message

Revelation 14:7 *Saying with a loud voice, Fear God, and give glory to him; for the hour of his judgment is come: and worship him that made heaven, and earth, and the sea, and the fountains of waters.*

We know from I Corinthians 15 that the gospel is the death, burial, resurrection, and proof of the resurrection of Christ. That is the good news that God offers. But in order to accept that good news, there are some other things we need to know, and this angel covers them pretty well:

Saying with a loud voice, Fear God...

This world is rapidly losing the reverential fear of Almighty God. There was a time when people would not so much as curse while driving by a church. Now they use the church parking lot as a place to drink and smoke on Saturday night. People are going through life with no fear of God, and one second after death, when their feet hit the fire, they will realize their eternal mistake.

Saying with a loud voice... give glory to him

Here is another thing the angel understood and proclaimed that men seem to have forgotten about. God expects to be glorified of us. I am amazed how many people will open their mouths to speak glowingly of a musician or a singer or a preacher or a teacher or a son or a daughter but clam up tight when it comes to glorifying God! It should not take an angel flying through heaven to remind men of that fact.

Saying with a loud voice... for the hour of his judgment is come.

The message of redemption is always honest. Because of that, it always includes the fact that judgment is coming for those who reject God. This is another thing that makes the "seeker-friendly" movement so dangerous. They would never dream of telling people uncomfortable things like, "You are headed for hell," or "You need to repent," or "God will not tolerate your wicked life," or "You reap what you sow," and things of that nature. But as surely as the sun rises in the east, there will come a day when the judgment of God falls on the unrepentant, and that part of the message of redemption must be preached!

Saying with a loud voice... and worship him that made heaven, and earth, and the sea, and the fountains of waters.

This part of the message of redemption deals with the fact that there is a Creator that we, the creation, are subject to. People hate this concept! Especially wealthy, self-important types who think that they are "self-made." They do not want to answer to anyone, especially God.

They can dislike it all they want, you can dislike it all you want, but if you get saved, it will be because you as a creature came and humbled yourself and worshipped Him as your Creator.

From 1905 to 1980, the world bore with an atheist and evolutionist named Jean-Paul Sartre. He refused to believe in God and refused to acknowledge himself as a creature subject to a creator. It is interesting; lots of people go through life like that, but few ever can look death in the face like that. Near the end of his life, Jean-Paul Sartre told Pierre Victor: "I do not feel that I am the product of chance, a speck of dust in the universe, but someone who was expected, prepared, prefigured. In short, a being whom only a Creator could put here..."*(The "scandalous"...* 2014)

You may be reading this book as a lost sinner, not even believing in the existence of God. But if you have any sense, you will pay attention to the message of redemption while it is being spoken by a man. Because if you wait until you hear it from that first angel flying through heaven, it will be too late for you.

A message of ruin

Revelation 14:8 *And there followed another angel, saying, Babylon is fallen, is fallen, that great city, because she made all nations drink of the wine of the wrath of her fornication.*

For fourteen-plus chapters in the book of the Revelation, we have been dealing with the raptured church, the 144,000 Jewish witnesses, the nation of Israel, and Gentile world powers. But verse eight of this chapter marks the first time the word Babylon appears in the book of The Revelation. This is a little bit amazing since the word Babylon occurs two hundred eighty-six times in Scripture, and the shortened form Babel occurs twice. This city is seen as far back as the eleventh chapter of Genesis, where it was the scene of the first organized rebellion against God.

This will not be the last time it is mentioned in the book of The Revelation. In fact, much of the last chapters of the book are devoted to it! Because of that, I am not going to say much about it by way of identifying it just yet. This verse just simply introduces it and then mentions its ruin and why it is ruined. So, for now, I am going to do the exact same thing. We have introduced the subject of Babylon during the Tribulation Period and will spend the rest of the time at this point looking at what God says about its ruin.

Strength does not prevent ruin

Revelation 14:8 *And there followed another angel, saying, Babylon is fallen, is fallen, that great city...*

Here is a quiz for you: in every single verse in the book of The Revelation that the word Babylon appears, another descriptive word always appears with it. What is that word?

Great.

We get our English word mega from the Greek word for great. Babylon historically, geographically, influentially, symbolically, has always been a great, strong city. Just look back at the Babylon of Nebuchadnezzar, and here is what you will find. Babylon was roughly the size of Houston, Texas, and had a population of more than a million people. Around the city there was an inner wall built, three hundred fifty feet high, eighty-seven feet thick. A half-mile further out, there was another wall built the exact same size. That made for thirty square miles of rich cropland in between. On top of the walls were two hundred fifty watchtowers, four hundred fifty feet high. Running around the wall was a deep-water moat, thirty feet wide. Filling the moat and running underneath the walls into and through the city was the Euphrates River. So this city had all of the food and water needed for any length of a siege and walls to protect them from any enemy. This was a strong city! So, it is no wonder that as you look back at Daniel 5, King Belshazzar, Nebuchadnezzar's grandson, was having a drunken party while the armies of the Medes and the Persians were gathered against him outside the wall. Belshazzar just knew that his city was too strong to fall.

But that night, that is exactly what happened. Babylon fell! The city of strength was captured, the king was killed, and a new kingdom took over the city.

Babylon has continued to exist in different forms throughout the years. Though the original city has been long buried somewhere in Iraq by the banks of the Euphrates, the name and spirit and ideas of Babylon have lived on, probably stronger than ever. Just to give you a little preview of things to come, Assyria later had a Babylon, Rome was repeatedly called Babylon, the world system of Antichrist will be a Babylon. Babylon lives on, and she is still very, very strong. Babylon, in its basest form, is any organized rebellion against God.

Babylon was strong, is strong, and will be strong, but strength does not prevent ruin:

One of the most powerful, dangerous men who has ever lived is Mike Tyson, the former heavyweight boxing champion of the world. Though he is just a shadow of his former self, there was a day when he was simply unbeatable. In short order, this young man went 37-0 with thirty-three knockouts. He is widely regarded as the best ever in terms of having both amazing speed and raw punching power. He could knock people out with either hand, and he usually did so within the first couple of rounds. Tyson was so tough and so confident that he sometimes put on all of his gold and diamond jewelry, a full-length fur coat, and walked through New York's downtown Central Park after dark, alone.

But on February 11, 1990, Iron Mike Tyson was knocked stupid by a 42-1 underdog named Buster Douglas. In the tenth round, Tyson found himself rolling around on the canvass, trying to put his mouthpiece back in but getting it upside down, and finally slumping down, unable to even get up.

Men may think that they are too strong to be taken by a Sovereign God, but no amount of strength can ever prevent ruin.

So what happened? How did Babylon fall, and how will she fall again? We saw that strength does not prevent ruin; now let's look at the fact that:

Sin does promote ruin

Let's go back for a moment to Belshazzar's drunken party. The year was 539 B.C., and Belshazzar was feeling comfortable and worry-free in his strong city. But all of the leaders were stoned drunk! No one was paying attention; people everywhere were engaging in open acts of fornication and lewdness. They had become so engrossed in sin that they did not even notice the water level of the Euphrates River dropping. You see, the Medo-Persians had divided the army into three sections. One was at the far end of the city, right where the water went back under the walls and back out into the desert. The second was at the near end of the city, where the water first went under the walls into the city. The third had gone several miles upstream and dug a channel that they opened up to divert some of the flow of the river. So as the water level fell, the armies simply marched under the walls and through the gates that they had bribed two men to open.

Not one bit of this would have been possible except for that little three-letter word, s-i-n.

Look again at what Revelation 14:8 says:

Revelation 14:8 *And there followed another angel, saying, Babylon is fallen, is fallen, that great city, because she made all nations drink of the wine of the wrath of her fornication.*

This Babylon to come will fall into ruin because of sin. Just in this one verse, we see wine and wrath and fornication mentioned. The Babylon of the past fell into ruin because of sin. And it was the same sins! Drunkness, wrath, fornication, among others. Nations fall into ruin today because of sin. No nation that embraces homosexuality and abortion and pornography and booze and drugs and fornication and adultery can hope to avoid ruin forever.

Churches fall into ruin today because of sin. Families fall into ruin today because of sin. Individuals fall into ruin because of sin.

A message of responsibility

Revelation 14:9 *And the third angel followed them, saying with a loud voice, If any man worship the beast and his image, and receive his mark in his forehead, or in his hand,* **10** *The same shall drink of the wine of the wrath of God, which is poured out without mixture into the cup of his indignation; and he shall be tormented with fire and brimstone in the presence of the holy angels, and in the presence of the Lamb:* **11** *And the smoke of their torment ascendeth up for ever and ever: and they* *have no rest day nor night, who worship the beast and his image, and whosoever receiveth the mark of his name.*

For the last several chapters, the mark of the beast has come up pretty regularly. It is one of the chief characteristics of the Tribulation Period. Remember that through this mark, the Antichrist will control every financial transaction on earth. No mark, no buying or selling whatsoever. If people want to buy food, they have to take the mark. If they want their power to stay on, they have to take the mark. If they want gas for their car, they have to take the mark. If they want the county water to keep flowing, they have to take the mark. If they want medical treatment, they have to take the mark. If they want their medications, they have to take the mark. If they want to stay in their house, they have to take the mark.

That will be an enormous incentive for people everywhere to brush the hair off of their foreheads or hold their hand out and take the mark of the beast. Every person on earth will either take the mark and be lost forever, or reject it and forfeit their lives.

What do you think people are going to do? I know what God thinks about that because He sends a third preacher to warn them against it. There will be some lost folks on the bubble, wondering whether they should accept Christ or accept the Antichrist. And while they are wondering, while they are debating, they are going to hear from the third angelic preacher:

"Don't do it! Don't do it! You'll die and go to hell if you take that mark, don't do it!"

This is a crystal-clear message of responsibility. This angel is telling men point-blank that they are responsible for their eternal destiny. God has done everything necessary for them to be saved. He came from heaven to earth, wrapped Himself in flesh, lived a sinless life in the face of all temptations; He was beaten, mocked, scourged, pierced, dehydrated, had a crown of thorns smashed onto His brow. He was wounded for our transgressions, He was bruised for our iniquities, it was the chastisement of our peace that was upon Him, and it is by His stripes we are healed. He died for us, His enemies, while we were sinners alienated from God. He has done everything He had to do to purchase and secure salvation for every one of us. If we reject God and die and go to hell, it will be our own fault, and not one of us will be able to rightfully blame God.

This text uses some brutal terminology to describe what people will endure when they of their own free will reject Jesus the Messiah. Verse ten says that *"The same shall drink of the wine of the wrath of God, which is poured out without mixture into the cup of his indignation."*

In many ancient cultures, to avoid wine becoming strong enough to be intoxicating, it was mixed four parts water to one part wine. But the cup of God's ultimate wrath will not be watered down like that. It will be wrath without mixture. God's wrath in our day has always been tempered and mixed with mercy and love and grace. But there will come a time when that is no longer true. There will come a point at which God says, "Enough! You have rejected Me, and rebelled against Me, and refused to serve Me, and time's up! Judgment falls now; time's up!" At that point, no watchmaker can turn back the clock, no lawyer can get you a stay of execution, no theologian can talk you out of the hell you are cast into.

I do not know how this will work, but verse ten says that whoever receives that mark "*shall be tormented with fire and brimstone in the presence of the holy angels, and in the presence of the Lamb.*" People who have rejected God will, at least for a time, look out through the searing flames and be able to see a Holy God and His holy angels and know that they were just that close to getting saved and escaping the fire.

Verse eleven tells us that even if this part of hell's fire is ever released from the presence of God and the angels, the smoke of their tormenting fire will ascend up forever. They will never rest. This applies to every lost person, not just those who go into the Tribulation Period and receive the mark. This is an awesome responsibility! You are responsible for either accepting or rejecting Christ, and as such, you are responsible for whether you go to heaven or hell.

Three angels fly through the heavens, three more preachers sent from the hand of a loving God to a dying world. And when they do, after they have delivered a scalding set of messages to a world that will largely reject them, then we hear something sweet and positive:

Revelation 14:12 *Here is the patience of the saints: here are they that keep the commandments of God, and the faith of Jesus.*

The last few verses have been pointing to the negative. They have been exposing wicked Babylon and those who will take the mark of the beast. But when we get to verse twelve, the entire focus changes. You see, not everyone is taking the mark. Not everyone rejects Christ. Not everyone is willing to lose their soul to save their life. Some people will do right in our day. Some people will do right even during the Tribulation Period. And this verse seems to be God's way of saying, "Don't get too discouraged. Let me show you some who are still standing for what is right. Let me show you another 7,000 like I had in Elijah's day, men who would not bow the knee, men who would not kiss Baal. Let me show you some stiff-spined, hard-headed, old-fashioned, Bible-believing children of God, loved by heaven, hated by hell, delightful to God, despised by the world."

I hope with all my heart you, even now, want to be in that kind of crowd!

You say, "But it costs so much to follow God!" You have no idea how much it can cost. It will cost the Tribulation saints their lives. They will not be insulted; they will be impaled. They will not be denied a fair shake; they will be decapitated. But for them, it will not be a loss; it will be a win:

Revelation 14:13 *And I heard a voice from heaven saying unto me, Write, Blessed are the dead which die in the Lord from henceforth: Yea, saith the Spirit, that they may rest from their labours; and their works do follow them.*

Just think of all that John had seen so far that will happen during this awful time. Christians starving, because they refused to take the mark. 144,000 Jews hunted down like animals. People saved one day and slaughtered the next. These people will be under a situation so bad that living itself becomes unbearable. And so God says, "It is enough. These people have been through enough; they've served me faithfully; blessed are they which die in the Lord from this point forward. It is reunion time in heaven. There's a godly old woman who needs to be reunited with her husband who was murdered by the Antichrist. There's a teenager who's still alive, but her mom and dad were killed for my name's sake. They need to be together again."

And in droves, the last of the Christians will begin to be killed. But even in death, they are still being followed. Not by the secret police of the Antichrist, though. No, according to verse thirteen, their works are following them. I guarantee you these humble servants of God are in for one more surprise. Just imagine when some dear saint has her head cut off and wakes up that very split second in eternity in the presence of Jesus. That will be surprising enough. But imagine when a second later that lady hears, "Make way, coming through," and she sees the UPS truck, the Unexpected Parcel Service, pull into the throne room. Imagine the big back door of the truck rolling up, and angels starting to unload box after box after box, right at the dear lady's feet. Cannot you see her as she turns to Jesus and says, "Lord, what's this?" And cannot you see as He smiles and says, "Child, those are your works. They followed you here. Over here is a box of heavenly stubbornness. It is from that day when you told the Antichrist that he was ugly, and his mama dressed him funny. Here's a box of evangelism, from all those people you won to God when they saw you refuse the mark. And here's a big parcel of Christlikeness. This comes from when you, even though you were starving, took your own food and gave it to your kids so they would not be hungry and would not be as tempted to take the mark."

Can you just imagine! Do you kind of wish you could get in on that? I have good news; you can:

1 Timothy 5:24 *Some men's sins are open beforehand, going before to judgment; and some men they follow after.* **25** *Likewise also the good works of some are manifest beforehand; and they that are otherwise cannot be hid.*

What Paul said about sins in verse twenty-four, he said another way about good works in verse twenty-five. Sometimes, sin or good works are open and visible and known here in this life. But sometimes, they just follow people into eternity. So we get the same privilege as the Tribulation saints! We get our own set of "boxes" of unexpected parcels.

It will be an incredible time when our packages arrive in glory!

Right now, you can pretty easily find any of a thousand preachers at a moment's notice. But not forever. There will come a day when all the preachers are gone. But things will not stay quiet for long because a loving God will launch a trio of angels, three more preachers to speak His Word to a lost and dying world.

Chapter Thirty-Two
Approaching Armageddon

Revelation 14:14 *And I looked, and behold a white cloud, and upon the cloud one sat like unto the Son of man, having on his head a golden crown, and in his hand a sharp sickle.* **15** *And another angel came out of the temple, crying with a loud voice to him that sat on the cloud, Thrust in thy sickle, and reap: for the time is come for thee to reap; for the harvest of the earth is ripe.* **16** *And he that sat on the cloud thrust in his sickle on the earth; and the earth was reaped.* **17** *And another angel came out of the temple which is in heaven, he also having a sharp sickle.* **18** *And another angel came out from the altar, which had power over fire; and cried with a loud cry to him that had the sharp sickle, saying, Thrust in thy sharp sickle, and gather the clusters of the vine of the earth; for her grapes are fully ripe.* **19** *And the angel thrust in his sickle into the earth, and gathered the vine of the earth, and cast it into the great winepress of the wrath of God.* **20** *And the winepress was trodden without the city, and blood came out of the winepress, even unto the horse bridles, by the space of a thousand and six hundred furlongs.*

In the few verses just prior to these, John saw three angels flying through the heavens with three messages for mankind. And it is very clear from the messages they preached that they were heralding the closing acts of the judgment of God on a wicked world. And as we segue from there into these verses, we will see a picturesque vision of part of that judgment, a very famous part of it, and just how devastating it will be. But we will also see a very sweet scene that occurs just before that judgment falls.

A sweet reaping

Revelation 14:14 *And I looked, and behold a white cloud, and upon the cloud one sat like unto the Son of man, having on his head a golden crown, and in his hand a sharp sickle.* **15** *And another angel came out of the temple, crying with a loud voice to him that sat on the cloud, Thrust in thy sickle, and reap: for the time is come for thee to reap; for the harvest of the earth is ripe.* **16** *And he that sat on the cloud thrust in his sickle on the earth; and the earth was reaped.*

If you are not careful in how you handle the text, you may assume these verses to be a part of the judgment in this chapter. But look at what immediately precedes them in the context:

Revelation 14:13 *And I heard a voice from heaven saying unto me, Write, Blessed are the dead which die in the Lord from henceforth:*

Yea, saith the Spirit, that they may rest from their labours; and their works do follow them.

The voice from heaven spoke of how blessed people would be to die in the Lord from that point forward. And immediately on the heels of that, we find a reaper on the clouds reaping the earth.

Revelation 14:14 *And I looked, and behold a white cloud, and upon the cloud one sat like unto the Son of man, having on his head a golden crown, and in his hand a sharp sickle.*

This first reaper is described as "like unto the Son of Man," and He is wearing a golden crown. A quick look at the very first chapter of the book of The Revelation will identify this individual for us very thoroughly.

Revelation 1:13 *And in the midst of the seven candlesticks one **like unto the Son of man**, clothed with a garment down to the foot, and girt about the paps with a golden girdle.* **14** *His head and his hairs were white like wool, as white as snow; and his eyes were as a flame of fire;* **15** *And his feet like unto fine brass, as if they burned in a furnace; and his voice as the sound of many waters.* **16** *And he had in his right hand seven stars: and out of his mouth went a sharp twoedged sword: and his countenance was as the sun shineth in his strength.* **17** *And when I saw him, I fell at his feet as dead. And he laid his right hand upon me, saying unto me, Fear not; I am the first and the last:* **18** *I am he that liveth, and was dead; and, behold, I am alive for evermore, Amen; and have the keys of hell and of death.*

That is very clearly speaking of Jesus, as is our current text in Revelation 14, which once again refers to Him as "like unto the Son of Man." So before the approaching judgment of Armageddon and all of the horrific bloodshed and destruction, Jesus will be reaping His crop, His saints, out of this world. And where the verses to follow speak in terms of grapes and uses the word winepress, these verses speak in terms of grain, a harvest, as verse fifteen puts it. Furthermore, the first reaper and sickle mention nothing of bloodshed; that is not mentioned until verse twenty, after the second reaper has swung his sickle. These are two different sickle bearers, two different sickles, two different things. In this first reaper, we clearly see Christ gathering His own to Himself, bringing home those who are martyred during this part of the Tribulation Period.

Will the Antichrist be killing them? Yes. But will Jesus be reaping them? Yes. Both are true at the exact same time. The devil may be putting them to death, but Jesus is gathering them home.

A sharp judgment

Revelation 14:15 *And another angel came out of the temple, crying with a loud voice to him that sat on the cloud, Thrust in thy sickle, and reap: for the time is come for thee to reap; for the harvest of the earth is ripe.* **16** *And he that sat on the cloud thrust in his sickle on the earth; and the earth was reaped.* **17** *And another angel came out of the temple which is in heaven, he also having a sharp sickle.* **18** *And another angel came out from the altar, which had power over fire; and cried with a loud cry to him that had the sharp sickle, saying, Thrust in thy sharp sickle, and gather the clusters of the vine of the earth; for her grapes are fully ripe.* **19** *And the angel thrust in his sickle into the earth, and gathered the vine of the earth, and cast it into the great winepress of the wrath of God.*

After the Son of Man, Jesus, finishes swinging His sickle and reaping His crop from the earth, the text once again turns to angels of judgment, one of which also carries a sickle. And where the sickle of Christ was a sweet sickle of gathering the harvest, the sickle of this angel is going to be a sharp sickle of judgment on the wicked world.

The Bible is a truly amazing book. We should all expect that from something authored by God. One of the things that makes it so amazing is that people who lived hundreds of years apart wrote about the exact same things, and even now, in our day, we can see those things that they prophesied thousands of years ago taking shape!

One major thing that is taking shape in our day was written about here in the book of the Revelation by John the apostle, and also hundreds of years before that by the prophet Joel. Notice how exactly it matches what we just read about in Revelation 14:

Joel 3:1 *For, behold, in those days, and in that time, when I shall bring again the captivity of Judah and Jerusalem,* **2** *I will also gather all nations, and will bring them down into the valley of Jehoshaphat, and will plead with them there for my people and for my heritage Israel, whom they have scattered among the nations, and parted my land.*

Joel 3:9 *Proclaim ye this among the Gentiles; Prepare war, wake up the mighty men, let all the men of war draw near; let them come up:* **10** *Beat your plowshares into swords, and your pruninghooks into spears: let the weak say, I am strong.* **11** *Assemble yourselves, and come, all ye heathen, and gather yourselves together round about: thither cause thy mighty ones to come down, O LORD.* **12** *Let the heathen be wakened, and come up to the valley of Jehoshaphat: for there will I sit to judge all the heathen round about.* **13** *Put ye in the sickle, for the harvest is ripe: come, get you down; for the press is full, the fats overflow; for their wickedness is great.* **14** *Multitudes, multitudes in the* *valley of decision: for the day of the LORD is near in the valley of decision.*

These are parallel passages. Joel 3:13 especially speaks of the sickle and the divine reaper, which is the exact same thing John spoke of in Revelation 14. And we find both the harvest in verse fourteen, as we did in Revelation 4:15, and the grapes and the winepress here in verse thirteen as well that correlates to the second sickle and the second sickle bearer. So what in the world are John and Joel talking about, especially in reference to the grapes and winepress? Let me show you.

Joel 3:2 *I will also gather all nations, and will bring them down into the valley of Jehoshaphat...*

Now look at verse fourteen of the same chapter:

Joel 3:14 *Multitudes, multitudes in the valley of decision: for the day of the LORD is near in the valley of decision.*

Three times you saw "the valley of." Twice it was the Valley of Decision, once it was the Valley of Jehoshaphat. So we are talking first of all about a place, a literal, physical place on this earth. One of the names it goes by is the Valley of Jehoshaphat, another name it goes by is the Valley of Decision, and it is also called the plain of Jezreel. It has even more names, but there is one name it bears that I guarantee you, you have heard before. Look at the next time it is mentioned in the book of The Revelation, in chapter sixteen and verse sixteen:

Revelation 16:16 *And he gathered them together into a place called in the Hebrew tongue Armageddon.*

You may never have heard of the Valley of Decision, or the Valley of Jehoshaphat, or the plain of Jezreel, but pretty much everyone living has heard of Armageddon. Most people think of it as an event, and in a way, it is, but the main thing it is, is a place. And in that place, God will hold the final showdown of this age. We will see the details of Armageddon when we cover Revelation 19.

But right here as we are introduced to the subject of Armageddon here in the book of Revelation, we should take a moment to look at a rather unique aspect of it, namely the draw of Armageddon. This thing that God alludes to here in Revelation 14 and then further elaborates on in Revelation 16 and Revelation 19, how does it happen? How will God get people there to it and for it? When we are talking about an angel of God reaping the earth, causing horrific death and bloodshed, when you are talking about what Revelation 14:19 calls *"the great winepress of the wrath of God,"* it is not like people are going to line up for such a thing voluntarily.

In Joel 3:3, God said that He would gather all nations into this valley. In verse twelve, He said that all the heathen would be there. In verse fourteen, He used the term multitudes twice in a row to show how many people would be there. In both Joel's account and what we see here in Revelation fourteen, the picture given is that of grapes so full they are about to pop. There will be multiplied millions at this place called Armageddon! And that brings us to one of the most amazing facts of prophecy.

There was a time when Armageddon was a natural draw, a place people literally could not stay away from. Armageddon is a Hebrew word that means "The Mound of Megiddo." Megiddo was an extremely important Old Testament city.

In 1 Kings 9, the great King Solomon raised a tax to build up three important cities. One was Hazor, one was Gezer, and the last one was Megiddo. Megiddo was the middle of those three cities. In fact, Megiddo was the middle of a lot of things. Truthfully, at that time, it was the center of the world! Israel lay right between Egypt and Mesopotamia (modern-day Iraq, Iran, etc.). These were the two biggest powers of the world, both militarily and in terms of commerce. But in order for them to trade with each other, they had to take the one and only pathway that lay between them. It was a road called the Via Maris, the way of the sea. Because of the Mediterranean Sea, there just was no other viable way between these two great lands. That road, the Via Maris, ran right through Israel. And there was exactly one point at which it could be controlled. The valley of Jehoshaphat, the Valley of Decision, the plain of Jezreel, Megiddo... Armageddon. So when Solomon gained control of that one valley, he took control of the commerce of the entire world. That may explain how God made him the richest man that ever lived.

This valley was the most important, desirable piece of real estate on the planet; it just made sense for all nations to gather there. But here is where things get really interesting: it has not been that way for more than two thousand years, and it certainly is not that way in our day. If you went to the valley of Armageddon today, let me tell you what you would find: not much of anything! Some croplands, maybe an archaeologist roaming around, a few rocks piled up, a stray sheep or two, but that is about it. There simply is no good reason for anyone to go there anymore. If someone in Iran wants to sell something to someone in Egypt, they take the order online, package it up, call UPS, put the box on a plane, cruise up to 35,000 feet, fly straight over Israel, and the package arrives the very next day. The valley of Armageddon has no influence whatsoever on world commerce anymore.

There is no financial value under Armageddon either. There are no wells pumping oil up from the ground of Armageddon because there is no known oil under that particular piece of ground.

There are no tourist attractions in Armageddon to bring in millions of foreign dollars. There is no Armageddon beach resort because there is no beach. There is no Armageddon high-rise hotel. There is no logical reason for anyone, much less everyone, to come to Armageddon. Yet God said that they will come, all of them. The prophet Ezekiel said that God will put hooks in their jaws to draw them to this spot.

And this spot He will draw them to is perfectly designed for one thing above all else: warfare. In fact, it was the scene of the first recorded warfare of nations in history, and has been a consistent site of warfare ever since, and will end up being the scene of the last warfare of this age!

The Battle of Megiddo is the first recorded battle on earth, taking place in the 15th century BC. It took place between Egyptian Pharoah Thutmose and Canaanite King Kadesh. From that battle on, history has played out in this valley. Jezebel was killed in this valley (2 Kings 9:10). King Josiah was killed in this valley (2 Chronicles 35:20-25). There was the Battle of Ain Julat between the Mongols and the Mamluks in A.D. 1260. Napoleon Bonaparte defeated the Ottomans here in 1799. Even a battle of WW1 was fought here between General Allenby and the Turks and Germans. In all, somewhere around two hundred battles have taken place in this valley, making it arguably the bloodiest battlefield in history. And God is going to use this site for the battle to end all battles before the thousand-year millennial reign of Christ begins. (Myatt, 2019)

How in the world will all this happen? What is the hook in the jaw? What is the draw that will bring all men to Armageddon? Here it is:

Luke 21:20 *And when ye shall see Jerusalem compassed with armies, then know that the desolation thereof is nigh.*

The draw of Armageddon will be raw hatred of the Jewish people. Armageddon will be the time when the armies of the world in general and the Middle East in particular band together and surround Israel, determined to finally destroy her.

And what will the result of that attempt be?

Revelation 14:19 *And the angel thrust in his sickle into the earth, and gathered the vine of the earth, and cast it into the great winepress of the wrath of God.* **20** *And the winepress was trodden without the city, and blood came out of the winepress, even unto the horse bridles, by the space of a thousand and six hundred furlongs.*

Nearly six thousand years ago, the first human blood was shed as Cain murdered his brother Abel. Since that first drop of blood was shed, more blood has been shed during wartime in the place called Armageddon than any other place on earth. More wars have been fought there than in any other place. Armageddon is the most natural battlefield on earth, and it has been used for that purpose time and time again. But all of the bloodshed up to this very time throughout history will pale in comparison to what happens at the battle of Armageddon.

According to Revelation 14:19-20, when the reaper swings his sickle at Armageddon, it will not be grape juice that flows; it will be human blood. It is going to flow some four feet deep in the center of the valley, and the flow will run for 1600 furlongs, which works out to about 200 miles!

This world has seen death.

But this world has never seen death like it will soon see at Armageddon.

Look again at what Joel called this valley:

Joel 3:14 *Multitudes, multitudes in the valley of decision: for the day of the LORD is near in the valley of decision.*

Armageddon is the valley of decision. But by the time the armies of the world march into that valley, the decision is already made. The only time they could have possibly chosen another course is to have chosen before they got there. But the decisions of world nations for the past seventy-plus years have been running us like a freight train towards Armageddon. Chief among those decisions has been the decision to hate and try to destroy Israel. Look at how God put it in the early part of Joel 3:

Joel 3:1 *For, behold, in those days, and in that time, when I shall bring again the captivity of Judah and Jerusalem,* **2** *I will also gather all nations, and will bring them down into the valley of Jehoshaphat, and will plead with them there for my people and for my heritage Israel, whom they have scattered among the nations, and parted my land.*

In God's sight, Armageddon will be all about how the nations of the world have treated His heritage, Israel.

When Israel became a nation in 1948, she was not allowed any breathing space to organize her forces. She was vastly outnumbered in troops, population, weapons, land mass, and had no allies. Experts proclaimed that within two months, the issue would be settled, and Israel would be no more. The Arabs would destroy her quickly and completely. The Arab forces lined up against her included Palestinians, Egypt, Jordan, Syria, Lebanon, and troops from Saudi Arabia. Azzam Pasha, Secretary General of the Arab League, boldly proclaimed to the world that, "This will be a war of extermination."

On May 25, 1965, Egyptian President Gamal Abdel Nasser issued a statement that said, "The Arab national aim is the elimination of Israel."

On October 6, 1973, on Yom Kippur, the Day of Atonement, the holiest day in the year to the Jewish people, Arab forces launched a surprise attack. Arabs rise up in anger when any bombs drop during Ramadan, but they themselves saw no problem with a sneak attack on Yom Kippur. 1,400 Syrian tanks rolled into the Golan heights, facing one hundred eighty Israeli tanks. Along the Suez Canal, 80,000 Egyptians went against five hundred Jewish defenders. Iraq, Saudi Arabia, Kuwait, Libya, Algeria, Tunisia, Lebanon, the Soviet Union, and Jordan all contributed either men, money, or equipment to the effort. Again, this was a battle Israel simply could not win, and again they won!

The type of conflict Israel most often faces has for, the last couple of decades, been one of terroristic guerrilla attacks. The main group behind this drive is the Palestinian Liberation Organization, the P.L.O. The P.L.O. was formed in 1964, and most of the violence you see in the middle east to this day will be the result of their hands or the hands of a newer group, Hamas. The Arabs have never ceased in their hatred for the Jew, and they never will.

In 2006, Iranian President Mahmoud Ahmadinejad said, "Israel has no right to even exist; they should be pushed off the face of the planet." America and Israel hater Cindy Sheehan said the same thing nearly word for word. Several young, prominent members of Congress openly despise Israel and advocate for starving them out economically. Hatred of Israel has many prominent advocates right here in America! People are making their decision; they are deciding to hate God, they are deciding to hate the people He loves, and they are deciding to hate America for standing with the people of God. That decision is sending this world right down the pathway to Armageddon. And the truth is, God, in His righteousness, is using that hatred as a hook in the jaws of the Gentiles around the world to pull a wicked world to judgment. Basically, this world has already made up its mind; it has decided.

There may be some reading this book who have never even left their hometowns, much less traveled outside the country, but who will one day be drawn to the place called Armageddon. And here is the truly frightening thought: Armageddon happens right near the end of the seven-year Tribulation Period. So if armies are already lining up around her, how near could we be to the coming of Christ? If you pass yet another day having rejected Christ, you may very shortly feel a pain in your jaw as God sets the hook and draws you to Armageddon.

Chapter Thirty-Three
Peace in the Storm

Revelation 15:1 *And I saw another sign in heaven, great and marvellous, seven angels having the seven last plagues; for in them is filled up the wrath of God.* **2** *And I saw as it were a sea of glass mingled with fire: and them that had gotten the victory over the beast, and over his image, and over his mark, and over the number of his name, stand on the sea of glass, having the harps of God.* **3** *And they sing the song of Moses the servant of God, and the song of the Lamb, saying, Great and marvellous are thy works, Lord God Almighty; just and true are thy ways, thou King of saints.* **4** *Who shall not fear thee, O Lord, and glorify thy name? for thou only art holy: for all nations shall come and worship before thee; for thy judgments are made manifest.* **5** *And after that I looked, and, behold, the temple of the tabernacle of the testimony in heaven was opened:* **6** *And the seven angels came out of the temple, having the seven plagues, clothed in pure and white linen, and having their breasts girded with golden girdles.* **7** *And one of the four beasts gave unto the seven angels seven golden vials full of the wrath of God, who liveth for ever and ever.* **8** *And the temple was filled with smoke from the glory of God, and from his power; and no man was able to enter into the temple, till the seven plagues of the seven angels were fulfilled.*

For my family and me, February 16, 2003, was a bad day in a lot of ways. First of all, there was a huge ice storm. Power was off all over the place. A church member had a wreck in the church van that we let him use and totaled it. And Dana and I were exhausted; we had hardly slept the night before. You see, that was the day after Alethia, our youngest child, was born.

But here is an interesting thing: despite everything everyone was going through, despite our exhaustion, despite the totaled van, despite the storm, despite the widespread power outages, that little girl did not care or worry a bit. She slept—like a baby! She had no fear and no worries. She had peace in the storm. She just laid there in mama or daddy's arms and trusted us to take care of her every need while everything raged on in the world around her.

That is an awesome picture of the privilege of being a child of God. No matter what storms may come, the child of God can have a peace that defies the circumstances:

Philippians 4:7 *And the peace of God, which passeth all understanding, shall keep your hearts and minds through Christ Jesus.*

No matter what storms may come, the child of God can have a peace that will never be taken away:

John 14:27 *Peace I leave with you, my peace I give unto you: not as the world giveth, give I unto you. Let not your heart be troubled, neither let it be afraid.*

No matter what storms may come, the child of God can have a peace that guides your heart right:

Colossians 3:15 *And let the peace of God rule in your hearts, to the which also ye are called in one body; and be ye thankful.*

There is nothing in the universe like the sweet peace of Almighty God taking hold in your heart.

As we have been looking through the book of The Revelation, we have been looking ahead to a time, a time I think is not too far away, when God will unload His fury on a disobedient world. We saw seven seal judgments, followed by seven trumpet judgments, among many other devastating things that take place during the Tribulation Period. Imagine this awesome time when the moon turns to blood, the wind is stopped, earthquakes destroy entire major cities, and satanic scorpions sting men for five months, yet God will not let them die. Imagine this awful time when people have to take the mark of the beast, 666, or die of starvation. Imagine a talking statue of the Antichrist looking down at people with piercing eyes, watching for anyone who refuses to bow down. Imagine a third of the vegetation on earth destroyed, a third of the ships sunk, and a third of the waters fouled. Imagine when the fallen star called Wormwood poisons the drinking water on earth, yet makes that water as addictive as cocaine so that people will drink it even knowing it is going to kill them. This will be a terrible time for this world.

And all of that makes me so glad that I got saved when I was nine years old. When God comes back to rapture His bride, I will be removed from this doomed world before all of that happens. If you have never been truly born again, you need to do so while you still have time and opportunity!

In Revelation 14, we were shown the approach to Armageddon, the time when all the nations of the world will descend on Israel to try and destroy her. But as we get into Revelation 15, God lets us drop back just a bit and see another scene, something that will take place while the nations of the world are getting ready to descend into the valley of Armageddon. At that time, God is going to unleash His final seven judgments, a storm of fury, and we will see the details of that storm in the next chapter. But in the midst of that storm, He shows us a picture of perfect peace.

The power of the storm

This storm of judgment puts an exclamation mark on the sentence of God's anger:

Revelation 15:1 *And I saw another sign in heaven, great and marvellous, seven angels having the seven last plagues; for in them is filled up the wrath of God.*

Those two words "filled up" are from one word in the language of the New Testament, the word *teleo*. It is an awesome word, and in this case, it means to finish something at full strength.

Think of a boxer who is pounding on his opponent, round after round, but even though he is in full control, he does not seem to be in any hurry to knock his opponent out. But then finally, after about seven rounds, he unleashes a series of shots to the body and the head, and they make such a sound when they connect, you know immediately that these are the hardest punches he has ever thrown, and he intends to end the fight right then and there. That is a good illustration of the word used here to describe the final judgments of God about to fall on earth.

Can you imagine this? After all the devastating judgments God has leveled on earth from the beginning of time until the end of the Tribulation, the last seven judgments are the hardest shots He will ever throw. This will be a powerful storm!

This storm of judgment changes the very nature of the sea of glass:

Revelation 15:2a *And I saw as it were a sea of glass mingled with fire:*

The sea of glass is mentioned only twice in the Bible, both times in the book of the Revelation. Let me remind you of the first time we saw it:

Revelation 4:6 *And before the throne there was a sea of glass like unto crystal: and in the midst of the throne, and round about the throne, were four beasts full of eyes before and behind.*

One chapter later, in Revelation 5:11, we saw that this sea is big enough for millions and millions of God's worshippers to crowd onto it to praise Him because that is exactly what they do. They are all gathered onto this sea of glass, but in Revelation 4, it simply looks as clear as crystal. It has no color in itself; it simply reflects the colors that shine into it. But in Revelation 15, the nature of that sea of glass had changed. Now it looks like it is glass mixed with a raging fire.

I think John got it exactly right: it looks like it is mingled with fire because it is mingled with fire. The fire of God's storm of wrath has mixed with the sea of glass. His anger is so hot with this wicked, rebellious, unrepentant world that even the sea of glass in heaven is affected by it. That is a powerful storm.

The peace of the saints

Revelation 15:2b... *and them that had gotten the victory over the beast, and over his image, and over his mark, and over the number of his name, stand on the sea of glass, having the harps of God.* **3** *And they sing the song of Moses the servant of God, and the song of the Lamb, saying, Great and marvellous are thy works, Lord God Almighty; just and true are thy ways, thou King of saints.* **4** *Who shall not fear thee, O Lord, and glorify thy name? for thou only art holy: for all nations shall come and worship before thee; for thy judgments are made manifest.*

The greatest storm of wrath this universe has ever seen is being poured out, and yet these dear saints of God are singing! Their sea of glass has become glass mingled with fire, yet they are praising God. According to verse two they have gotten the victory over the beast, and over his image, and over his mark, and over the number of his name.

They gained that victory at cost of their lives.

And because of that, while the storm rages, they have what we need even now, peace in the storm. How in the world do these saints have this peace in the midst of the storm? How can we have that kind of peace in the midst of our storms? Here are a few things I see:

<u>They have already learned conclusively that everything will end up coming out all right:</u>

Revelation 15:2 *And I saw as it were a sea of glass mingled with fire: and them that had gotten the victory over the beast, and over his image, and over his mark, and over the number of his name, stand on the sea of glass, having the harps of God.*

Remember again who these people are. They are Tribulation-era saints. They are people who had not heard and rejected the gospel previous to the Rapture and because of that, were able to get saved after the Rapture. And because they accept Christ during that time, they run afoul of the Antichrist and are killed. Yet the Bible says that they "got the victory" over him.

What does that mean? Again, it does not mean that they survived. In fact, it means just the opposite. Every one of them will get murdered by Antichrist! These people are going to be like the saints during the Medieval Period that refused to bow to the pope. They are going to be beheaded, they are going to be tortured, they are going to be burned at the stake, they will be killed in all kinds of different and awful ways, but God says, "They win!" They got the victory!

These people will try to survive, they will try to live, they will try to keep their families safe, and it will not work. But the second that blade falls across their neck and their head rolls off of their kneeling bodies, they will look up to see a pair of nail-scarred feet, and they will feel their head still on their shoulders, and they will breathe in heavenly air; they do not lose, they win!

May I apply this to you who are going through the storm? No matter what happens in the first quarter, second quarter, third quarter, fourth quarter, even if you feel like you are losing one hundred seventy to zero, when the final whistle blows, you will find out that everything is all right after all! Once we truly understand this, peace in the storm is much easier to come by.

They have learned to trust both the works and the ways of God.

Revelation 15:3 *And they sing the song of Moses the servant of God, and the song of the Lamb, saying, Great and marvellous are thy works, Lord God Almighty; just and true are thy ways, thou King of saints.*

After God brought Israel safely through the Red Sea and used that same Red Sea to destroy those pursuing them, Moses, in Exodus 15, taught the children of Israel a song of victory to commemorate that. These Tribulation saints will sing an adaptation of that song, tailored for their great delivery from their Pharaoh, the Antichrist.

In that song, they will specifically sing about God's works, calling them marvelous, and His ways, calling them just and true. God's works are the things He does; God's ways are the way He does them. All of God's works are great and marvelous, and all of His ways are just and true. That fact gives these saints peace in the storm, and here is why. God is specifically getting ready to level judgment. He is so angry that the sea of glass these saints are standing on is now mingled with fire. He is so furious that He has added his own wrath to the plagues of the angels. God's work in this judgment truly is going to be great and marvelous. When we get to the details of the seven vial judgments in the next chapter, it will be utterly breathtaking.

As these things are getting ready to fall, please remember that there is something happening in heaven. The sea of glass these saints are standing on is now mingled with fire because of how angry God is. If you were looking at that, what might you assume? God is angry with everybody! Everyone is about to get it!

Are you, by chance, a parent that has ever done the "Alright, since none of you will admit who did it, everybody gets a spanking?"

thing? Have you ever been in an entire school class that got paddled for the offence of one or a small few?

Many years ago, a friend of mine from college and a friend of his in the same dorm was in that dorm room with a thief, and no one knew who. People kept on having money and other things stolen, and no one could catch the thief, and no one would confess.

My friend, by the way, was huge. And his buddy in the dorm was about the same. So finally, they called everyone in the dorm for a meeting. It went like this: "Alright, we are tired of the stealing. And since no one will confess to it, we just wanted to let you know that if anything at all of ours gets taken, I mean even so much as a paper clip, everybody is getting a beating."

Nothing was ever stolen again.

These are examples of indiscriminate judgment, judgment that is leveled against anyone and everyone, guilty or innocent. If you were standing on that sea of glass, clear as crystal, and suddenly you saw it turn red with the wrath of God, I suspect you might get a little nervous...

But these saints are not nervous. They have peace in the storm. They know that the work of God, His judgment, is about to be "great and marvelous." But they also know that His ways are always true and just! In other words, they are not the least bit worried about the judgment of God falling on them. They know that nothing He does is random or indiscriminate.

Dear saint, God judged your sin when He sent Christ to Calvary. The fire of God's wrath fell on Jesus, the perfect sacrifice. I know this world is wicked, I know the storm clouds of God's wrath are gathering, but I also know that none of it is directed towards me. When He sees me, He sees His Son, not my sin. When you finally realize that God is not angry with you anymore, when you understand that your sins are cast as far as the east is from the west, when you come to know that you are loved with an everlasting love and underneath are the everlasting arms, the sea of glass can turn as red as the flames of hell itself, and you will still have peace, sweet peace, right in the midst of the storm.

These saints have peace in the storm because they have already learned conclusively that everything will end up coming out all right and because they have learned to trust both the works and the ways of God. But there is yet another reason they have peace in the storm.

<u>They know they are not going to have enemies for very much longer.</u>

Revelation 15:4 *Who shall not fear thee, O Lord, and glorify thy name? for thou only art holy: for all nations shall come and worship before thee; for thy judgments are made manifest.*

This, to me, is stunning beyond measure. These saints are claiming some things. They are claiming that everyone is going to come and glorify the name of the Lord. Think of every God-hating or even God-denying person on earth bowing before the King; oh, how wonderful this is going to be!

These saints are also telling us that all nations are going to come and bow before Him. Think of the list of atheistic, communistic nations that includes!

These saints on the fiery sea of glass have peace in the storm because they know all of their enemies are about to be singing the same tune they are! I know we sometimes encounter storms of circumstances: sickness, finances, etc. But if you think about it, about ninety percent of the storms you ever face have something to do with people behaving as enemies. I have had roof problems as a pastor and plumbing problems as a pastor, but ninety percent or better of my problems have been people problems. You Christians that sit in a pew to worship each week have had sickness problems, aging problems, and all kinds of other problems, but I just bet that most of your problems have been people problems.

Sometimes we all want to echo the words of that world-famous theologian, Rodney King, "Can't we all just get along?" And I have good news for you; one day, we will. There is coming a day when all doctrinal issues are settled... there is coming a day when all personality conflicts are over... there is coming a day when all national hatred is laid aside... there is coming a day when there is only one political party, the party of King Jesus.

As you face your enemies from day to day, I want you to remember this: there is coming a day when every knee shall bow, and every tongue shall confess that Jesus Christ is Lord to the glory of God the Father. There is coming a day when the only flag flying will be the flag of heaven. There is coming a day when everyone that has battered you for your faith in God will kneel before the same God you have been praying to all these years. Those people may be putting you through a storm now, but that storm will stop at the feet of Jesus as they bow and acknowledge Him as King.

The plagues of the seven

Revelation 15:5 *And after that I looked, and, behold, the temple of the tabernacle of the testimony in heaven was opened:* **6** *And the seven angels came out of the temple, having the seven plagues, clothed in pure and white linen, and having their breasts girded with golden girdles.* **7** *And one of the four beasts gave unto the seven angels seven golden vials full of the wrath of God, who liveth for ever and ever.* **8** *And the temple* *was filled with smoke from the glory of God, and from his power; and no man was able to enter into the temple, till the seven plagues of the seven angels were fulfilled.*

The Holy of Holies on earth was merely a representation of the real Holy of Holies in heaven. There is in heaven a real temple, with the real holy place, the real Holy of Holies, the real Ark of the Covenant, the real mercy seat. Twice in the book of The Revelation, we see that holy place opened up. The first one was in Revelation 11:

Revelation 11:19 *And the temple of God was opened in heaven, and there was seen in his temple the ark of his testament: and there were lightnings, and voices, and thunderings, and an earthquake, and great hail.*

But here is the difference. In Revelation 11, the temple of God is opened; we see into it, we hear things from inside it, but we do not see anyone come out of it. Now look again at Revelation 15:5-6

Revelation 15:5 *And after that I looked, and, behold, the temple of the tabernacle of the testimony in heaven was opened:* **6** *And the seven angels came out of the temple, having the seven plagues, clothed in pure and white linen, and having their breasts girded with golden girdles.*

There are right now in heaven seven holy angels within the veil, in the heavenly holy place. For all we know, they may have been there for all eternity past. But when we get to the final storm of God's judgment, God will send these angels out from His presence to rain down the final judgments of God on earth.

In verses one and six, these seven angels already have the plagues they are to unleash on earth. But now look at verse seven:

Revelation 15:7 *And one of the four beasts gave unto the seven angels seven golden vials full of the wrath of God, who liveth for ever and ever.*

We have seen these four beasts many times in the book of the Revelation. We saw that they are a unique kind of creature, having characteristics of both Seraphim and Cherubim. At this point in the Tribulation Period, when these seven angels come out of the temple carrying the seven last plagues, one of those beasts comes over to them and hands them each a vial, an old style of a bowl, full of the wrath of God. Their plagues are going to be mixed with God's wrath!

I have worked with torches for a lot of years. The main combination I have used is either Acetylene and Oxygen or Propane and Oxygen. Early on, the guys teaching me about the torch taught me this: oxygen is not flammable. Propane is flammable. Acetylene is flammable, but oxygen is not flammable. So why do we use it? Why not use just Propane or just Acetylene?

Here is why. Oxygen is what is called an accelerant. In other words, when I put a flame in front of a torch spitting out propane, I get a soft, orange flame. But when I add oxygen to the mix, I get a violent, hissing, sharp, hot blue flame. The oxygen makes the other gas burn a lot harder and hotter.

This is the picture of what we see here in Revelation 15. The plagues would be bad enough, but when God mixes His wrath in those vials with them, Katie bar the door, things are about to break loose. It is a fearful thing to rebel against God.

Revelation 15:8 *And the temple was filled with smoke from the glory of God, and from his power; and no man was able to enter into the temple, till the seven plagues of the seven angels were fulfilled.*

One other time in the Bible, men could not enter into the house of God, and it was for the exact opposite reason as what we see here:

2 Chronicles 5:13 *It came even to pass, as the trumpeters and singers were as one, to make one sound to be heard in praising and thanking the LORD; and when they lifted up their voice with the trumpets and cymbals and instruments of musick, and praised the LORD, saying, For he is good; for his mercy endureth for ever: that then the house was filled with a cloud, even the house of the LORD;* **14** *So that the priests could not stand to minister by reason of the cloud: for the glory of the LORD had filled the house of God.*

This is one of my favorite passages in the entire Bible. It recalls the time when people got to worshipping and singing and praising God, and it got so thick with Holy Ghost smoke that the clergy could not even do their job.

But in Revelation 15, smoke fills the house of God again; people cannot even get in, it is so thick, but this time it is not because of how pleased God is; it is because of how angry He is.

Can we even grasp that? Can we really wrap our minds around the concept that God can get so angry over sin on earth that He will not even let anyone into the temple in heaven?

Let this sink deeply into your heart; our God is a holy God. He truly hates sin. Our God hates drinking and drugging and fornicating and homosexuality and adultery and cursing and lying and stealing and gossiping and disobeying the authorities He has placed over us and pornography and every other sin; God just hates it! He is not some soft, blond-haired, blue-eyed, laid-back surfer dude who tolerates everything. He said, "Be ye holy, for I am holy!" God hates sin, and the sin of this wicked world will soon cause a storm so powerful it will keep even good men from the immediate presence of God until the plagues are finished.

You think you have a bad storm in your life? You think the waves are rolling and the winds blowing and the sea raging? You have not ever seen anything like the storm to come in Revelation 15.

But while it will bring pain to the world, it will bring peace to the children of God.

So rage on, storm, rage on.

Chapter Thirty-Four
The First Four Vials

Revelation 16:1 *And I heard a great voice out of the temple saying to the seven angels, Go your ways, and pour out the vials of the wrath of God upon the earth.* **2** *And the first went, and poured out his vial upon the earth; and there fell a noisome and grievous sore upon the men which had the mark of the beast, and upon them which worshipped his image.* **3** *And the second angel poured out his vial upon the sea; and it became as the blood of a dead man: and every living soul died in the sea.* **4** *And the third angel poured out his vial upon the rivers and fountains of waters; and they became blood.* **5** *And I heard the angel of the waters say, Thou art righteous, O Lord, which art, and wast, and shalt be, because thou hast judged thus.* **6** *For they have shed the blood of saints and prophets, and thou hast given them blood to drink; for they are worthy.* **7** *And I heard another out of the altar say, Even so, Lord God Almighty, true and righteous are thy judgments.* **8** *And the fourth angel poured out his vial upon the sun; and power was given unto him to scorch men with fire.* **9** *And men were scorched with great heat, and blasphemed the name of God, which hath power over these plagues: and they repented not to give him glory.*

In chapter fifteen of the book of The Revelation, we saw seven mighty angels make their way out of the Holy of Holies in heaven. They were carrying seven plagues to cast on the earth. But we then heard that God added His own wrath to those plagues, making them hotter and more intense through His righteous anger.

In the midst of all that, though, God focused our attention on the saints on the sea of glass, who had perfect peace right in the midst of the storm. It did not matter to them that the sea of glass had turned red with the fire of God's anger; they were not worried a bit. They had already experienced the fact that everything will turn out all right, they had learned to trust both the works and ways of God, and they knew they were not going to have enemies very much longer.

As chapter sixteen begins, those judgments that God alluded to in chapter fifteen will be unleashed on this wicked world. What we could only guess at in the last chapter will be revealed in this one. We will split Revelation 16 into three parts, covering the first four vials in this chapter then vials five and six, and then vial seven after that.

The great preacher H.A. Ironside told the true story of a young woman who chose to reject God. This young woman, who had been brought up in a Christian home and who had often had very serious convictions in regard to the importance of coming to Christ, chose instead to take the way of the world. Much against the wishes of her godly mother, she insisted on keeping company with a wild, partying crowd, who lived only for the moment and determined to ignore eternity.

Again and again, people pleaded with her to turn to Christ, but she would not listen, did not care, and demanded to be left alone.

But one day, unexpectedly, she got deathly ill. All the best doctors came, she got all the best medicine, but it soon became evident that the case was hopeless; she was not going to live. People continued to beg her to repent, but she was as hard as a stone, as stubborn as a mule, and did not want anything to do with God.

But one night, she awoke suddenly out of a sound sleep, a frightened look in her eyes and sweat on her fevered brow. She looked up in horror at her mother, who was there by her bedside, and said, "Mother, what is Ezekiel 7:8-9?"

Her mother said, "What do you mean, my dear?"

She replied that she had had the most vivid dream. There was a holy Presence in the room, who very solemnly said to her, "Read Ezekiel 7:8-9." The mother did not know those verses by memory, so she reached for a Bible. As she opened it, her heart sank as she saw the words, but she read them aloud to the dying girl:

"Now I will shortly pour out my fury upon thee, and accomplish mine anger upon thee: and I will judge thee according to thy ways, and will recompense thee for all thine abominations. And mine eye shall not spare, neither will I have pity: I will recompense thee according to thy ways and thine abominations that are in the midst of thee; and ye shall know that I am the Lord that smiteth."

That dying girl, with a look of horror on her face, sank back on the pillow, exhausted and used up, and in a few short moments, she was in eternity facing the God that she rejected. (31-32)

It is a fearful and deadly thing to reject the God who made you, and loved you, and died for you, and has been calling you, and will one day end up judging you because you turned Him away.

That is very much what we will see in the sixteenth chapter of the book of The Revelation. The world in our day is presently rejecting God except for a minority of people who still love Him dearly. But by Revelation sixteen, this world will have rejected Him wholesale, they will have ignored His messengers, destroyed His remnant, and nothing will be left except the sure and sudden judgment of the last seven vials and the battle of Armageddon. As to timing, everything you see here will almost certainly be right near the end of the Tribulation Period, right as men are gathering for Armageddon. Given the nature of devastation here,

I do not see much of a way that earth could ever simply recover and continue on.

The first vial produces a sore

Revelation 16:1 *And I heard a great voice out of the temple saying to the seven angels, Go your ways, and pour out the vials of the wrath of God upon the earth.* **2** *And the first went, and poured out his vial upon the earth; and there fell a noisome and grievous sore upon the men which had the mark of the beast, and upon them which worshipped his image.*

As we begin looking at the last seven judgments, I am struck again by the thought that even as powerful as angels are, they still come under their proper authority. These angels holding these seven vials do not make a move with them until a great voice from the Holy of Holies, and I believe clearly that this is the voice of God Himself, tells them to go.

When the first angel pours out his vial, the Bible says that *"there fell a noisome and grievous sore upon the men which had the mark of the beast, and upon them which worshipped his image."*

When this happens, people will not have any excuse or any reason to blame God. They will not be able to say, "You never told me this would happen!" because He did tell them. In fact, He told them by the mouth of an angel flying through heaven, shouting at the top of his lungs:

Revelation 14:9b *...If any man worship the beast and his image, and receive his mark in his forehead, or in his hand,* **10** *The same shall drink of the wine of the wrath of God, which is poured out without mixture into the cup of his indignation...*

People will be warned, but they will take the mark and worship the image of Antichrist anyway. And sometime thereafter, when this angel steps out onto the scene of time and space and pours out his vial, they will regret what they have done. Verse two says there will fall on them a noisome and grievous sore.

When you think of the word "sore," you probably aren't thinking of anything remotely like what is described here. This is not some little bug bite; it is not some poison ivy rash; it is not a wart or a blood blister. This word for sore means an open ulcer, a running wound, a giant boil. Think of what covered Job's body. Think of the wounds of the beggar Lazarus, and you are getting close to the picture.

But there are two more descriptive words used here that will help you better understand what we are dealing with. The text first of all says that this sore is a noisome sore. It is from the Greek word *kakon*, meaning something that is incredibly bad and destructive. This Greek word has forty-three different forms and occurs one hundred fifty-seven times in the New Testament. It is usually translated bad, evil, wicked, or something like that. Out of all those one hundred fifty-seven occurrences, this is the one and only time it is ever translated as noisome. In fact, this is the only time the English word noisome occurs in the New Testament.

The translators of our Bible grasped something that they wanted us to understand very clearly: there has never ever been a sore like this one. Just using the word bad would not convey that. Using the word evil would not convey that. Using the word awful would not convey that. They used the word noisome because it had never been used before, and only a word that has not been used of anything else could possibly describe a sore that is worse than any other sore ever! And think of how perfect and picturesque this word is. With a sore like this falling on men and women around the earth, if it is going to be anything, it is going to be noisome.

Imagine men and women by the untold millions writhing on the floors of their homes, laying in the gutters of the streets in agony, pulling over on the side of the road to roll in the grass in torments, screaming and crying and foaming at the mouth in pain from this sore.

The Bible also describes it here as a grievous sore. It is from the word *ponayron,* and it means a pressing, a great evil, an unbearable hardship.

All of this because men choose to reject God and take the mark of the beast, and worship his image.

How fitting are the judgments of God? Imagine how the skin of men will be marked and scarred by this noisome and grievous sore. They took the mark of the beast *willingly*; now they will be forced to take the marks caused by this noisome and grievous sore *unwillingly*.

By the way, we are all currently on this side of the Tribulation, on this side of the Rapture, but the truth taught here still applies even for our day; there are consequences for every action and every decision. You can choose your deeds, but you cannot choose your consequences; those are all built in. It is a package deal.

The second vial pollutes the sea

Revelation 16:3 *And the second angel poured out his vial upon the sea; and it became as the blood of a dead man: and every living soul died in the sea.*

There is almost no way to overestimate how important the oceans are to us. There are probably some of you reading this who have never seen the ocean in person. Yet without the oceans, you would be in a world of trouble where you sit.

Roughly seventy-five percent of our world is covered in water, and the vast majority of that water is found in the ocean. There is really only one ocean; all of the names we give it (Atlantic, Pacific, etc.) are just names of regions of that one ocean. Eighty-five percent of all plant life on earth is in the ocean. Eighty percent of all life of all kinds on earth is in the ocean. (Ocean Syrup, 2020)

In 2018, the ocean produced one hundred seventy-nine million metric tons of food for humanity. (Holland, 2020)

Much of our chemicals and minerals come from the oceans. Oceans help to regulate the weather. Oceans are some of the primary lanes for shipping and transporting goods and people. If the oceans ever die, people will not be far behind.

There will come a day when they will. When this second angel pours out his vial on the sea, the Bible says that it will become as the blood of a dead man. It will not turn some vibrant, living red; it will become a thick, putrid, awful-smelling mess. Every living creature in every drop of the ocean on earth, from the biggest whale to the smallest piece of plankton, will die. Every crab, shrimp, lobster, sea bass, snapper, everything good for food will be gone.

Albert Barnes takes the correct view of this word "soul." We normally think of that in regard to a human when it is used in Scripture, but on certain occasions, that is not the case, and this is one of those occasions. Barnes says:

> "Here the destruction is more general; the calamity is more severe and awful. It is as if every living thing had died. No emphasis should be put on the word soul here, for the word means merely a creature, a living thing, an animal, Ac 2:43; 3:23; Ro 13:1; 1Co 15:45. The sense here is, that there would be some dreadful calamity, as if the sea were to be changed into dark blood, and as if every living thing in it were to die."
(Linder)

The reason it will seem like that is because that is exactly what will happen. The sea is going to die. Everything in it is going to die.

People will not be ninety-five percent naked, sunbathing in the sand at the beach; the beach will be closed down due to the smell. There will not be any pleasure cruises to the Bahamas; resorts will close down, people will abandon their beachfront homes and move inland to live in shelters.

This judgment will show beyond any doubt the awesome power of God. Do you realize that we humans could not destroy the ocean if we tried? If we piled all of our garbage into it, if we dropped bombs on it, we are still not powerful enough to destroy or pollute all of the ocean water on earth; we are not powerful enough to destroy all of the sea creatures. But the God who made it all will, with just the dropping of a heavenly bowl of anger, wipe it out entirely.

Doesn't it kind of make you wonder? Why is it that God so often has to drop the heavenly hammer to get people to remember how awesome and powerful He is?

Shouldn't Bethlehem itself do that?

Shouldn't Calvary itself do that?

Shouldn't the empty tomb do that?

It may not do it for the lost world, but it should definitely do it for you. You and I need not ever forget how powerful our God is. We need not ever go off into sin and cause His chastening hand to fall on us before we remember that He is not to be trifled with.

If the almighty God has to break or ruin something for you, He will. If God has to turn your ocean into a putrid red mess, He will. But it seems like it would be a whole lot better for you and me to live right, love God, and learn about His power from reading His word rather than from coming under His judgment.

The third vial parches the soul

Revelation 16:4 *And the third angel poured out his vial upon the rivers and fountains of waters; and they became blood.* **5** *And I heard the angel of the waters say, Thou art righteous, O Lord, which art, and wast, and shalt be, because thou hast judged thus.* **6** *For they have shed the blood of saints and prophets, and thou hast given them blood to drink; for they are worthy.* **7** *And I heard another out of the altar say, Even so, Lord God Almighty, true and righteous are thy judgments.*

When the oceans become like the blood of a dead man, it will be devastating. Roughly ninety-nine percent of the water on earth is ocean water. But did you realize that the remaining one percent, the fresh water on earth, sustains all of our lives? A human can go roughly three weeks without food, but only about three days without water in some form. So when this third judgment falls, it will be catastrophic. All of the rivers and fountains on earth will not become like blood; they will actually become blood. We do not know how long it will last, we do not know how deeply it will affect ponds or self-contained water supplies, but we do know that the vast majority, probably better than ninety-five percent of drinking water on earth, comes from rivers and fountains. So basically, ninety-five percent of the one percent of water on earth that is fresh water, will not be fresh water anymore. It is incalculable how many people will die from dehydration. It is staggering to think how many people will get so thirsty that they will drink blood to try and stay alive. And far from being "unjust" or "cruel," look again at what verse five says:

Revelation 16:5 *And I heard the angel of the waters say, Thou art righteous, O Lord, which art, and wast, and shalt be, because thou hast judged thus.*

God has certain angels designated for certain things. One of those angels is the "angel of the waters." Remember that the next time you take a sip of cool, clear, water. God has had an angel in charge of that water since time began.

But as time begins to end, that water is going to be ruined. It is going to be turned to blood. And the angel that has been keeping it clear and drinkable for 6,000 years is going to look at that destruction and say, "You've done right, Lord. This needed to happen. This is appropriate."

Why? Why would he feel that way? The next verse gives us the why:

Revelation 16:6 *For they have shed the blood of saints and prophets, and thou hast given them blood to drink; for they are worthy.*

This is why. For thousands of years, wicked men have been killing the saints of God, shedding their blood by the gallon, and now they are going to be forced to drink blood because of it. They are worthy of it. They deserve it.

In A.D. 690, 100,000 Bible-believing Paulicians were murdered by the church of Rome for holding to the belief that the Bible alone is our final authority.

In A.D. 1163, the Roman Church determined that the city of Braziers was home to some "Bible-only heretics." Rather than even try to sort them out, the papal legate looked out over a city of 40,000 people and said, "Kill them all; God knows His own."

The Waldensians of the twelfth century were slaughtered en masse for refusing to bow to the pope. Spain in the fourteenth century, England during the fifteen hundreds, all of the Middle East to this very day, whether it be by Rome or Islam or Communism, God's people have been hunted down in packs and killed without mercy since the stoning of Stephen nearly 2,000 years ago. Wicked men have shed blood, so they are going to be made to drink blood.

When that verdict is read, another voice is going to speak up:

Revelation 16:7 *And I heard another out of the altar say, Even so, Lord God Almighty, true and righteous are thy judgments.*

Do you remember who that "voice out of the altar" is? Way back in Revelation 6, we saw a bunch of souls under the altar, people who had been killed during the Tribulation Period. They were crying out, asking God how long it was going to be until their blood was avenged:

Revelation 6:10 *And they cried with a loud voice, saying, How long, O Lord, holy and true, dost thou not judge and avenge our blood on them that dwell on the earth?*

Do you remember how God answered them?

Revelation 6:11 *And white robes were given unto every one of them; and it was said unto them, that they should rest yet for a little season, until their fellowservants also and their brethren, that should be killed as they were, should be fulfilled.*

In other words, not yet, be patient for a while longer.

But when you get to Revelation 16, the wait is over. And the voice from the altar says in so many words, "That's good. Give it to them, Lord! Let them have it!"

You who suffer in some way because of your faith in Christ, may I remind you that when God said in Romans 12, "Vengeance is mine saith the Lord, I will repay," that He meant it, and He will do it?

One day it may get so bad that you and I have our heads laid across a chopping block by a hooded Islamic terrorist and hear the air splitting as the sword comes down across our necks, sending us out into eternity. But that will not happen a single time without God taking note of it and marking a date for divine retribution.

The fourth vial punishes with the sun

Revelation 16:8 *And the fourth angel poured out his vial upon the sun; and power was given unto him to scorch men with fire.* **9** *And men were scorched with great heat, and blasphemed the name of God, which hath power over these plagues: and they repented not to give him glory.*

Ninety-three million miles from us, there is an everyday reminder that God is real and that He is in charge. Our sun in relation to our earth is a marvel. If our sun was just a teeny bit farther away, our world would turn into a dead ball of ice. If it was just a little bit closer, our world would be engulfed in flames. It is in the absolute perfect spot for there to be life on earth.

But there will come a day when the sun in the sky, our greatest natural ally, becomes man's worst enemy. A mighty angel is going to fly from the Holy of Holies in heaven, and he is going to pour his vial out on the sun. Whatever comes out of that vial, the heat from the sun will not evaporate it or bother it in any way. But the contents of that vial will bother the sun. When that angel pours out his vial, the sun itself is going to get exponentially hotter. People are literally going to be scorched from the heat.

Think of the worst sunburn you have ever gotten, and imagine it a hundred times worse, and you are starting to get the idea. There will not be any fornicating going on when that happens; everyone on earth will be in "don't touch me" mode. Water will be boiling in ponds and lakes, people will be dying from the suffocating heat, and men who have always thought that they were in control of everything will suddenly realize that they cannot get anywhere near that angel, they cannot stop him from turning the sun up on high, and there is no cave low enough to hide in to keep themselves from being burned by the sun's scorching heat. Every air-conditioning unit on earth will blow up after a matter of minutes trying to deal with these unreal temperatures. This will shut earth down as long as it lasts.

It seems like, if nothing else convinced man to repent, this would do it. But it will not:

Revelation 16:9 *And men were scorched with great heat, and blasphemed the name of God, which hath power over these plagues: and they repented not to give him glory.*

Let this sink in! These men know that the God who unleashed these plagues has power over the plagues. Yet instead of repenting, instead of begging for forgiveness, they literally look up into heaven and shake their fist at God and blaspheme His name. They refuse to give Him glory. They refuse to repent. They will lay there and die in the heat rather than accept and obey Christ.

This reaction sums up our own day, unfortunately. It makes me want to ask, "If you are not saved yet, what will it take to make you finally bow down and accept Christ? If you are not living right, what will it take to make you repent and live right? What will it take to make men glorify God rather than blaspheme Him?"

God can turn up the heat on you more than you can ever imagine. He can turn up the heat at work, at home, in your finances, in your relationships, in your health, in your emotions, God can pour out showers of blessings, or He can pour out vials of judgment. While you have time, you need to get all the way right with God. Showers of blessings are much preferable to vials of judgment.

Chapter Thirty-Five
The Fifth and Sixth Vials

Revelation 16:10 *And the fifth angel poured out his vial upon the seat of the beast; and his kingdom was full of darkness; and they gnawed their tongues for pain,* **11** *And blasphemed the God of heaven because of their pains and their sores, and repented not of their deeds.* **12** *And the sixth angel poured out his vial upon the great river Euphrates; and the water thereof was dried up, that the way of the kings of the east might be prepared.* **13** *And I saw three unclean spirits like frogs come out of the mouth of the dragon, and out of the mouth of the beast, and out of the mouth of the false prophet.* **14** *For they are the spirits of devils, working miracles, which go forth unto the kings of the earth and of the whole world, to gather them to the battle of that great day of God Almighty.* **15** *Behold, I come as a thief. Blessed is he that watcheth, and keepeth his garments, lest he walk naked, and they see his shame.* **16** *And he gathered them together into a place called in the Hebrew tongue Armageddon.*

Vials one through four have been covered, and we now move into the next two judgments of this chapter, the fifth and sixth vials.

The fifth vial darkens a kingdom

Revelation 16:10 *And the fifth angel poured out his vial upon the seat of the beast; and his kingdom was full of darkness; and they gnawed their tongues for pain,* **11** *And blasphemed the God of heaven because of their pains and their sores, and repented not of their deeds.*

It is sometimes funny to think of the conclusions we could come to if we did not actually study the meaning of the words in the Bible. This is an excellent example of that. We have taught our children that one word they can use for their posterior is "seat." What a joy it would be to think of God judging the "butt of the beast!"

But when this verse uses the word seat, it actually means a throne or a place from which one rules. This chapter in the book of The Revelation is describing events near the end of the Tribulation Period. For right at seven years, by this point in the text, the Antichrist has been ruling, murdering, blaspheming, and having his way with men. Through his kingdom, made up of ten nations, he has dominated the world.

When God pours this fifth vial out on the kingdom of the beast, it is going to be a divinely ironic judgment. Since he began his rule, the Antichrist has enslaved the entire world in pitch-black spiritual darkness.

So when God judges him and his kingdom, He will do so by making the beast's kingdom as dark physically as it has been spiritually.

Notice a couple of things about this darkness.

First of all, it is particular.

This darkness is going to be localized to just the kingdom of the beast. It will be absolutely unnatural. The sun will not affect it. The edges of it will not gradually fade into the light. If you were standing on the outside of it, it would literally look like a wall of black. It will be dark only in the kingdom of the beast and light everywhere else. This may sound amazing, and it is, but it will not be the first time it has happened:

Exodus 10:21 *And the LORD said unto Moses, Stretch out thine hand toward heaven, that there may be darkness over the land of Egypt, even darkness which may be felt.* **22** *And Moses stretched forth his hand toward heaven; and there was a thick darkness in all the land of Egypt three days:* **23** *They saw not one another, neither rose any from his place for three days: but all the children of Israel had light in their dwellings.*

This was one of the plagues that God brought on Egypt. For three days, darkness was only in the Egyptian portion of the land, but in Goshen, where the Jews lived, it was light. God did it once, and He will do it again, only this time on a much larger scale, engulfing at least ten nations.

Secondly, it is painful.

This is where the darkness on the kingdom of the beast during the Tribulation Period will be worse than what fell on Egypt. In Egypt, there was darkness, and the Bible says that it could be "felt." But in the book of the Revelation, this darkness is not just darkness that is so thick you can feel it; it is so dark that it actually causes intense physical pain:

Revelation 16:10 *And the fifth angel poured out his vial upon the seat of the beast; and his kingdom was full of darkness; and they gnawed their tongues for pain,* **11** *And blasphemed the God of heaven because of their pains and their sores, and repented not of their deeds.*

You may have experienced some very serious darkness, but I guarantee you that no one in this world has ever gone through a darkness that produced actual physical pain that is severe enough to make them chew on their own tongues, pain that causes brutal sores.

This is an excellent example of the law of sowing and reaping. The beast has been sowing darkness, his followers have been sowing darkness, and now they are reaping a brutal, supernatural darkness. It is clear that even man-made lights will not be able to shine in and against this darkness. Nothing at all will give anyone the smallest amount of light during this time.

Please do not ever forget; you will reap what you sow.

What is truly amazing, though, is how stubborn people can be. In spite of the darkness, in spite of the terrible physical pain, in spite of the fact that God Himself is clearly behind it, men will still refuse to repent. They will refuse to back down. From their darkened rooms, in their pitch-black towns, in their black as sin countries, they will scream blasphemies through the darkness, cursing the God who is punishing them. If you want a good idea of what hell will be like, this is it: men engulfed in the darkness, in incomprehensible pain, cursing God at the top of their lungs. It is nowhere a sane person would ever want to be.

The sixth vial dries up a river

Revelation 16:12 *And the sixth angel poured out his vial upon the great river Euphrates; and the water thereof was dried up, that the way of the kings of the east might be prepared.*

In Eastern Turkey, a river begins. It is 1,780 miles long and flows through Turkey, Syria, and Iraq. It is one of the four great rivers that originally flowed from the garden of Eden, and it is one of the few landmarks that survived Noah's flood. That river eventually empties out into the Persian Gulf. At its widest point, the Euphrates is more than four hundred yards wide. That river is used for drinking water, for business, and for recreation. When this verse describes it as the great river Euphrates, it truly is a GREAT river.

This river, for thousands of years, has also served as a geographical barrier. It is not too very far from Israel, and it is between them and Iran, between them and much of Iraq, between them and Russia, between them and Pakistan, between them and China, between them and North Korea, it is between them and a lot of nations that have always hated them.

Even people that do not believe the Bible could look at the modern news and not have much trouble believing that Israel could be the scene of the last best war on earth. It seems like all of the hatred on earth is focused on that one little piece of land. But one thing that would seem to stand in the way of that happening is the Euphrates River. It may not be that hard to fly planes over a river and drop bombs, but if you are going to move actual troops into an area, a major river could be a major problem. But God Himself will eliminate that problem with this sixth vial.

Look carefully at the exact wording of this verse. In the Old Testament, we read about the Jordan river having its waters backed up by God so that the Jews could pass over, and then the water was released and went back to flowing. That is not what will happen in this case. This verse does not say that the Euphrates River will be backed up; it says that it will be dried up. This will be one of the most stunning miracles ever when a 1780-mile-long river simply dries up! There is no other explanation for this other than God Himself turning off the water.

The reason why this will be done is in order to make it easy for the nations east of Israel to come there in battle. This eastern force will be one portion of the troops at the battle of Armageddon that we started talking about in chapter fourteen. Basically, God will grease the skids for them to slide to their doom. But not only will God make it easy for them to come, the devil himself will make it impossible for them to refuse:

Revelation 16:13 *And I saw three unclean spirits like frogs come out of the mouth of the dragon, and out of the mouth of the beast, and out of the mouth of the false prophet.* **14** *For they are the spirits of devils, working miracles, which go forth unto the kings of the earth and of the whole world, to gather them to the battle of that great day of God Almighty.*

It is a bit stunning to realize how far the one third of the angels who followed Lucifer in his rebellion have fallen. At least three of these formerly glorious creatures now bear the appearance of frogs. Oh, how costly a thing is rebellion against a gracious Creator!

But their appearance is not the main point of this verse. The main point is that the devil's hatred for Israel is going to move him against God's people yet again.

Israel has a unique history as far as their enemies go. They are the only nation that first of all never falls to their enemies when they are right with God. Secondly, they are the only nation that, even when they do displease God and experience defeat and capture, always has God judge the nations that defeated them as soon as Israel gets right! It has always been an impossibly dangerous thing to fight against Israel.

So why, after thousands of years of a history like that, would the kings of the east ever march into Israel for one final battle?

There are many details we will see about this in the next few chapters, but the main reason is found right here. You may be dumb enough not to believe in demons, but they are real. And there will be three of them sent out, one by Satan, one by Antichrist, and one by the false prophet just before Armageddon. These demons will go out with one purpose, to seduce world leaders to bring their armies to this one last battle. By means of unspecified miracles, they will convince world leaders to embark on a march to their own doom.

This phenomenon of seducing spirits in the last days was prophesied by Paul:

1 Timothy 4:1 *Now the Spirit speaketh expressly, that in the latter times some shall depart from the faith, giving heed to seducing spirits, and doctrines of devils;*

Everyone is looking for "inner guides" these days, but very specifically not God. My warning to those going that way is this: you better be careful; you may find one that is not what he seems.

In the last days of the Tribulation Period, three smooth-talking demons will play a significant role in convincing all world leaders to show up at this last battle, in the place called Armageddon. Knowing this, God gave a warning that will be good for that day but is also very good for our day:

Revelation 16:15 *Behold, I come as a thief. Blessed is he that watcheth, and keepeth his garments, lest he walk naked, and they see his shame.* **16** *And he gathered them together into a place called in the Hebrew tongue Armageddon.*

It is not surprising when a thief can break in unawares and catch men not watching for him. But when he has announced the time of his coming, no one should be caught off guard. Yet here, speaking of the end of the Tribulation Period, Armageddon, and the time when God comes back openly as King of kings and Lord of lords, a day that will happen seven years after the Tribulation Period begins, no one should ever be caught off guard—but they will be. And they will be walking in both physical and spiritual nakedness because they were not preparing themselves for the coming of "they," (verse fifteen), meaning Christ, His angels, and His saints.

That admonition is equally applicable for today. How many people, even today, when it is pretty clear that Christ could come back at any moment, are going to be found walking in spiritual nakedness when the trumpet sounds?

Chapter Thirty-Six
The Seventh Vial

Revelation 16:17 *And the seventh angel poured out his vial into the air; and there came a great voice out of the temple of heaven, from the throne, saying, It is done.* **18** *And there were voices, and thunders, and lightnings; and there was a great earthquake, such as was not since men were upon the earth, so mighty an earthquake, and so great.* **19** *And the great city was divided into three parts, and the cities of the nations fell: and great Babylon came in remembrance before God, to give unto her the cup of the wine of the fierceness of his wrath.* **20** *And every island fled away, and the mountains were not found.* **21** *And there fell upon men a great hail out of heaven, every stone about the weight of a talent: and men blasphemed God because of the plague of the hail; for the plague thereof was exceeding great.*

Every July Fourth, there is a moment that just makes my jaw drop. I love watching fireworks, and yes, they are impressive. But at the very end of the show, it is like they shoot off a million explosives all at one time and just light up the entire sky. During the show, people are talking, eating, making calls, generally only about half paying attention. But at that moment, the fireworks are just too great to ignore.

And that is just a tip-of-the-iceberg illustration of what this last judgment will be like.

The declaration of the seventh vial

Revelation 16:17 *And the seventh angel poured out his vial into the air; and there came a great voice out of the temple of heaven, from the throne, saying, It is done.*

Looking at the seventh vial, the first interesting thing to notice is that it is poured out into the air. The other vials were poured out on specific places or things: the sun, the rivers, the kingdom of the beast, and so on. This one is not going to be so localized. This one is going to have full dispersion. It will be like a poison traveling on the wind, spreading across the entire world.

Notice the fact that as it is poured out, God Himself shouts from off the throne. His declaration is, *"It is done!"* The word He uses for this phrase is incredible. It is not *tetelestai*, it is finished, but *gegonen*, another perfect tense word meaning "it has come to be."

Why this word? Here is why: God has been prophesying all of this, the Rapture, the Tribulation, Armageddon, all of the end-time judgments, for thousands of years. And for all of those years, people have been mocking what He said:

2 Peter 3:3 *Knowing this first, that there shall come in the last days scoffers, walking after their own lusts,* **4** *And saying, Where is the promise of his coming? for since the fathers fell asleep, all things continue as they were from the beginning of the creation.*

People in general may say they believe the Bible, but they turn into scoffers pretty quickly when they hear about all of the cataclysmic judgments of the Tribulation Period, the second coming, etc. So when the end finally does come, and the last, greatest judgment falls on the entire world, God basically says, "You may have doubted it, but it's done; it has come to be even though you said it would not."

Sometimes I wonder when people will finally grasp the fact that when God says it, it is as good as money in the bank!

You can doubt the Rapture if you want, but mark this down, it is as good as done.

You can doubt the Tribulation judgments if you want, but mark this down, it is as good as done. You can doubt the second coming if you want, but mark this down, it is as good as done.

That is the declaration of the seventh vial.

The destruction of the seventh vial

Revelation 16:18 *And there were voices, and thunders, and lightnings; and there was a great earthquake, such as was not since men were upon the earth, so mighty an earthquake, and so great.*

How frightening will it be to hear voices from the air? Not a voice, singular, but voices, plural. How frightening will these thunders and lightnings be? These things will be epic in the worst sort of way.

But most of all, there will be the earthquake of all earthquakes.

According to this verse, this will be the worst earthquake ever. How significant is that?

In 856, an earthquake in Damhgan, Iran, killed 200,000 people.

In 1138, in Syria, an earthquake killed 230,000.

In 1976 in Tangsahn, China, there was a 7.6 that killed 255,000.

In 2004 in Sumatra, there was a 9.1 that killed 283,000

In 1556 in Shansi, China, the most destructive earthquake ever killed 830,000 people.

Yet here is God telling us that, as destructive as that earthquake in China was that took nearly a million lives, this last earthquake will make it seem tame in comparison.

Did you realize that no matter how hard things have ever been in times past, God can make it much, much worse?

Men are so proud; they have built their giant buildings, centers of commerce, government, entertainment, education. So many of them are filled with defiance and disbelief toward God. But every one of them is built on the ground. And God is going to shake down all of those buildings!

The direction of the seventh vial

Revelation 16:19 *And the great city was divided into three parts, and the cities of the nations fell: and great Babylon came in remembrance before God, to give unto her the cup of the wine of the fierceness of his wrath.*

In the book of the Revelation, the phrase "great city" occurs ten times. The first time, in Revelation 11:8, it refers to Jerusalem. But the final nine times, it refers to a city called Babylon.

There have been a few Babylons in history: Babylon in Assyria, the famous Babylon of the Chaldeans, and Babel of Nimrod that was the first of all. But you also find that throughout the Bible, cities are called by the name of other cities when God wants to send a message. For instance, right here in the book of the Revelation:

Revelation 11:8 *And their dead bodies shall lie in the street of the great city, which spiritually is called Sodom and Egypt, where also our Lord was crucified.*

In what city was Jesus crucified? Jerusalem, which is here called Sodom and Egypt.

When you read the description of Babylon in the book of the Revelation, the odds are that it is not one of the old Babylons rebuilt but a new Babylon, most likely the city of Rome.

Political Babylon in the book of the Revelation will be the city from which the Antichrist rules, and that city that has given itself to the evil one will be targeted by God. This great earthquake will shake the whole world, but it will be centered in the great city that will go by the name Babylon. The entire city will be broken into three parts; the gaps in the ground from this earthquake will literally separate the landmass of this city into three separate entities.

None of God's judgments are haphazard; they are laser beam precise; the earth will shake, the cities of the nations will fall, but it will be evident that it all centers in and radiates outward from this new Babylon.

The disappearance of the seventh vial

Revelation 16:20 *And every island fled away, and the mountains were not found.*

There are literally tens of thousands of islands on earth. There are mountains more than five miles high. There is no way our human minds can fully wrap around this, but at this last judgment, earth as we know it will not be earth as we know it anymore. Kings Mountain will be gone, as will the Blue Ridge Parkway, the Rockies, Crowders Mountain, even Mount Everest.

Grenada will be gone, and so will Hawaii, and Trinidad and Tobago, and St. Lucia, and the Philippines. Much of the earth as we know it will simply disappear because of this earthquake.

This is a good reason not to get too attached to this old world. We are only passing through, and this hotel earth that we have been staying on is on its last few days. It is about to be torn down to make way for a much better model.

The dropping of the seventh vial

Revelation 16:21 *And there fell upon men a great hail out of heaven, every stone about the weight of a talent: and men blasphemed God because of the plague of the hail; for the plague thereof was exceeding great.*

Different parts of the world regarded the "talent" weight differently, but the smallest talent was around 55 pounds. Falling from the sky, there is no building or structure on earth that will withstand this assault. Wicked men will see their loved ones bombed out of existence, they will know they are in the line of fire, and again they will blaspheme rather than repent.

It never had to be this way. Adam did not have to eat the fruit, and no one since has had to rebel against God, either. It has been a choice. All have been offered salvation in Christ. Yet this world even now is pushing God away just as hard as it can. And seven years into the Tribulation Period, this world will be taking the final blows of judgment from the loving yet holy God that they have hated and rejected.

Chapter Thirty-Seven
Hell's Harlot

Revelation 17:1 *And there came one of the seven angels which had the seven vials, and talked with me, saying unto me, Come hither; I will shew unto thee the judgment of the great whore that sitteth upon many waters:* **2** *With whom the kings of the earth have committed fornication, and the inhabitants of the earth have been made drunk with the wine of her fornication.* **3** *So he carried me away in the spirit into the wilderness: and I saw a woman sit upon a scarlet coloured beast, full of names of blasphemy, having seven heads and ten horns.* **4** *And the woman was arrayed in purple and scarlet colour, and decked with gold and precious stones and pearls, having a golden cup in her hand full of abominations and filthiness of her fornication:* **5** *And upon her forehead was a name written, MYSTERY, BABYLON THE GREAT, THE MOTHER OF HARLOTS AND ABOMINATIONS OF THE EARTH.* **6** *And I saw the woman drunken with the blood of the saints, and with the blood of the martyrs of Jesus: and when I saw her, I wondered with great admiration.*

When you study through the book of The Revelation, please remember that it is not always in chronological order. There are times when the narrative is interrupted by parenthetical passages. Revelation seventeen is one of those passages. We have already looked in the book of The Revelation at things that will happen right at the very end of it. But this chapter will go back and show us something that will be present from the very beginning of the Tribulation Period, something that is very clearly taking shape even now in our day. The Tribulation Period will be a time when the world sees something it has never yet seen: an entire world following the exact same religion. The devil himself will be in the church business, and business will be booming.

The description of the harlot

Revelation 17:1 *And there came one of the seven angels which had the seven vials, and talked with me, saying unto me, Come hither; I will shew unto thee the judgment of the great whore that sitteth upon many waters:*

While many of the chapters in the book of The Revelation have described very literal events, fantastic though they may be, this is one of the chapters in the book that employs heavy symbolism throughout. It is evident that there is no human female prostitute that is so large that she is sitting upon many waters and with whom the kings of the earth have committed fornication. The whore that is spoken of here is very clearly a religious system. In fact, that very terminology was incredibly familiar to John as he wrote this since it is used in the Old Testament time and time again to describe heathen and idolatrous religions:

Exodus 34:15 *Lest thou make a covenant with the inhabitants of the land, and they go a whoring after their gods, and do sacrifice unto their gods, and one call thee, and thou eat of his sacrifice;*

Leviticus 17:7 *And they shall no more offer their sacrifices unto devils, after whom they have gone a whoring. This shall be a statute for ever unto them throughout their generations.*

Leviticus 20:5 *Then I will set my face against that man, and against his family, and will cut him off, and all that go a whoring after him, to commit whoredom with Molech, from among their people.*

1 Chronicles 5:25 *And they transgressed against the God of their fathers, and went a whoring after the gods of the people of the land, whom God destroyed before them.*

These are just a small number of the great many references in the Old Testament to idolatrous religions being described as whoredom. In fact, there is an entire book of the Old Testament that deals with it as such. The whole book of Hosea uses the physical whoredom of Gomer, Hosea's wife, as a picture of the spiritual whoredom that the nation of Israel was committing against God by following heathen, idolatrous religions:

Hosea 4:12 *My people ask counsel at their stocks, and their staff declareth unto them: for the spirit of whoredoms hath caused them to err, and they have gone a whoring from under their God.*

Hosea 9:1 *Rejoice not, O Israel, for joy, as other people: for thou hast gone a whoring from thy God, thou hast loved a reward upon every cornfloor.*

When you see all of this, and then you see the angel of Revelation 17 speaking of the "*great whore that sitteth upon many waters,*" you know immediately that what is being spoken of is an enormous, anti-God religious system encompassing the entire world. The word "great" here is from the word *megas,* we get our English word "mega" from it. This will be the ultimate mega-church! And when verse fifteen tells us that, "*The waters which thou sawest, where the whore sitteth, are peoples, and multitudes, and nations, and tongues,*" we learn that this hellish "church" will have campuses literally all over the earth! There will be no competition for members; she will have them all.

Yes, there is a political Babylon mentioned throughout the book of The Revelation, but this particular Babylon is clearly a religious Babylon. She will accomplish what Nimrod very nearly accomplished at the first Babel until God scattered the people and confounded their language. And God, right here at the outset, has determined to judge her. He is not simply going to "be tolerant and accept her." He is going to utterly ruin her. He would not allow the first Babel/Babylon to stand unjudged, nor will He allow this one to do so.

The defilement of the harlot

Revelation 17:2 *With whom the kings of the earth have committed fornication, and the inhabitants of the earth have been made drunk with the wine of her fornication.*

As we begin to examine this hellish religion that will be present everywhere during the Tribulation Period, it is interesting that we find the word fornication twice, wine once, and drunk once. In case it is not painfully obvious why that is so ironic, just try to imagine seeing a new church built in your town, and then when the sign goes up, you see "Wine Loving, Falling Down Drunk, Double Fornicating Church."

This one-world religion of the Antichrist is going to have none of the holiness, none of the Biblical preaching, none of the righteous expectations of any true church that has ever come before it. Both literally and symbolically, there will be fornication and drunkenness not just tolerated but actually woven into the religious fabric. It will be absolutely filthy.

It will also, though, be exceptionally popular. Verse two tells us that both the kings of the earth and just the regular inhabitants of the earth are involved in it.

Another interesting thing to consider about this looming one-world religion is that, while it will not be officially chartered until after the Rapture, it has actually been taking shape for a very long time now, thousands of years, in fact. Both *"have committed fornication"* and *"have been made drunk"* are past tense phrases in English, aorist tense phrases in Greek, and indicate something that has already happened. As we work our way through the entire text of Revelation 17, you will find many more indications that this does not simply spring up during the Tribulation Period; it has actually been brewing for a very long time.

On a practical note, we should not leave this verse before we observe the fact that fornication and alcohol are tied together here. Once again, that is a very common refrain in Scripture:

Genesis 19:31 *And the firstborn said unto the younger, Our father is old, and there is not a man in the earth to come in unto us after the manner of all the earth:* **32** *Come, let us make our father drink wine, and we will lie with him, that we may preserve seed of our father.* **33** *And they made their father drink wine that night: and the firstborn went in,* *and lay with her father; and he perceived not when she lay down, nor when she arose.* **34** *And it came to pass on the morrow, that the firstborn said unto the younger, Behold, I lay yesternight with my father: let us make him drink wine this night also; and go thou in, and lie with him, that we may preserve seed of our father.* **35** *And they made their father drink wine that night also: and the younger arose, and lay with him; and he perceived not when she lay down, nor when she arose.* **36** *Thus were both the daughters of Lot with child by their father.*

Proverbs 23:29 *Who hath woe? who hath sorrow? who hath contentions? who hath babbling? who hath wounds without cause? who hath redness of eyes?* **30** *They that tarry long at the wine; they that go to seek mixed wine.* **31** *Look not thou upon the wine when it is red, when it giveth his colour in the cup, when it moveth itself aright.* **32** *At the last it biteth like a serpent, and stingeth like an adder.* **33a** *Thine eyes shall behold strange women...*

Hosea 4:11 *Whoredom and wine and new wine take away the heart.*

Habakkuk 2:15 *Woe unto him that giveth his neighbour drink, that puttest thy bottle to him, and makest him drunken also, that thou mayest look on their nakedness!*

No one has ever said, "I have a great idea; let's all of us stay away from alcohol completely so that we can be more likely to fornicate!" Alcohol has ever been the ally of fornication, not the enemy of it.

The designation of the harlot

Revelation 17:3 *So he carried me away in the spirit into the wilderness: and I saw a woman sit upon a scarlet coloured beast, full of names of blasphemy, having seven heads and ten horns.* **4** *And the woman was arrayed in purple and scarlet colour, and decked with gold and precious stones and pearls, having a golden cup in her hand full of abominations and filthiness of her fornication:* **5** *And upon her forehead was a name written, MYSTERY, BABYLON THE GREAT, THE MOTHER OF HARLOTS AND ABOMINATIONS OF THE EARTH.*

In the first two verses of this chapter, the angel has been speaking to John and asking him to come with him to see this great harlot. So thus far, John has heard about her, but he has not yet seen her. But now, in verses three through five, John finally gets to see this filthy harlot, this one world religion, with his own two eyes.

Notice that the angel carries him away in his spirit, not literally and physically, into the wilderness. John is now in a symbolic place, seeing a symbolic picture. And the place that he has been taken to is exceptionally interesting. He does not see this woman in a royal city or in the halls of luxury; he sees her in the wilderness.

The word for wilderness is *eraymos*, and it means a solitary, lonely, desolate, uninhabited place.

This woman, this harlot, this one-world religion that has been so wildly successful, is actually in a desolate wilderness and is just not spiritually perceptive enough to realize it.

It is entirely possible for a religion or even for a church to be wildly successful by man's standards and yet be so abhorrent to God that it is actually in a spiritual wilderness.

When John arrived in that wilderness to view this harlot, he said that he saw "*A woman sit upon a scarlet coloured beast, full of names of blasphemy, having seven heads and ten horns.*"

Be aware that at this point in the text, we still do not know what the woman herself looks like. The description in this verse is actually of the beast that she is sitting on. It is the beast that is scarlet-colored, it is the beast that is full of names of blasphemy, and it is the beast that has seven heads and ten horns. So to put it in very common terms, we are looking at the woman's ride in this verse, not at the woman herself.

Based on the description of verse eight, the beast is both the Antichrist and the political kingdom and power of the Antichrist. This harlot, this one world religion, is supported entirely by government. She rides to power on his back. The Antichrist is going to attempt to be what only Christ is qualified to be, both the spiritual and political leader of the entire world all at once.

When we read that the beast will be full of names of blasphemy, it means that it is covered with names and titles that are injurious to God, either by insulting God or by taking the glory of God to itself.

This should not be surprising considering what Scripture has already told us about the coming Antichrist:

2 Thessalonians 2:3 *Let no man deceive you by any means: for that day shall not come, except there come a falling away first, and that man of sin be revealed, the son of perdition;* **4** *Who opposeth and exalteth himself above all that is called God, or that is worshipped; so that he as God sitteth in the temple of God, shewing himself that he is God.*

What a great "convenience" it will be for mankind to have one unified worldwide "church" preaching to it about its "god," and to have that god right there in the flesh to be seen and worshipped, and for that god to be telling all of them all of the things they already want to hear and none of the things that they do not.

Verse three ends by telling us that the beast has seven heads and ten horns. We have seen that symbolism twice so far in the book of the Revelation:

Revelation 12:3 *And there appeared another wonder in heaven; and behold a great red dragon, having seven heads and ten horns, and seven crowns upon his heads.*

Revelation 13:1 *And I stood upon the sand of the sea, and saw a beast rise up out of the sea, having seven heads and ten horns, and upon his horns ten crowns, and upon his heads the name of blasphemy.*

In that first passage, Revelation 12:3, we are seeing the devil as he was in eternity past when he led a rebellion against God. His seven heads and ten horns and seven crowns were twenty-four high-ranking angelic powers of three different ranks that followed him in that rebellion.

He continues his patterns on earth. The beast of Revelation 13, the Antichrist, has that same ranking system with human leaders that accompany him, doubtless indwelt by the twenty-four demons that followed Satan.

So as we arrive at Revelation 17, remember again that horns, heads, and crowns in the Bible speak of powers and leaders. That is what we see here. These ten crowns are the same thing as the ten toes described in the book of Daniel.

We have been through four gentile world kingdoms so far. The Babylonians were first. The Medo-Persians were second. The Greeks were third. The Roman Empire was fourth. What we are waiting for now is what is known as the revived Roman Empire. It will be a federation of ten nations, some strong, some weak, mixed together. Those kingdoms are the ten toes of Daniel 2 and the ten horns of Revelation 13 and 17. The crowns are not mentioned here because the emphasis in this passage is not on the political apparatus but on the religious apparatus that the political apparatus is carrying.

In verse four, we begin to find the description of the woman herself. We are told, "*the woman was arrayed in purple and scarlet colour, and decked with gold and precious stones and pearls, having a golden cup in her hand full of abominations and filthiness of her fornication.*"

There are some things that are noteworthy about the items on this list. To begin with, all of it has been seen for years in the Roman Catholic Church.

Right away, let me say this. I do not think the Roman Catholic Church, by itself, is the great whore of the book of The Revelation. It seems reasonably clear that she will be the most prominent part of it, but she will not be all of it.

But even though people may not like to hear it, this list does describe the Catholic Church through the centuries very well. The color scarlet was reserved for popes and cardinals by that church. Pope Paul II made it illegal for anyone but cardinals to wear hats of scarlet. The Roman Ceremonial book compiled several centuries ago by Marcellus, a Romish archbishop, and dedicated to Leo X, enumerated five different articles of dress of scarlet color. A vest is mentioned studded with pearls. The Pope's miter is of gold and precious stones. The eucharist takes place with a golden cup. All of this fits with the description of verse four. (Jamieson, 710)

So why do I say that the Catholic Church is not, by herself, the great harlot? Because this will be a true one-world religion, and the entire world is not going to become Catholic, at least not in name. This will be a brand-new religion, at least outwardly. We are going to see later in the chapter that Rome will head it up. But this will amalgamate every world religion into one. Antichrist, that greatest of diplomats, will manage to merge every world religion into one and have himself at the center of it.

The second remarkable thing about it to notice is its incredible wealth. Again, notice the list: Purple, scarlet, gold, precious stones, pearls, golden cup.

This one-world religion will have a world of wealth. Can you imagine what it will be like, when every religion on earth merges, and everyone is completely devoted to it, no one is allowed to miss services, and everyone is willing to give everything they have for it? This will be buying power like you have never seen.

The description of the cup she is carrying is also worthy of note. We read, *"having a golden cup in her hand full of abominations and filthiness of her fornication."*

Remember, this is a religion that we are talking about. She will be called Babylon in verse five, and she has this golden cup in her hand. All of that has also been seen previously in Scripture:

Jeremiah 51:7 *Babylon hath been a golden cup in the LORD'S hand, that made all the earth drunken: the nations have drunken of her wine; therefore the nations are mad.*

God used old Babylon as a judgment, and He will use the new religious Babylon in the same way. Just like the church of Rome has a cup that is always a front and center in its worship, a cup that everyone drinks out of, the one world religion symbolically will do the same. But it will be a cup full of filthiness. God will allow the devil to run his own church as a judgment on this wicked world that has rejected the true church.

The last part of her designation is found in verse five:

Revelation 17:5 *And upon her forehead was a name written, MYSTERY, BABYLON THE GREAT, THE MOTHER OF HARLOTS AND ABOMINATIONS OF THE EARTH.*

A mystery in Scripture is something that is hidden or veiled. So this harlot that is being described here, once again, is a symbolic thing. She is not a woman; she is a system. She is Babylon, but not Babylon the city, Babylon the great. She is not just a harlot; she is the mother of harlots and abominations of the earth.

You can go all the way back to Babel in Genesis 11 and trace most every aberrant religious doctrine on earth today back to it. Just as God has always had true religion, the devil has always produced counterfeit religion. And what started at Babel has sprung off into thousands of different world religions, all of which will come back together to their mother during the Tribulation Period.

All beliefs are not equal and valid. There is true, and there is false. And this one-world religion, which for the devil will be the culmination of at least 4,000 years of effort on earth from the time of Nimrod until now, is not something to be respected. God has never had any respect for that which defies Him, nor should we. This religion is and will be the mother of harlots and abominations; her building may be on earth, but her foundation is in hell.

The destruction of the harlot

Revelation 17:6 *And I saw the woman drunken with the blood of the saints, and with the blood of the martyrs of Jesus: and when I saw her, I wondered with great admiration.*

The last thing you would ever expect from a church is to find it "drunken with the blood of the saints, and with the blood of the martyrs of Jesus." But that is exactly what you get when the devil goes into the church business.

In case you do not know, the slaughter of Christians began at the hands of the religious and has continued to be primarily at the hands of the religious through the millennia. Jesus' death was brought about by the priests of Israel. Stephen's death was brought about by the priests of Israel.

The Paulicians of the seventh century held to the Bible-only belief. Because of that, the Roman Church in A.D. 690. slaughtered more than 100,000 of them. (Christian, 51)

Another group of Bible believers, known as the Albigenses, lived in France, in the little city of Albi, in the district of Albigeois. The Roman Church deemed them as heretics for their refusal to baptize babies, for their teaching that men could not be converted by the sword, for their belief in salvation by grace through faith, for their teaching that there was no need of priests, especially wicked ones, and for their teaching that the sacraments of Rome could not save a man. The Roman Church became so enraged that in the years 1139, 1163, and 1180 decrees of persecution were published against them. The second crusade against them lasted twenty years. In it, the first city captured was that of Braziers, which had some 40,000 residents. Consider the wrath of Rome. When the Earl of Leicester asked the papal legate what to do with these 40,000 people, he replied, "Kill them all. God knows His own." (Christian, 63

The Waldensians of the twelfth century also received this type of treatment from Rome, being slaughtered en masse for refusing to bow to the whims of Popes and Priests.

Bloody Mary. England, France, Spain, all of Europe is stained with the blood of Christians killed by the Roman Church. And now, Christians are being slaughtered across the middle east and Asia at the hands of Islam.

The one-world religion of the Tribulation will be the last form of this harlotry. Millions upon millions will die as this evil harlot has her biggest drunken binge ever.

Seeing this, John said, *"And when I saw her, I wondered with great admiration."*

When we use the word "admiration," it is almost always in a positive context. But here it simply means that he was astonished; we would say he was stunned. It was simply hard for him to believe that this harlot could be responsible for such evil and bloodshed.

Do you realize what is so shocking about that? He was there the day the multitudes screamed "crucify him!" about Jesus.

But what did Jesus Himself say as He was being led up to Calvary?

Luke 23:31 *For if they do these things in a green tree, what shall be done in the dry?*

What shall be done in the dry, indeed.

For a long time now, people have been saying very foolish things like, "Religion is responsible for all of the blood shed on earth." There will come a day where real religion is gone, along with its grace and mercy and compassion and forgiveness and love and kindness, and all that is left is a compulsory one-world religion that will shed and drink the blood of saints until everybody is positively drunk from their satanic cup. This will indeed be Hell's Harlot. And you can see by the push for all religions to abandon doctrine and unify around feelings that it is already taking shape in our day.

Chapter Thirty-Eight
It Takes an Angel to Explain a Woman

Revelation 17:7 *And the angel said unto me, Wherefore didst thou marvel? I will tell thee the mystery of the woman, and of the beast that carrieth her, which hath the seven heads and ten horns.* **8** *The beast that thou sawest was, and is not; and shall ascend out of the bottomless pit, and go into perdition: and they that dwell on the earth shall wonder, whose names were not written in the book of life from the foundation of the world, when they behold the beast that was, and is not, and yet is.* **9** *And here is the mind which hath wisdom. The seven heads are seven mountains, on which the woman sitteth.* **10** *And there are seven kings: five are fallen, and one is, and the other is not yet come; and when he cometh, he must continue a short space.* **11** *And the beast that was, and is not, even he is the eighth, and is of the seven, and goeth into perdition.* **12** *And the ten horns which thou sawest are ten kings, which have received no kingdom as yet; but receive power as kings one hour with the beast.* **13** *These have one mind, and shall give their power and strength unto the beast.* **14** *These shall make war with the Lamb, and the Lamb shall overcome them: for he is Lord of lords, and King of kings: and they that are with him are called, and chosen, and faithful.* **15** *And he saith unto me, The waters which thou sawest, where the whore sitteth, are peoples, and multitudes, and nations, and tongues.* **16** *And the ten horns which thou sawest upon the beast, these shall hate the whore, and shall make her desolate and naked, and shall eat her flesh, and burn her with fire.* **17** *For God hath put in their hearts to fulfil his will, and to agree, and give their kingdom unto the beast, until the words of God shall be fulfilled.* **18** *And the woman which thou sawest is that great city, which reigneth over the kings of the earth.*

Women are very, VERY hard to explain...

Some years ago, my wife and I were driving down the road, talking, and she randomly said, "Our greatest enemy is right around this corner."

Well, now, that can shake a guy up! I nearly slammed the brakes but instead kept enough composure to say, "What do you mean? What enemy is right around the corner?" She just got this blank look on her face and said, "Huh?"

So I reminded her of what she had just said five seconds earlier. As it just so happens, she and I were studying for our scuba diving exam. One of the questions is about panic, which is, in fact, your greatest enemy when you are scuba diving. But in the middle of giving me that quick, impromptu pop quiz, she decided to also give me directions to our destination, Dogget's Shoe Store. And thus, "Our greatest enemy is right around this corner."

That one took a bit of effort to sort out!

Yes, I know that men can sometimes be hard to explain as well, but you have to admit that, for the most part, women are much harder to explain than men. When you ask a man what's wrong, and he says, "Nothing," he means "nothing." When you ask a woman what's wrong, and she says, "Nothing," she means "something is wrong, but I will not be satisfied unless you figure it out on your own." When you ask a man what he wants to eat, and he says, "It doesn't matter," he means "it doesn't matter." When you ask a woman what she wants to eat, and she says, "It doesn't matter," she means, "It does matter, and you need to guess somewhere between five and fifteen times before you finally figure out a place that I'm willing to eat at right now."

When a guy breaks up with a girl and says, "We can still be friends," he means, "we can still be friends." When a girl breaks up with a guy and says, "We can still be friends," she means "don't call me, don't text me, don't look at me, don't think about me, move very far away if you possibly can, and I am going to say embarrassing things about you to everyone I meet for the next three years..."

So yes, women are very hard to explain.

That is especially true about the woman spoken of in Revelation 17 and 18. Look again at the description of her that we have been given already:

Revelation 17:1 *And there came one of the seven angels which had the seven vials, and talked with me, saying unto me, Come hither; I will shew unto thee the judgment of the great whore that sitteth upon many waters:* **2** *With whom the kings of the earth have committed fornication, and the inhabitants of the earth have been made drunk with the wine of her fornication.* **3** *So he carried me away in the spirit into the wilderness: and I saw a woman sit upon a scarlet coloured beast, full of names of blasphemy, having seven heads and ten horns.* **4** *And the woman was arrayed in purple and scarlet colour, and decked with gold and precious stones and pearls, having a golden cup in her hand full of abominations and filthiness of her fornication:* **5** *And upon her forehead was a name written, MYSTERY, BABYLON THE GREAT, THE MOTHER OF HARLOTS AND ABOMINATIONS OF THE EARTH.* **6** *And I saw the woman drunken with the blood of the saints, and with the blood of the martyrs of Jesus:*

What a description! No wonder the next thing we read is John saying, *"And when I saw her, I wondered with great admiration."*

John was amazed, perplexed, and even a bit bewildered about this woman. And that is when he got some help:

Revelation 17:7 *And the angel said unto me, Wherefore didst thou marvel? I will tell thee the mystery of the woman, and of the beast that carrieth her, which hath the seven heads and ten horns.*

An angel came to John and volunteered to tell him everything he needed to know about this woman.

This is a good news/bad news situation. The good news is that the angel explained this woman, and we can understand her. The bad news is, as far as we know, he is not going to show up again and explain any women for any man today. So let's just love the women that we have yet cannot understand, and also work our way through this text so that we can understand the woman that we would not have even if we could.

The ride of the woman

Revelation 17:8 *The beast that thou sawest* [which verse three says the woman is riding on] *was, and is not; and shall ascend out of the bottomless pit, and go into perdition: and they that dwell on the earth shall wonder, whose names were not written in the book of life from the foundation of the world, when they behold the beast that was, and is not, and yet is.*

This beast represents both the Antichrist and the one-world government of Antichrist. But why does it say that he was, and is not, and shall ascend out of the bottomless pit?

Earlier in this book, I explained that riddle. But in case you have forgotten, here is why I believe the Bible describes the beast, the Antichrist, this way:

2 Thessalonians 2:3 *Let no man deceive you by any means: for that day* [the Tribulation Period] *shall not come, except there come a falling away first, and that man of sin be revealed, the son of perdition;* **4** *Who opposeth and exalteth himself above all that is called God, or that is worshipped; so that he as God sitteth in the temple of God, shewing himself that he is God.*

Do you remember the word apocalypse that we said our English word Revelation comes from? That is the same word used here when we are told the Antichrist must be revealed before the Tribulation begins. Antichrist will not just slowly appear on the scene, gradually gaining power and prestige over many years until he takes over. This man will explode onto the scene and be in charge so fast it will make heads spin.

Notice that he is called the son of perdition. The word perdition means absolute destruction. It describes what he causes and what is going to happen to him. This phrase "the son of perdition" is found exactly twice in the entire Bible. Let me show you the other time it is used. It came when Jesus was thinking about and praying for His disciples in the immediate moments after Judas left to betray Him:

John 17:12 *While I was with them in the world, I kept them in thy name: those that thou gavest me I have kept, and none of them is lost, but the son of perdition; that the scripture might be fulfilled.*

John 17:12 calls Judas the, not a, son of perdition. 2 Thessalonians 2:3 calls Antichrist the, not a, son of perdition.

This is certainly not a major issue, but these passages lead me to believe that a resurrected Judas Iscariot will be the Antichrist.

But on a doctrinal note, the more important thing to notice from verse eight is the description of these men as those who have not had their names written in the Book of Life from the foundation of the world. The Tribulation era beast worshippers, unlike the saved, and the lost from other ages as we will see in Revelation 20:10, never had their names in that book at all. They were never even there to be blotted out.

As Lenski observed, God foresaw that most evil of choices and made a choice of his own.

> "The reason that the names of these earth dwellers were never entered in the Book of Life is stated here: they ever bow in admiration and adoration before the antichristian world power (the beast). How could God, whose foreknowledge saw all from eternity, have their names entered in this blessed Book that is to be read at the last day (20:12)? Their eternal fate is that of the beast and of the dragon." (401)

But as to the beast, this beast was, and is not, and shall ascend out of the bottomless pit. And this woman, the one-world religion, will ride him and his political apparatus to power.

Revelation 17:9 *And here is the mind which hath wisdom. The seven heads are seven mountains, on which the woman sitteth.*

To modern American readers, this woman sitting on "seven mountains" might make them scratch their heads. But to John the apostle, who wrote the book of the Revelation, there was no head scratching going on. This woman, this harlot, had already been clearly identified as a city. Verse five called her "Babylon." But not literal Babylon, "mystery" Babylon. In other words, this woman was a religion, and a city, a city like Babylon, but not Babylon itself. So we are looking for a religious city, sitting on seven mountains. Let me assure you; John had no trouble at all identifying that city. That city and her emperor were responsible for him being exiled to Patmos! That city was Rome, and everyone in that day knew it. It is the only major city on earth to ever be built on seven mountains! The Greeks called Rome the city of seven tops. Varro called her Septiceps, the city of seven heads. Others called her Septem Collis, the seven-hilled city. She was often called Septicollis Roma. The ancient Romans themselves held a festival called Septimontium, the feast of the seven-hilled city.

People can like it or not like it, but the one-world religion will be headed by Rome. There are still more than a billion people on earth that believe the Pope is infallible. And one day, the Antichrist will use that devotion, merge all religions into one brand-new religion through his diplomatic skills, and have Rome leading the way in the only religion left on earth.

Revelation 17:10 *And there are seven kings: five are fallen, and one is, and the other is not yet come; and when he cometh, he must continue a short space.*

This, too, might make people today shake their heads and wonder what the Bible is talking about. But John knew. In Bible days, kings were synonymous with kingdoms, mostly because every great nation is always associated with one truly great leader. Let me illustrate; what nation do you think of when I say George Washington? America. Hitler? Germany. Churchill? Great Britain. Napoleon? France. As I observed, every great nation is always associated with one truly great leader. So when the Bible here speaks of seven kings, five of which had fallen, John could immediately think of great powers of the world that were tied into everything prophetic. Egypt had dominated the world but had fallen into obscurity. Assyria had controlled it all and was now gone. The Chaldean Empire with the capital city of Babylon, headed by Nebuchadnezzar, had come and gone. The Medo-Persian Empire, headed by Cyrus, had ascended to the heights and then been defeated. The Greek Empire of Alexander the Great had conquered the entire world and then met her match when Rome, the sixth great empire, came onto the scene. Look at what verse ten says again: five are fallen (Egypt, Assyria, Chaldea, Medo-Persia, Greece) and one is (Rome).

When John was putting pen to parchment, he knew that Rome, the sixth great empire, was right then in his day in existence. The seventh empire was "not yet." It would come after John's day. Way after his day. It would come in the days when the Tribulation falls on the earth, most likely in our day! Since the days of the Roman Empire, there has not been a single nation that has ruled the world. But there will be. And according to the prophecies of Daniel, it will be a revived form of the Roman empire. It will begin in earnest during the Tribulation Period, which will only last seven years. That is not a very long time for an empire to rule the entire world. That is why verse ten also says this,

"...and when he [the last king and kingdom] *cometh, he must continue a short space."*

The Bible is flawless, matchless, incredible! Had there been a single nation to rule the entire world at any time since the fall of Rome, then the numbers simply would not have matched. But God knew that it would not happen. He knew that the last empire to ever rule the world would only have seven short years to do it, right at the end of this age.

Revelation 17:11 *And the beast that was, and is not, even he is the eighth, and is of the seven, and goeth into perdition.*

This last form of government, this revived Roman Empire, will be the seventh great world-dominating empire on earth. The Antichrist will head it. But get this tricky little detail: whereas every empire and king before it was pretty much equal, Antichrist will be so much more the focus than his kingdom that he is regarded as number eight, not number seven. His kingdom is number seven; he is number eight. But he is, specifically, of the seven. Not of "the seventh," of "the seven." In other words, he is the living combination of everything evil and powerful and deceitful and terrifying about all the seven put together. He is the end-all-be-all of wicked human dictators. This is the ruler the one-world religion will be riding on.

Revelation 17:12 *And the ten horns which thou sawest are ten kings, which have received no kingdom as yet; but receive power as kings one hour with the beast.*

This is very simple; we have already seen this earlier in the book of the Revelation and in the book of Daniel. This will be the ten-nation federation that makes up the revived Roman Empire. The fact that they receive power for "one hour" goes back to what you saw in verse ten, which said, *"...and when he cometh, he must continue a short space."*

How long is that "short space?" Seven years. This "one hour" is symbolic for the short period of seven years that the Antichrist will rule during the Tribulation Period. This woman's ride will be a dark hour, but it will be a short hour as well, just a few years long.

Revelation 17:13 *These have one mind, and shall give their power and strength unto the beast.*

Most world alliances are tenuous at best, with everyone having their own self-interests at heart. But this alliance that the Antichrist melds together will be the most unique of political things, a situation in which everyone else has his, the Antichrist's, best interests at heart. And what will their alliance with Antichrist lead them into?

Revelation 17:14 *These shall make war with the Lamb, and the Lamb shall overcome them: for he is Lord of lords, and King of kings: and they that are with him are called, and chosen, and faithful.*

This political alliance will gather all of their combined armies and gather them into the valley of Armageddon to fight against God Himself! Maybe they figure they can take Him; after all, this verse does describe Him as a Lamb. How powerful can a Lamb be?

But this Lamb is not any ordinary lamb; this Lamb is also Lord of lords and King of kings, and He has an army of saints with Him who are called and chosen and faithful.

Do you understand the significance of this? We get to be with Him when this last battle takes place. We get to be there when Antichrist loses and Jesus Christ wins. This woman, this harlot, this one-world religion, her ride is not going to survive.

But interestingly enough, she will not even survive as long as her ride does. We will see that in a few verses, but I do not want us to get too far ahead of ourselves. We have seen the ride of the woman, so for now, let's go to verse fifteen and see:

The ruled of the woman

Revelation 17:15 *And he saith unto me, The waters which thou sawest, where the whore sitteth, are peoples, and multitudes, and nations, and tongues.*

We have observed this already in our study of The Revelation. This verse simply reminds us that the impossible is going to become a reality. One religion is going to draw in Catholicism and Islam and Hinduism and Buddhism and the New Age and Protestantism and everything else from everywhere else on earth. There is hardly any way we can even wrap our minds around this, but there will come a day when everyone agrees on every religious matter. No more arguing over which holy book to follow, no more debating which city to pray towards, no more Jihad against infidels; everyone will look to Rome and Antichrist for guidance. This woman, the one-world religious system, will be sitting on every nation and people on earth. The one-world religion will be riding the one-world government, and she will be thrilled with the arrangement. On the surface, everything seems to be perfect.

But politicians hate to share power. They always have, and they always will. And that is why we now come to:

The ruin of the woman

Revelation 17:16 *And the ten horns which thou sawest upon the beast, these shall hate the whore, and shall make her desolate and naked, and shall eat her flesh, and burn her with fire. 17 For God hath put in their hearts to fulfil his will, and to agree, and give their kingdom unto the beast, until the words of God shall be fulfilled. 18 And the woman* *which thou sawest is that great city, which reigneth over the kings of the earth.*

It always amazes me how there really is no safety among sinners. Sinners will always eventually turn on their very own.

The one-world government will at first tolerate the one-world religion because she serves their purpose. But eventually, they will get tired of the game, tired of the pageantry, tired of the things that even they know are not true, and especially tired of bowing to her when they feel like she should be bowing to them.

God will be behind this. He will be the one that first moves them to follow her and then turns them to ruin her. And thus, the same one-world government that carried the one-world religion will turn and destroy her. This will be a satanic civil war, something only God could cause.

This passage has given us a great many facts and figures about the one-world religion to come. But whether or not you remember all of those facts is not really as important to me as you learning this one application of those facts: wicked friends are not really friends at all. And the same crowd sinners are being carried by will one day destroy them if they do not forsake them and turn to Christ. It may take an angel to understand a woman, but it takes someone utterly bereft of any common sense to ignore this obvious fact to the point of their own ruin.

Chapter Thirty-Nine
The Fall of Babylon

Revelation 18:1 *And after these things I saw another angel come down from heaven, having great power; and the earth was lightened with his glory.* **2** *And he cried mightily with a strong voice, saying, Babylon the great is fallen, is fallen, and is become the habitation of devils, and the hold of every foul spirit, and a cage of every unclean and hateful bird.* **3** *For all nations have drunk of the wine of the wrath of her fornication, and the kings of the earth have committed fornication with her, and the merchants of the earth are waxed rich through the abundance of her delicacies.* **4** *And I heard another voice from heaven, saying, Come out of her, my people, that ye be not partakers of her sins, and that ye receive not of her plagues.* **5** *For her sins have reached unto heaven, and God hath remembered her iniquities.* **6** *Reward her even as she rewarded you, and double unto her double according to her works: in the cup which she hath filled fill to her double.* **7** *How much she hath glorified herself, and lived deliciously, so much torment and sorrow give her: for she saith in her heart, I sit a queen, and am no widow, and shall see no sorrow.* **8** *Therefore shall her plagues come in one day, death, and mourning, and famine; and she shall be utterly burned with fire: for strong is the Lord God who judgeth her.* **9** *And the kings of the earth, who have committed fornication and lived deliciously with her, shall bewail her, and lament for her, when they shall see the smoke of her burning,* **10** *Standing afar off for the fear of her torment, saying, Alas, alas, that great city Babylon, that mighty city! for in one hour is thy judgment come.* **11** *And the merchants of the earth shall weep and mourn over her; for no man buyeth their merchandise any more:* **12** *The merchandise of gold, and silver, and precious stones, and of pearls, and fine linen, and purple, and silk, and scarlet, and all thyine wood, and all manner vessels of ivory, and all manner vessels of most precious wood, and of brass, and iron, and marble,* **13** *And cinnamon, and odours, and ointments, and frankincense, and wine, and oil, and fine flour, and wheat, and beasts, and sheep, and horses, and chariots, and slaves, and souls of men.* **14** *And the fruits that thy soul lusted after are departed from thee, and all things which were dainty and goodly are departed from thee, and thou shalt find them no more at all.* **15** *The merchants of these things, which were made rich by her, shall stand afar off for the fear of her torment, weeping and wailing,* **16** *And saying, Alas, alas, that great city, that was clothed in fine linen, and purple, and scarlet, and decked with gold, and precious stones, and pearls!* **17** *For in one hour so great riches is come* *to nought. And every shipmaster, and all the company in ships, and sailors, and as many as trade by sea, stood afar off,* **18** *And cried when they saw the smoke of her burning, saying, What city is like unto this great city!* **19** *And they cast dust on their heads, and cried, weeping and wailing, saying, Alas, alas, that great city, wherein were made rich all that had ships in the sea by reason of her costliness! for in one hour is she made desolate.* **20** *Rejoice over her, thou heaven, and ye holy apostles and prophets; for God hath avenged you on her.* **21** *And a mighty angel took up a stone like a great millstone, and cast it into the sea, saying, Thus with violence shall that great city Babylon be thrown down, and shall be found no more at all.* **22** *And the voice of harpers, and musicians, and of pipers, and trumpeters, shall be heard no more at all in thee; and no craftsman, of whatsoever craft he be, shall be found any more in thee; and the sound of a millstone shall be heard no more at all in thee;* **23** *And the light of a candle shall shine no more at all in thee; and the voice of the bridegroom and of the bride shall be heard no more at all in thee: for thy merchants were the great men of the earth; for by thy sorceries were all nations deceived.* **24** *And in her was found the blood of prophets, and of saints, and of all that were slain upon the earth.*

All throughout chapter seventeen of the book of The Revelation, we examined the one-world religion that will exist during the Tribulation Period. She is called Mystery Babylon, Great Babylon, the Great Whore, the Harlot.

We saw that this one-world religion will be headed by Rome.

After centuries in power, the last hundred years have not been kind to the Roman Catholic Church, largely because of world-wide exposure of her child abuse sexual scandals.

But during the Tribulation Period, the Antichrist will mold her into a new version of an old heresy, and every religion on earth will come under her lead. But as we saw at the end of chapter seventeen, the one-world political system that she is riding on will eventually turn on her and destroy her. And chapter eighteen will deal with her destruction in extensive detail.

A sentence declared

Revelation 18:1 *And after these things I saw another angel come down from heaven, having great power; and the earth was lightened with his glory.* **2** *And he cried mightily with a strong voice, saying, Babylon the great is fallen, is fallen, and is become the habitation of devils, and the hold of every foul spirit, and a cage of every unclean and hateful bird.* **3** *For all nations have drunk of the wine of the wrath of her fornication, and the kings of the earth have committed fornication with her, and the* *merchants of the earth are waxed rich through the abundance of her delicacies.*

Over and over in the Bible, God describes Himself as "jealous." He does not like having any other so-called god worshipped. You may remember that He said so in the very first of the ten commandments:

Exodus 20:2 *I am the LORD thy God, which have brought thee out of the land of Egypt, out of the house of bondage.* **3** *Thou shalt have no other gods before me.*

He also mentioned it in the second commandment:

Exodus 20:4 *Thou shalt not make unto thee any graven image, or any likeness of any thing that is in heaven above, or that is in the earth beneath, or that is in the water under the earth:* **5** *Thou shalt not bow down thyself to them, nor serve them: for I the LORD thy God am a jealous God, visiting the iniquity of the fathers upon the children unto the third and fourth generation of them that hate me;*

God does not like "rivals." So when the world eagerly chases after the religion of Antichrist, God is not one bit pleased with it. And when it falls, it will not take long for heaven to express an opinion. An angel will come down from heaven, visible for all to see. In fact, verse one tells us that the entire earth will light up with his glory when he appears. This angel will already have everyone's attention when he shouts with a strong voice, *"Babylon the great is fallen, is fallen!"*

When things are repeated twice in the Bible, it is both to show emphasis and to show certainty. There is no question about it; the one-world religion will fall.

Look at what the angel says next. Babylon *"is become the habitation of devils, and the hold of every foul spirit, and a cage of every unclean and hateful bird."*

This wording that describes the fall of "Mystery Babylon" is almost identical to the wording that described the fall of literal Babylon thousands of years ago:

Isaiah 13:20 *It shall never be inhabited, neither shall it be dwelt in from generation to generation: neither shall the Arabian pitch tent there; neither shall the shepherds make their fold there.* **21** *But wild beasts of the desert shall lie there; and their houses shall be full of doleful creatures; and owls shall dwell there, and satyrs shall dance there.* **22** *And the wild beasts of the islands shall cry in their desolate houses, and dragons in their pleasant palaces: and her time is near to come, and her days shall not be prolonged.*

Everything Isaiah prophesied came true.

Cyrus the Persian took the city of Babylon by diverting the waters of the Euphrates which ran through the midst of it and entering the place at night by the dry channel. But the river was never restored afterward to its proper course. So it overflowed the whole country and made it little better than a swamp. This and the fact that the Persians slaughtered multitudes of the city's inhabitants was the first step to the ruin of ancient Babylon. The Persian monarchs were always leery of the city, so they kept it in disarray and took care to prevent it from recovering its former greatness. A few years later, a man named Darius Hystaspes severely punished it for a revolt, depopulated it, lowered the walls, and demolished the gates. Xerxes later destroyed all the temples of Babylon. Then there was a city built nearby, Seleucia, on the Tigris River. That exhausted Babylon because so many people left Babylon for the new city. A king of the Parthians soon after carried away into slavery a great number of the remaining inhabitants and burned and destroyed the most beautiful parts of the city. Later writers testify to the fact that Babylon became just an overgrown jungle, lived in by animals. (Clarke 4: 79) So when Isaiah 13:20 prophesied that great Babylon would reach such a state of ruin that it would be regarded as utterly desolate, he was right! No one would have ever believed it, yet it happened.

The same thing will happen to Babylon, the one-world religion. Verse two says that she is going to become desolate; like a destroyed city filled with devils, demons, crows, and ravens.

Again, God despises anything that competes for the attention that you and I should be giving Him! And inevitably, everything that draws attention away from God can be described the same way that God described great Babylon in the next verse:

Revelation 18:3 *For all nations have drunk of the wine of the wrath of her fornication, and the kings of the earth have committed fornication with her, and the merchants of the earth are waxed rich through the abundance of her delicacies.*

Drunkenness, fornication (which means sexual sins), and then materialism. As we saw in the last chapter, the merchants of earth will get filthy rich off of her. She will be the biggest customer on the planet, a church with billions of totally devoted members!

No matter. Her riches will not save her; her popularity will not sway God; His sentence declared on her is that she is going to be destroyed.

A separation demanded

Revelation 18:4 *And I heard another voice from heaven, saying, Come out of her, my people, that ye be not partakers of her sins, and that ye receive not of her plagues.* **5** *For her sins have reached unto heaven, and God hath remembered her iniquities.*

This is God demanding that His people on earth not have anything to do with apostate religion. But why would He even have to say this?

Here is why. Especially during difficult times, the temptation to toss sound doctrine out the window and just get along with everyone can be enormous! Think of how hard it will be during the Tribulation Period on true believers. They are being hunted like animals; they do not have church buildings to meet in anymore; they are murdered as soon as anyone finds out they are Christians. And then a neighbor invites them down to the "revival meeting" at the First Apostolic Ecumenical Church of the Devil Himself...

How tempting must it be to finally quit taking a stand and just decide to get along with everybody, even when everybody is not getting along with God?

The temptation will be awesome. I know this because even today, the pressure is huge to do just that!

Much of mainstream evangelicalism is now wholly given over to unity over truth. It tolerates everything except unwavering Biblical truth. And if a person or a church says such divisive things as "Jesus Christ is the only way to heaven, and those who reject Him go to hell," they will immediately be labeled as "un-Christlike" for quoting Christ Himself. And oftentimes, people are threatened with the loss of job and livelihood for being vocal about Biblical truth. So, yes, the pressure is enormous. But we cannot give in to it, not for a moment, not for a second, because we all must give an account of ourselves before the Judgment Seat of Christ. And He is not going to be looking to see how well we got along with apostates. Here, among other things, is what He will be looking to see:

2 Corinthians 6:17 *Wherefore come out from among them, and be ye separate, saith the Lord, and touch not the unclean thing; and I will receive you,* **18** *And will be a Father unto you, and ye shall be my sons and daughters, saith the Lord Almighty.*

Romans 16:17 *Now I beseech you, brethren, mark them which cause divisions and offences contrary to the doctrine which ye have learned; and avoid them.*

1 Timothy 1:3 *As I besought thee to abide still at Ephesus, when I went into Macedonia, that thou mightest charge some that they teach no other doctrine,*

Let me repeat the warning of the angel in verse four. No matter what the cost, we cannot ever hold hands with those that deny the doctrines of the faith.

And this will be abundantly true with Mystery Babylon, the one-world religion, during the Tribulation Period. Those believers who are somehow mixing and mingling with her are at risk of being plagued along with her because, according to verse five, "...*her sins have reached unto heaven, and God hath remembered her iniquities.*"

Remember, this is a religion that we are dealing with. Religion is not always righteous, but in this case, it would be more accurate to say religion is not at all righteous!

Revelation 18:6 *Reward her even as she rewarded you, and double unto her double according to her works: in the cup which she hath filled fill to her double.* **7** *How much she hath glorified herself, and lived deliciously, so much torment and sorrow give her: for she saith in her heart, I sit a queen, and am no widow, and shall see no sorrow.* **8** *Therefore shall her plagues come in one day, death, and mourning, and famine; and she shall be utterly burned with fire: for strong is the Lord God who judgeth her.*

The very first phrase of verse six is almost shocking when we consider to whom it is directed. In context, it unmistakably goes back to those directly addressed in verse four:

Revelation 18:4 *And I heard another voice from heaven, saying, Come out of her,* **my people**, *that ye be not partakers of her sins, and that ye receive not of her plagues.*

The "*my people*" of verse four are the ones commanded to "*Reward her even as she rewarded you*" in verse six. In our dispensation, God clearly takes the right of vengeance away from us and holds it to Himself:

Romans 12:19 *Dearly beloved, avenge not yourselves, but rather give place unto wrath: for it is written, Vengeance is mine; I will repay, saith the Lord.*

But near the end of the Tribulation Period, when God's people have suffered so much at the hands of the one-world church of Antichrist, God is going to instruct those believers who remain to participate in His vengeance on their oppressors!

What the church of Antichrist will do is violent and terrible. Millions of new Christians will be tortured and killed during the Tribulation Period. But what she and her leaders do will come back to haunt them; they will get treated exactly twice as bad as they have treated the people of God!

God despises this apostate religion. One reason for that, according to verse seven, is that she regards herself as a queen; she believes herself to be royal and untouchable, eternal, everlasting.

Because of that, God says that her destruction will come in one single day! How in the world is it possible for a one-world religion to fall in a single day? Verse eight answers that question: *strong is the Lord that judgeth her*.

No wicked religion and no persecutor of the righteous will ever get by forever. Payday is coming.

A sorrow displayed

Revelation 18:9 *And the kings of the earth, who have committed fornication and lived deliciously with her, shall bewail her, and lament for her, when they shall see the smoke of her burning,* **10** *Standing afar off for the fear of her torment, saying, Alas, alas, that great city Babylon, that mighty city! for in one hour is thy judgment come.* **11** *And the merchants of the earth shall weep and mourn over her; for no man buyeth their merchandise any more:* **12** *The merchandise of gold, and silver, and precious stones, and of pearls, and fine linen, and purple, and silk, and scarlet, and all thyine wood, and all manner vessels of ivory, and all manner vessels of most precious wood, and of brass, and iron, and marble,* **13** *And cinnamon, and odours, and ointments, and frankincense, and wine, and oil, and fine flour, and wheat, and beasts, and sheep, and horses, and chariots, and slaves, and souls of men.* **14** *And the fruits that thy soul lusted after are departed from thee, and all things which were dainty and goodly are departed from thee, and thou shalt find them no more at all.* **15** *The merchants of these things, which were made rich by her, shall stand afar off for the fear of her torment, weeping and wailing,* **16** *And saying, Alas, alas, that great city, that was clothed in fine linen, and purple, and scarlet, and decked with gold, and precious stones, and pearls!* **17** *For in one hour so great riches is come to nought. And every shipmaster, and all the company in ships, and sailors, and as many as trade by sea, stood afar off,* **18** *And cried when they saw the smoke of her burning, saying, What city is like unto this great city!* **19** *And they cast dust on their heads, and cried, weeping and wailing, saying, Alas, alas, that great city, wherein were made rich all that had ships in the sea by reason of her costliness! for in one hour is she made desolate.*

I want you to notice some interesting things here. First of all, notice the list of things that this harlot trades in, namely gold and silver, precious stones, pearls, fine linen, purple, silk, scarlet, thyine wood, all manner of vessels of ivory, all manner of vessels of most precious wood, brass, iron, marble, cinnamon, odors, ointments, frankincense, wine, oil, fine flour, wheat, beasts, sheep, horses, chariots, slaves, and souls of men.

Does anything strike you as interesting about that list? How about this: these will be the primary things that she buys and sells in at least the twenty-first century! Not computers, not jet planes, not yachts, not anything that John could even describe as some kind of high technology.

Why is that? Because all these things listed in these verses through the years have been used for religious purposes. Gold, silver, gemstones, fine linen, purple, silk, scarlet, precious woods, ivory, brass, iron, marble, cinnamon, fragrances, ointments, frankincense, wine, oil, fine flour, wheat, animals, chariots, these things especially have the Roman Church written all over them. Every one of these has been used by Popes and priests for centuries.

How about slaves? Yes, those too. Rome was a big player in the slave trade and will be again during the Tribulation Period.

But how about the last one on the list, the souls of men? That one nails it down conclusively. When you consider that the church of Rome has owned the souls of men by the selling of indulgences, the granting or withholding of "grace" (through the sacraments), and the doctrine of penance, this one-world religion will continue that pattern. I wonder what price a man will pay for his "soul" during the Tribulation Period? No wonder this will be the wealthiest "church" ever!

But please notice also the secular/economic facet of all of this, namely how the merchants of earth react to her destruction. They are literally wailing and mourning over the fall of this religion.

Mind you; they do not really care about religion falling; they care about losing the customer that has made them all filthy rich. During the Tribulation Period, economics is going to become very "old school." Again, it will not be electronic gadgets that all the world is buying; it will be religious paraphernalia made of actual, tangible goods. So when she falls, the money-making scheme falls with her.

These merchants are standing far off from her. They are watching her burn from their cargo ships out at sea. But pay attention to the fact that both verse ten and verse fifteen say that they are standing far off from her "for fear of her torment." They are scared to get near her, lest her torment falls on them. Remember that God destroys Babylon, Rome, but He does so by letting the ten leaders of Antichrist's one-world government do it. They do it by physical means, by military means. And the way that they do it makes the city burn and smoke and makes everyone scared to get too close. That seems to be almost certainly a description of a nuclear strike. That would undoubtedly do the job, and it would do it in the "one hour" that verse nineteen speaks of, which in this case is to be taken literally since it is men using the term.

These men, these merchants, are broken-hearted because their best customer has been destroyed. Politics and religion and business have now clashed, politics has come out of the fight as the undisputed holder of all power on earth, religion has been destroyed entirely, and business is left powerless and weeping.

They can cry all they want to, but God will lower the hammer on wickedness eventually.

A sovereign decree

Revelation 18:20 *Rejoice over her, thou heaven, and ye holy apostles and prophets; for God hath avenged you on her.* **21** *And a mighty angel took up a stone like a great millstone, and cast it into the sea, saying, Thus with violence shall that great city Babylon be thrown down, and shall be found no more at all.* **22** *And the voice of harpers, and musicians, and of pipers, and trumpeters, shall be heard no more at all in thee; and no craftsman, of whatsoever craft he be, shall be found any more in thee; and the sound of a millstone shall be heard no more at all in thee;* **23** *And the light of a candle shall shine no more at all in thee; and the voice of the bridegroom and of the bride shall be heard no more at all in thee: for thy merchants were the great men of the earth; for by thy sorceries were all nations deceived.* **24** *And in her was found the blood of prophets, and of saints, and of all that were slain upon the earth.*

When this one-world religion finally falls, God decrees a celebration. It is time to rejoice over the fact that people are not being duped anymore. It is time to rejoice that the saints are not being hunted by her anymore. It is time to thank God that there are no rivals for His glory anymore.

In verse twenty-two, the angel gives the world a visual picture of the destruction of this city and the one world religion that is based out of her. He picks up a gigantic stone and casts it into the sea. Great Babylon will sink forever out of memory just as the stone sinks forever out of sight.

In verses twenty-two and twenty-three, the angel lists the things that will never be seen or heard in this city again, namely harpers, musicians, pipers, trumpeters, craftsmen, the sound of a millstone the light of a candle and the voice of the bridegroom and of the bride.

All of these things are primarily religious in nature. Religion that makes a hefty profit for those involved, but religion nonetheless. And all of that money-making mockery of God will be destroyed in an hour, taking most of the world economy with it.

Verse twenty-four then reminds us that *"in her was found the blood of prophets, and of saints, and of all that were slain upon the earth."*

This combination world-wide religion/Ponzi scheme is full of money, but it is all blood money. Just as individual religions before her, particularly Rome and Islam, have slain so many in the pursuit of power and profit, this final man-made religion will be utterly soaked in the blood of victims who stood in her way.

And the God who heard the cry of the blood of just one, Abel, will hear the cry of the blood of the multitudes slain at the hand of the harlot.

Babylon will fall; weep not at all for her.

Chapter Forty
The Shouting Before the Showing

Revelation 19:1 *And after these things I heard a great voice of much people in heaven, saying, Alleluia; Salvation, and glory, and honour, and power, unto the Lord our God:* **2** *For true and righteous are his judgments: for he hath judged the great whore, which did corrupt the earth with her fornication, and hath avenged the blood of his servants at her hand.* **3** *And again they said, Alleluia. And her smoke rose up for ever and ever.* **4** *And the four and twenty elders and the four beasts fell down and worshipped God that sat on the throne, saying, Amen; Alleluia.* **5** *And a voice came out of the throne, saying, Praise our God, all ye his servants, and ye that fear him, both small and great.* **6** *And I heard as it were the voice of a great multitude, and as the voice of many waters, and as the voice of mighty thunderings, saying, Alleluia: for the Lord God omnipotent reigneth.* **7** *Let us be glad and rejoice, and give honour to him: for the marriage of the Lamb is come, and his wife hath made herself ready.* **8** *And to her was granted that she should be arrayed in fine linen, clean and white: for the fine linen is the righteousness of saints.* **9** *And he saith unto me, Write, Blessed are they which are called unto the marriage supper of the Lamb. And he saith unto me, These are the true sayings of God.* **10** *And I fell at his feet to worship him. And he said unto me, See thou do it not: I am thy fellowservant, and of thy brethren that have the testimony of Jesus: worship God: for the testimony of Jesus is the spirit of prophecy.*

In the last chapter, we finished covering Revelation 17 and 18, which dealt with the one-world religion that the Antichrist will institute during the Tribulation Period. Chapter eighteen showed us the destruction of the one-world religion, which the Bible calls the Great Whore.

We have already seen the buildup to Armageddon, and we have seen all twenty-one of the judgments that God is going to unleash during the Tribulation Period. So we are nearing the end of time by this point in the book; we are nearing the second part of the second coming of the Lord. The first will be unseen when He comes in the Rapture and removes His bride at the beginning of the Tribulation Period. The second will be shown to all when He comes to take charge of the world.

Just imagine what a time that will be! We are looking forward to that showing.

But before the showing, there will be some shouting.

Shouting over a condemnation

Revelation 19:1 *And after these things I heard a great voice of much people in heaven, saying, Alleluia; Salvation, and glory, and honour, and power, unto the Lord our God:* **2a** *For true and righteous are his judgments...*

Verses one through seven of this chapter comprise what could best be described as a shouted song, a heavenly choral arrangement both powerful and pointed. Each verse starts with an "Alleluia," or as we would put it in our language, Hallelujah.

The introductory notes to the song start with the words "*After these things,*" meaning after John saw the destruction of the harlot, after the fall of the one-world religion whose roots extend all the way back to Babel of Genesis 11. After all of this, John heard a great voice of much people in heaven. This is not a quiet nod of agreement steeped in dignity and decorum; this is a sound of shouting loud enough to make the heavens ring.

That kind of thing is often scoffed at by people who are far too impressed with themselves. But before anyone criticizes them, please take note of the fact that they are in heaven. They do not even have a sin nature anymore. They do not have the ability to be wrong anymore. They are not influenced by the world anymore. They are perfect and perfectly wise and perfectly Christ-like, and they are shouting at the top of their lungs.

In other words, they are better authorities on the subject of praise and worship than anyone in our world today, including lofty doctors of the law who view that type of thing as "indecent and out of order."

Notice the content of their shouting.

They first of all cry, "Alleluia!" and it means "praise ye the Lord." It is a rightful command that we praise the Lord. Praise is every bit as much of a command in Scripture as tithing and praying and studying and winning souls. And heaven will have no problem obeying that command and calling for others to do so.

Then the multitude in heaven says, "*Salvation, and glory, and honour, and power, unto the Lord our God.*"

The reference to salvation in this praise chorus means that salvation belongs to Him; He is the author and finisher of it.

Glory is from the word *doxa*, and it means glory and splendor and brightness. All of this and more belongs to Him; it is perfectly accurate to say that we cannot possibly praise Him enough.

Honor comes from the word *timay*, and it means a high valuation. Simply put, God is worthy of being held in utter reverence

Power belongs to God as well, and this is from the word *dunamis*. Not just His, but all of our power belongs to Him.

This is the content thus far, but what is the motivation behind the content? Why are they saying what they are saying? The answer to that question begins to be given in verse two:

Revelation 19:2 *For true and righteous are his judgments:*

In other words, it is perfectly acceptable to shout and praise God when we see His enemies judged because His judgments are always totally warranted and pinpoint accurate.

While there is still hope for a wretched sinner or even an entire world that is wilfully defying God, pray for them with all your heart. When judgment has finally fallen, you may as well stop praying and rejoice in what God has done.

In this case, there will be a specific judgment that these inhabitants in heaven are rejoicing over:

Revelation 19:2b... *for he hath judged the great whore, which did corrupt the earth with her fornication, and hath avenged the blood of his servants at her hand.*

Remember that this is the one world religious system of Antichrist. These heavenly saints, many of whom died at her hand, see this and rejoice! And when they do, verse two of the song begins:

Revelation 19:3 *And again they said, Alleluia. And her smoke rose up for ever and ever.*

What a thing to say: "*Alleluia. And her smoke rose up for ever and ever.*" All of that is coming from the mouths of the multitude. In other words, "We have already looked into eternity, and we have seen that God will never stop judging her. The fire and smoke of earth now will give way to the fire and smoke of the lake of fire later; hallelujah, glory to God, the Antichrist has lost, and our God reigns supreme and forever!"

Up to this point in the shouting, we have only been made aware of a general great multitude in heaven. But as verse four of the text begins, we once again find a very specific group of people among them:

Revelation 19:4 *And the four and twenty elders and the four beasts fell down and worshipped God that sat on the throne, saying, Amen; Alleluia.*

For the twelfth and final time in the book of The Revelation, we read of the twenty-four elders, the representatives of the church that first appeared in the early verses of chapter four. Along with them, we once again find the four glorious beasts who attend around the throne of God. The elders and the beasts add their "amen," their "so be it, we agree" to all that has been shouted thus far, and then they add their own shout of alleluia to begin the next verse of the song.

And they did so with movement; they fell down and worshipped before the throne. For the fifth time in the book of The Revelation, in fact, they fell down before the throne.

In the "professionally polished church world" today, it is common to have people glare at you or even derisively call you names like "ignorant and emotional" if you shout or put your face on the floor or raise your hands or any a great number of other things that people in Scripture actually did.

If that ever happens, simply lament the fact that you are exactly as ignorant and emotional as those elders and angelic beasts in heaven. It will give you a bit of consolation over not being as "intelligent" as all of the theological peacocks here on earth.

As the third verse of the shouted song continues, a new voice joins the chorus:

Revelation 19:5 *And a voice came out of the throne, saying, Praise our God, all ye his servants, and ye that fear him, both small and great.*

This verse does not tell us who utters this command, though we will learn a bit more about him in just a few verses. The throne in heaven is more than just a seat, like that of a king on earth. It is the seat and everything in near proximity to it. It is an area, not just a piece of furniture.

So we do not know whose voice this is. But we do know, since it comes from the throne, the place where God Himself sits and the highest of His creation attends to praise, that it comes from a higher place than a local church pulpit. It also comes from a higher place than the lectern of a Bible college. It comes from a much higher place than a podcast. It comes directly from the throne of God.

So for anyone who does not believe that we should, in the words of this verse, "*Praise our God, all ye his servants, and ye that fear him, both small and great,*" I have a word for you:

Overruled.

And it is interesting that when a command comes from the throne, true servants obey. Look at the buildup to the fourth verse of the shouted song and then the content of that verse itself:

Revelation 19:6 *And I heard as it were the voice of a great multitude, and as the voice of many waters, and as the voice of mighty thunderings, saying, Alleluia: for the Lord God omnipotent reigneth.*

Once again, alleluia means "praise ye Lord." And the "for" of this, the "why" is, "*for the Lord God omnipotent reigneth.*" There are four straight words of authority in that phrase: Lord, God, omnipotent, reigneth; *kurios, theos, pantokrator, ebasiluese*. These words together show His absolute charge over His creation and provide a reason for everyone who knows how good of a thing that is to shout "hallelujah!"

But this was not merely an intellectual exercise for them, nor should it be for us. That actually shouted those words. And we should too.

Try this for practice, sometime, shouting "Alleluia: for the Lord God omnipotent reigneth! Alleluia: for the Lord God omnipotent reigneth! Alleluia: for the Lord God omnipotent reigneth!"

God likes it, and that is really all that matters.

All of this praising, all of this shouting, and in this case, it is because of a condemnation.

Shouting over a celebration

Revelation 19:7 *Let us be glad and rejoice, and give honour to him: for the marriage of the Lamb is come, and his wife hath made herself ready.*

The song now moves from judgment to joy. And just about the only way this can be described is "heart-stopping." Do you understand what has happened here? This whole book, the Bible, has always been about Christ and His desire to take a bride. This is the grandest love story of all eternity, and it is all true.

Yet things have been so dark for so long. You see, a great and powerful enemy has been at work. He first tried to destroy the groom. The rebellion in heaven near the beginning of time... Herod the Great and the slaughter of Bethlehem... he tried; he tried his very best to destroy the groom. But he failed.

And having failed at that, he then turned his attention to destroying the bride. The last 2,000 years have been a constant attempt to stamp out the bride. All of the Tribulation Period, he is engaged in yet another attempt to, among other nefarious things, stamp out the bride.

Yet in the darkest hour, the Tribulation Period, when the enemy is at his strongest and seems on the verge of victory, the groom, the champion wades into the battle and begins swinging the sword on behalf of His beloved. God had been gathering saints to make up His bride for so long, and there were seven years left to do so, and it looked like the bride during the Tribulation was going to take quite a beating.

But now, just before He shows Himself in battle, He wades into the battle unseen to human eye just yet. He will be seen in just a few verses by all, but He wades in on behalf of the last of His bride, brings her home through martyrdom, and destroys Satan's play toy, the worldwide religion that killed so many saints. And the bride, for her part, according to verse seven, has "made herself ready."

That is an incredibly important phrase. Properly understood, it deals in deathblow to the pseudo-spiritual belief that God Himself does or causes everything Himself and that we are really nothing more than puppets on a string dancing to His whims.

Yes, the bride is purchased by Christ; but having been purchased, she prepares herself to meet Him. In other words, just as He freely offered Himself to absolutely anyone in the entire world and gave absolutely everyone a free will to receive Him or reject Him, He continues to give us free will in the closeness of our relationship with Him.

This eternal marriage will not be some preprogrammed, choreographed stage production; it, it will be an actual relationship with Him, just as it is now.

And now, after all that blood and havoc, after the bride prepares herself to meet her groom, John hears a sound. The voice says, "The bride is ready." But do you see her anywhere in here? No, we are just told that she has made herself ready. In fact, do you realize that we are not given a single sight of her in the Bible? On earth, the groom cannot see the bride before the wedding; in heaven, none of us can see her yet, even though we are her!

It should go without saying to you men, of course, that you are not going to become a girl. The bride of Christ is all of the saved, men and women, gathered together in heaven to love Christ and be loved of Him forever. But there will still be a wedding; only every one of us individually has already said "I do" the day that we got saved, and that made us espoused to Christ. Now we are just waiting for the actual wedding ceremony.

Revelation 19:8 *And to her was granted that she should be arrayed in fine linen, clean and white: for the fine linen is the righteousness of saints.*

This, a pure white garment symbolizing the purity of the person wearing it, is what every bride should be able to rightly wear. It is still God's command that every man and woman be a virgin when they get to the marriage altar.

The bride in heaven, though, the saved, are in a bit of a different situation. We have our "right to white" not because of what we do or do not do but because of what He did. We were born sinners, chose to act on that sin, and could never by any number of acts of righteousness undo so much as a single one of our acts of unrighteousness. Romans 4 repeatedly tells us that we have the righteousness of Christ imputed to our accounts through our faith in Him.

Thus, this bride in heaven will be arrayed in the spotless white righteousness of the saints, which is nothing else but the righteousness of Christ Himself imputed to us, which results in right living coming from us:

2 Corinthians 5:17 *Therefore if any man be in Christ, he is a new creature: old things are passed away; behold, all things are become new.*

There is a change of behavior when a person gets saved, and that will be reflected in the white wedding gown of heaven.

Revelation 19:9 *And he saith unto me, Write, Blessed are they which are called unto the marriage supper of the Lamb. And he saith unto me, These are the true sayings of God.*

There is a tiny word that we now need to give some consideration to, the word "he." Who exactly is this "he" that is now commanding John to write these words? The context of Revelation 17-19 really leaves us only two choices. It could be the angel that begins talking with him in 17:1, or it could be the individual in Revelation 19:5 who spoke from the throne.

But Revelation 19:10 eliminates the angel as a possibility when he says, *"See thou do it not: I am thy fellowservant, and of thy brethren that have the testimony of Jesus."* This is, therefore, a human being, a glorified saint, one who has been spending his time in eternity near to the God who sits on the throne. And that will become important as we get to the text of verse ten.

As this individual began speaking to John, he tells him to write the words, *"Blessed are they which are called unto the marriage supper of the Lamb."* There is not a specified group or individual pointed to in this verse; it is merely left as a general statement. In other words, whoever gets to be there for the marriage supper of the Lamb, in whatever capacity, bride, attendants, servants, friends, are blessed indeed! Imagine just getting to be there, even as an angel! It will be so grand, the voice had to say, *"These are the true sayings of God."*

Revelation 19:10 *And I fell at his feet to worship him. And he said unto me, See thou do it not: I am thy fellowservant, and of thy brethren that have the testimony of Jesus: worship God: for the testimony of Jesus is the spirit of prophecy.*

We now find that the possessor of the unseen voice from the throne has walked to where John is to speak to him. Seeing him, John's immediate reaction was to fall down and worship him. That means that John assumed this individual to be none other than the Lord Jesus Christ

Himself. And that led to the saint saying, "Stop, don't do that. I have prophesied this, but I am one of you! I am a man that Jesus used as a prophet, don't worship me, worship God."

What makes that so significant is the realization that one who spends their time being very close to Christ will invariably become very Christlike.

Oh, to be so Christlike that we could actually be mistaken for Him!

The last thing the saint told John is a bit of a unique phrase, *"For the testimony of Jesus is the spirit of prophecy."* It means that prophecy has, as its chief design, testifying of Jesus. Prophecy contains things like the Antichrist and the mark of the beast and judgments upon the world, but it is not about the Antichrist and the mark of the beast and judgments upon the world, nor is it about anyone who would proclaim those things from a pulpit or just one-on-one as this saint did for John; it is about Jesus, it is designed to point people to Him.

Many years ago, when Alethia, my daughter, was still very young, Dana and I let her watch our wedding video. The next day, at lunch, she had a salt shaker and pepper shaker draped in white napkins, moving them around the table. She was so fascinated by what she had seen that she was "playing wedding."

One day, for her, it will be real. One day, for all of the saints, it will be equally real.

Chapter Forty-One
The Second Coming

Revelation 19:11 *And I saw heaven opened, and behold a white horse; and he that sat upon him was called Faithful and True, and in righteousness he doth judge and make war.* **12** *His eyes were as a flame of fire, and on his head were many crowns; and he had a name written, that no man knew, but he himself.* **13** *And he was clothed with a vesture dipped in blood: and his name is called The Word of God.* **14** *And the armies which were in heaven followed him upon white horses, clothed in fine linen, white and clean.* **15** *And out of his mouth goeth a sharp sword, that with it he should smite the nations: and he shall rule them with a rod of iron: and he treadeth the winepress of the fierceness and wrath of Almighty God.* **16** *And he hath on his vesture and on his thigh a name written, KING OF KINGS, AND LORD OF LORDS.* **17** *And I saw an angel standing in the sun; and he cried with a loud voice, saying to all the fowls that fly in the midst of heaven, Come and gather yourselves together unto the supper of the great God;* **18** *That ye may eat the flesh of kings, and the flesh of captains, and the flesh of mighty men, and the flesh of horses, and of them that sit on them, and the flesh of all men, both free and bond, both small and great.* **19** *And I saw the beast, and the kings of the earth, and their armies, gathered together to make war against him that sat on the horse, and against his army.* **20** *And the beast was taken, and with him the false prophet that wrought miracles before him, with which he deceived them that had received the mark of the beast, and them that worshipped his image. These both were cast alive into a lake of fire burning with brimstone.* **21** *And the remnant were slain with the sword of him that sat upon the horse, which sword proceeded out of his mouth: and all the fowls were filled with their flesh.*

This world is heading shortly for the defining moment of history. Soon and very soon, Jesus is coming back to earth, and this time He will not be coming to lay down His life; He will be coming to lay down the law.

Jesus Himself spoke of this to His disciples:

Matthew 24:30 *And then shall appear the sign of the Son of man in heaven: and then shall all the tribes of the earth mourn, and they shall see the Son of man coming in the clouds of heaven with power and great glory.*

He spoke of it to His enemies:

Matthew 26:64 *Jesus saith unto him, Thou hast said: nevertheless I say unto you, Hereafter shall ye see the Son of man sitting on the right hand of power, and coming in the clouds of heaven.*

The Old Testament prophet Zechariah spoke of it:

Zechariah 12:9 *And it shall come to pass in that day, that I will seek to destroy all the nations that come against Jerusalem.* **10** *And I will pour upon the house of David, and upon the inhabitants of Jerusalem, the spirit of grace and of supplications: and they shall look upon me whom they have pierced...*

Peter told us that only scoffers doubt the second coming:

2 Peter 3:3 *Knowing this first, that there shall come in the last days scoffers, walking after their own lusts,* **4** *And saying, Where is the promise of his coming? for since the fathers fell asleep, all things continue as they were from the beginning of the creation.*

James, the half-brother of Jesus, wrote about it:

James 5:7 *Be patient therefore, brethren, unto the coming of the Lord. Behold, the husbandman waiteth for the precious fruit of the earth, and hath long patience for it, until he receive the early and latter rain.* **8** *Be ye also patient; stablish your hearts: for the coming of the Lord draweth nigh.*

Titus spoke of it as well:

Titus 2:13 *Looking for that blessed hope, and the glorious appearing of the great God and our Saviour Jesus Christ;*

Paul told the Thessalonian Church about it:

2 Thessalonians 2:1 *Now we beseech you, brethren, by the coming of our Lord Jesus Christ, and by our gathering together unto him,*

He also told the church at Corinth about it:

1 Corinthians 15:23 *But every man in his own order: Christ the firstfruits; afterward they that are Christ's at his coming.* **24** *Then cometh the end, when he shall have delivered up the kingdom to God, even the Father; when he shall have put down all rule and all authority and power.*

Isaiah looked ahead to it:

Isaiah 9:6 *For unto us a child is born* [Bethlehem], *unto us a son is given* [Calvary]: *and the government shall be upon his shoulder: and his name shall be called Wonderful, Counsellor, The mighty God, The everlasting Father, The Prince of Peace.* [The Second Coming.]

An angel told the disciples about it:

Acts 1:9 *And when he had spoken these things, while they beheld, he was taken up; and a cloud received him out of their sight.* **10** *And while they looked stedfastly toward heaven as he went up, behold,* *two men stood by them in white apparel;* **11** *Which also said, Ye men of Galilee, why stand ye gazing up into heaven? this same Jesus, which is taken up from you into heaven, shall so come in like manner as ye have seen him go into heaven.*

Repeatedly, the Bible speaks clearly about the Second Coming of the Lord Jesus Christ. If a person does not believe in the Second Coming, he may as well not believe in heaven either. If one does not believe in the Second Coming, he may as well not believe that God answers prayer. In fact, anyone who does believe in the Second Coming may as well not even believe in God because God told us that He was coming again, and if He is God, which He is, then He does not lie.

The world we live in is right now spiraling out of control, and it will only get worse once the church has been removed and the Antichrist takes control. And the only bright spot that can be seen on that horizon is this: at the end of it all, Jesus is coming back.

Scientists tell us that the universe is unraveling and will end up destroyed after a few billion more years or so, but that just is not quite right. You see, according to the Bible, we are not looking for a slow collapse; we are looking for a Second Coming.

The coming

Revelation 19:11 *And I saw heaven opened, and behold a white horse; and he that sat upon him was called Faithful and True, and in righteousness he doth judge and make war.*

There is no grammatical or contextual reason to take this verse figuratively or metaphorically. As much as the devil despises it, it must be taken literally. As much as liberal theologians deny it, it still must be taken literally. What John saw is what this world will actually see. There is coming an awesome day when every eye will look upward as the sky we see with our eyes literally rips open as Jesus makes His way to earth.

He could come any way He chooses. He could simply speak the word and be standing on the ground. He could have a legion of angels carry Him on their shoulders. He could be transported by a whirlwind. But He has chosen to make His way back to earth riding a white horse right through the atmosphere. Horses can jump, but they do not fly. This one, though, will ride as easily on the air as any horse ever did across the ground.

When John saw Jesus like this, he knew that we would know who He was, but he wanted to tell us anyway. And out of all the names he could have chosen, he called Him "Faithful and True." There could not be a better name or description given to Him at that point. Just think about it; how many scoffers have said He was not coming? How many saints have been looking for that coming and yet perhaps growing doubtful as the years drag on? But He is coming; He said He was, and He is Faithful and True.

When He comes, He will not be coming for peace; He will be coming for war. There will not ever be real peace until we finally have real war. Peace does not come from two sides tentatively agreeing to make nice; it comes from one side being totally defeated and not ever wanting to fight again. That is exactly what is going to happen, and it will not be a bad or evil thing. Verse eleven says, *"In righteousness he doth judge and make war."*

It will be right for Him to judge His enemies as worthy of death. It will be equally right for Him to make war on them and carry out the sentence.

Revelation 19:12 *His eyes were as a flame of fire, and on his head were many crowns; and he had a name written, that no man knew, but he himself.* **13** *And he was clothed with a vesture dipped in blood: and his name is called The Word of God.*

The eyes are the most expressive parts of the body. If you took a closeup video of just someone's eyes, you could look just at their eyes and figure out if they are happy, sad, angry, a thousand emotions are reflected in the eyes.

When Jesus comes, there will be very clear anger in His eyes. They will be "as a flame of fire." Those eyes that were so tender towards Jerusalem, and little children, and repentant sinners, will look like flames of fire.

On His head will be not one crown, but many crowns. There are two different types of crowns in the Bible: one was a stephanos, which was a garland or wreath type of a crown. That was given to a lot of common people as trophies at sporting events and the like.

The second was a diadem, a crown usually made of precious metals and gems and worn by royalty. That is the kind of crown spoken of here. A king that had conquered another king or territory would often take and wear the crown of those he had conquered. There are two really awesome things to think of here:

By His love He has conquered us, His friends, and He will be wearing our crowns:

Revelation 4:10 *The four and twenty elders fall down before him that sat on the throne, and worship him that liveth for ever and ever, and cast their crowns before the throne, saying,* **11** *Thou art worthy, O Lord, to receive glory and honour and power: for thou hast created all things, and for thy pleasure they are and were created.*

Remember that these twenty-four elders are the representatives of a much larger group, the church!

He has also conquered every enemy He has ever faced and will be wearing their crowns:

Exodus 15:3 *The LORD is a man of war: the LORD is his name.*

In addition to the fiery eyes and the many crowns, John also noted that Jesus had a name written that no man knew except Him. This name was open, visible, millions were seeing it, including John, yet no one knew it. How is that possible, and what does it mean?

Commentators are all over the board on this one. Some regard it as a reference to the new name of Christ referenced in Revelation 2:17. Others view it as Jehovah, claiming that the true pronunciation has been lost through the years, and only God Himself knows it. Whatever it is, the most important thing about it for us at this moment is what it lets us know about what we cannot know!

Have you ever noticed how people often think that they know it all? When it comes to Jesus, you have not even scratched the surface. The longer you know Him, the more you will learn that you still have a lot more to learn. He is at once the most transparent and simple yet complex and unfathomable person you will ever know. And that will be true in this instance, where, somehow, He has a visible new name for Himself written, likely on garment or accouterments, and yet somehow, though everyone can see it, no one can yet know it.

People often worry that eternity will be boring. That is a totally unfounded fear. Jesus, who will be our focus, will for all eternity never be totally figured out by any of us!

John saw that He had fiery eyes and many crowns and a new name written, and then he noted that Jesus was wearing clothing that had been dipped in blood. This was prophesied by Isaiah:

Isaiah 63:2 *Wherefore art thou red in thine apparel, and thy garments like him that treadeth in the winefat?* **3** *I have trodden the winepress alone; and of the people there was none with me: for I will tread them in mine anger, and trample them in my fury; and their blood shall be sprinkled upon my garments, and I will stain all my raiment.*

This was the picture of one who had just returned from a recent slaughter. He allowed His own blood to be shed during His first coming. It will be the blood of others at His second. The Jesus that has been remade in our day, fabricated into a timid, soft, easy-going surfer dude, is not even close to the truth of the real Jesus. He will be as willing to shed the blood of His enemies at His second coming as He was in shedding His own blood for His enemies at His first coming.

Then we are told that His name is called "The Word of God." If you had any doubts as to whether or not this is Jesus, this should settle it forever. Look at what this very same John wrote in the gospel that bears his name:

John 1:1 *In the beginning was the Word, and the Word was with God, and the Word was God.* **2** *The same was in the beginning with God.* **3** *All things were made by him; and without him was not any thing made that was made.*

John 1:14 *And the Word was made flesh, and dwelt among us, (and we beheld his glory, the glory as of the only begotten of the Father,) full of grace and truth.*

That's Him! When God wanted to "give us a Word," He gave us His Son:

Hebrews 1:1 *God, who at sundry times and in divers manners spake in time past unto the fathers by the prophets,* **2** *Hath in these last days spoken unto us by his Son, whom he hath appointed heir of all things, by whom also he made the worlds;*

Jesus was and is the living Word of God.

Revelation 19:14 *And the armies which were in heaven followed him upon white horses, clothed in fine linen, white and clean.*

These armies in heaven are none other than the saints themselves. We are His soldiers (2 Timothy 2:3). We are the ones described in the book of the Revelation as wearing white linen. Here is another verse that makes that same tie-in:

Revelation 17:14 *These shall make war with the Lamb, and the Lamb shall overcome them: for he is Lord of lords, and King of kings:* and **they that are with him are called, and chosen, and faithful**.

This is a clear description of the redeemed, not of angels. While angels themselves certainly fight, as is seen many times in Scripture, the saints themselves will be this heavenly army following our Captain and King to battle. We will be riding white horses through the sky with Him, and not one of us will be afraid of the heights. It will, though, be a battle whose outcome does not depend in the least on us, as the next verse makes clear:

Revelation 19:15 *And out of his mouth goeth a sharp sword, that with it he should smite the nations: and he shall rule them with a rod of iron: and he treadeth the winepress of the fierceness and wrath of Almighty God.*

In case you have forgotten, this is Armageddon we are reading about. All the nations of all the world will be there, and Christ the King will be there in all of His anger to smite the nations with His spoken word, the sword that comes out of His mouth, and then rule them with a rod of iron as will be seen beginning in Revelation 20.

Revelation 19:16 *And he hath on his vesture and on his thigh a name written, KING OF KINGS, AND LORD OF LORDS.*

The vesture is the upper garment. The thigh would be the lower garment, the side of the leg. Jesus the King will not be exercising any humility here, nor would it be at all appropriate. The world will see, written in bold letters, the title, the name, the claim of Jesus, "I am the King of kings; I am the Lord of lords." In so many words He is saying, "I am the boss. I am in charge. I am here to take over."

The calling

Revelation 19:17 *And I saw an angel standing in the sun; and he cried with a loud voice, saying to all the fowls that fly in the midst of heaven, Come and gather yourselves together unto the supper of the great God;* **18** *That ye may eat the flesh of kings, and the flesh of captains, and the flesh of mighty men, and the flesh of horses, and of them that sit on them, and the flesh of all men, both free and bond, both small and great.*

Oh, does God ever know how to get the world's attention! Here is Jesus, coming through heaven on a white horse, we are following with Him, and then John sees an angel standing in the sun. The picture is that of John looking directly at the sun, which is bright enough to blind a man pretty quickly, and somehow, he sees an angel standing there. We could view this as meaning that he was standing in the sky directly in front of the sun, but the simple wording of the text seems to indicate otherwise. And why should it be a shocking thing for a spirit to stand in the sun and be seen and heard? If God can make a universe of two trillion galaxies, He can clearly make an angel capable of such a comparatively smaller task.

The angel is big enough to see. He is not being consumed. He is able to speak loudly enough to be heard from 93,000,000 miles away, and the world can both see and hear him.

But he is just an invitation bearer. His job is to call birds. He is calling them to the valley of Armageddon. You see, there is about to be a slaughter, and every bird on earth will be needed to help with the cleanup. Buzzards and vultures and crows and hawks will be eating the flesh of kings, captains, generals, mullahs, imams, potentates, cooks, slaves, privates, corporals, and paper pushers. If you close your eyes, you can almost hear the noise of tens of millions of birds crowing and cawing and flying and flapping, and if you look up, you can almost see the sky grow dark with all of them.

The contest

Revelation 19:19 *And I saw the beast, and the kings of the earth, and their armies, gathered together to make war against him that sat on the horse, and against his army.* **20** *And the beast was taken, and with him the false prophet that wrought miracles before him, with which he deceived them that had received the mark of the beast, and them that worshipped his image. These both were cast alive into a lake of fire burning with brimstone."*

Oh, what an assemblage! The beast, Antichrist, is there. Every king and ruler on earth is there. Every soldier of every army is there. They are almost assuredly there for the same reason armies are always there; to attack Israel and anyone who may yet be defending her.

And yet, as they arrive and turn their eyes upward, all of these different nations and armies are suddenly bound together instantly as one for a different purpose. They all have one goal—defeat and destroy Jesus and His army. The evil spirits who drew them to this time and place knew that this would be the actual fight (Revelation 16:14).

This will be the biggest battle ever. There will be warplanes and tanks and battleships and nuclear weapons and bombs and foot soldiers and horses, a mixture of every weapon, ancient and modern. And yet, rather than an account of a long, uncertain, drawn-out battle, we simply read in verse twenty, *"And the beast was taken, and with him the false prophet that wrought miracles before him, with which he deceived them that had received the mark of the beast, and them that worshipped his image. These both were cast alive into a lake of fire burning with brimstone."*

Notice that the beast and the false prophet will be taken right out of the midst of the untold millions who have come to fight. Somehow Jesus will not have any trouble knowing exactly who they are and where they are in the midst of everyone else.

Their fate is swift and breathtaking; they are cast alive into the lake of fire.

Revelation 19:21 *And the remnant were slain with the sword of him that sat upon the horse, which sword proceeded out of his mouth: and all the fowls were filled with their flesh.*

The remnant, the rest, will see their two human leaders taken and judged right before their eyes. And it is the last thing they will ever see on this earth because they will, one and all, be slain in the very next moment. This is not metaphorical; God goes to graphic lengths to remind us that their bloody, rotten carcasses will be dinner for every scavenger bird of the sky.

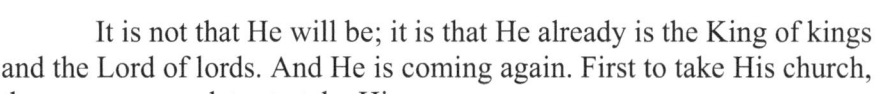

It is not that He will be; it is that He already is the King of kings and the Lord of lords. And He is coming again. First to take His church, then seven years later to take His vengeance.

Chapter Forty-Two
The Millennial Reign of Christ

Revelation 20:1 *And I saw an angel come down from heaven, having the key of the bottomless pit and a great chain in his hand.* **2** *And he laid hold on the dragon, that old serpent, which is the Devil, and Satan, and bound him a thousand years,* **3** *And cast him into the bottomless pit, and shut him up, and set a seal upon him, that he should deceive the nations no more, till the thousand years should be fulfilled: and after that he must be loosed a little season.* **4** *And I saw thrones, and they sat upon them, and judgment was given unto them: and I saw the souls of them that were beheaded for the witness of Jesus, and for the word of God, and which had not worshipped the beast, neither his image, neither had received his mark upon their foreheads, or in their hands; and they lived and reigned with Christ a thousand years.* **5** *But the rest of the dead lived not again until the thousand years were finished. This is the first resurrection.* **6** *Blessed and holy is he that hath part in the first resurrection: on such the second death hath no power, but they shall be priests of God and of Christ, and shall reign with him a thousand years.*

I believe he probably cries from heaven each time he sees a beautiful rose here on earth, and maybe if you listened closely, you could even hear him say, "It's my fault." I suspect that while you and I look at a rainbow in awe, with smiles spilling across our faces from ear to ear, he groans in agony, knowing that he is responsible for that too. Whenever a mighty lion chases down a gazelle in the plains of Africa, we film it and make a nature documentary, extolling the power and grace of the lion.

But not Adam. Adam knows that something is drastically wrong and that he caused it. You see, in the world Adam was given, roses did not have thorns, there was never any need for the rain that now causes rainbows, and all of the animals ate plants rather than each other. On earth before Adam sinned, the temperature was always perfect; there was never a need for a coat or an air conditioner. There were no diseases or infirmities, no children on crutches or old people in wheelchairs. There were no eyeglasses, no hearing aids, no aspirin, no doctors, and no dieticians. There was no diabetes, no aids, no cancer, no heart disease, and no common cold. There were no sniffles, no earaches, no arthritis. Teeth never fell out; men never went bald; ladies never got osteoporosis. There was no need for vitamins or health-food stores.

Adam lived in paradise on earth. All of the earth was a paradise, and he lived in the nicest part of that paradise, the garden of Eden.

But then, sin came calling, and Adam answered.

As God was leveling judgment, He made this statement concerning the earth itself:

Genesis 3:17 *And unto Adam he said, Because thou hast hearkened unto the voice of thy wife, and hast eaten of the tree, of which I commanded thee, saying, Thou shalt not eat of it: cursed is the ground for thy sake; in sorrow shalt thou eat of it all the days of thy life;* **18** *Thorns also and thistles shall it bring forth to thee; and thou shalt eat the herb of the field;* **19** *In the sweat of thy face shalt thou eat bread, till thou return unto the ground; for out of it wast thou taken: for dust thou art, and unto dust shalt thou return.*

At that point, paradise began to unravel. It did not all happen in a single day; it took place over time. Year by year, the flowers produced ever more thorns. Year by year, the ground got harder, less willing to yield. Year by year, the lifespan decreased, while diseases and infirmities increased. Year by year, weeds took over, and pollution grew. By the time Paul was living, he had this to say about our world:

Romans 8:22 *For we know that the whole creation groaneth and travaileth in pain together until now.*

Earth is literally hurting. As pretty as our world can often be, with the sunrises and sunsets and white sand beaches and majestic mountains, it still is not nearly what it used to be, and it is getting worse year by year. Go to any beach, and you will find a million busted shells from creatures who have died and decayed. On any mountain, you will find fallen and rotting trees with fungus growing on them. Breathe the air anywhere on earth, and you are breathing in dust and dander and pollen.

Leave your lawn alone for a month in summer, and it will be an overgrown jungle for you to tame. Forget to water your garden, your plants will wither and die. Forget to spray pesticide, and bugs will kill them. Leave a little family pet in the yard, and a bigger animal or bird will have it for lunch.

And then there are the people problems. When Adam sinned, it did not just scar the earth; it caused every one of their kids and their descendants to be born as sinners. That is why their oldest son ended up killing their younger son, Abel. The bloodshed has been going on ever since. Our world is home to murder, terrorist attacks, war, racial hatred, ethnic cleansing, genocide, and the Holocaust. It is enough to make people ask, "Will it ever stop? Will there ever be a single day when earth is as it should be?"

And the answer is no; there will not be a single day of it.

There will be *a thousand years of it!*

Our text tells us of a glorious time that will begin right after the Tribulation Period ends, a thousand years when Christ will rule and reign on earth. We call that one-thousand-year period The Millennial Reign of Christ.

Before we begin to dissect the text, let's deal a bit with an issue of timing. When any discussion of the Millennial Reign comes up, you will find that there are three primary and differing opinions concerning it. There is the premillennial position, the postmillennial position, and amillennial position. In greatly simplified form, here is what those positions mean.

The premillennial position is that the Millennial Reign of Christ is a yet future event and that Christ will return to earth to start it. The post-millennial position is that it will not be Christ that triumphs over evil by bringing the Millennial Reign to earth; it will be the gospel that brings that wonderful period of one thousand years, and then Christ will return after that. The amillennial view is that there will not actually be a literal one-thousand-year reign of Christ.

It should not be difficult at all to determine which of those views is both sensible and Scriptural. The amillennial view directly contradicts Scripture which plainly states that there will be a one-thousand-year reign of Christ. The postmillennial view expects us to believe that there can be a kingdom without the King, and I think we have ample evidence from the past two thousand years that that is a ridiculously unfounded hope. Only the premillennial view takes the Scripture literally and makes sense of the world around us.

So as we study this text, we are looking at a very literal future set of events.

The removal of Satan

Revelation 20:1 *And I saw an angel come down from heaven, having the key of the bottomless pit and a great chain in his hand.* **2** *And he laid hold on the dragon, that old serpent, which is the Devil, and Satan, and bound him a thousand years,* **3a** *And cast him into the bottomless pit, and shut him up, and set a seal upon him...*

People are forever trying to make society a better place. President Lyndon B. Johnson started a "war on poverty," yet even after taking a few trillion dollars out of the pockets of one group of Americans and handing that money over to others, we still have poverty. Law enforcement has built jails by the thousands, court is held somewhere all day every day, prisoners are given free college education to aid in their rehabilitation, yet we still have crime. Medical scientists have given us condoms and vaccines, yet we still have dozens of STDs. After all of the character training in schools, people still curse and lie and steal. After all of the many years and thousands of dollars people have spent on psychiatrists and psychoanalysts and psychotherapists and psychologists, we still have depression and phobias and doubts and guilt and despair. Society is not getting any better; in fact, it is getting worse.

And there is a reason for that: mankind has a very real, very living, very powerful and dangerous enemy. His name is Satan, the devil. He has wreaked havoc for more than 6,000 years now, and he is good at whipping sinful mankind up into a frenzy.

Realizing that, it is very tempting to say, "Somebody needs to do something about him!"

And someone will. Verse one of our text tells us that there is coming a wonderful day when the devil is going to get collared. Empowered by Almighty God, an angel is going to come down from heaven right after the battle of Armageddon and snatch that snake up by the neck. This angel has two things in his hands: a key and a giant chain.

That chain is to bind Satan. There has never been a chain quite like this one. Satan is a spirit, a demon, a fallen angel. Yet God has designed a chain that will hold a spirit. It is not some little thing you would hold a tractor on a trailer with; verse two calls it a *great* chain. It is big enough and strong enough to bind the second most powerful being in the universe.

Can you imagine the horror of being free and unbound and second in power only to God for your entire existence and then finding yourself bound by a great chain that you in all your power cannot break? According to verse two, that is going to happen to the devil, and it will be a literal one-thousand-year sentence he will be serving for his crimes. All the while the King is sitting on His throne on earth, the devil will be bound and helpless.

But the angel also has a key in his hand. It is a very special key, one like no locksmith on earth could ever produce. This key is to a literal, physical place which the Bible calls the bottomless pit. This key like no other fits the lock that opens a door into a place like no other, a place miraculously designed by God to hold the devil himself. The devil has been tripping men up and helping them to fall for thousands of years, so now he is going to have to experience what it is like to fall. Not for a few seconds, not for a minute or two, but for one thousand years, he will fall.

Once that gate has been shut, verse three says that the angel will put a seal on him. In other words, God will put His divine signet marking on that pit, which will refuse entrance to anyone who would open it from the outside and let the devil out. That may not seem like it would be necessary to you, but one little additional detail will let you know why this has to be.

When the Tribulation Period ends, there will still be some people alive after all the judgments have fallen. All the people in all of the armies have been destroyed, but those who were too young or too old or too infirmed to fight will still be alive, and those people are lost!

So let this sink in. When Christ sets up shop to rule all of humanity, as far as actual, normal, unglorified people go, He will be beginning His reign ruling over the lost! A whole bunch of lost people will live during the Millennial Reign of Christ, and they will produce lost children. And then, like now, everyone will have a choice of whether to accept or reject Christ. He will be visible and present, and yet the same choice afforded to us now by faith will be afforded to them then as He is visibly present among them.

And many will reject Him. They will not be able to behave badly during that time because Christ will be ruling the earth with a rod of iron. But in their hearts, they are still wicked. And if they could, if there was any way, they would head straight for that pit, pry that gate open, and set their wicked commander free for another fight against God. So God has a seal put on that pit and sovereignly decrees that for one thousand years, Satan will be removed.

The rediscovery of truth

Revelation 20:3b*... that he should **deceive the nations no more**, till the thousand years should be fulfilled: and after that he must be loosed a little season.*

Contrary to popular modern belief, there is such a thing as absolute, objective truth. And let me show you how the devil has always felt about truth:

John 8:44 *Ye are of your father the devil, and the lusts of your father ye will do. He was a murderer from the beginning, and abode not in the truth, because there is no truth in him. When he speaketh a lie, he speaketh of his own: for he is a liar, and the father of it.*

The devil has spent years denying absolute truth. He has fought it in every way imaginable. But he is fighting a losing battle because if there is a God, then there has to be an absolute truth, and the very universe around us screams out that God is real.

I could write an encyclopedia on the lies the devil has told, and I would not be able to cover them all. But here are a few of his favorite ones:

He says you can sin without consequence

Genesis 3:4 *And the serpent said unto the woman, Ye shall not surely die:*

He says evil is good, and good is evil

Isaiah 5:20 *Woe unto them that call evil good, and good evil; that put darkness for light, and light for darkness; that put bitter for sweet, and sweet for bitter!*

He says you have plenty of time

Acts 24:25 *And as he reasoned of righteousness, temperance, and judgment to come, Felix trembled, and answered, Go thy way for this time; when I have a convenient season, I will call for thee.*

People have listened to and believed these lies for years! Isaiah put it this way:

Isaiah 59:14b... *for truth is fallen in the street, and equity cannot enter.*

Truth was fallen in his day, and it is still fallen in our day, but there is coming a time, a wonderful 1000 years when truth will be rediscovered, and the very Father of Lies will be banished. During that time, if you ever have to argue about anything, it will not be the devil's fault because God will not allow him to deceive the nations.

The reward of the faithful

Revelation 20:4 *And I saw thrones, and they sat upon them, and judgment was given unto them: and I saw the souls of them that were beheaded for the witness of Jesus, and for the word of God, and which had not worshipped the beast, neither his image, neither had received his mark upon their foreheads, or in their hands; and they lived and reigned with Christ a thousand years.*

This lengthy verse brings up a question for us and also proceeds to answer it. John saw thrones, plural, set up during the Millennial Reign of Christ. But who are those thrones for? According to the end of the verse, they are for those who were martyred for Christ during the Tribulation Period because of their refusal to worship the beast and his image and because of their refusal to receive his mark.

These saints who were killed will live again during the Millennial Reign, and the Christ who is omnipotent to handle everything Himself will instead use them as His governors over various parts of the earth. They showed the ultimate faithfulness and paid the most drastic price for following Christ, and they will be amply rewarded for what they did. They will not just enjoy the Millennial Reign; they will rule all during it.

Revelation 20:5 *But the rest of the dead lived not again until the thousand years were finished. This is the first resurrection.* **6** *Blessed and holy is he that hath part in the first resurrection: on such the second death hath no power, but they shall be priests of God and of Christ, and shall reign with him a thousand years.*

The rest of the dead, meaning all of those who died lost during the Tribulation Period, will stay dead during the Millennium. Their souls will be in hell; their bodies will be in the grave. Those who died saved during the Tribulation Period get to live again and enjoy the Millennial Reign. Those who died lost during the Tribulation Period do not; God will not have them infecting His world along with the lost living. But they will be raised after it is over to face judgment, which will result in them being cast into the Lake of Fire.

The restoration of paradise

John did not give us a description of what the world will be like during the Millennial Reign, mostly because everyone already knew; Isaiah had already written about it in detail nearly eight hundred years earlier in Isaiah 35. Briefly, then, let us look at those details and plug them into our text and study of Revelation. What will things be like during this one-thousand-year period of time that Revelation 20:1-6 tells us about?

Earth will be medically perfect

Isaiah 35:5 *Then the eyes of the blind shall be opened, and the ears of the deaf shall be unstopped.* **6a** *Then shall the lame man leap as an hart, and the tongue of the dumb sing:*

Earth will be topographically perfect

Isaiah 35:6b *...for in the wilderness shall waters break out, and streams in the desert.* **7** *And the parched ground shall become a pool, and the thirsty land springs of water: in the habitation of dragons, where each lay, shall be grass with reeds and rushes.*

Earth will be behaviorally perfect

Isaiah 35:8 *And an highway shall be there, and a way, and it shall be called The way of holiness; the unclean shall not pass over it; but it shall be for those: the wayfaring men, though fools, shall not err therein.*

Earth will be zoologically perfect

Isaiah 35:9a *No lion shall be there, nor any ravenous beast shall go up thereon, it shall not be found there;*

Earth will be religiously perfect

Isaiah 35:9b *...but the redeemed shall walk there:* **10** *And the ransomed of the LORD shall return, and come to Zion with songs and everlasting joy upon their heads:*

Earth will be emotionally perfect

...they shall obtain joy and gladness, and sorrow and sighing shall flee away.

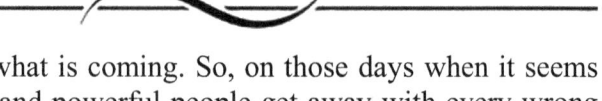

All of this is what is coming. So, on those days when it seems like evil always wins and powerful people get away with every wrong thing they ever do, just remember, the King is coming. On those days when it seems like the clouds never clear up, and you have forgotten what a blue sky looks like, just remember, the King is coming. On those days when your body is falling apart, and the doctor has only bad news for you, just remember, the King is coming.

The King is coming!

Chapter Forty-Three
God's Sewage System

Revelation 20:7 *And when the thousand years are expired, Satan shall be loosed out of his prison, 8 And shall go out to deceive the nations which are in the four quarters of the earth, Gog and Magog, to gather them together to battle: the number of whom is as the sand of the sea. 9 And they went up on the breadth of the earth, and compassed the camp of the saints about, and the beloved city: and fire came down from God out of heaven, and devoured them.*

We just finished examining verses one through six of Revelation 20, which along with Isaiah 35, describe the literal, physical, one-thousand-year reign of Christ on earth that will follow the Tribulation Period. It is during that time that all of the Old Testament prophecies to the nation of Israel will be fulfilled. They will own and occupy all of the land that was promised to them, and Jesus the King will rule from the throne of His father David. It is during that time period that the earth will be restored to its Edenic state. No more thorns, no diseases, no sickness, no storms, all of nature will be perfect. It is during that time period that, according to Revelation 19:15, Jesus will rule the nations with a rod of iron.

But why is there even a need for that last part? Because there will be some lost people who survive the Tribulation Period and go into the Millennial Reign. They will produce children during that time, and many of their children will follow their lead and refuse to accept King Jesus. But for one thousand years, though men may be wicked inwardly, they will not be able to show it outwardly. Not one act of rebellion or disobedience or violence will be allowed. It will be absolute peace, safety, calm, and quiet. The earth that was ravaged during the Tribulation Period will be healed and whole. The devil will be locked away in the bottomless pit for every second of that one thousand years and will not be able to lead one person astray.

You would think that after all that, people would decide that God's ways are best after all. But unfortunately, that will not be the case.

An unleashed enemy
Revelation 20:7 *And when the thousand years are expired, Satan shall be loosed out of his prison,*

The thousand years have a definite beginning, and they will have a definite ending. We are told here that they will "expire." What an awful thought! Those will be some very good years. But as we will see in the next couple of chapters, and as you probably already know, the eternity to follow will make those one thousand years pale in comparison.

Satan will have been bound for all of those one thousand years. No wonder it will be such a tremendous time!

But there is an incredibly practical lesson to learn from that. There will still be lost people on earth during the one thousand years, but there will not be any overt problems. When you take away the ringleader, you do not have near as many problems with the followers. In any setting, church, work, school, you name it, you can deal with followers all day, every day, and you will never, ever see things get better. But if you can ever deal with the ringleader, you will find that things get infinitely more peaceful.

For one thousand years, there will be wicked, lost people all over the place, and yet everything will still be peaceful and calm because they will have no ringleader.

At the end of the one thousand years, though, Satan, the ringleader, will be released from his prison for a while. It is interesting to me that he could not get loose on his own. He had one thousand years to try. This is the creature that said he would be like God! This is the dragon that said that he would exalt his throne above the stars of God, yet in one thousand years of trying, he could not get loose from his chain or find a way out of the pit.

But after one thousand years, the enemy, the accuser of the brethren, the deceiver of the world, is going to be unleashed. And it will not be man that opens the door; it will be God.

That is such an interesting thought. Why would God open the door to that? In the answer to that question, we are actually reminded of the answer to the very same question that we often ask about the early chapters of Genesis. Why did God open the door to let Satan in amongst humanity the first time?

It is called free will. God wanted man to have a legitimate choice.

We know how that worked out. And we often are tempted to belittle Adam and Eve since what they did plunged all of humanity into sin and under the curse. But in Revelation 20:7-9, we find hard proof that we would have done no better than they did. They had days or weeks in paradise to see how good God was, and yet they still followed after Satan's lies. In mankind's future, we will have one thousand years in paradise to see how good God is and yet will once again fall for Satan's lies anyway. God will open the pit, a choice will be offered, and as we will see in the next few verses, it will not go well for us.

An unchanged character

Revelation 20:8 *And shall go out to deceive the nations which are in the four quarters of the earth, Gog and Magog, to gather them together to battle: the number of whom is as the sand of the sea.*

Do you ever sometimes wonder, "What will it take for people to finally learn?" After one thousand years of judgment, it would seem like the devil would finally have learned and changed his ways. But after all that, his character will be unchanged.

May I make an observation? The devil is the devil is the devil, and he will never change.

The flood did not change his character. The dispersion of Babel did not change his character. His loss to Jesus in the wilderness temptation did not change his character. Calvary did not change his character. The resurrection did not change his character. If none of that changed his character, then a thousand years of torment, a million, a hundred million years of torment still will not change it.

But man's character will also be unchanged. This, to me, is as stunning as the devil is predictable. You can expect the devil to never change through a thousand years of punishment, but man will not change through a thousand years of paradise! After the entire Millennial Reign, the devil will be able to go out into every corner of the globe and find a countless number of people; verse eight says their number is as "the sand of the sea," to rebel against God. Hundreds of millions, perhaps even billions of people, will immediately follow Satan into battle against the God who has brought them nothing but peace and prosperity.

It is interesting at this point to notice a couple of unusual names in verse eight. When the Bible speaks here of the countless people who will come from all the corners of the earth to rebel against God one last time, Gog and Magog are mentioned, indicating that, humanly speaking, they will be running the show.

Who are Gog and Magog? Both of those names mean high, exalted, lifted up, mountainous. That is an indication of their pride and power. Look at the first time Magog is mentioned in the Bible:

Genesis 10:2 *The sons of Japheth; Gomer, and Magog, and Madai, and Javan, and Tubal, and Meshech, and Tiras.*

Magog was the son of Japheth, who is the father of the Gentiles. So automatically, when the Bible speaks of Magog being part of the last battle, you know we are dealing with Gentiles.

Now notice what Ezekiel had to say of this:

Ezekiel 38:2 *Son of man, set thy face against Gog, the land of Magog, the chief prince of Meshech and Tubal, and prophesy against* him, **3** *And say, Thus saith the Lord GOD; Behold, I am against thee, O Gog, the chief prince of Meshech and Tubal:*

In this verse, you see that Gog was a person, a title, rather. Gog is the human leader of Magog, the Gentiles. But what else do you notice in Ezekiel 38 that is also in Genesis 10? Meshech and Tubal. These were two more sons of Japheth, two more divisions of the Gentiles. This last battle will be led humanly by a Gentile leader, with a bunch of Gentiles following him.

But Magog is also the name of an area. The Bible always describes it as being to the North, and that always means to the general direction of the North of Israel. Josephus tells us that the Scythians used to live in the area known as Magog. That area is Russia. The bear may be a little weak today, but at the end of the one thousand years, she will be leading the last fight against God. America is the only superpower today, but whatever she will be called after the Millennium, Russia will be in charge and will lead the world against God.

An untamed God

Revelation 20:9 *And they went up on the breadth of the earth, and compassed the camp of the saints about, and the beloved city: and fire came down from God out of heaven, and devoured them.*

After the Millennial Reign, the world will see a sight it has not seen for more than 1000 years: columns of armies marching in formation.

After one thousand years of peace and safety, Jerusalem, which has throughout history been the bloodiest city on earth but has finally enjoyed real peace for a while, will be surrounded by enemies.

This has happened before. In A.D. 70, Jerusalem was surrounded by enemies, just like this. Titus laid siege to the city and leveled it to the ground. His armies ripped up men, women, and children. They destroyed the temple; they melted the gold off of the blocks of the temple; they left nothing.

But there is a difference. In A.D. 70, they had just thrown out their King. They rejected Him; they crucified Him; they demanded that His blood be on their hands. When the devil is let out of his prison, the King of the Jews will be sitting on the throne of Jerusalem, not hanging on a cross outside the gates. And that makes all the difference. That is why this battle will fall out this way:

Revelation 20:9 *And they went up on the breadth of the earth, and compassed the camp of the saints about, and the beloved city: and fire came down from God out of heaven, and devoured them.*

The camp of the saints and the beloved city is Jerusalem. It is the most targeted city on earth in our day, and that will not change even after one thousand years of Christ ruling from that spot and making all of the earth perfect. Every hypocrite who spent hundreds of years bowing before Christ while hating Him in his heart will be there. They will be ready for battle, but instead they will get, *"and fire came down from God out of heaven, and devoured them."*

Gone. At this point, every sinner on earth is gone. God's sewage system will work perfectly. Junk has been hiding in the pipes for a thousand years, and God is going to flush it all out, and He is going to use the devil to do it.

Man's environment is not the problem. It has never been the problem. Man's heart is the problem. But there is coming a day when only the redeemed, the pure of heart, will be left. God will allow one thousand years for people to get saved and become a part of that number, but after that, He will close the curtain on that phase of existence and leave nothing but Himself and His own.

Chapter Forty-Four
The Message I Want the Devil to Hear

Revelation 20:10 *And the devil that deceived them was cast into the lake of fire and brimstone, where the beast and the false prophet are, and shall be tormented day and night for ever and ever.*

This chapter will cover just one verse. Not because it is complicated; it really is not. Not because it will take a whole lot of explaining for you to understand it; the truth is that you probably already understand it quite well. The reason I am going to take an entire chapter to cover this one verse is because the devil has had more than 6,000 years to cause problems, and I just flat out enjoy writing about him finally getting what is coming to him.

The description of the devil

Revelation 20:10 *And **the devil** that deceived them was cast into the lake of fire and brimstone, where the beast and the false prophet are, and shall be tormented day and night for ever and ever.*

The word devil comes from the word *diabolos*. It means "slanderer." It is a perfect description of him as we have already seen many times in Scripture:

Revelation 12:10 *And I heard a loud voice saying in heaven, Now is come salvation, and strength, and the kingdom of our God, and the power of his Christ: for the accuser of our brethren is cast down, which accused them before our God day and night.*

Job 1:9 *Then Satan answered the LORD, and said, Doth Job fear God for nought?* **10** *Hast not thou made an hedge about him, and about his house, and about all that he hath on every side? thou hast blessed the work of his hands, and his substance is increased in the land.* **11** *But put forth thine hand now, and touch all that he hath, and he will curse thee to thy face.*

Zechariah 3:1 *And he shewed me Joshua the high priest standing before the angel of the LORD, and Satan standing at his right hand to resist him.* **2** *And the LORD said unto Satan, The LORD rebuke thee, O Satan; even the LORD that hath chosen Jerusalem rebuke thee: is not this a brand plucked out of the fire?*

Everything you have ever done, the devil has tattled on you for. He will even tattle to other people about things you have not done! He is not in the least bit concerned with honesty or even accuracy; he just wants to say hurtful things about you.

The damage of the devil

Revelation 20:10 *And the devil **that deceived them** was cast into the lake of fire and brimstone, where the beast and the false prophet are, and shall be tormented day and night for ever and ever.*

Everything the devil accomplishes, he accomplishes through some form of deceit. He is a liar! Look what Jesus said about him:

John 8:44 *Ye are of your father the devil, and the lusts of your father ye will do. He was a murderer from the beginning, and abode not in the truth, because there is no truth in him. When he speaketh a lie, he speaketh of his own: for he is a liar, and the father of it.*

The devil deceives people into rejecting Christ. The devil deceives men and women into wrecking their homes. The devil deceives people into living one way in church and another way the rest of the week. The devil deceives people into giving up their purity. The devil deceives people into swallowing false doctrine.

Yes, James was correct when he said, *"Every man is tempted, when he is drawn away of his own lust,"* but that does not in the least change the fact that the devil is a great deceiver of men. He knows we have our own lusts, and he deceives people into acting on those lusts rather than submitting to Christ. But it never works out like he promises.

It is reported that in the late 1860s, President Ulysses S. Grant gave a cigar to Horace Norton, philanthropist and founder of Norton College. Because of his respect for the President, Norton chose to keep the cigar rather than smoke it. Upon Norton's death, the cigar passed to his son, and later it was bequeathed to his grandson. It was Norton's grandson who, in 1932, chose to light the cigar ceremoniously during an oration at Norton College's 70th-anniversary celebration. Waxing eloquent, Norton lit the famous cigar and proceeded to extol the many virtues of Grant until...Boom! The renowned cigar exploded! Over sixty years earlier, Grant had passed a loaded cigar along to a good friend, and at long last, it had made a fool of his friend's grandson. (Today, 39)

No matter what the devil offers you, trust me, it is a lie that will eventually blow up in your face.

The defenselessness of the devil

Revelation 20:10 *And the devil that deceived them **was cast** into the lake of fire and brimstone, where the beast and the false prophet are, and shall be tormented day and night for ever and ever.*

Cast. Thrown like a piece of trash. This monster, who has seemed unstoppable for so long, gets "cast." He will be absolutely defenseless.

Some years ago in our church, I heard some very high-pitched screaming. I rushed to investigate and found some of our young girls squealing as they pointed to a particular spot. Finally I was able to make out the word "mouse."

I caught him. By the tail.

And then I walked to the back door with him and executed a perfect, NFL style punt, sending him rocketing airborne into the woods behind the church.

One day, God is going to do something akin to picking the devil up by the tail, and punting him into hell. What a day that will be!

The destination of the devil

Revelation 20:10 *And the devil that deceived them was cast **into the lake of fire and brimstone**, where the beast and the false prophet are, and shall be tormented day and night for ever and ever.*

A lake brings up pictures of water, but there is no water where the devil is going. What there is, though, is fire. There is also brimstone. Brimstone is burning sulfur, which melts almost anything in its path and stinks horribly.

This is where the devil is going. This is his destination. It is a very literal place, and it is where the devil will spend forever.

He deserves this. He will reap what he has sown in sending so many to hell throughout the years.

The decreasing of the devil

Revelation 20:10 *And the devil that deceived them was cast into the lake of fire and brimstone, **where the beast and the false prophet are**, and shall be tormented day and night for ever and ever.*

Behold, the greatest threat of all time and eternity, now reduced to the same station as two mere, tormented mortals! And lest you think that he arrives in that place as some celebrity, or even as lord over it, notice what Isaiah told us of this event:

Isaiah 14:12 *How art thou fallen from heaven, O Lucifer, son of the morning! how art thou cut down to the ground, which didst weaken the nations!* **13** *For thou hast said in thine heart, I will ascend into heaven, I will exalt my throne above the stars of God: I will sit also upon the mount of the congregation, in the sides of the north:* **14** *I will ascend above the heights of the clouds; I will be like the most High.* **15 Yet thou shalt be brought down to hell, to the sides of the pit. 16 They that see thee shall narrowly look upon thee, and consider thee, saying, Is this the man that made the earth to tremble, that did shake kingdoms;*

People in hell and the lake of fire will not be impressed by Satan in the least. He will arrive as a loser, stripped of his power and prestige.

My father-in-law, Don, is a decent-sized man and also a man with a pretty sharp sense of humor. Some years ago, he was in an auto parts store in Alabama, sitting at the counter waiting on some parts.

A man came in, and as soon as the door shut behind him, he started teasing everyone in a rude sort of way, almost like a dog marking his territory for dominance.

Don did not say anything; he just sat there at the counter, fidgeting with a smooth stone he always kept in his pocket. Finally, the man got around to him, saw the stone, and loudly said, "And watcha got there, mister?"

He replied calmly, "Oh, it's just my Indian medicine stone."

Clearly intrigued, the loud-mouthed man said, "Really? What does it supposedly do?"

Don answered, "You put it on some sore area of your body, and it absorbs the pain."

The man laughed, snorted, and said, "I don't believe that junk for a second."

By now, everyone in the place, employees and customers, was paying close attention to the exchange.

"I don't care whether you believe it or not; it works," my father-in-law stated simply.

"Give me that and let me try," the man said, and Don handed it over to him, saying, "Put it on your forehead, and you should feel it working."

The man put it on his forehead and said, "This is stupid; I don't feel anything."

Don replied, "Well, try this. The tongue is the most sensitive part of the body, so just touch it to the tip of your tongue."

Amazingly, the man did so. Then he scoffed and said, "This thing doesn't work at all."

To which my father-in-law then replied, "I know for a fact that it does because I had it on my hemorrhoids just a few minutes ago!"

Everyone in the place fell in the floor laughing, except the loud-mouthed antagonist who had (according to the employees of the store) never been cut down to size like that.

That has to be a pretty good proximity to how foolish and ridiculous the devil will look when he arrives in the lake of fire.

The doom of the devil

Revelation 20:10 *And the devil that deceived them was cast into the lake of fire and brimstone, where the beast and the false prophet are,* ***and shall be tormented*** *day and night for ever and ever.*

It may be tempting to feel sorry for him, but he deserves to be tormented forever, and he will. His rebellion against God was planned and chosen by him, and so is every bit of damage he has done since that time.

As to what this tells us about the nature of the lake of fire, it is clear proof that this is not mythological, psychological, or allegorical. It is real and active torment caused by real and active fire.

The duration of the devil

Revelation 20:10 *And the devil that deceived them was cast into the lake of fire and brimstone, where the beast and the false prophet are, and shall be tormented* **day and night for ever and ever.**

The devil will live forever in the lake of fire, in constant torments, wanting to cease to exist but not being allowed to do so. Every moment that we will be enjoying heaven, he will be screaming in that awful place.

I just want you to picture this in your mind. For 6,000 years, Satan has been in open rebellion against God, and so often, it has seemed like he was getting away with it. He has wrecked literally billions of lives and homes, ruined churches, destroyed nations, killed babies, and so much more. And it has looked like he will never be slowed, much less stopped.

But all of a sudden, time is up, and he is dragged in chains before the King of kings. He looks up and growls, saliva dripping off of his blood-stained fangs. This once angelic being, now scarred and stained by his own sin, is no longer glowing white, but marred and soiled in the presence of the great King. He seems drawn, and haggard, and a look of desperation creeps over his face. He knows better than anyone what God is capable of. The King looks down at him and pronounces judgment. Strong arms reach out for him and drag him toward the lip of the pit of the lake of fire. He screams and struggles, but it is no use. This creature that once used to fly through the heavens is now thrown through the air like a piece of heavy garbage. All of the saints of heaven watch in amazement as he gets smaller and smaller as he falls away from them. They see the lake of fire splash and ripple outward as he lands right in the middle of it. One last scream... and the devil is never heard from again. The lake of fire disappears from sight, and the devil is lost to all memory.

King of kings, Hallelujah, Hallelujah, Lord of lords, hallelujah, hallelujah, Christ reigneth, forever, He is Lord!

Chapter Forty-Five
The Great White Throne Judgment

Revelation 20:11 *And I saw a great white throne, and him that sat on it, from whose face the earth and the heaven fled away; and there was found no place for them.* **12** *And I saw the dead, small and great, stand before God; and the books were opened: and another book was opened, which is the book of life: and the dead were judged out of those things which were written in the books, according to their works.* **13** *And the sea gave up the dead which were in it; and death and hell delivered up the dead which were in them: and they were judged every man according to their works.* **14** *And death and hell were cast into the lake of fire. This is the second death.* **15** *And whosoever was not found written in the book of life was cast into the lake of fire.*

In our day, wickedness is very hard to deal with because it is so very scattered. You gain a victory when a godly person wins a political office over an ungodly person, but at the exact same time, a liberal judge strikes down some good law that a state legislature has put into place. You catch some local child pornographer, but overseas a jihadist imam is in a mosque telling his followers to become suicide bombers. Some drunk gets saved, and God totally changes his life, but in the local school, there is a demon-possessed teacher trying to convince little boys that they are actually little girls and little girls that they are actually little boys. A drug dealer in your local town gets convicted, but cartels continue to send mules across the southern border with even more. A pastor stands in his pulpit and preaches that people ought to stay sexually pure; Hollywood stars stand in front of cameras and teach the entire world to be sexually impure.

It is like playing the world's largest never-ending game of whack-a-mole.

But it has not always been like that, and one day it will cease to be like that again. Sin entered into the human experience with all of humanity, both of them, standing in front of a tree. Sin will be expunged from the human experience with all of humanity, countless billions of them, standing in front of or around a throne.

In all of time or eternity, there will never be an experience so ominous and awe-inspiring as the Great White Throne Judgment of God.

But when it is done, evil is done. The passage that we are going to study marks the eternal end of all wickedness. If you want to know at what point there will be no more lying and cheating and stealing and cursing and murdering and gossiping and hating and drunkenness and fornicating and adultery and pornography and wicked politics and everything else that is wrong, this is that point.

So let's examine the Great White Throne Judgment of God.

An awesome sight

Revelation 20:11a *And I saw a great white throne, and him that sat on it...*

As John begins to unfold this vision of the future, he gives us an object and an occupant and two descriptive words about the object of the occupant. He said that he saw a great white throne. It is beyond dispute that this is the throne of God that he is seeing.

The fact that it is great refers both to its size and its stature. This throne of God is utterly enormous and would be breathtaking even if it were empty.

The fact that it is white obviously gives us its color, but it also indicates that it is gleaming. In other words, it is a white whiter than any white we have ever yet seen on earth. It is so white that it shines and would affect human eyes to even look at it.

It is great, it is white, but above all, it is a throne, THE throne. It is the seat of all power in all of existence.

John was not the first living human being to be given a glimpse of it:

Isaiah 6:1 *In the year that king Uzziah died I saw also the Lord sitting upon a throne, high and lifted up, and his train filled the temple.* **2** *Above it stood the seraphims: each one had six wings; with twain he covered his face, and with twain he covered his feet, and with twain he did fly.* **3** *And one cried unto another, and said, Holy, holy, holy, is the LORD of hosts: the whole earth is full of his glory.* **4** *And the posts of the door moved at the voice of him that cried, and the house was filled with smoke.* **5** *Then said I, Woe is me! for I am undone; because I am a man of unclean lips, and I dwell in the midst of a people of unclean lips: for mine eyes have seen the King, the LORD of hosts.*

Daniel saw it as well and got a good look at the person on the throne:

Daniel 7:9 *I beheld till the thrones were cast down, and the Ancient of days did sit, whose garment was white as snow, and the hair of his head like the pure wool: his throne was like the fiery flame, and his wheels as burning fire.* **10** *A fiery stream issued and came forth from before him: thousand thousands ministered unto him, and ten thousand times ten thousand stood before him: the judgment was set, and the books were opened.*

Jesus Himself spoke of it:

Matthew 25:31 *When the Son of man shall come in his glory, and all the holy angels with him, then shall he sit upon the throne of his glory:* **32** *And before him shall be gathered all nations: and he shall separate them one from another, as a shepherd divideth his sheep from the goats:* **33** *And he shall set the sheep on his right hand, but the goats on the left.* **34** *Then shall the King say unto them on his right hand, Come, ye blessed of my Father, inherit the kingdom prepared for you from the foundation of the world:*

As to Christ being the occupant of this throne, that also is very clear both from the passage above and from many other portions of Scripture. Here is one that says a lot about Christ on this throne and what He will be doing:

John 5:22 *For the Father judgeth no man, but hath committed all judgment unto the Son:* **23** *That all men should honour the Son, even as they honour the Father. He that honoureth not the Son honoureth not the Father which hath sent him.* **24** *Verily, verily, I say unto you, He that heareth my word, and believeth on him that sent me, hath everlasting life, and shall not come into condemnation; but is passed from death unto life.* **25** *Verily, verily, I say unto you, The hour is coming, and now is, when the dead shall hear the voice of the Son of God: and they that hear shall live.* **26** *For as the Father hath life in himself; so hath he given to the Son to have life in himself;* **27** *And hath given him authority to execute judgment also, because he is the Son of man.* **28** *Marvel not at this: for the hour is coming, in the which all that are in the graves shall hear his voice,* **29** *And shall come forth; they that have done good, unto the resurrection of life; and they that have done evil, unto the resurrection of damnation.*

So this awesome sight that John saw, that all of humanity will one day see, was a great white throne with Jesus Christ the risen Savior, the Lamb of God, the King of kings, and the Lord of lords, sitting on it. It is the ultimate hope of every child of God and the ultimate horror of everyone who has rejected God. We love the very thought of it; they loathe the very thought of it.

But love it or loathe it, no one can stop it. This moment is coming, this event is sure, and it will change everything forever.

An amazing disappearance

Revelation 20:11b*... from whose face the earth and the heaven fled away; and there was found no place for them.*

Let your eyes rest on those words for a moment, and let your mind truly consider them.

In case you do not really grasp them, allow me to help you to do so. The ground under your feet is going away. The sky over your head is going away. The entire universe around you is going away. Everything that currently exists by way of a material universe is going to disappear in a moment of time as if it had never been. And it will not be some scientific and predictable thing that the laws of physics dictate. Quite the contrary; the material universe will flee away from the face of the Lord Jesus Christ as He sits on His throne. His word brought this universe into existence; His gaze will remove the universe from existence.

As to how it will happen, the apostle Peter was given that information by revelation. Look at it, and take note of several dramatic words and phrases as you do:

2 Peter 3:10 *But the day of the Lord will come as a thief in the night; in the which the heavens shall pass away with a **great noise**, and **the elements shall melt with fervent heat**, the earth also and the works that are therein shall be **burned up.** 11 Seeing then that all these things shall be **dissolved**, what manner of persons ought ye to be in all holy conversation and godliness, 12 Looking for and hasting unto the coming of the day of God, wherein the heavens being **on fire** shall be **dissolved**, and **the elements shall melt with fervent heat?***

One hot gaze from the Son of God is going to make all the universe melt with a fervent heat, burn up, and be dissolved all the way down to the very elements. No wonder Peter said that it would be a "great noise." At that point, somehow, someway, all that is going to be left is God and His heavenly creatures and all of the human souls who have ever lived. There will be more later; there will be a new heaven and a new earth with all of the good things and none of the bad things of the old heaven and the old earth. But for that moment of time, for that event, all that will exist is God and His heavenly creatures and all of the human souls who have ever lived, and everything and everyone will therefore be gathered around or in front of the throne.

Nowhere to run. Nowhere to hide. No way to cover up. It will be God and you.

An assembled multitude

Revelation 20:12 *And I saw the dead, small and great, stand before God...*

You will find the dead mentioned four times in this handful of verses. It is the dead that will be standing before His throne to be judged. The living will be with God, not standing before Him. At this point in time, everything is black and white, neatly divided. All of the living are the saved; all of the dead who are now brought up to answer for their lives are the lost.

Remember that the entire universe has just passed away with a great noise and a fervent heat. Even the elements are gone. So anyone that had perchance not been there to be destroyed at the last battle of Revelation 20:7-10 is destroyed when God burns down the universe in an instant. And as we will learn in just a couple more verses, all of the dead of earth, whether in the ground or in the sea, are delivered up to God the instant before everything is melted away.

In short, every human soul from the Garden of Eden until the last second of earth's existence will be brought up to stand before God all at once at this moment. There are currently nearly eight billion people alive on earth at this moment. It is almost hard to imagine how massive a crowd will be standing before God when we are talking about seven thousand years of human history or more by that point. We do not know the number, but we do know the percentage; one hundred percent of the people who have ever lived will be either standing before God or standing with God at that moment. No one will be left out—absolutely no one.

An accounting of life

Revelation 20:12b... *and the books were opened: and another book was opened, which is the book of life: and the dead were judged out of those things which were written in the books, according to their works.*

A very telling and dramatic scene now takes place. As all of the unsaved dead stand before Christ their judge, books, and a book, are opened.

That wording sounds so odd; it seems like the text would just say, "Books were opened." Or, if we wanted to distinguish the book of life from the other books, we may be tempted to say, "Books were opened, and one of them was the book of life."

But that is not what the text says. It clearly distinguishes between books, plural, and the one book, the book of life.

As to the fact that there are actual books opened, it is amazing to consider that in light of the omniscience of God. God knows everything; God remembers everything; so why the need for the books? But perhaps a better question would be, "If the omniscient God who knows and remembers everything nonetheless chooses to utilize the written word on the page, why is it that many so-called theologians in our day minimize the written word on the page? Why is it that so many of them denigrate the written word that God gave us when God Himself is clearly so big on the written word?"

But back to the scene at hand in the text, all of the lost dead are standing before God, books are opened, and the book of life is opened.

The identity of the book of life is not hard to figure out since the text clearly states it for us. Verse fifteen tells us that it is simply a book with names written in it, specifically the names of all of the saved. And while the books, plural, are not given a name, their identity is also not hard to figure out since the text clearly states that for us as well. Verse thirteen says, "*and the dead were judged out of those things which were written in the books, according to their works.*" These books, then, contain all of the sinful deeds that all of mankind has ever committed, along with all of the written law of God that they have violated. These books will be an exposure of sin along with the scriptural references that mankind was responsible for knowing that labeled those activities as sin.

We are talking about billions of people. Can you imagine the number of volumes and the size of the books that we are talking about?

The text tells us that "*the dead were judged out of those things which were written in the books, according to their works.*" Every lie, every petty theft, every perverted act, every wrong thing a person has ever done will have to be given account for.

I have no earthly idea how this works, but then again, I also have no earthly idea how God destroys the entire universe and then has everyone standing before His throne to be judged. But I know that that is exactly what is going to happen, and I know that the scene before the Great White Throne Judgment is also going to happen. I would suspect that, while such a thing would take billions of years for man in time, it will not take long at all for God in eternity. But whether it takes ages or just moments, it will be an utterly horrifying experience. Mankind has thumbed his nose at God for so long and has lived like the devil in his pride and arrogance. But there will be no pride and arrogance at the Great White Throne Judgment; there will just be anguish as everyone looks at a perfectly holy God and has Him expose all of their life of wickedness, every bit of which was written in those books.

These books are a testimony to the importance of salvation. You see, only the works of the lost dead are in those books. If you are saved, your works are no longer in there:

Colossians 2:13 *And you, being dead in your sins and the uncircumcision of your flesh, hath he quickened together with him, having forgiven you all trespasses;* **14 Blotting out** *the handwriting of ordinances that was against us, which was contrary to us, and took it out of the way, nailing it to his cross;*

Those words "blotting out" are pretty important, and they are not the last time we will see them in this context. But for now, just understand that as God opens those books before the unsaved dead, He sees very clear entries as to all of their sin, and mixed in with all of that, He sees entries that have been completely blotted out by the blood of Christ. You can either answer for every single one of your sins before a holy God, or you can have Christ answer on your behalf based on the sacrifice He made for you on Calvary. You can either be standing before God on that day with all of your sins still clearly visible in those books, or you can be standing around the throne of God on that day with all of your sins blotted out of those books.

An arising to judgment

Revelation 20:13 *And the sea gave up the dead which were in it; and death and hell delivered up the dead which were in them: and they were judged every man according to their works.*

We need to do a little bit of work in this verse to make sure we arrive at a proper understanding of some things. We are told that the sea and death and hell deliver up the dead to judgment. But at first blush, it seems as if there is a redundant set in those words, death and dead.

The sea and hell will help to define death for us in this instance. The sea is an actual physical place. Hell is an actual physical place. Therefore death, in that first half of the verse, is also a physical place. In this case, it is referring to the grave.

As commentator Adam Clarke observed:

> The sea and death have the bodies of all human beings; hades has their spirits. That they may be judged, and punished or rewarded according to their works, their bodies and souls must be reunited; hades, therefore, gives up the spirits; and the sea and the earth give up the bodies. (1057)

This verse obliterates the cultish doctrine of annihilationism. Human beings, made in the image of God, will never cease to exist even for a moment. And lost human beings will be reunited with their bodies just as surely as saved human beings, judged in those bodies, and then be cast into the lake of fire to live forever in conscious, eternal torment, either somehow still in those bodies or just in their soul and spirit which still have all the same five senses as those bodies.

An addition to punishment

Revelation 20:14 *And death and hell were cast into the lake of fire. This is the second death.*

Preachers sometimes get swollen up in chronological pride and love to spend their time trying to poke holes in what "older and less educated clergy before them" famously said and preached. And in recent years, one attack that I have heard with very regular frequency is one that goes like this:

"These preachers that talk about people burning in hell forever really should study their Bibles. Hell is a temporary place; it is the lake of fire in which people will burn forever."

Before we even get to the scriptural fallacy of that, just the logical fallacy alone should be obvious. When you throw fire into fire, you do not get less fire; you get more fire. Hell is not going to be extinguished when it is cast in the lake of fire; it is going to be expanded.

Ample scriptural evidence teaches us that hell is currently in the center of the earth. But since the heaven and the earth are burned up just prior to this judgment, God is going to take hell, which He prepared for the devil and his angels (Matthew 25:41) and, rather than destroy it, preserve it and then cast it into the lake of fire. Furthermore, look at what Jesus Himself specifically said about hell:

Mark 9:43 *And if thy hand offend thee, cut it off: it is better for thee to enter into life maimed, than having two hands to go into hell,* ***into the fire that never shall be quenched****:*

Taking issue with people who say the lost will suffer in hell forever simply because hell is in this text cast into the lake of fire completely misses the point. The lost will still be in hell, and hell will be in the lake of fire. This is an addition to punishment. This is when hell gets even worse than it has ever been and stays that way for the rest of eternity.

An absence of hope

Revelation 20:15 *And whosoever was not found written in the book of life was cast into the lake of fire.*

We have focused on the books, and now our attention is drawn to the book. And it is at this point that we must take note of the word blotted or blot once again.

In reference to the books, the books of our works, the lost will find in horror that their works have not been blotted out. The saved will find in happiness that their works have been blotted out. And what this tells us is that every work that mankind has ever done is already written in those books before they ever do them. In order for the saved to have the handwriting of ordinances which was against us blotted out, those works first had to be written in.

God is omniscient. He does not foreordain sin as the Calvinist so horribly says and infers; everyone has a choice every moment that they live as to whether or not they will do right or wrong. But though God does not foreordain sin, He does foreknow sin. And before you ever do it, it is already written down that you did it. And the book of life is handled in the exact same way. Look at two passages concerning this:

Exodus 32:32 *Yet now, if thou wilt forgive their sin--; and if not, blot me, I pray thee, out of thy book which thou hast written.*

Revelation 22:19 *And if any man shall take away from the words of the book of this prophecy, God shall take away his part out of the book of life, and out of the holy city, and from the things which are written in this book.*

That first passage showed Moses asking God either to forgive the sin of the people or to blot him out of the book. Do remember, in this, that the Holy Spirit worked much differently in the Old Testament era than He does in the new. The second passage gives a warning to lost mankind not to take away any of the words of Scripture (for the saved would never do so) and a warning that if they do, God will take away their part out of the book of life.

Do you understand what this means? It is not that our names are written in the Lamb's book of life when we get saved; it is that God so much wanted every man and woman and boy and girl to be saved that even before mankind was created, the names of every single one of them were already pre-written in the Lamb's book of life. And then when we receive Christ, we and our names are *"sealed unto the day of redemption."* (Ephesians 4:30) The only exception to this, as we saw in Revelation 17:8, seems to be those that God foresaw as worshipping the beast during the Tribulation Period. Not one verse of Scripture anywhere says that our names are written in the book when we get saved, not one. Our names are already written in the book when we are born, then sealed when we get saved: our names are blotted out of the book when we reject Christ for the last time.

The great tragedy of the Great White Throne Judgment will be that everyone standing lost before God had their names written in that book of life and yet chose to reject Christ and caused their own names to be blotted out of that book. No wonder this will be a scene with an utter absence of hope. One by one, people will stand before God lost, having rejected the payment for their sin and will be shown the place where their name once was, a place that now has just a blot marking out that name. And each and every one of them will then be cast into the lake of fire, never to escape and likely never even to be remembered.

Chapter Forty-Six
All Things New

Revelation 21:1 *And I saw a new heaven and a new earth: for the first heaven and the first earth were passed away; and there was no more sea.* **2** *And I John saw the holy city, new Jerusalem, coming down from God out of heaven, prepared as a bride adorned for her husband.* **3** *And I heard a great voice out of heaven saying, Behold, the tabernacle of God is with men, and he will dwell with them, and they shall be his people, and God himself shall be with them, and be their God.* **4** *And God shall wipe away all tears from their eyes; and there shall be no more death, neither sorrow, nor crying, neither shall there be any more pain: for the former things are passed away.* **5** *And he that sat upon the throne said, Behold, I make all things new. And he said unto me, Write: for these words are true and faithful.*

Let me remind you of the last thing that John saw:

Revelation 20:15 *And whosoever was not found written in the book of life was cast into the lake of fire.*

At the end of all history, John saw the Great White Throne Judgment. Please remember that at that time, all of the earth and the universe is rolled up like a scroll and melted away with a fervent heat. By the end of Revelation 20, there is nothing left but God, His angels and heavenly creatures, and the saved. There is nowhere to put your feet down; there is nothing to grab hold of.

For God, that is definitely not a problem. But for us, we who are used to having ground under our feet and substance that we can touch with our hands could tend to struggle with that. And so a loving God, who is concerned for our comfort and welfare, remakes all things brand new.

God really does "new" right

There are four references to "new" in these verses:

Revelation 21:1 *And I saw a **new** heaven and a **new** earth: for the first heaven and the first earth were passed away; and there was no more sea.* **2** *And I John saw the holy city, **new** Jerusalem, coming down from God out of heaven, prepared as a bride adorned for her husband.* **3** *And I heard a great voice out of heaven saying, Behold, the tabernacle of God is with men, and he will dwell with them, and they shall be his people, and God himself shall be with them, and be their God.* **4** *And God shall wipe away all tears from their eyes; and there shall be no more death, neither sorrow, nor crying, neither shall there be any more pain:*

for the former things are passed away. **5** *And he that sat upon the throne said, Behold, I make all things* **new**. *And he said unto me, Write: for these words are true and faithful.*

In all four instances of the word "new" in this passage, it is not from the word *neos*, which would be new in relation to time; it is from the word *kainos*, which means new in relation to quality and substance.

There is a heaven now; there is an earth now. There will be a heaven then and an earth then. Those will not be new concepts. It is just that the heaven and the earth then will be brand new in their quality. It will be like trading up from a 1973 Gremlin to a brand-new Cadillac Escalade. They are both vehicles, but the quality is completely different!

By the way, let me show you another place in the Bible where we see this kind of "new:"

2 Corinthians 5:17 *Therefore if any man be in Christ, he is a new creature: old things are passed away; behold, all things are become new.*

When you get saved, all things take on a new quality. Likewise, the heaven and the earth to come are absolutely new. The names may be the same, but the quality will be oh, so very different.

It is interesting to note that in order for there to be a new heaven and earth, according to verse one, the old had to pass away. Again, what a parallel to 2 Corinthians 5:17:

2 Corinthians 5:17 *Therefore if any man be in Christ, he is a new creature: old things are passed away; behold, all things are become new.*

Without the old "passing away," there cannot be the new!

When God makes everything new, the sea is gone

Revelation 21:1 *And I saw a new heaven and a new earth: for the first heaven and the first earth were passed away; and there was no more sea.*

For all the years I have read this, it has been mildly traumatic for me since I love the ocean. But please understand some things. To John, the sea was an everyday prison on every side of Patmos. It is what kept him in exile for eighteen long months. The sea also, in the book of the Revelation and elsewhere in Scripture, represented the troubled and unsettled world of men.

Furthermore, what has the sea been like since the fall? Simply put, it has been more and more polluted and tumultuous every year.

The sea, as it stands and in what it represents, is really a negative thing. As much as we love it, it is not good to God, or in symbolism, or even in relation to what it once was when it was first created.

But understand this as well; God did not say there would be no more beaches, nor did He say there would be no more huge bodies of water. He said there would no more sea. If you go to the great lakes, you will see an ocean-sized body of water, but it is fresh water. Every part of it is usable.

In the new heaven and earth, there will almost certainly be ocean-sized bodies of water, but there will not be any undrinkable, dark, murky, dangerous water. There will not be any water that will burn your eyes or hurt when you swallow it. You will be able to look down for miles and read the date on a heavenly coin. The fish in eternity will not be less vibrant and colorful than the fish now in the oceans of this fallen world; they will be more so.

Trust me, the loss of the sea will not be a big deal.

God's favorite city, Jerusalem, will also be brand new

Revelation 21:2 *And I John saw the holy city, new Jerusalem, coming down from God out of heaven, prepared as a bride adorned for her husband.*

This is the only city that we are told makes it into the new creation. There is no new Paris, or new New York, or new Rome, or new Chicago, or new Moscow, or new London. Of all of the cities that earth has ever known, the only one that will have a new version of itself in the new heaven and new earth is Jerusalem. And it is equally interesting to consider the fact that God, who in a moment of time makes a brand-new universe, a new heaven, and a new earth, could have easily made that new Jerusalem already sitting on the new earth. But instead, He allows her to make a grand entrance. The New Jerusalem will come down from God out of heaven. It is His capital city, and He will bring it from heaven to earth.

Jerusalem, through the years, has been hot, dusty, bloody, and violent. But on this glorious day to come, she will be as beautiful as a new bride. Please notice, God does not say she is "the bride,"; it says she is prepared as a bride. Even a few verses further on, when this term bride is used again, it does not refer to the city but to the saved who are living in the city, those mentioned in verse twenty-four. Christ will not be the groom to a city; He will be the groom to the people within the city.

Nonetheless, when this New Jerusalem comes down from God out of heaven, this city will be as beautiful and breathtaking as a new bride.

The way that God relates to us will also be brand new

Revelation 21:3 *And I heard a great voice out of heaven saying, Behold, the tabernacle of God is with men, and he will dwell with them,* *and they shall be his people, and God himself shall be with them, and be their God.*

Here is a shocking statement: there will not be any theological faith in heaven. We will not need it! Why would we need faith to believe in someone that we can see and hear and touch? God is going to live together with us. His tabernacle will be with us. It will not be at all like it has been in the Old Testament, the New Testament, and even today. We will literally, physically, eternally live with God, walk with God, talk with God. We will enjoy forever what Adam and Eve only enjoyed for a short while.

When all things are made new, there will be some things that are conspicuously absent

Revelation 21:4 *And God shall wipe away all tears from their eyes; and there shall be no more death, neither sorrow, nor crying, neither shall there be any more pain: for the former things are passed away.*

There will be no tears in our eternal home unless they are happy tears. There will be no death whatsoever. There will be no sorrow at all of any kind. There will be no crying, and that word indicates an outcry, a clamor. In other words, no wailing, no complaining, no unpleasant sounds or interactions.

There will also be no more pain of any kind. No physical pain, no emotional pain, no mental pain, nothing. And there will be none of those things because they are all in the class of "former things," things relating to this wicked and broken world, and therefore are passed away. Former things do not get to invade our eternal home.

We have word from the highest level that these things are true

Revelation 21:5 *And he that sat upon the throne said, Behold, I make all things new. And he said unto me, Write: for these words are true and faithful.*

Having seen all of this, John now looks into the face of our King on the throne and hears Him say, "*Behold, I make all things new. And he said unto me, Write: for these words are true and faithful.*" So this is not something we have to cross our fingers and hope for, is an absolute certainty. It is going to happen. There will be a new heaven, there will be a new earth, there will be a new Jerusalem, all of the former dirty and horrible and painful things of this life will be gone forever; our God is going to make all things new.

Chapter Forty-Seven
Alpha and Omega

Revelation 21:6 *And he said unto me, It is done. I am Alpha and Omega, the beginning and the end. I will give unto him that is athirst of the fountain of the water of life freely.* **7** *He that overcometh shall inherit all things; and I will be his God, and he shall be my son.* **8** *But the fearful, and unbelieving, and the abominable, and murderers, and whoremongers, and sorcerers, and idolaters, and all liars, shall have their part in the lake which burneth with fire and brimstone: which is the second death.*

A few years back, there was a wrestler who called himself the "total package." He was tall, blonde, muscled up—and had an enormous nose. I mean a big red puffy thing. To me, it sort of seems like the "total package" would not have the same nose as Otis the town drunk!

The funny thing about humans is that there really is not a perfect one anywhere.

Michael Jordan was the greatest basketball player ever—and then he tried to play baseball.

Albert Einstein was an incredible genius—who could not figure out how to comb his hair.

All of you who are married know that there is no total package. Your "perfect" spouse has flaws!

There is no perfect human; there is no "total package."

Can you imagine what a total package would be like, someone who is perfect in every way; physically, spiritually, emotionally, intellectually? If there were such a person, that would truly be someone you could rely on.

And there is.

As John came near the end of the very last Revelation of God ever to be given to man, he was told something beyond incredible. There will be a Great White Throne Judgment, the heaven and earth will pass away, all will be remade brand new.

After being told something that hard to imagine, it is little wonder that God chose to re-introduce Himself to John the very way that He introduced Himself to him at the very beginning of the book:

Revelation 1:8 *I am Alpha and Omega, the beginning and the ending, saith the Lord, which is, and which was, and which is to come, the Almighty.*

Revelation 21:6 *And he said unto me, It is done. I am Alpha and Omega, the beginning and the end. I will give unto him that is athirst of the fountain of the water of life freely.*

He is Alpha and Omega. He is the total package.

A certainty

Revelation 21:6a *And he said unto me, It is done...*

God tells John that it, meaning the destruction and re-making of all things, is done. The way He says this is with the word *gegonen*. It means just what it says, it is done. But it is not just in any tense; it is in the perfect tense. It means that it is done, and it can never be undone.

And He says this before it comes to pass! While John was standing there looking at Him 2,000 years ago, God proclaimed that the destruction of all there is in the entire universe and the remaking of a new heaven and a new earth is a done deal.

You and I cannot even assure anyone that we will have lunch today because we may not even make it, or if we do, we may or may not even be able to eat. So how can He do this? As we will begin to see in the next verse, He can do so because He is Alpha and Omega.

A credential

Revelation 21:6b... *I am Alpha and Omega, the beginning and the end.*

Oddly, I learned the Greek alphabet at about seven years old. That is not exactly standard fare for a nobody of a kid from North Carolina.

One of the first things I learned is that Alpha is the first letter of the Greek alphabet, and Omega is the last. But in this context, what in the world does that even mean? Why is Jesus saying, "I am the first and last letter of the Greek alphabet?"

This saying is much older than even the Greek language. It used to be that the Old Testament Jews would say, "That is the Aleph to the Tau of the matter." Aleph was the first letter of the Hebrew alphabet, and Tau the last. We do the exact same thing today. We will say, for instance, "That covers it from A to Z." Whether it is Aleph to Tau, Alpha and Omega, A to Z, the meaning is exactly the same:

There is nothing that Jesus needs that He does not have. In divine character, attributes, and abilities, He lacks nothing whatsoever.

It also means that without Him, there would be nothing.

It also means that He will not "give out somewhere in the middle." He is A all the way to Z!

It means that He can be so deep and complex that we can never fully grasp Him (tetrachlorohydroquinone) and yet so simple a child can get hold of Him (l-o-v-e)

It means that He is "the whole matter," or as we often put it in song, it really is all about Him!

It means that in any language across the world, He is all you need to know.

That is a pretty lofty multi-faceted credential, one that only Christ holds!

A comfort

Revelation 21:6c... *I will give unto him that is athirst of the fountain of the water of life freely.*

Ponce de Leon was rumored for a long time to have sought for the fabled fountain of youth, though there is little proof of it. Tales from cultures around the world have spoken of various fountains of such a nature, but for obvious reasons, none has ever been found.

But there is something better, or at least there will be something better. In the new heaven and new earth, God will give whoever is thirsty water from the fountain of the water of life freely. What is that water like? Scripture does not say, and I do not know. But we do know that, since it is given to thirsty souls, it will quench that thirst.

These words served, and serve, as a comfort to those who are on this side of eternity; there will be no thirst of any kind that is unquenchable on the other side of eternity.

A conquering

Revelation 21:7 *He that overcometh shall inherit all things; and I will be his God, and he shall be my son.*

It is easy to get the wrong idea when we see that word "overcome" in Scripture. We get the idea of people hanging on for dear life and somehow managing to survive through it all. But that is the exact wrong idea based on this word. It is from the word *nikao*; we get the brand name Nike from it, and it literally means to overcome by conquering the foe. So how can we do this? Let me answer that by showing you another place in Scripture where that word is used:

Romans 8:35 *Who shall separate us from the love of Christ? shall tribulation, or distress, or persecution, or famine, or nakedness, or peril, or sword?* **36** *As it is written, For thy sake we are killed all the day long; we are accounted as sheep for the slaughter.* **37** *Nay, in all these things we are more than* **conquerors** *through him that loved us.*

We do not overcome by hanging on for dear life; we overcome through Christ and the love that He has for us. That has always been the case and will never be otherwise. And that makes the overcoming of the believer a certainty rather than a probability or possibility. And because He has made us overcomers, we will inherit all things, God will be our God, and we will be His sons

That is quite a list! So how can He promise all that? Simply because He is Alpha and Omega.

A condemnation

Revelation 21:8 *But the fearful, and unbelieving, and the abominable, and murderers, and whoremongers, and sorcerers, and idolaters, and all liars, shall have their part in the lake which burneth with fire and brimstone: which is the second death.*

We now find the second of two potential categories for eternity. In verses six and seven, we saw the conquerors, and now in verse eight, we see the condemned.

The conquerors are given the fountain of the water of life; The condemned are given a lake of fire.

Eight markers of the condemned, the lost, are given here. Clearly, this list of eight sins does not give every single sin in Scripture or creation. It does list eight rather significant ones that serve as common markers of the lost, as well as umbrella terms that encompass all others.

The fearful, those who for fear of man refused God, will be condemned.

The unbelieving, those who were presented with the truth of God and yet chose not to receive that truth by faith, will be condemned.

The abominable, those who engage in practices that God finds disgusting and putrid, will be condemned.

Murderers, those who snuff out innocent human life, will be condemned.

Whoremongers, those who engage in sexual activity outside the bonds of marriage, will be condemned.

Sorcerers, those who engage in witchcraft and seek out drugs for that purpose (it is from the word *pharmakea*, we get the word pharmaceutical from it), will be condemned.

Idolaters, those who worship someone or something other than God, will be condemned.

All liars, those who intentionally utter falsehoods with sinful intent, will be condemned.

They will one and all be cast into the lake of fire. They will suffer the second death, eternal separation from God in conscious torment.

The conquerors and the condemned are going to be separated forever. And from our perspective, it is going to be as beneficial as it will be detrimental to them. We are never going to have to deal with the junk from a single sinner ever again. All people problems will be forever over. How can He promise this? Because He is Alpha and Omega...

Chapter Forty-Eight
Showing Off the Bride

Revelation 21:9 *And there came unto me one of the seven angels which had the seven vials full of the seven last plagues, and talked with me, saying, Come hither, I will shew thee the bride, the Lamb's wife.*

It was 1983, when I was all of thirteen years old. I was playing softball. Third base. The guy at the plate hit a ground ball my way, which was an easy play except for one thing; it was at that very moment that I began to really notice girls...

There was a new girl in school. She walked by as that guy hit the ball, she looked back at me... and smiled. That ball went screaming across the ground, right towards me, right between my legs, and out into left field. I knew right then that man does not live by softball alone but must eventually take a bride.

That began a long journey for me. I did not have anyone to tell me what to do in the "pursuit of a mate" game, so I had to figure things out as I went along. I did not know any better, so I did the whole pursue/go steady/break up/get back together/break up again/find somebody new/start the entire cycle over thing. I did it over and over and over. I wish someone had pulled me aside and taught me just to focus on my relationship with Christ and let Him bring me the right one in His time and in His way.

But since no one did, I dated. Boy did I date. Now the funny thing about all that dating is this: when you date and break up a lot, you end up with a lot of exes. And no matter how spiritual you think you are, all of us inwardly want to marry well enough that when our exes see us, they get jealous and wish they had done as well as we did. You ladies out there, when you see an ex-boyfriend, you hope that he has gotten bald and out of shape and has to wear Coke bottle classes, and that his wife has bad breath and acne. You guys, when you see an ex out there, you hope she looks like the before picture in an extreme weight loss ad, and that her husband works the Guess Your Age booth at the county fair.

In April of 1993, I met Dana Sessions. I knew at once that I wanted to take her out. I knew at once I wanted to marry her. I knew at once that this was the very woman that I wanted to spend my entire life with parading in front of every ex-girlfriend that ever broke up with me.

I knew that this was the woman I wanted to be seen with by every guy anywhere around. Ladies, your husband picked you out at least partially because he figured that you make him look good. There is Biblical justification for this:

1 Corinthians 11:7a... *but the woman is the glory of the man.*

You can think it immature if you like, but it is what God made it to be: a man who regards his wife as pretty just seems to walk around a little straighter and poke his chest out a little more than a man who wakes up one morning and looks over at his wife and screams, "AGGGGH! What have I done?!?"

Dana and I were married on March 5, 1994. I have spent the last twenty-eight years enjoying every moment that I get to go out in public with this woman. I do not mind saying it; she makes me look good. She is my glory. I like showing her off. She is never inappropriate, she is never gaudy or immodest, but she is always beautiful, and I still get a thrill going out in public to a restaurant, walking around and opening her door, and knowing that people are impressed when she steps out of the vehicle. I like walking to a table with her, pulling out her chair, helping her into it, and brushing her shoulder as I go to my side of the table. After all these years, I still like showing off my bride. And maybe not in much else, but at least in this, I am like Christ. Our dear Savior loves showing off His bride. Look at our text verse again:

Revelation 21:9 *And there came unto me one of the seven angels which had the seven vials full of the seven last plagues, and talked with me, saying, Come hither, I will shew thee the bride, the Lamb's wife.*

At the request of Jesus Himself, at the request of the Groom, an angel of glory focused John's attention so that God could show off His bride. According to Ephesians 5 and many other passages, the bride of Christ is those who are saved by the blood of the lamb. God has spent countless years gathering His bride together out of every tribe and race and kindred and tongue. He has given His all so that there can one day be the wedding to end all weddings, when Jesus Christ the Son of God takes His bride to wed in Heaven itself. And when He does, He just cannot help but say, "Hey John, check this out. You and I were close on earth, and I want you to see this. This is what it was all about, John. John, come see my bride."

The bride is shown off by contrast

Notice the intentionally identical wording that is used in two different verses here in the book of the Revelation:

Revelation 17:1b... *Come hither; I will shew unto thee the judgment of the great whore...*

Revelation 21:9b... *Come hither, I will shew thee the bride, the Lamb's wife.*

This angel that came to show John the bride had already shown him another woman, another bride. He had shown him, in fact, the devil's bride, the one world-religious system of the Antichrist, which was represented by the city of Babylon:

Revelation 17:1 *And there came one of the seven angels which had the seven vials, and talked with me, saying unto me, Come hither; I will shew unto thee the judgment of the great whore that sitteth upon many waters:* **2** *With whom the kings of the earth have committed fornication, and the inhabitants of the earth have been made drunk with the wine of her fornication.* **3** *So he carried me away in the spirit into the wilderness: and I saw a woman sit upon a scarlet coloured beast, full of names of blasphemy, having seven heads and ten horns.* **4** *And the woman was arrayed in purple and scarlet colour, and decked with gold and precious stones and pearls, having a golden cup in her hand full of abominations and filthiness of her fornication:* **5** *And upon her forehead was a name written, MYSTERY, BABYLON THE GREAT, THE MOTHER OF HARLOTS AND ABOMINATIONS OF THE EARTH.* **6** *And I saw the woman drunken with the blood of the saints, and with the blood of the martyrs of Jesus: and when I saw her, I wondered with great admiration.*

This woman was "great," she was not some anonymous female. This woman was known worldwide, "sitting upon many waters." This woman was immoral, fornicating with the kings of the earth. This woman was dressed in all of the world's finery. This woman had on all the jewels that her sin had bought her. This woman was "tattooed" on the forehead. This woman was a murderer.

But for all this, this woman could still amaze a man, and John was truly amazed at what he saw.

Why would God show us a woman like that in His Word? Because true beauty is always at its most beautiful when it is contrasted against something opposite. This angel that showed John the whore of Revelation 17 which was represented by the city of Babylon, then turned around and showed him the bride in Revelation 21 which is represented by the New Jerusalem. That whore may have seemed truly amazing to John—until he saw the bride.

This whore was "great;" she was not some anonymous female. But the bride of Christ is humble, not seeking her own glory.

This whore was known worldwide, "sitting upon many waters," but the bride of Christ does not mind being unknown, as long as everyone knows her groom.

This whore was immoral, fornicating with the kings of the earth, but the bride is washed clean in the blood of the Lamb and has neither spot nor blemish.

This whore was dressed in all of the world's finery, but the bride is dressed in the righteousness of Christ.

This whore had on all the jewels that her sin had bought her, but the bride has on a jeweled crown that she turns and casts at the feet of her dear Jesus.

This whore was even "tattooed" on the forehead with 666 or the name of Antichrist. The bride has a new name written for Jesus, which no one knows but her.

This whore was a murderer, but the bride is a lifesaver, giving herself over and over to rescue the perishing.

Miss America may be beautiful, but let her stand beside some bile-spewing, manly, leftist hag, and she is positively stunning. The bride of Christ is beautiful, but put her beside the whore, the devil's bride, and she is drop-dead, knock your socks off gorgeous.

The bride is shown off by commandment

Revelation 21:9 *And there came unto me one of the seven angels which had the seven vials full of the seven last plagues, and talked with me, saying,* **Come hither***, I will shew thee the bride, the Lamb's wife.*

Those two words "come hither" are from the Greek word *duero*. That word is an imperative command. Sometimes, when my son was young, I would say, "Caleb, come here, buddy." Sometimes, I would say, "Caleb, come see this." But sometimes I would say, "Caleb, come... here... now." That last one is not optional; it is imperative. I will not let him off the hook; he is coming.

That is the message that God sent to John by this angel. "John, come here now! You are going to see this!"

Has it ever dawned on you, Christian, that God wants to show you off? I wonder how many times he pulls out that heavenly wallet, pulls out a beat-up picture of you, and says, "Hey Abraham, come over here. I want you to see Lucy. Man, isn't she something else?"

God is not going to let it be optional; all the world will see His bride.

The bride is shown off by commitment

Revelation 21:9 *And there came unto me one of the seven angels which had the seven vials full of the seven last plagues, and talked with me, saying, Come hither, I will shew thee* **the** *bride, the Lamb's wife.*

Oh my, the stupid things that the ancient patriarchs did.

Abraham and Sarah... and Hagar.

Jacob and Leah... and Rachel and Zilpah and Bilhah.

David and Bathsheba... and Michal and Merab and Abigail and Ahinoam and Eglah and and and and.

Solomon and seven hundred wives and three hundred concubines. If they had some ancient version of our modern Valentine's Day, it had to bankrupt those guys. And none of that was planned by or approved by God. With God, the plan was always "one man, one woman, for life."

And God lives by what He planned. He practices what He preached. When it comes wedding day, it is **the** bride, the Lamb's wife. There is only one.

God is not a polygamist. He is not going to marry Christianity and Islam and Buddhism. He has taken Himself a bride by the blood of the Lamb. He has purchased His bride the church, and there is no other.

Think about it; you are the only one.

And who would have it any other way? My wife has never shown any particular liking for the idea of me marrying all of my ex-girlfriends and moving them in with us.

That is how committed Christ is to you. You are His only one.

If there is ever anyone who could be "man" enough for more than one bride, it would surely be Jesus the King of kings. But He looked down from eternity past and said, "I don't want any other. Just give me the blood-bought church of God of every race and tribe, redeemed from sin and abject wickedness, yanked out of the jaws of hell; that's who I want. Just give me my bride, my one and only; the devil can have all the rest."

The bride is shown off by conflict

Just two verses before our text, God said something about His bride, the church:

Revelation 21:7 *He that overcometh shall inherit all things; and I will be his God, and he shall be my son.*

That word "overcometh" indicates that they were in a great battle, a terrible trial, and yet they came through as conquerors. And that should bring up a question in your mind: if God loves His bride, and He does, why does He even let them go through conflict to start with? David asked that question all through the Psalms, especially Psalm 37. Job asked that question many times in his difficulties. That has always been the age-old question, why do the righteous suffer? Why do they undergo such great conflicts in this life if God loves His bride?

Let me tell you why: because God loves showing off His bride. And it is far easier to show someone off in their time of trials than in times of ease. Anyone can live for God when the skies are blue, but it takes a really beautiful bride of Christ to live for God when the storms are raging.

While in the horrible Ravensbruck concentration camp, Corrie Ten Boom often observed how horrible all of the emaciated bodies looked. But when God saw them, and saw them living for Him even in those horrific circumstances, they were beautiful. And as we look back on them and read about them now, they are beautiful to us.

Paul asked three times to have a thorn in the flesh removed, and God told him no three times, and Paul said, "No problem, I'll just glory in my infirmities." God loves showing off His bride.

John was boiled in oil and exiled to Patmos when he was old enough to be in a nursing home, and he said, "No problem, I'll just let God use me to write the entire book of The Revelation." God loves showing off His bride.

John Bunyan was imprisoned for thirteen years just for preaching, his children grew up without him, and John Bunyan said, "No problem, I'll just use this time to write *The Pilgrim's Progress*." God loves showing off His bride.

Child of God, I do not know what you are going through, but I do know that your Groom is calling all of heaven alongside, looking over the railings of glory and saying, "Take a look at my bride! Isn't she pretty?"

The bride is shown off by ceremony

Revelation 21:10 *And he carried me away in the spirit to a great and high mountain, and shewed me that great city, the holy Jerusalem, descending out of heaven from God,*

We will cover this verse more in the next chapter, but for now I just want you to see that John was caught up, and was carried way up high into a mountain. This was God putting John in the pew so he could see the ceremony.

Then heaven opened up, and New Jerusalem, carrying the bride, started coming down.

There is a moment in every wedding that just takes your breath away. Everyone is seated in the church. The candles are glowing. The scent of fresh roses fills the air. The organist has been playing sweet songs. The groom makes his way out and stands beside the pastor. Then the groomsmen make their way in and stand proud and tall beside him. From the other door, here come the bridesmaids. They are radiant, smiling from ear to ear, slippers shuffling across the carpet, carrying bouquets.

And then everything stops. There is a split second of silence where you could hear a pin drop—and then the wedding march starts. The back doors open, and every eye in the church turns to see the bride.

There has never been a sight so breathtaking. Spotless white dress, a veil that she is positively glowing through, and at that moment, no one sees anything but her.

And then, a few minutes later, the wedding is done, and the pastor says, "I now present unto you Mr. and Mrs. Whosit." And that husband takes his wife by the arm and heads down the aisle to start forever with his bride.

One day, the very doors of heaven will be opened. We who are saved are already betrothed to be married to Christ. One day that wedding will take place, and there will be a grand ceremony as we come down from heaven in the New Jerusalem. Jesus will stick out His chest in pride, look over at the angels of glory and say, "Look what I've got! The world hated her, her enemies battered her, her families forsook her, her critics slandered her, her circumstances rattled her, but I loved her, and I asked her to marry me, and she said yes. Now I've healed her wounds, I've replaced her tattered garments with a robe of white, I've prepared a place for her, look at my bride! Look at my bride! Look at my bride!

Jesus loves showing off His bride.

Are you part of that bride?

Chapter Forty-Nine
A Little Slice of Heaven

Revelation 21:10 *And he carried me away in the spirit to a great and high mountain, and shewed me that great city, the holy Jerusalem, descending out of heaven from God,* **11** *Having the glory of God: and her light was like unto a stone most precious, even like a jasper stone, clear as crystal;* **12** *And had a wall great and high, and had twelve gates, and at the gates twelve angels, and names written thereon, which are the names of the twelve tribes of the children of Israel:* **13** *On the east three gates; on the north three gates; on the south three gates; and on the west three gates.* **14** *And the wall of the city had twelve foundations, and in them the names of the twelve apostles of the Lamb.* **15** *And he that talked with me had a golden reed to measure the city, and the gates thereof, and the wall thereof.* **16** *And the city lieth foursquare, and the length is as large as the breadth: and he measured the city with the reed, twelve thousand furlongs. The length and the breadth and the height of it are equal.* **17** *And he measured the wall thereof, an hundred and forty and four cubits, according to the measure of a man, that is, of the angel.* **18** *And the building of the wall of it was of jasper: and the city was pure gold, like unto clear glass.* **19** *And the foundations of the wall of the city were garnished with all manner of precious stones. The first foundation was jasper; the second, sapphire; the third, a chalcedony; the fourth, an emerald;* **20** *The fifth, sardonyx; the sixth, sardius; the seventh, chrysolite; the eighth, beryl; the ninth, a topaz; the tenth, a chrysoprasus; the eleventh, a jacinth; the twelfth, an amethyst.* **21** *And the twelve gates were twelve pearls; every several gate was of one pearl: and the street of the city was pure gold, as it were transparent glass.* **22** *And I saw no temple therein: for the Lord God Almighty and the Lamb are the temple of it.* **23** *And the city had no need of the sun, neither of the moon, to shine in it: for the glory of God did lighten it, and the Lamb is the light thereof.* **24** *And the nations of them which are saved shall walk in the light of it: and the kings of the earth do bring their glory and honour into it.* **25** *And the gates of it shall not be shut at all by day: for there shall be no night there.* **26** *And they shall bring the glory and honour of the nations into it.* **27** *And there shall in no wise enter into it any thing that defileth, neither whatsoever worketh abomination, or maketh a lie: but they which are written in the Lamb's book of life.*

Are you looking forward to going to heaven? I rather suspect so, or you likely would not have read this far in this book! But do you realize that the Bible never really describes heaven for us? If God had chosen to describe heaven for us, I suspect that the Bible would have to be about a hundred volume set, hardback, in very small print. The only vivid description we have of "heaven" in the Bible is really just a description of one tiny piece of heaven, and that description is found right here in the last two chapters of the Bible.

And while the old earth and old heaven have passed away by this point, it is reasonable to assume that the current heaven is pretty well represented by what we see here in this portion of the new heaven.

The symbol of Heaven

Revelation 21:10 *And he carried me away in the spirit to a great and high mountain, and shewed me that great city, the holy Jerusalem, descending out of heaven from God,*

New Jerusalem, one city out of all of heaven, is the representative of heaven for us. She symbolizes the glory of all of heaven. We will not know what heaven is like until we get there, but just judging by one city out of all of it, heaven is going to be amazing! And what an entrance she will make. This entire city comes down from the sky, from God out of heaven, and will be established on the new earth.

The shining of Heaven

Revelation 21:11 *Having the glory of God: and her light was like unto a stone most precious, even like a jasper stone, clear as crystal;*

Here, cities have the glory of man. San Francisco has the glory of Sinatra. Memphis has the glory of Elvis.

But the new Jerusalem has the glory of God!

Here, cities have man-made light.

But there, the light is generated by God, and it glows like a clear Jasper stone. The Jasper is a beautiful sea-green color. The city glows with a clear, sea-green glow!

Aren't you looking forward to going?

The structure of Heaven

Revelation 21:12 *And had a wall great and high, and had twelve gates, and at the gates twelve angels, and names written thereon, which are the names of the twelve tribes of the children of Israel:* **13** *On the east three gates; on the north three gates; on the south three gates; and on the west three gates.* **14** *And the wall of the city had twelve foundations, and in them the names of the twelve apostles of the Lamb.*

This city is laid out in a square. It has a wall going around it, twelve gates, three on each side, and an angel at each gate. The wall itself has twelve foundations, twelve layers that it sits upon.

Verse twelve tells us that the wall is "great and high." And yet it is only there for looks! No one is going to break in, no one wants to get out, and no armies are left to attack. It is there simply because God likes it.

The wall that surrounds the city has twelve gates. Each gate has an angel standing at it as a sentry. Each gate is named after one of the twelve tribes of Israel.

The wall has not one but twelve foundations. What a wall to require that many layers of a foundation! Every foundation layer has the name of one of the twelve apostles of the Lamb, meaning the twelve original apostles, with Mathias having taken the place of Judas.

Judas could have had his name forever etched on one of those foundations in eternity. Oh, what people give up when they set their eyes on the baubles of this world! For a handful of coins, Judas gave up permanent, eternal glory.

The size of Heaven

Revelation 21:15 *And he that talked with me had a golden reed to measure the city, and the gates thereof, and the wall thereof.* **16** *And the city lieth foursquare, and the length is as large as the breadth: and he measured the city with the reed, twelve thousand furlongs. The length and the breadth and the height of it are equal.* **17** *And he measured the wall thereof, an hundred and forty and four cubits, according to the measure of a man, that is, of the angel.*

The measurements given here are breathtaking. This city is a perfect square of 1200 furlongs. That is 1500 miles long, wide, and high! Seeing these measurements, many commentators through the years have objected to them on the basis that earth could never support such a structure. And if we were talking about *this* earth, they would be correct!

But *this* earth will be gone.

The new Jerusalem, coming down from God out of the new heaven, will be sitting on a new earth. And clearly, the new earth will be many times more massive than the current earth. Our current earth is just a speck of dust in the vast expanse of the universe. The new earth, since the capital city of heaven will be here, will most assuredly be the biggest and most impressive thing out there.

The city wall, though, is merely one hundred forty-four cubits, which is about two hundred sixteen feet high. Does that strike you as interesting? Think of those two sizes in relation to each other; the wall is tiny in relation to the size of the city! Does that remind you of something Jesus said?

Matthew 5:14 *Ye are the light of the world. A city that is set on an hill cannot be hid.*

God did not intend for heaven to be hidden behind a wall. Nor did God intend for us to be hidden behind walls here and now! A church must reach out beyond the walls. A church must make itself as visible as possible, rather than hiding out to "be safe."

Heaven will be massive; heaven will be incredibly visible.

The scenery of Heaven

Revelation 21:18 *And the building of the wall of it was of jasper: and the city was pure gold, like unto clear glass.* **19** *And the foundations of the wall of the city were garnished with all manner of precious stones. The first foundation was jasper; the second, sapphire; the third, a chalcedony; the fourth, an emerald;* **20** *The fifth, sardonyx; the sixth, sardius; the seventh, chrysolite; the eighth, beryl; the ninth, a topaz; the tenth, a chrysoprasus; the eleventh, a jacinth; the twelfth, an amethyst.* **21** *And the twelve gates were twelve pearls; every several gate was of one pearl: and the street of the city was pure gold, as it were transparent glass.*

What does the new Jerusalem, this little slice of heaven, look like? What will capture our eyes?

Color; lots and lots of vibrant color.

The wall is made out of solid, clear jasper, that beautiful stone with the lovely sea-green color. Both the city and the street are made of pure gold. The gold we have on earth is tainted and cannot be seen through. The gold of heaven is pure and translucent; it looks like golden yellow glass.

The foundation layers and colors (as far as we know based on our knowledge of these stones on this earth) of the walls are as follows:

1. Jasper - Sea Green
2. Sapphire - Dark Blue
3. Chalcedony - Bluish white
4. Emerald - Deep green
5. Sardonyx - Light red
6. Sardius - Blood red
7. Chrysolite - Yellow
8. Beryl - Bluish green
9. Topaz - Greenish yellow
10. Chrysoprasus - Yellowish blue
11. Jacinth - Cinnamon color
12. Amethyst - Deep purple

Additionally, these foundation layers of solid, lovely stones, are each garnished with all manner of unspecified other lovely stones. Further, each of the twelve massive gates of the city will be made of one massive pearl. Once again, such a thing is impossible in our tiny world today but will be no problem at all in the enormous world of the future.

The superiority of Heaven

Revelation 21:22 *And I saw no temple therein: for the Lord God Almighty and the Lamb are the temple of it.* **23** *And the city had no need of the sun, neither of the moon, to shine in it: for the glory of God did lighten it, and the Lamb is the light thereof.*

Throughout the book of the Revelation thus far, when looking at the heaven that now is, we have seen repeated references to the temple that is in heaven. But when the current heaven is burned up and remade, the new heaven will be lacking a temple in it. And the simple reason for that is that it will no longer be needed. In the words of verse twenty-two, *"for the Lord God Almighty and the Lamb are the temple of it."*

This phrase serves to let us know that God will be open and visible and forever fellowshipping with His people in the new heaven. We will not have to go to the house of God and worship; the Father and Son will be walking and talking with us every moment of the day.

Verse twenty-three gives us another likely absence of heaven, that of the sun and the moon. The reason I refer to it as a likely absence is that the verse does not specifically say there will be no sun and moon, but it does say that there will be no need of the light of the sun or the moon. It could potentially be that God has a sun and a moon for the earth and the city, but that they are simply overshadowed by the light and glory of God, or it could indeed be that there will be no sun and no moon. Either way, not only will the new heaven and earth be superior in worship, not having a temple, it will also be superior in lighting, having no need of sun or moon.

The safety of Heaven

Revelation 21:24 *And the nations of them which are saved shall walk in the light of it: and the kings of the earth do bring their glory and honour into it.* **25** *And the gates of it shall not be shut at all by day: for there shall be no night there.* **26** *And they shall bring the glory and honour of the nations into it.* **27** *And there shall in no wise enter into it any thing that defileth, neither whatsoever worketh abomination, or maketh a lie: but they which are written in the Lamb's book of life.*

And now we behold the bride as represented by the city. It is the nations of them which are saved, the blood-bought believers of earth, who are the bride of Christ. In eternity, all of them, even the kings of the earth that rule and reign under Christ the King, will make their way time and again to bring glory to the great King who redeemed them and created this new world for them to live in.

And as verse twenty-seven observes, under no circumstances will anything or anyone that could possibly dirty it up make their way into it. All of that and all of those are gone, already cast into the lake of fire. All that is left are those that are written in the Lamb's book of life.

And this is just *A Little Slice of Heaven*.

Chapter Fifty
Settling into Eternity

Revelation 22:1 *And he shewed me a pure river of water of life, clear as crystal, proceeding out of the throne of God and of the Lamb.* **2** *In the midst of the street of it, and on either side of the river, was there the tree of life, which bare twelve manner of fruits, and yielded her fruit every month: and the leaves of the tree were for the healing of the nations.* **3** *And there shall be no more curse: but the throne of God and of the Lamb shall be in it; and his servants shall serve him:* **4** *And they shall see his face; and his name shall be in their foreheads.* **5** *And there shall be no night there; and they need no candle, neither light of the sun; for the Lord God giveth them light: and they shall reign for ever and ever.*

There are times when big changes take place. For instance, try spending twenty or more years of your life being single and then getting married. Then try going from being a young married couple, footloose and fancy-free, coming and going as you please, and then having several children! You will go from going to the beach on the spur of the moment to having it take two hours just to get to the car in the morning.

As big as these changes are, imagine how big of a change it will be to go from time to eternity! All of you who are so busy each and every day, all of you who are getting older and wonder where your youth is going or has gone, just consider this:

No alarm clocks forever.
No deadlines.
No obnoxious jerks.
No insurance policies.
No traffic lights.
No elections.
No computers.
No telephones.
No diapers. (For babies or adults!)
No kidney stones.

We are talking about a "place" where no one is ever in a hurry, stress is non-existent, yet everything is always exciting and new. It will be so very different than anything we have ever known. Take your best vacation ever, make it never-ending, and you are still not even close to scratching the surface of eternity for the saved.

Revelation 21:1-5 is almost like an orientation for eternity. Let's work our way through it without getting in a hurry; somehow, getting in a hurry to get through a passage on eternity just would not seem right!

Eternity has a river

Revelation 22:1 *And he shewed me a pure river of water of life, clear as crystal, proceeding out of the throne of God and of the Lamb.*

This river of life, eternity's river, is totally pure.

When backpacking, you will learn that just because water in some river looks clear and is cool, that does not necessarily make it so. There are nasty little things like Cryptosporidium, Giardia, and other tiny critters that will either kill you or make you wish you were dead! But that will never be a problem with eternity's river. The water of eternity is pure to the sight, and it is also pure beyond sight!

It will taste good, it will satisfy the thirst, and no one will be bottling it and selling it for $2.99 a bottle!

The river of life, eternity's river, is doubtless enormous.

If everything else in eternity is huge (like the city itself) imagine the size of the river! I guarantee you that our current earth has nothing even close in size to it.

The river of life, eternity's river, is not just any water; it is the water of life.

What does this mean? Among other things, it means that it is flowing water, not stagnant. More importantly, though, it means that the water itself has life-giving and life-enhancing qualities to it.

This is not by necessity; it is what it is because God likes it. He could simply speak the word, and we would have the same effects without drinking the water. But He knows that we are used to enjoying our five senses. So He will allow this water to stimulate all five of our senses: taste, touch, smell, hearing, seeing.

This water will be pure joy to drink. It will be pure joy to wade out into it and splash around. Everyone will be perfect and therefore able to swim like a fish in eternity, so there will be no worries about drowning. Dive down as deep as you like, stay under as long as you like, chase the fish, lay on the bottom, enjoy!

The river of life, eternity's river, has as its fountainhead the very throne of God.

Just think about this. Every river on earth starts with a water source. Snow on the mountain melts and trickles down into little channels, and on into little waterways, and then into creeks, and then the creeks eventually run together to make a river. That is a logical, understandable source. But this river is not sourced like that at all. In eternity, we will be looking at the throne, and this mighty, awesome river will be running out from the base of the throne!

You say, "That doesn't make sense!" It makes more sense than you think. What is the source of water itself? God!

John 1:3 *All things were made by him; and without him was not any thing made that was made.*

Since God is the source of water, it makes perfect sense that the great river of eternity will spring right out of His throne at full strength!

Eternity has a tree

Revelation 22:2 *In the midst of the street of it, and on either side of the river, was there the tree of life, which bare twelve manner of fruits, and yielded her fruit every month: and the leaves of the tree were for the healing of the nations.*

As far as we can tell from the Garden of Eden, there was only one singular tree of life. After all, there were only two people! But in eternity, this tree is seen growing in the middle of the street of gold and on both sides of this mighty river. There may be countless millions of them. It is kind of like what we might read today in a book on botany if it said, "The mighty oak tree is found from the mountains of the midwest to the shore of Florida." Even though "oak tree" is singular, we know that the singular is representative of the plural. That is a common grammatical practice.

There may be, doubtless will be, many kinds of trees in eternity, but the tree will be the Tree of Life!

This one tree bears twelve different kinds of fruit. And it does not do this by grafting; it does it by nature! Think of how colorful that will be, think of how sweet the fruit will be, think of the variety. One thing is obvious; we will be eating in eternity!

And we will never get fat. We will never feel bloated like we have overeaten. We will never get sick to our stomachs from eating this fruit. There are no pesticides on it because there are no pests.

This tree yields fruit every month. And, at this point, may I point out something that is so obvious that most people miss it? Even though there is no "time" in eternity, in a weird sort of way, there is time in eternity! The Bible just told us that the tree would yield fruit every single month! Here is the difference, though. Here, time has a barrier on each end. It has a starting point, and it has a stopping point. In eternity, there is no stopping point. That is why we call it eternity! Days will give way to months, months to years, years to decades, decades to centuries,

centuries to millennia, millennia to eons, and when ten trillion times ten trillion of what we now call years have passed, we will still have just as much "time" left as when we started! There is literally no end to it at all!

And every month in eternity, this tree will produce its crop of fruits. I wonder what those blooms are like? You know they look more beautiful and smell more fragrant than anything we have on earth. And every month, the inhabitants of eternity will gather in and have their feast of fruit. And we will not eat because we have to; we could keep living forever without it and never feel a single hunger pang. No, we will eat it just because it tastes so good that we want to!

The leaves of the trees are as valuable as the fruit. Look at a phrase in verse two again:

Revelation 22:2 *and the leaves of the tree were for the healing of the nations.*

Now, this needs to be looked at. We are talking about eternity; why is there any need for healing? Here is why. What just happened right before eternity began? The very last battle. Remember that Satan had been bound for one thousand years during the Millennial Reign, and then he was loosed for a little season. He incited one last rebellion and gathered a massive army against God. God destroyed that army and sent Satan to the lake of fire forever.

During that last battle, it seems like the nations, the people that followed God against the devil and his army, one last time will experience the injuries and ravages of war as they fight for and alongside of our King. Again, God could just simply make all of those injuries go away with a word. It is interesting that right after that battle, He destroys the heaven and earth, and in a moment of time, remakes everything brand new. Yet apparently, He leaves these injuries to be perfectly healed in a marvelous way by the leaves of that tree.

Imagine a battle-scarred veteran of this last battle. God looks at him and sees the wounds he has suffered for His cause and says, "Son, remember when you were a little boy and used to go running and jumping into a pile of freshly raked leaves? There's a big pile over there; go have a ball. He does and comes running back healed like brand new!

And notice something that God said way back in Eden about this tree:

Genesis 3:22 *And the LORD God said, Behold, the man is become as one of us, to know good and evil: and now, lest he put forth his hand, and take also of the tree of life, and eat, and live for ever:*

Again, just because God wants it that way, one of the things that will give us eternal health and the ability to never die in Heaven is that amazing tree!

Eternity has a God

Revelation 22:3 *And there shall be no more curse: but the throne of God and of the Lamb shall be in it; and his servants shall serve him:* **4** *And they shall see his face; and his name shall be in their foreheads.*

Did you notice that contrast? In eternity there will be no more curse, speaking of the curse on nature. Remember that the curse was suspended during the Millennial Reign. But there was sin after the Millennial Reign since the devil got man to rebel one last time. So you could assume that since the first sin brought a curse on creation, the last one might as well. But that is not the case because of that word "but." Verse three says, *"And there shall be no more curse:* **but** *the throne of God and of the Lamb shall be in it..."*

When God is on the throne, in the midst, there is no curse!

Notice that we will, for the first time ever, be able to see God the Father. This is a drastic change. Look at what Jesus said while walking among men:

John 1:18 *No man hath seen God at any time; the only begotten Son, which is in the bosom of the Father, he hath declared him.*

But in eternity, in our glorified bodies, we will be able to see what man has never seen; we will be able to see God the Father.

The throne of God the Father and the throne of Jesus the Lamb will be there. Eternity is going to have the universe centered around a piece of furniture, the throne of God!

His name will be in our foreheads. The devil marks his own, and God marks His own. You may think, "I don't like that!" If you do, let me put it in perspective: He was lashed for me, He was pierced for me, he was scarred for me, and those marks and scars will still be there in eternity. So let me be marked!

Eternity has light

Revelation 22:5a *And there shall be no night there; and they need no candle, neither light of the sun; for the Lord God giveth them light:*

There are some things to like about the night, but day is better than night. When night comes, we turn on the lights. You never hear of anyone "turning on the darks." There will be no night and no darkness in the new Jerusalem, the capital city of eternity, because God Himself will forever give light. And this will be pure light, not like a candle, a light bulb, or even the sun. Everything will be illuminated perfectly. The light will not hurt your eyes. It will give perfect, comforting warmth but will never get hot.

God has great experience with this matter of light. Do you remember the very first thing He is ever recorded as saying?

Genesis 1:3 *And God said, Let there be light: and there was light.*

And may I remind you that when He said this, He had not created the sun yet, or the stars or moon yet, and Edison had not invented the lightbulb yet. God made light with only Himself as the source, and that is the kind of light that will exist again in eternity!

Eternity has things to do

Revelation 22:3b*... and his servants shall serve him:*
Revelation 22:5b*... and they shall reign for ever and ever.*

Are you worried about boredom in eternity? Don't be. We will serve, and we will reign.

Let's look at the last one first, the fact that we will reign in eternity. Let me remind you that God made man to rule over His creation in the very beginning:

Genesis 1:26 *And God said, Let us make man in our image, after our likeness: and let them have dominion over the fish of the sea, and over the fowl of the air, and over the cattle, and over all the earth, and over every creeping thing that creepeth upon the earth.* **27** *So God created man in his own image, in the image of God created he him; male and female created he them.* **28** *And God blessed them, and God said unto them, Be fruitful, and multiply, and replenish the earth, and subdue it: and* **have dominion** *over the fish of the sea, and over the fowl of the air, and over every living thing that moveth upon the earth.*

God made man to have dominion, to rule over creation. We blew it the first time...

But that will not happen again since even the temptation towards sin will be removed forever! We will finally do what Adam could not; we will rule over God's creation in perfect righteousness. And when you consider that our current universe has approximately two trillion galaxies and two hundred billion trillion stars, who knows how many worlds there will be and what wondrous things we will rule over in the new universe, which will be even bigger and better!

We will also serve in eternity.
God Himself came to serve:

Mark 10:45 *For even the Son of man came not to be ministered unto, but to minister, and to give his life a ransom for many.*

And He has always expected us to serve:

Mark 10:44 *And whosoever of you will be the chiefest, shall be servant of all.*

In eternity, God will finally get us to do what we are already supposed to be doing now, truly serving Him. We will explore and create and tend to a new universe under His supervision. Yes, we will rest, but there will also be more to do then than there is now, so boredom will never be an issue. We will serve in eternity.

But lest you decide to wait on that one, please remember that God expects us to be serving even now.

Thank you, ladies and gentlemen, and I hope you have enjoyed your orientation meeting for eternity!

Chapter Fifty-One
The End

Revelation 22:6 *And he said unto me, These sayings are faithful and true: and the Lord God of the holy prophets sent his angel to shew unto his servants the things which must shortly be done.* **7** *Behold, I come quickly: blessed is he that keepeth the sayings of the prophecy of this book.* **8** *And I John saw these things, and heard them. And when I had heard and seen, I fell down to worship before the feet of the angel which shewed me these things.* **9** *Then saith he unto me, See thou do it not: for I am thy fellowservant, and of thy brethren the prophets, and of them which keep the sayings of this book: worship God.* **10** *And he saith unto me, Seal not the sayings of the prophecy of this book: for the time is at hand.* **11** *He that is unjust, let him be unjust still: and he which is filthy, let him be filthy still: and he that is righteous, let him be righteous still: and he that is holy, let him be holy still.* **12** *And, behold, I come quickly; and my reward is with me, to give every man according as his work shall be.* **13** *I am Alpha and Omega, the beginning and the end, the first and the last.* **14** *Blessed are they that do his commandments, that they may have right to the tree of life, and may enter in through the gates into the city.* **15** *For without are dogs, and sorcerers, and whoremongers, and murderers, and idolaters, and whosoever loveth and maketh a lie.* **16** *I Jesus have sent mine angel to testify unto you these things in the churches. I am the root and the offspring of David, and the bright and morning star.* **17** *And the Spirit and the bride say, Come. And let him that heareth say, Come. And let him that is athirst come. And whosoever will, let him take the water of life freely.* **18** *For I testify unto every man that heareth the words of the prophecy of this book, If any man shall add unto these things, God shall add unto him the plagues that are written in this book:* **19** *And if any man shall take away from the words of the book of this prophecy, God shall take away his part out of the book of life, and out of the holy city, and from the things which are written in this book.* **20** *He which testifieth these things saith, Surely I come quickly. Amen. Even so, come, Lord Jesus.* **21** *The grace of our Lord Jesus Christ be with you all. Amen.*

I have read a lot of books. I have read a lot of different kinds of books, everything from Frank Peretti novels to the Swiss Family Robinson to Le Morte d'Arthur to Louis L'Amour westerns to Dr. Suess! Those books have very little in common. But almost every book has two words in common, found on the very last page:

The End

But when Louis L'Amour put "the end" on the last page of a Sackett novel, he would turn right around and write another Sackett novel! So it was not really the end.

When God penned the last chapter of the book of the Revelation, He really did make it "the end." In fact, look at how serious He was about this:

Revelation 22:18 *For I testify unto every man that heareth the words of the prophecy of this book, If any man shall add unto these things, God shall add unto him the plagues that are written in this book:* **19** *And if any man shall take away from the words of the book of this prophecy, God shall take away his part out of the book of life, and out of the holy city, and from the things which are written in this book.*

God wrote about everything we needed to know all the way through the end of time and into the beginning of eternity, which is why the title of this last chapter is simply *The End*.

The speed of the end

Revelation 22:6 *And he said unto me, These sayings are faithful and true: and the Lord God of the holy prophets sent his angel to shew unto his servants the things which must shortly be done.* **7** *Behold, I come quickly: blessed is he that keepeth the sayings of the prophecy of this book.* **8** *And I John saw these things, and heard them. And when I had heard and seen, I fell down to worship before the feet of the angel which shewed me these things.* **9** *Then saith he unto me, See thou do it not: for I am thy fellowservant, and of thy brethren the prophets, and of them which keep the sayings of this book: worship God.* **10** *And he saith unto me, Seal not the sayings of the prophecy of this book: for the time is at hand.* **11** *He that is unjust, let him be unjust still: and he which is filthy, let him be filthy still: and he that is righteous, let him be righteous still: and he that is holy, let him be holy still.* **12** *And, behold, I come quickly; and my reward is with me, to give every man according as his work shall be.* **13** *I am Alpha and Omega, the beginning and the end, the first and the last.*

From our perspective, a couple of thousand years seems like such a long time. But when God spoke of these things, He regarded the time as short! And isn't it? It used to be that a couple of decades seemed like an eternity. But for anyone over fifty, I bet a couple of decades has passed in the blink of an eye!

Revelation 22:6 *And he said unto me, These sayings are faithful and true: and the Lord God of the holy prophets sent his angel to shew unto his servants the things which must **shortly** be done.* **7a** *Behold, I come **quickly**...*

Both "shortly" in verse six and "quickly" in verse seven indicate speed and suddenness. Obviously, this has led to a great many faulty eschatological schemes through the years since those words are now nearly 2,000 years old, and none of this has come to pass. But once again, remember that God does not view time like we view time. For the God who already knows what eternity is like, a couple of millennia is indeed a very quick thing. And for us, now, it is also pretty obviously going to be a quick and sudden thing!

As God began to speak to John about the speed of the end, He took a moment to attach a blessing to the book of the Revelation:

Revelation 22:7 *Behold, I come quickly: blessed is he that keepeth the sayings of the prophecy of this book.*

The word "keep" in this verse is from the word *tereo*, and it means to attend carefully to, to closely observe. The book of The Revelation may not be as inspirational as Ruth or as practical as Proverbs, but it is so important to God that He attached a promise of blessings to those who read and observe it.

At this point, John, overwhelmed by what information he had been given, tried to worship the angel, as verse eight calls him, and was forbidden to do so:

Revelation 22:8 *And I John saw these things, and heard them. And when I had heard and seen, I fell down to worship before the feet of the angel which shewed me these things.* **9** *Then saith he unto me, See thou do it not: for I am thy fellowservant, and of thy brethren the prophets, and of them which keep the sayings of this book: worship God.*

This teaches us something of which we should take particular note. This angel speaking to John was not an angel in the way that we normally take the word. He was, in fact, a fellow Christian and a fellow prophet. The word *angellos* from whence we derive our word angel simply means a messenger. Often times, those messengers are literal angels, cherubim or seraphim, but occasionally they are human.

And in this case, the heavenly messenger standing in front of John was human and would never dream of receiving worship. Nor would the literal angels, by the way.

As we further examine the speed of the end, we find that when it begins, the end will be so sudden that no one who has rejected the revelation of Scripture will have time to change their ways:

Revelation 22:10 *And he saith unto me, Seal not the sayings of the prophecy of this book: for the time is at hand.* **11** *He that is unjust, let him be unjust still: and he which is filthy, let him be filthy still: and he that is righteous, let him be righteous still: and he that is holy, let him be holy still.*

Hundreds of years before, when Daniel was given his prophecy, the companion book to the book of The Revelation, God told him to "shut up the words, and seal the book, even to the time of the end." But this messenger at the direction of God gave John the exact opposite message, telling him not to seal up the sayings of the book because the time was at hand.

From our perspective, 2,000 years have come and gone since John received this message. But from the perspective of the messenger in verse eleven, and looking at the end as it will be, he once again reiterated that it would come with such speed and suddenness that no one would have time to change even if they could.

The last battle and the remaking of heaven and earth will be merely a grain of sand falling through the eternal hourglass.

For good or bad, reward day is coming. And as Christ Himself began to speak in verse twelve, He once again reiterated through the usage of the word "quickly" that we will not have long to wait:

Revelation 22:12 *And, behold, I come quickly; and my reward is with me, to give every man according as his work shall be.*

As He has done in so many other portions of Scripture, God now reiterates for us that, while our salvation is entirely dependent on Christ, our rewards or lack thereof are entirely dependent on us. Christ is coming, He is bringing His reward with Him, and He will *"give to every man according as his work shall be."*

All of this is guaranteed by the Alpha and Omega:

Revelation 22:13 *I am Alpha and Omega, the beginning and the end, the first and the last.*

It will all happen, it will all happen quickly, and we know that it will all happen because the Alpha and Omega has promised it.

The separation of the end

Revelation 22:14 *Blessed are they that do his commandments, that they may have right to the tree of life, and may enter in through the gates into the city.* **15** *For without are dogs, and sorcerers, and whoremongers, and murderers, and idolaters, and whosoever loveth and maketh a lie.*

We find another indication in these verses of how ridiculous it is to claim to be saved yet not obey His commandments. Jesus said, *"Blessed are they that do his commandments, that they may have right to the tree of life, and may enter in through the gates into the city."*

This is not proof that we are saved by good works, but proof that the saved will demonstrate good works.

On the other side of the coin, verse fifteen tells us that there is a place for dogs, meaning those with wicked hearts, and for sorcerers, whoremongers, murderers, idolaters, and those who lie and love lying. And that place is not heaven! These are without, meaning in the lake of fire.

This matches with what Paul told the church at Corinth:

1 Corinthians 6:9 *Know ye not that the unrighteous shall not inherit the kingdom of God? Be not deceived: neither fornicators, nor idolaters, nor adulterers, nor effeminate, nor abusers of themselves with mankind,* **10** *Nor thieves, nor covetous, nor drunkards, nor revilers, nor extortioners, shall inherit the kingdom of God.*

The end will truly bring a great separation.

The star of the end

Revelation 22:16 *I Jesus have sent mine angel to testify unto you these things in the churches. I am the root and the offspring of David, and the bright and morning star.*

Jesus is the authority behind everything this angel told John. And these words specifically went out to the churches, plural. Here in the very last chapter of the very last book of the Bible, God once more shows us how important the local church is!

So many pious-sounding people who are nonetheless lacking in Scriptural understanding want to go away from the local church in our day. They want to "worship at home and let father be the priest." They speak in lofty terms about the "universal church" and say things like, "We don't go to church; we are the church!"

But God bled and died for the church; God promised to build His church; God sent the entire book of The Revelation to the church. And here at the end of the book, as He did way back in chapters two and three at the beginning of the book, it is very clear that it is the local church He is speaking of.

At the end of verse sixteen, He reminds us that the star of the end is the bright and morning star, the root and offspring of David. Jesus is qualified to be the star of the end! He is also qualified to be the star of our every day here and now.

We should take a moment, though, to look at those exact terms, "root and offspring of David," because they are one more excellent indicator of the nature of Christ. This phrase tells us that David came from Christ, and then Christ came from David! Jesus was the root that produced David, and Jesus was also the fruit that came from David. The former shows His absolute deity, and the latter shows His absolute humanity.

There is simply no one like Him!

The summons of the end

Revelation 22:17 *And the Spirit and the bride say, Come. And let him that heareth say, Come. And let him that is athirst come. And whosoever will, let him take the water of life freely.*

John knew about the Spirit, and John had just viewed the bride. And now Jesus informed him that both the Spirit and the bride were uttering an invitation for whosoever will come.

Both the saved and the one who seals the saved understand that salvation is a "whosoever will" matter and want everyone to be part of that whosoever will.

Jesus also, though, gave a command in this verse that, *"let him that heareth say, Come."* In other words, child of God, our fulfillment of the great commission should be just as fervent as the desire of the Holy Spirit Himself and of the saved who are already in glory.

The Scripture of the end

Revelation 22:18 *For I testify unto every man that heareth the words of the prophecy of this book, If any man shall add unto these things, God shall add unto him the plagues that are written in this book:* **19** *And if any man shall take away from the words of the book of this prophecy, God shall take away his part out of the book of life, and out of the holy city, and from the things which are written in this book.*

As God closed out the book of The Revelation, which tells us everything we need to know all the way to the end of time and into the beginning of eternity, He sealed up the canon of Scripture and put His "The End" on it. He used these verses to let us know that no more revelation would be coming. There would not be another "Word of God." And if you understand this, you will never fall prey to Islam, or the Jehovah's Witnesses, or Mormonism, or the Seventh Day Adventists, or Christian Science, or anyone else that has, since John finished the book of The Revelation, produced another writing that they call the word of God.

He was so serious about revelation being closed that He added a dual condemnation to His "the end." He said in verse eighteen that if anyone adds to the words of Scripture, God will add to them the plagues that are written in this book. In verse nineteen, He said that if anyone takes away from the words of Scripture, He will take away their part out of the book of life and the holy city. We know by this that he is talking about the lost, for the saved would never tamper with Scripture in such manner. It is a warning that once they go that far into unbelief and rebellion, their name will be blotted out and there will be no more chance to be saved. Nonetheless, this passage serves as another reminder of how important the written Word of God is to God Himself and therefore how important it should always be to us.

The sentiment of the end

Revelation 22:20 *He which testifieth these things saith, Surely I come quickly. Amen. Even so, come, Lord Jesus.* **21** *The grace of our Lord Jesus Christ be with you all. Amen.*

Sixty-six books. 1,189 chapters. More than three-quarters of a million words. And when it is all said and done, the sentiment that John closes this book with is

EVEN SO, COME, LORD JESUS!

Come! Do not wait for another second. Come! We want to see you. Come! Let us kneel and kiss your feet. Come! End this madness that has taken over humanity. Come! Put Satan into hell, clear the air, make all things new. Come! Your grace is wonderful, we want it to be with us, but what we really want is for you to be with us. Come, we want to see our loved ones again. Come and get eternity started. Come, Lord, Come tonight. There is nothing to hold us here, come, come, come.

And then to those who would read the book of The Revelation then in his day, throughout the ages, and now in our day, John said, *"The grace of our Lord Jesus Christ be with you all. Amen."*

The End

Works Cited

Anistoriton Journal of History. Anistoriton Journal of History, Archaeology, Arthistory: An essay. (n.d.). Retrieved November 18, 2022, from http://www.anistor.gr/english/enback/e043.htm

Bett, J. (2021, June 25). *Woman mourns after her dolphin husband dies and says she will never remarry*. mirror. Retrieved November 16, 2022, from https://www.mirror.co.uk/news/weird-news/woman-mourns-after-dolphin-husband-24395652

Broussard-Simmons, V., & Hunt, L. E. (2001, October 24). *Guide to the Ivory Soap Advertising Collection*. Smithsonian Online virtual Archives. Retrieved November 16, 2022, from https://sova.si.edu/record/NMAH.AC.0791#:~:text=There%20 was%20immediate%20demand%20for,made%20thee%20glad .%22%20Chemical%20analyses

Chilver, G. E. F. (2022, October 22). *Domitian*. Encyclopædia Britannica. Retrieved November 18, 2022, from https://www.britannica.com/biography/Domitian

Christian, J. T. (1992). *A history of the Baptists, together with some account of their principles and practices*. Bogard Press.

Clarke, Adam. *The Holy Bible, Containing the Old and New Testaments, the Text Carefully Printed from the Most Correct Copies of the Present Authorized Translation, Including the Marginal Readings and Parallel Texts: with a Commentary and Critical Notes Designed as a Help to a Better Understanding of the Sacred Writings*. Vol. 6 Set, Abingdon, 1977.

Foxe, J. (1989). *Foxe's Christian Martyrs of the world*. Barbour Books.

Goldbaum, E. (2015, June 18). *Earth's mysteriously light core contains brimstone*. LiveScience. Retrieved January 4, 2022, from https://www.livescience.com/51249-earth-core-contains-brimstone.html

Henry, Matthew. *Matthew Henrys' Commentary of the Whole Bible.* Vol. 6, Fleming H Revell Company.

Holland, J. (2020, June 9). *UN: The world is producing and consuming more seafood, but overfishing remains rife.* SeafoodSource Official Media. Retrieved November 16, 2022, from https://www.seafoodsource.com/news/supply-trade/un-the-world-is-producing-and-consuming-more-seafood-but-overfishing-remains-rife

Ironside, H.A., *Illustrations of Bible Truth*, Moody Press, 1945

Jamieson, R., Fausset, A. R., & Brown, D. (2008). *A commentary on the old and new testaments* (Vol. 3). Hendrickson Publishers.

Keller, N. H. M., & Ibn-al-Naqib, A. ibn L. (2011). *Reliance of the Traveller: The Classic Manual of Islamic Sacred Law.* Amana Publications.

Lenski, R. C. H. (1963). *The Interpretation of St. John's Revelation.* Augsburg Publishing House.

Limbaugh, R. (2007, November 13). *Danson: I lied, Oceans didn't die.* The Rush Limbaugh Show. Retrieved November 16, 2022, from https://www.rushlimbaugh.com/daily/2007/11/13/danson_i_lied_oceans_didn_t_die2/

Linder, P. (n.d.). Power Bible CDVersion (5.9).

Myatt, A. (2019, August 9). *What is the Valley of Armageddon?* Immanuel Tours. Retrieved November 16, 2022, from https://www.immanuel-tours.com/israel/what-is-the-valley-of-armageddon

Nevres, M. Ö. (2021, October 13). *Seven wonders of the world.* Our Planet. Retrieved July 27, 2022, from https://ourplnt.com/seven-wonders-of-the-world/#axzz71rqsShbN

Nostalgia Travel. (n.d.). Retrieved November 16, 2022, from https://www.nostalgia.gr/varia-artemis.html

Ocean Syrup. (2020, April 28). *How deep do plants grow in the ocean?* Ocean Syrup. Retrieved November 16, 2022, from https://oceansyrup.com/how-deep-plants-grow-ocean/

Of the ten bloody persecutions which the Christians suffered under the HEA then emperors of rome; the first of which began in the reign of nero, A. D. 66. Of The Ten Bloody Persecutions Which The Christians Suffered Under The Hea Then Emperors Of Rome; The First Of Which Began In The Reign Of Nero, A. D. 66. (n.d.). Retrieved November 16, 2022, from https://www.homecomers.org/mirror/martyrs011.htm

Orr, J. (1952). *The International Standard Bible Encyclopaedia. James Orr, general editor* (Vol. 5). W.B. Eerdmans Pub. Co.

Parliament and Crown - UK parliament. UK Parliament. (n.d.). Retrieved November 16, 2022, from https://www.parliament.uk/about/how/role/relations-with-other-institutions/parliament-crown/

Public Broadcasting Service. (2014, May 29). *The Great Fire of Rome ~ background.* PBS. Retrieved August 5, 2021, from https://www.pbs.org/wnet/secrets/great-fire-rome-background/1446/

Reyes, R. (2021, September 17). *Outrage as maskless 'hypocritical' San Francisco mayor and BLM co-founder party at Nightclub.* Daily Mail Online. Retrieved November 16, 2021, from https://www.dailymail.co.uk/news/article-10001951/Outrage-maskless-hypocritical-San-Fran-Mayor-BLM-founder-party-nightclub.html

Smallwood, K. (2015, March 29). *The truth about the origin of floating soap.* Today I Found Out. Retrieved November 16,

2022, from http://www.todayifoundout.com/index.php/2015/03/truth-floating-soap/

The "scandalous" religious conversion of Jean-Paul Sartre. Union of Catholic Christian Rationalists. (2014, December 11). Retrieved November 16, 2022, from https://www.uccronline.it/eng/2014/12/11/the-scandalous-conversion-of-jean-paul-sartre/

Today in the Word, Moody Bible Institute, July 1989.

Vedder, H. C. (1907). *A short history of the Baptists.* American Baptist Publication Society.

WebMD. (n.d.). *Wormwood: Overview, uses, side effects, precautions, interactions, dosing and reviews.* WebMD. Retrieved December 31, 2021, from https://www.webmd.com/vitamins/ai/ingredientmono-729/wormwood

Webster, A. (2020, January 2). *Three Arguments for the Existence of God.* House to House Heart to Heart. Retrieved November 16, 2022, from https://housetohouse.com/three-arguments-for-the-existence-of-god/

Wolff, J. S. (n.d.). *St. Irenaeus.* Heritage History | Stories of Saints and Martyrs by Jetta S. Wolff. Retrieved November 26, 2022, from https://www.heritage-history.com/index.php?c=read&author=wolff&book=martyrs&story=irenaeus

Other Books by Dr. Bo Wagner

Daniel: Breathtaking
Esther: Five Feast and the Fingerprints of God
James: The Pen and the Plumb Line
Jonah: A Study in Greatness
Nehemiah: A Labor of Love
Proverbs: Bright Lights from Dark Sayings - Volume 1
Proverbs: Bright Lights from Dark Sayings - Volume 2
Romans: Salvation From A-Z
Ruth: Diamonds in the Darkness

More Books by Dr. Bo Wagner

Beyond the Colored Coat
Don't Muzzle the Ox
From Footers to Finish Nails
I'm Saved! Now What???
Learning Not to Fear the Old Testament
Marriage Makers/Marriage Breakers

Books in the Night Heroes Series

Cry From the Coal Mine (Vol. 1)
Free Fall (Vol. 2)
Broken Brotherhood (Vol. 3)
The Blade of Black Crow (Vol. 4)
Ghost Ship (Vol. 5)
When Serpents Rise (Vol. 6)
Moth Man (Vol. 7)
Runaway (Vol. 8)
Terror by Day (Vol. 9)
Winter Wolf (Vol. 10)

Devotionals

DO Drops Volume 1
DO Drops Volume 2
DO Drops Volume 3
DO Drops Volume 4
DO Drops Volume 5
DO Drops Volume 6
DO Drops Volume 7
DO Drops Volume 8

Zak Blue and the Great Space Chase Series:
Falcon Wing (Vol. 1)
Enter the Maelstrom (Vol. 2)

www.ingramcontent.com/pod-product-compliance
Lightning Source LLC
Chambersburg PA
CBHW050417170426
43201CB00008B/440